The ITIL® Process Manual
Key Processes and their

Other publications by Van Haren Publishing

Van Haren Publishing (VHP) specializes in titles on Best Practices, methods and standards within four domains:
- IT management
- Architecture (Enterprise and IT)
- Business management and
- Project management

Van Haren Publishing offers a wide collection of whitepapers, templates, free e-books, trainer material etc. in the **Van Haren Publishing Knowledge Base**: www.vanharen.net for more details.

Van Haren Publishing is also publishing on behalf of leading organizations and companies: ASLBiSL Foundation, CA, Centre Henri Tudor, Gaming Works, Getronics, IACCM, IAOP, IPMA-NL, ITSqc, NAF, Ngi, PMI-NL, PON, Quint, The Open Group, The Sox Institute, Tmforum.

Topics are (per domain):

IT (Service) Management / IT Governance
ABC of ICT
ASL®
BiSL®
CATS CM®
CMMI®
CoBIT
Frameworx
ISO 17799
ISO 27001
ISO 27002
ISO/IEC 20000
ISPL
IT Service CMM
ITIL®
ITSM
MOF
MSF
SABSA

Architecture (Enterprise and IT)
Archimate®
GEA®
SOA
TOGAF®

Business Management
Contract Management
EFQM
eSCM
ISA-95
ISO 9000
ISO 9001:2000
OPBOK
Outsourcing
SAP
SixSigma
SOX
SqEME®

Project/Programme/ Risk Management
A4-Projectmanagement
ICB / NCB
MINCE®
M_o_R®
MSP™
P3O®
PMBOK® Guide
PRINCE2®

For the latest information on VHP publications, visit our website: www.vanharen.net.

The ITIL® Process Manual

Key Processes and their Application

Colophon

Title:	The ITIL® Process Manual
Author:	James Persse
Copy editor:	Jane Chittenden
Publisher:	Van Haren Publishing, Zaltbommel, www.vanharen.net
Design & layout:	CO2 Premedia Bv, Amersfoort – NL
ISBN Hardcopy:	978 90 8753 650 3
ISBN eBook copy:	978 90 8753 650 1
Edition:	First edition, first impression, July 2012
Copyright:	© Van Haren Publishing, 2012

All rights reserved. No part of this publication may be reproduced in any form by print, photo print, microfilm or any other means without written permission by the publisher.
Although this publication has been composed with much care, neither author, nor editor, nor publisher can accept any liability for damage caused by possible errors and/or incompleteness in this publication.

TRADEMARK NOTICES
ITIL® is a registered trade mark of the Cabinet Office.
The ITIL Swirl logo™ is a trade mark of the Cabinet Office.

Foreword

Establishing ITIL in a business already running IT operations can seem like an overwhelming challenge to many technology organizations. As reliance on IT continues to grow, many businesses have turned to ITIL to help ensure smooth, continuous availability of critical systems. ITIL, as an internationally recognized codex of best practices, offers a logical, planned approach to ensure that you:
1. Truly understand what your IT customers need;
2. Can effectively plan for those needs;
3. Gauge how well you are meeting those needs; and
4. Improve your offerings to remain viable and competitive.

The IT industry has adopted ITIL because it provides a straightforward, business-oriented view regarding how IT services can integrate with business objects. ITIL has achieved a proven track record of success since its introduction in the early late 1980s. Its concepts have continued to evolve with the emergence of new technologies; and from it have also grown a well-designed training and certification path. However, when you read the available books, attend the classes, or study the material it can be difficult to relate the concepts to what you do as an IT professional on a daily basis. Relax. You are not alone.

With the *ITIL Process Manual* Dr. James Persse has laid out practical ideas that can help you translate ITIL into a workable solution for your business.
As a Solutions Architect for Lockheed Martin, I have worked with James on a number of ITIL initiatives for government agencies. James and I have worked closely to both develop new operational processes and revise existing processes which help to invoke culture changes within organizations seeking to establish ITIL. With a clear path and an adoptive approach to the ITIL concepts, I have successfully been able to adopt ITIL automation tools based on the groundwork laid out in James' processes.
Too often I see attempts to define process that spring from a tool's particular capabilities, and this can lead to disjointed process adherence or confusing and rapid changes to process flows. Taking the better path, when you start with a set of defined activities – process first -- it becomes easier to see the intersections, responsibilities, and capability needed. Now you are ready to make a plan, and it is ITIL that gives you the basis for that plan.

While there are a number of volumes on what ITIL is, this book is unique in that it helps define a practical and workable approach. James understands that ITIL is not necessarily a word-for-word definition of what an organization must do to be successful, but rather a group of common practices that can be adopted to fit your organization. In the workshops I have conducted, and the innovations I have been a part of, I hear a lot of comments to the effect of *"the ITIL definition says..."*, and while that may technically be true, is any organization obligated to take on such a literal definition? Are IT teams ready to make a hard cutover from the typical tower mentality to a shared responsibility model? The likely answer is no. So instead, take the theme of an ITIL-specific process and align to your objectives in such a way so that it can to be easily adopted.

I know that many will say: "*easier said than done*". But the key to this concept is captured in this book (and practiced daily) by James and I. In addition, this book helps you understand that by starting with a vision and tackling achievable goals will be more likely to result in success than trying to be too aggressive. Remember too, that ITIL incorporates a continual improvement philosophy, so you don't necessarily need to be perfect right out of the gate, or have an elaborate thirty page deep process document to get started. Sometimes starting with a familiar set of activities and translating those into repeatable steps, coupled with a plan to revisit them and improve, is the easiest way forward.

With these concepts, infused with real world examples from the projects I have collaborated with him on, his numerous other assignments, and other bodies of written work on ITIL, James has created a true manual for a manageable, scalable rollout of ITIL. We have used this same approach to develop a repeatable method for instilling culture change, solid process development, and automation in the pursuit of efficient ITIL oriented organizations for our customers.

Tobi J. Leiker
IT Service Management Solution Architect
Lockheed Martin
Washington, D.C.

Acknowledgements

This title has been one of the hardest publishing projects we have engaged in. On the face of it, the ITSM processes described in ITIL and also ISO 20000 are basic common sense and should be easy for the user to work with in a practical environment. In practice, there are, rightly, many different approaches to adopting ITSM process within an organizational environment. It is our great fortune that the Author and also the Reviewers used their considerable knowledge and expertise to guide and support the project. Always positive and always open to feedback on the subtleties and nuances in the market, the Publisher is indeed extremely grateful to all involved for making this 'delivery' project a real pleasure.

We would like to thank James Persse for his very considerable patience, expertise and attention to detail. His broad shoulders took on much feedback and the quality manuscript reflects this dedication and experience.

We would also like to thank our ever dedicated review team as follows:

Clair Agutter	ITIL Training Zone
Theo Bosselaers	Mitopics
Rob van der Burg	Microsoft
Michael Busch	IT Solution Crew
David Jones	Pink Elephant UK
Ali Makahleh	Microsoft
Mark O'Loughlin	IT Alliance
Rita Pilon	EXIN
Mart Rovers	InterProm USA

Contents

Foreword V
Acknowledgements VII

Introduction 1

1. **Overview of ITIL v3, 2011 edition** 7
   1.1. Brief history of ITIL 8
   1.2. Structure of ITIL 9
   1.3. Core components of IT Service Management 26

2. **Steps towards implementing an ITIL-based IT Service Management program** 29
   2.1. Know the model 30
   2.2. Appreciate the value 30
   2.3. Obtain commitment 30
   2.4. Establish a service-based organization 31
   2.5. Select the program's scope 32
   2.6. Assess the organization 32
   2.7. Create your ITIL-based IT Service Management program ... 32
   2.8. Implement the program 33
   2.9. Support program use 33
   2.10. The ongoing care and maintenance of your program: Plan-Do-Check-Act 35
   2.11. Some practical tips 36
   2.12. Implementation checklist 38

3. **Business Relationship Management** 41
   3.1. Business Relationship Management activities 42
   3.2. Process inputs and outputs 45
   3.3. Processes related to Business Relationship Management ... 47
   3.4. Tools and techniques 48
   3.5. Key Performance Indicators 49
   3.6. Critical Success Factors 50
   3.7. Business Relationship Management roles 52
   3.8. Benefits of effective Business Relationship Management ... 54
   3.9. Implementation challenges and considerations 55
   3.10. Typical assets and artifacts of a Business Relationship Management program 57

4. **Service Level Management** 59
   4.1. Service Level Management work products 60
   4.2. Service Level Management activities 62

  4.3. Process inputs and outputs 68
  4.4. Processes related to Service Level Management 70
  4.5. Tools and techniques 71
  4.6. Critical Success Factors 72
  4.7. Key Performance Indicators 74
  4.8. Service Level Management roles 75
  4.9. Benefits of effective Service Level Management 77
  4.10. Implementation challenges and considerations 79
  4.11. Typical assets and artifacts of a Service Level Management program ...81

5. Capacity Management 85
  5.1. Process activities for Capacity Management 87
  5.2. Process inputs and outputs 92
  5.3. Processes related to Capacity Management 94
  5.4. Tools and techniques 96
  5.5. Key Performance Indicators 97
  5.6. Critical Success Factors 98
  5.7. Capacity Management roles 100
  5.8. Benefits of effective Capacity Management 102
  5.9. Implementation challenges and considerations 104
  5.10. Typical assets and artifacts of a Capacity Management program 106

6. Availability Management 109
  6.1. Availability Management activities 111
  6.2. Process inputs and outputs 116
  6.3. Processes related to Availability Management 118
  6.4. Tools and techniques 120
  6.5. Key Performance Indicators 121
  6.6. Critical Success Factors 123
  6.7. Availability Management roles 124
  6.8. Benefits of effective Availability Management 127
  6.9. Implementation challenges and considerations 129
  6.10. Typical assets and artifacts of an Availability Management program ...131

7. IT Service Continuity Management 135
  7.1. IT Service Continuity Management activities 137
  7.2. Process inputs and outputs 141
  7.3. Processes related to IT Service Continuity Management 143
  7.4. Tools and techniques 145
  7.5. Key Performance Indicators 146
  7.6. Critical Success Factors 148
  7.7. IT Service Continuity Management roles 149
  7.8. Benefits of effective IT Service Continuity Management 152
  7.9. Implementation challenges and considerations 153
  7.10. Typical assets and artifacts of an IT Service Continuity Management program 155

8. Information Security Management.................................159
   8.1.   Information Security Management activities 161
   8.2.   Process inputs and outputs 166
   8.3.   Processes related to Information Security Management 168
   8.4.   Tools and techniques 170
   8.5.   Key Performance Indicators 171
   8.6.   Critical Success Factors 173
   8.7.   Information Security Management roles..................175
   8.8.   Benefits of effective Information Security Management..........177
   8.9.   Implementation challenges and considerations 179
   8.10. Typical assets and artifacts of an Information Security
          Management program 181

9. Change Management..............................185
   9.1.   Change Management activities....................187
   9.2.   Process inputs and outputs 196
   9.3.   Processes related to Change Management 197
   9.4.   Tools and techniques 200
   9.5.   Critical Success Factors 201
   9.6.   Key Performance Indicators 202
   9.7.   Change Management roles 203
   9.8.   Benefits of effective Change Management 206
   9.9.   Implementation challenges and considerations 208
   9.10. Typical assets and artifacts of a Change Management program 210

10. Service Asset and Configuration Management..........................213
   10.1. Configuration Management activities 214
   10.2. Process inputs and outputs 219
   10.3. Processes related to Configuration Management.................221
   10.4. Tools and techniques 222
   10.5. Key Performance Indicators 223
   10.6. Critical Success Factors 225
   10.7. Configuration Management roles..................226
   10.8   Benefits of effective Configuration Management..................229
   10.9   Implementation challenges and considerations 231
   10.10 Typical assets and artifacts for a Configuration Management program .233

11. Release and Deployment Management 237
   11.1. Release and Deployment Management activities..................238
   11.2. Process inputs and outputs 244
   11.3. Processes related to Release and Deployment Management 246
   11.4. Tools and techniques 247
   11.5. Key Performance Indicators 248
   11.6. Critical Success Factors 250
   11.7. Release and Deployment Management roles 251
   11.8. Benefits of effective Release and Deployment Management 254

11.9. Implementation challenges and considerations 255
11.10. Typical assets and artifacts of a Release and
       Deployment Management program 257

12. Incident Management 261
12.1. Incident Management activities 263
12.2. Process inputs and outputs 268
12.3. Processes related to Incident Management......................269
12.4. Tools and techniques 272
12.5. Key Performance Indicators 273
12.6. Critical Success Factors 275
12.7. Incident Management roles.....................................277
12.8 Benefits of effective Incident Management......................280
12.9. Implementation challenges and considerations 281
12.10 Typical assets and artifacts of an Incident Management program......284

13. Problem Management 287
13.1. Problem Management activities 288
13.2. Process inputs and outputs 292
13.3. Processes related to Problem Management.......................294
13.4. Tools and techniques 296
13.5. Key Performance Indicators 297
13.6. Critical Success Factors 300
13.7. Problem Management roles......................................301
13.8. Benefits of effective Problem Management......................303
13.9. Implementation challenges and considerations 304
13.10. Typical assets and artifacts of a Problem Management program.......307

14. Service Desk 311
14.1. Service Desk responsibilities..................................312
14.2. Processes related to Service Desk 315
14.3. Tools and techniques 317
14.4. Key Performance Indicators 318
14.5. Critical Success Factors 319
14.6. Service Desk roles 321
14.7. Benefits of a well-executed Service Desk function 324
14.8. Implementation challenges and considerations 325
14.9. Typical assets and artifacts of a Service Desk function................327

15. Service Management and Service Improvement..........................331
15.1. Service Improvement activities.................................332
15.2. Process inputs and outputs 335
15.3. Processes related to Service Improvement 337
15.4. Tools and techniques 338
15.5. Key Performance Indicators 339
15.6. Critical Success Factors 340

15.7.	Service Improvement roles	341
15.8.	Benefits of effective Service Improvement	343
15.9.	Implementation challenges and considerations	345
15.10.	Typical assets and artifacts of a Service Improvement program	346

16. Implementing a basic Process Quality Assurance function 349
    16.1.   Objectivity and independence...................................349
    16.2.   PQA activities..350
    16.3.   The value of PQA...353
    16.4.   Summary: ensuring success....................................353

Introduction

Since its introduction in the mid-1980s, ITIL® has attained worldwide prominence as the leading process model for the management of IT infrastructures. At the same time, as technology infrastructures have reached into every nook and cranny of corporate operations, senior executives are seeing the value of management through the use of structured IT controls. The result has been more and more companies adopting ITIL.

As is true with any improvement initiative, adopting ITIL in an effective manner requires a set of actions that may not be familiar to many IT organizations, especially those new to process management. For that reason, this book has been prepared: *The ITIL® Process Manual*.

Purpose of this book

This book was written to give IT executives, managers, and process analysts a comprehensive view on how to implement an IT Service Management program using the core components of ITIL as a baseline. In line with that aim, this book is designed to achieve four general objectives:

- Present an overview of ITIL and its role in IT Service Management
- Point you to the key ITIL processes and functions
- Present practical tips and techniques for adopting the processes in an IT organization
- Highlight the relationships and flexibility inherent in the framework

Present an overview of ITIL
The first purpose of this book is to give the reader an overview of ITIL, to describe its focus, shape, and content. This will provide the background necessary for understanding ITIL's core components and for planning the design of a Service Management program. Here we discuss each of the model's five lifecycle phases and then briefly review the processes in each phase.

Orient you to key ITIL processes and functions
There are 26 processes and four functions in the full ITIL framework. Each of these occupies an important place in an IT Service Management program. But not all organizations need to adopt the full set and when it comes to new programs, any expert will advise starting with a carefully selected subset and then growing from there. This book makes an effort to establish that basic subset. It presents the core processes that are essential for delivering, controlling, releasing, and maintaining IT services. Each process is described in full detail, covering process activities, roles, metrics, assets, and artifacts.

Present practical tips and techniques for implementation

The primary purpose of this book is a practical, tactical one. We will explore a series of tips and techniques that you can use to help design, build, and implement your program. These tips and techniques come from practitioners in the industry who have designed and implemented many similar programs, not just ITIL-based programs, but others as well – the PMI's PMBOK, SEI's CMMI, Six Sigma, ISO 9001, and others. These programs share similar success traits with ITIL, as they are all based in the fundamentals of process improvement and organizational change. The tips and techniques presented here help you make the most of your efforts while avoiding some of the common pitfalls that can stall or even derail a program. These tips and techniques are featured across all chapters and cover inception through implementation on to adoption by your organization. This advice is geared toward helping promote a successful, well-focused operational design and facilitate a smooth implementation as the program is rolled out to live operation.

Highlight the relationships and flexibility inherent in the framework

A couple of traits of ITIL that are often overlooked, or at least under-stressed, are the interrelationships that exist among its elements and the amount of flexibility you have in putting those elements together. Some IT organizations tend to adopt ITIL processes independently of one another, as if they were standalone entities. That approach can work but it usually results in operational redundancies, duplicate work, or operational gaps. In this book we will point out where ITIL elements naturally overlap. By highlighting these relationships, this book can help you make the most of commonalities among all the core components. At the same time the book will highlight the degree of flexibility you have in interpreting the best way to adopt each in your organization. One of the strengths of ITIL is that it is not prescriptive; it does not set out obligatory requirements. It presents proven recommendations. It is your insight and experience that are needed to determine how to best integrate these recommendations across your functional groups. These two together – the interrelationships, and the flexibility – should help you create a streamlined, value-driven program, one that exploits ITIL's insights while accommodating your own cultural traits.

The audience for this book

This book is written primarily for IT professionals who need to acquire a good understanding of the core components of ITIL V3. Because the emphasis is on implementation of ITIL-based processes, this audience is made up of four groups of stakeholders and these stakeholders typically represent those in an IT organization who will assume most of the responsibility for taking a program from concept to realization. They are Chief Technology Officers (CTOs), IT Service Managers, IT Service Management program managers and analysts, and those who will work with the program at the line level. Let's take a quick look at each of these groups.

Chief Technology Officers

In today's business and economic climates, more and more are being asked to establish quality controls throughout their organizations. Many factors are contributing to this. Statutory requirements like those in the Sarbanes-Oxley Act (SOX) make implementing such controls in certain organizations mandatory. Then there is the basic fiduciary responsibility allied with IT spending. Corporate leadership, investors and even industry analysts expect controls to be in place. Then there's the basic issue of managing complex environments that are likely to be growing more complex by the week. Such executives can benefit from this book with its emphasis on practical implementation. Using it, they should be able to position their teams for an effective Service Management design, development, and implementation effort.

IT Service Managers

The managerial heart of an IT Service Management program may be found in the role of the IT Service Managers. These are the people whose job it is to oversee the design and delivery of IT services, anything from email to smartphones to payroll runs. By default they also oversee execution of the IT Service Management program. For that reason it is important they know the IT Service Management program well. In fact, it is important that they help *build* the program. This book can help managers understand the scope of ITIL's core processes, grasp the details that may need to be accounted for in their service areas, and then establish a program designed for success.

ITSM Process Program Managers.

Process Program Managers are those people typically charged with taking an executive vision (the strategy) and making its quality goals and workflows real in the organization (through tactics). Such program owners will find in this book a structural approach to Service Operation that emphasizes the purpose and function of each component while highlighting opportunities for integration. Through this an effective program scope can be established. Process Owners work with senior managers to introduce process elements; they tend to own one or more components of a program. They'll find this book helpful because, especially in Chapters 3 through 14, it presents a tactical picture of how each ITIL process can be accounted for. 'Accounted for' is not simply to be consistent with ITIL recommendations, but designed to be right-sized; that is, to fit well within the organizational culture, to make best use of existing best practices, and to allow for future growth and refinement.

Those who work within an IT Service Management program

Finally, this book should be helpful to those staff members required to operate within an IT Service Management program. While it is not necessary for everyone in an organization to understand the details of ITIL, key staff (e.g. team leads) would benefit from having some exposure to the framework and access to the detail as required. This will help them to appreciate the focus that ITIL brings to Service Management and understand how their IT duties may contribute to success on a broader level. Such a big-picture appreciation can help them operate more effectively and lead their teams in a more informed and directed manner.

How this book is organized

This book is organized in three parts. Part 1 presents an overview of ITIL and general considerations for how process programs can be implemented. Part 2 contains descriptions of each of the core ITIL processes. Part 3 presents a discussion on the importance of continual process improvement and of ITIL's relation to ISO/IEC 20000. The chapters break down as follows.

Chapter 1 presents a high level overview of ITIL. This is in place to give you a feeling for the scope of the framework across its five lifecycle phases and to provide context for the discussions of the core components. For this book the core components are the following processes:
- Service Level Management
- Capacity Management
- Availability Management
- IT Service Continuity Management
- Information Security Management
- Change Management
- Service Asset and Configuration Management
- Release and Deployment Management
- Incident Management
- Problem Management
- Continuous Service Improvement

Chapter 2 presents a series of steps and considerations helpful for initiating and implementing a process program. Because practical implementation is the focus of this book this chapter presents a high level implementation architecture that can be used as a management umbrella for the implementation approach contained in the chapters describing the individual processes.

Chapters 3 through 15 present discussions of each of the core processes or functions. The chapters are organized to contain the following details:
- Introduction – a description of the process in its operational context
- Activities – steps recommended for this process
- Inputs/outputs – typical inputs, entry criteria, outputs, and exit criteria for the process
- Related processes – other core processes that might interact with or influence this process
- Tools and techniques – common tools and techniques to help with process implementation
- Key Performance Indicators – a set of conventional measures that can be used to gauge the performance of the process
- Critical Success Factors – a set of measures to determine the operational success of the process
- Roles – a description of the kinds of job roles that organizations commonly use for process activities and management

- Benefits – a description of the kinds of organizational benefits that can be realized through effective process implementation.
- Implementation challenges and considerations – descriptions of the kinds of typical hurdles that may have to be addressed in order to maximize process effectiveness
- Typical assets and artifacts – a listing of the typical assets and artifacts commonly associated with process implementation and use

Chapter 16 supports program implementation and governance with a discussion of how to establish a basic process quality assurance function in the organization.

That is the structure of this book. There is also a theme that runs through the book. It rests on five general points of principle that lie at the heart of IT Service Management both as a discipline and a management philosophy. These five points are:
- Technology assets in a business domain are the same, in spirit, as any other corporate asset and, like other assets, should be deployed in pursuit of defined business objectives.
- The activities required for harnessing technology assets to the needs of the business should be considered 'services' that the IT organization provides on an ongoing basis.
- The IT organization (with executive support) should forge a close partnership with its business customers in order to determine as a team what technology services are needed and how they ought to perform.
- The IT organization should regularly measure the performance of its service-related activities and report its achievements back to the business.
- Together, IT management and business management should periodically review performance measures and seek in the data opportunities for improvement.

ITIL, with its focus on Service Management and its integration of industry best practices, can help you realize each of those five points. As you begin the process of implementing your ITIL-based program you will see how each of the five points demonstrably contributes to the levels of quality, control, consistency, and predictability one would expect to see in a well-managed IT environment. To begin our look at implementation let's start with an overall high-level look at ITIL.

1. Overview of ITIL v3, 2011 edition

ITIL is the acronym for the Information Technology Infrastructure Library, a collection of five volumes that set out proven practices for how organizations can effectively manage IT infrastructures. But while it is a collection of practices, it is not a process program, as is sometimes thought. Rather, ITIL is a framework that organizations can use to construct their own custom-built process programs. From the standpoint of focus, ITIL is designed to support IT Service Management. This is a management approach that treats the delivery of IT capabilities in much the same way that, say, the power company delivers electricity into homes - as a service.

That is not the way IT has traditionally been regarded. The traditional view sees technology as a specialized function within an organization, one whose mission may be to support the business but whose domain remains somewhat separate from the business. In this view, IT management tends to make technology decisions based mainly on technological considerations. How this view came about is easy to understand. Computing, and information technology in general, is relatively new to the world of business. The digital transformation began less than fifty years ago – practically a blink when considering that accounting practices have been around for 9,000 years. And when computers were first harnessed for business they *were* a specialized function. They performed very select jobs; they needed meticulous care; they required a new breed of employee. On top of that, technology by necessity had to be separate from the company – set apart in sealed, air-conditioned rooms with raised floors. That naturally bred the view that technology should be treated as a meta-function to the business.

Of course that is not the case today. The personal computer (PC) revolution of the 1980s changed that forever. Since then technology use, and the influence on technology's direction, has moved steadily out from the sealed rooms onto the desks of accounting, marketing, manufacturing, human resource, and distribution workers. In that time technology has certainly grown more specialized and exponentially more sophisticated, but it can no longer be isolated from the business. It is too important to the business. In many ways it *is* the business. Today business and technology have become so intertwined it is often difficult to distinguish where technology ends and business begins. The result is that the power of computing has become singularly important to business users. Paradoxically, it is also their desire that it becomes invisible.

The value of IT Service Management is based in that duality. Users need technology but they should not need technology's technicalities. They just want to flip the switch and see the lights come on. When they send an email they just want to know that it arrives. What goes on behind the scenes in order for that email to arrive may be quite complex. Software, servers, network lines, routers, switches – all these have to work in harmony. It is the job of the infrastructure (and the people who manage and operate the infrastructure) to establish and maintain that harmony, and thus –and this is key – allow business processes to flow.

What's new here is the view required of management. The software, servers, routers and switches should no longer be seen as independent devices, to be configured and maintained in isolation. Now they should be seen as the integrated components of an IT service, in this case an email service. In order for that email service to be delivered in a consistent and reliable way those components need to be managed as a continuous stream of capability. This requires close cooperation and collaboration between technical teams, a level not readily achieved in steeply separated IT organizations. But more importantly, in this new paradigm the IT organization is required to become a closely allied partner with most aspects of the business. Technology decisions should now be based mainly on business drivers. The voice of the customer should be echoed in every service configuration. The IT organization's responsibility is to deliver demonstrable value to the business; its job is not to be technologically astute so much as it is to become market savvy. And that's where ITIL comes in.

1.1. Brief history of ITIL

ITIL was developed in the mid-1980s by the UK Central Computer and Telecommunications Agency (CCTA), subsequently renamed the Office of Government Commerce (OGC)[1]. OGC at that time was not satisfied with the level of service that the UK government was receiving from its many IT contractors. In response, OGC commissioned the creation of a set of guidelines that could be followed by IT service providers to enhance consistency, establish common performance goals, and – ultimately –improve delivery quality. OGC was not interested in a proprietary standard. It wanted instead to borrow practices already proven in the IT industry and build the guidelines around those good practices; this is the path that was taken. The first version of ITIL appeared in 1989. It was a collection of guides across a series of management areas. Some of the earliest were Service Level Management, Contingency Planning, and Change Management.

Right from the start ITIL proved popular, and many IT organizations began adopting it. About 10 years later, OGC released ITIL V2. Version 2 was not much different in content from V1, but there was a structural improvement. The guides were presented in two domains, Service Support and Service Delivery. With Version 2, ITIL began to reach an international audience, and its popularity and adoption rates rose significantly. It was during this time that ITIL became recognized as the emerging framework when it came to service design, development, deployment, and

---

1 Since 2000 OGC has been the custodian of the Best Management Practice (BMP) portfolio, including ITIL, on behalf of UK Government. In June 2010 as a result of UK Government reorganization the Minister for the Cabinet Office announced that the BMP functions have moved into Cabinet Office.

IT operations. Then in 2007 OGC released ITIL V3. Version 3 greatly expanded the scope of ITIL and also embedded a strong emphasis on service management as an extension of business mission management. There was also another structural shift. OGC grouped ITIL processes and functions into a series of five lifecycle phases. Lastly, in the late summer of 2011, a refreshed edition of the library set was released, known as ITIL 2011 (developed by the UK Cabinet Office, which now owns ITIL along with other best practices). The 2011 edition presents more stylistic updates than actual content changes. Consistencies have been introduced across lifecycle phases and processes; clarifications and amplifications have been added. The biggest change content-wise is that business relationship management, a topic treated inferentially in the former framework, has now been treated explicitly as its own process. (See Chapter 3.) Version 3's 2011 edition is the version available today, and the one on which this book is based.

ITIL today is recognized as the de facto standard as the basis for implementing an IT Service Management program. The five volumes that comprise the library cover a broad field of information, the overriding theme being effective and responsive management of IT infrastructures. At its detailed base, ITIL is a collection of proven practices organized into processes, a process being a set of ordered activities designed to achieve a goal. In addition to processes, ITIL also describes functions. In ITIL terminology a function is an organizational unit that may use one or more processes - the Service Desk is a ready example of a function. The processes and functions in ITIL can be implemented in their entirety or selectively, depending on the needs of the organization.

1.2. Structure of ITIL

From a structural standpoint ITIL interprets IT Service Management as operating through a series of lifecycle phases with service maturity moving through a sequence of managed stages. For each stage there is a varying mix of processes, functions, and activities an IT organization should consider for each service it builds and moves towards production. In the Service Strategy phase, the organization views new or enhanced services in light of what exists in its IT portfolio already. The focus here is on complementary and value-added expansion. The Service Design phase introduces processes that deal with the kinds of scope and performance considerations that need to be accounted for as services are being designed. Service Transition includes those preparatory activities that need to be done in order to move a service from development into production. Service Operation features those processes and functions that guide how services are managed and maintained while they are being delivered to customers. Running through all four of these phases is Continual Service Improvement. This is the process improvement phase and it is here that ITIL presents practices for improving service features, performance, and quality.

In the next sections we'll take a brief look at these lifecycle phases and explore what processes ITIL defines for each. This will provide the context we need to investigate the core components of ITIL and view those areas with an angle on how to build them for use in your IT organization.

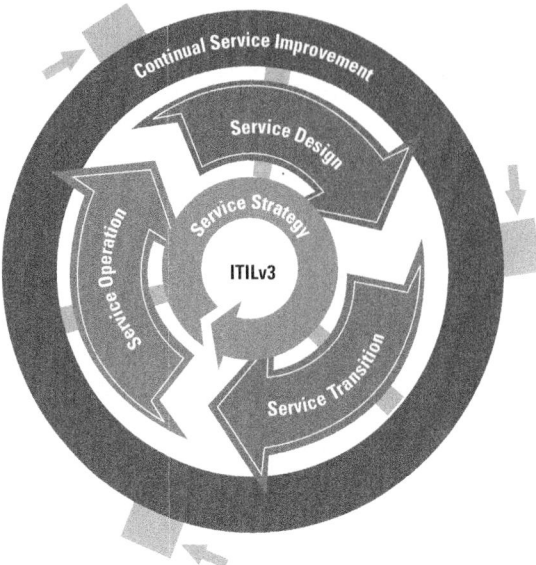

Figure 1.1 The five ITIL lifecycle phases
© Crown copyright 2011.

ITIL bases its structure on five lifecycle phases: Service Strategy, Service Design, Service Transition, Service Operation, and Continual Service Improvement.

Service Strategy

The Service Strategy phase is designed to provide an organization with processes useful for directing the form and function of an IT Service Management program. The scope of this direction includes evolving the shape of the infrastructure as well as applying techniques for designing, transitioning, and operating IT services. It is here that elements are set into place to support what might best be described as competitive service delivery, service delivery that combines cost effectiveness with maximized efficiency. At the same time, Service Strategy helps the organization frame its service offerings in a manner appropriate for its customer base. Five processes are presented here. They are:

- Strategy Management for IT Services
- Service Portfolio Management
- Demand Management
- Financial Management for IT Services
- Business Relationship Management

Strategy Management for IT Services. This process assesses the service provider's offerings and capabilities, together with an assessment of competitors, current and potential market spaces to develop a strategy for services to customers. Once the strategy has been defined, Strategy Management for IT Services is also responsible for ensuring the implementation of the strategy.

Process scope:
- Assessment of current offerings and capabilities
- Assessment of competitors and market space
- Definition of strategy for services to customers
- Implementation of strategy

Service Portfolio Management. The purpose of Service Portfolio Management is to strategically manage all the assets that make up the organization's infrastructure in a way that contributes to business success. Service Portfolio Management takes a holistic view of the organization's full suite of IT service offerings. The portfolio itself can be seen as consisting of three types of assets: those services that are available for customer use, those that are in the process of being newly released (the pipeline), and those that have been retired. Each of these represents in its own way a tangible value to the organization. The focus of Service Portfolio Management is on maximizing this value. Its practices work to make sure that the service mix is not redundant, that its components are complementary and not in conflict, and that plans and designs for new services take as much advantage as possible of what is already in place in the portfolio.

Process scope:
- Establishing the Service Catalogue
- Managing the service pipeline and overseeing service delivery
- Defining and analyzing new and enhanced services
- Chartering new and enhanced services

Demand Management. Demand Management is structured to ensure that the Service Portfolio is sized and configured in the most effective way as to balance demand (present and future) with operating costs. This process is closely associated with Financial Management and thus helps shape subsequent Service Design, Transition, Operation and Continual Service Improvement lifecycles. The purpose of Demand Management is to help the organization understand the level of demand associated with any particular service. High demand services will be likely to warrant robust and feature-rich designs and therefore significant levels of investment – with expectations for high returns. Low demand services will be likely to require less rigor and lower investment. The aim of Demand Management is to match the investment to the demand, and in doing so ensure that the infrastructure operates without a surplus or deficit of capacity, availability, and continuity as it grows and evolves over time.

Process scope:
- Provisioning service packages
- Managing lines of business

Financial Management for IT Services. The Financial Management for IT Services process is designed to ensure that investments made to create or enhance services are appropriately balanced against potential Return on Investment (ROI), demand, and the market needs of the organization. The design, delivery, and operation of IT services is the primary mission of IT Service Management. In order to do this the organization is required to invest in all the various components necessary for those activities to occur. That is where Financial Management for IT Services comes in. Financial Management for IT Services introduces a series of practices that guide how service provision is supported financially. This support is balanced between two criteria: investments appropriate to the needs of the marketplace and investments appropriate to the maturity of the organization. Effective Financial Management for IT Services results in cost-effective IT services that carry in them the potential for a positive ROI.

Process scope:
- Conducting business impact analyses
- Classifying and categorizing costs
- Budgeting
- Financial Management

Business Relationship Management. The purpose of this process is to maintain a positive and proactive relationship with customers; its primary concern is customer satisfaction. Business Relationship Management identifies the needs of existing and potential customers and ensures that appropriate services are developed to meet their evolving needs.

Process scope:
- Establishing and maintaining relationships with customers
- Identifying customers' evolving service requirements
- Improving customer satisfaction and handling of complaints

Service Design
Service Design provides a set of processes intended to ensure that core service attributes are accounted for and that they meet both the technical and business needs of the organization. This second phase in ITIL's lifecycle contains a series of eight processes that focus on considerations that go into designing a new service or enhancing an existing one. The emphasis across the seven processes is on production reliability, assuring that once a service is deployed it is appropriately secure, that it is consistently available, it is dependably capable of handling the required capacity, and it is quickly recoverable. The processes in this lifecycle phase are:
- Design Coordination
- Service Catalogue Management
- Service Level Management
- Availability Management
- Capacity Management
- IT Service Continuity Management

- Information Security Management
- Supplier Management

Design Coordination. This process aims to coordinate all service design activities, processes and resources. Design Coordination ensures the consistent and effective design of new or changed IT services, Service Management information systems, architectures, technology, processes, information and metrics.

Process scope:
- Design coordination support
- Service design planning, coordination and monitoring
- Technical and organizational service design
- Service Design review and Request for Change submission

Service Catalogue Management. The aim of Service Catalogue Management is to define, publish, and distribute a catalogue of current service offerings. The Service Catalogue is a subset of the Service Portfolio. The Service Catalogue contains descriptions of those business and technical services that the organization is prepared to deliver to a customer. This includes services already in production as well as new ones being prepared for production. Because IT services change over time, managing and maintaining the Service Catalogue is an important ongoing activity. Its service descriptions need to be kept current so that delivery commitments can be honored. And its component contents need to be kept current so that the right mix of offerings can be presented. (There may be some services scheduled for retirement in the Service Catalogue; when fully retired they will be located in the Service Portfolio and withdrawn from the Service Catalogue.) The practices that ITIL sets for this process help achieve both of these aims.

Process scope:
- Defining the Business Service Catalogue
- Defining the Technical Services Catalogue
- Publishing and distributing the Service Catalogue
- Maintaining the Service Catalogue

Service Level Management. Service Level Management is in place to establish agreements between IT and its customers about the scope of services and the quality of service delivery. Service Level Management is a cornerstone ITIL process. It is through Service Level Management that Service Level Agreements (SLAs) are put in place. SLAs define the performance thresholds that each service must meet in order to be deemed acceptable. Both parties (customer and service provider) participate in negotiating SLAs; the result is a mutually agreed definition of service levels. This definition provides an unambiguous and objective view of what quality means to both sides. The practices defined for this process help set service requirements, document SLAs, and provide for periodic reviews of both over time.

Process scope:
- Establishing service level requirements
- Establishing Service Level Agreements
- Monitoring service performance
- Measuring customer satisfaction
- Reporting on service performance and customer satisfaction
- Maintaining customer relationships

NOTE: Service Level Management is covered in detail in Chapter 4 of this book.

Availability Management. This process is designed to help ensure that services are designed in such a manner that the customer's availability needs are accounted for and met. Availability is a key characteristic of any service. The practices ITIL recommends for Availability Management promote the definition and implementation of availability requirements. However, any one service may be made up of any number of infrastructure components; determining availability requirements and designing them can be a complex undertaking. To facilitate this, ITIL promotes the early identification of vital business functions (VBFs). VBFs account for the major business processes that a service supports. By focusing on these VBFs first, a design team is more likely to effectively identify and realize critical requirements, and successfully incorporate them into services.

Process scope:
- Accounting for throughput, uptime, serviceability, maintainability, redundancy
- Identifying Vital Business Functions
- Establishing availability designs
- Implementing availability designs
- Analyzing and assessing availability performance

NOTE: Availability Management is covered in detail in Chapter 5 of this book.

Capacity Management. This process is structured to ensure that services are designed in such a manner that the customer's capacity needs (people, data and throughput) are accounted for and met, now and in the future. Capacity Management is closely associated with Availability Management. In the same way that services operate under certain availability requirements, so too they have capacity requirements. The concept of capacity involves a number of considerations. Among these are storage space, processing power, response time, and throughput. As with Availability Management, designing for Capacity Management can be quite complex. The practices recommended here by ITIL guide design teams through steps for identifying capacity requirements at the business, service, and service component levels. They also include testing performance against those requirements, and monitoring capacity performance in the field.

Process scope:
- Accounting for data storage, concurrency, service data
- Establishing capacity designs
- Implementing capacity designs
- Analyzing and assessing capacity performance

NOTE: Capacity Management is covered in detail in Chapter 6 of this book.

IT Service Continuity Management. This process is in place to ensure that technical service continuity is maintained if there are disruptive events so that business activity may be protected. The role of IT Service Continuity Management deals with designing (and deploying) services so that factors such as redundancy, failover, and restores are matched with reliability and dependability. A particular issue is the requirement to maintain availability, capacity, etc, even in the event of a disaster. In fact, in many organizations the term Continuity Management is synonymous with disaster recovery. The practices ITIL recommends for this process cover a spectrum of considerations, from ensuring a service's ability to forestall service interruptions to establishing pre-defined response actions so that services, once interrupted, can quickly recover. In this light, IT Service Continuity Management can be seen as a strategic extension of Availability Management.

Process scope:
- Defining continuity needs
- Establishing continuity plans
- Implementing continuity plans
- Periodically testing continuity plans

NOTE: IT Service Continuity Management is covered in detail in Chapter 7 of this book.

Information Security Management. Information Security Management ensures that the integrity of business data, services, and service components are protected from threats through appropriate access and configuration schemes. This process addresses the security requirements of a service. The practices recommended here cover such topics as system security, data security, identity profiles, security monitoring, and security policies. Since each kind of service is likely to have its own security needs, Information Security Management may be either a straightforward process or one that is intricately involved. The goal here, however, is not merely one of security; more fully it is one of security completeness: verifying that all facets of system and service security have been considered as a routine part of service design.

Process scope:
- Identifying information security needs
- Establishing security policies and methods
- Implementing security policies and methods
- Monitoring system access and use

NOTE: Information Security Management is covered in detail in Chapter 8 of this book.

Supplier Management. The intention of this process is to help select and manage suppliers in a way that promotes a partnership between IT management and its IT service providers, one that contributes to meeting defined service levels. Supplier Management deals with the coordination and collaboration activities necessary when working with third party suppliers. The focus is selecting and then engaging with those suppliers most qualified to realize service requirements as they relate to customer needs. Practices under this process have been established to help the organization identify and document supplier-related requirements, identify suitably qualified suppliers, select suppliers using verifiable criteria, regulate contracts and agreements, manage supplier work and deliverables, and evaluate supplier performance. As with the other components of ITIL, Supplier Management stresses a cooperative relationship, one in which both parties work to define common performance and quality expectations.

Process scope:
- Identifying qualified suppliers
- Negotiating with suppliers
- Establishing underpinning contracts
- Monitoring supplier performance

Service Transition

Service Transition provides a set of processes intended to ensure that new or enhanced services are deployed to the operational environment in such a way as to minimize downtime and protect infrastructure operability. Service Transition is the third phase in the service lifecycle. At this point a service is ready to move from concept into production. The idea of 'transition' provides that this move is made in a coordinated and controlled manner, one that minimizes risk to the operational environment. Seven processes are included here, which cover the progression from transition planning to change management through to performance evaluation. A brief description of each of these seven processes follows.

- Transition Planning and Support
- Change Management
- Service Asset and Configuration Management
- Release and Deployment Management
- Service Validation and Testing
- Change Evaluation
- Knowledge Management

Transition Planning and Support. ITIL provides this process to establish a management capability within the organization for transitioning services from design to live operational service. Here the organization establishes an overall transition strategy, then provides its teams with scheduling and coordination methods and tools. These teams are tasked with following through on transition activities so that service deployment occurs in a consistent, planned, and controlled manner, one that emphasizes the efficient use of capital outlay and resource allocation.

Process scope:
- Establishing a transition strategy
- Setting up a release approach
- Implementing the release approach
- Monitoring release management performance

Change Management. Change Management provides the organization with a method for introducing change in a coordinated and collaborative manner. This process deals with providing mechanisms to control change in the organization, particularly changes to the IT infrastructure. ITIL recommends a series of activities to support this. These include providing a way for users to submit requests for change, establishing a change control authority to assess and approve requests, and implementing a method to track active change requests. When integrated with other transition activities, these activities promote accountability and responsibility so that change can be made in a responsive and effective way.

Process scope:
- Coordinating the submission of Requests for Change (RFCs)
- Assessing the impact of RFCs
- Decision-making regarding RFCs
- Incorporating approved changes into releases

NOTE: Change Management is covered in detail in Chapter 9 of this book.

Service Asset and Configuration Management. This process helps ensure that the organization's operational assets are tracked in a way that reflects their current states and configurations. It provides practices for two areas: the identification of the components that make up the infrastructure – the assets; and documentation of the configuration of those items. An important starting point for this process is to plan for the configuration management activity, including the scope of work, and then to create an inventory of all those assets the organization currently owns (or controls). Next is establishing a baseline of the proper configurations of that inventory. Once these are in place the baselines should be protected; that is, changes to either the records or the actual components cannot be made without organizational approval. There are also periodic audits to verify that the descriptions of the inventory and corresponding configurations precisely match those in the operational environment. Through these practices the organization is better able to plan for and manage infrastructure growth and change.

Process scope:
- Planning configuration management activity
- Identifying configuration items (CIs)
- Controlling CIs

- Accounting for CI status
- Auditing and verifying CI status

NOTE: Service Asset and Configuration Management is covered in detail in Chapter 10 of this book.

Release and Deployment Management. ITIL provides this process to ensure that adequate plans exist for moving new or enhanced services into production. The focus here is on establishing an organizational release capability, then providing methods for smoothly deploying services under that capability. As part of this, ITIL recommends practices that ensure release packages meet the criteria for moving to the live operational environment; that is, that they have been inspected, tested, and validated. There are also practices that relate to how releases should be scheduled and coordinated so that deployment work has the least impact on operational uptime. And then there are practices that deal with the activities that implementation teams should undertake when installing services. The overriding goal of Release and Deployment Management is to make the transition from service potential to service performance as transparent and trouble-free as possible.

Process scope:
- Scheduling releases
- Planning deployments
- Deploying releases
- Conducting Post Implementation Reviews (PIRs)
- Providing Early Life Support (ELS)

NOTE: Release and Deployment Management is covered in detail in Chapter 11 of this book.

Service Validation and Testing. The purpose of Service Validation and Testing is to ensure that new or enhanced services are thoroughly tested and verified against operating requirements before deployment. This facet of ITIL is sometimes called a process and sometimes a function. It is often integrated with other ITIL processes, such as Release and Deployment Management or Evaluation. But wherever it resides, its mission remains the same. The job here is to document fitness-for-purpose and fitness-for-use, to validate that a service, has been properly tested before deployment, and that those test results demonstrate production readiness. Fitness-for-purpose means that the service (or service component) as designed meets the customer's original requirements. Fitness-for-use means that the service has been shown to work properly (that it integrates well) in the operating environment. Taken together these two traits help ensure service integrity and provide for anticipated service performance.

Process scope:
- Configuring test environments
- Establishing test plans

- Executing test plans
- Reviewing and assessing test results

Change Evaluation. The Change Evaluation process provides a way to verify that a service's performance meets the intended operating parameters and contributes to business missions as intended. This process can be seen as an extension of Service Validation and Testing. Here the organization is concerned with measuring the service's potential to deliver on an expected ROI. This is done in two steps. First, the service is run in a pre-production environment where its performance is measured and evaluated. If it hits ROI targets, it is next moved into live operational service. There, and for a limited time, its performance is once again measured and evaluated. If the returns continue to materialize, the service is left to fulfill its mission. If the operational targets are not met, management can then establish options to reconfigure, redeploy, or perhaps redesign the service. The practices under this process help management gain an objective understanding of service performance so that service commitments can be made with confidence.

Process scope:
- Planning evaluation activity
- Evaluating pre-production performance
- Evaluating operational performance
- Reviewing and assessing evaluation results

Knowledge Management. Knowledge Management is designed to provide the organization with a repository of knowledge that can be referenced as an aid to managing the infrastructure in an effective manner. Knowledge management introduces the concept of the knowledge-base. The acronym DIKW is at the heart of this process: Data, Information, Knowledge, and Wisdom. This is the evolutionary path a knowledge-based organization moves through as it seeks to collect, organize, and distribute the kinds of informative articles and performance statistics that contribute to effective Service Management. The knowledge-base can be used by analysis teams wishing to gain insight into service design and performance considerations. Transition teams can access the repository to acquire support for service enhancements and new releases. Operations personnel can use the repository as they deal with problems and incidents, and perform regular maintenance. A knowledge management program typically covers three areas. The first area is a knowledge strategy, which deals with defining the kinds of information needed to support IT services. The second is the collection approach that specifies how information will be amassed and organized. And the third is the method for knowledge transfer, implementing ways for people to access the knowledge-base promptly and efficiently.

Process scope:
- Establishing a knowledge content strategy
- Establishing a distribution strategy
- Establishing a knowledge management system
- Publishing knowledge articles

Service Operation

Service Operation provides a set of processes and functions to ensure IT services are managed in production in a manner that results in expected service performance - that is, high levels of quality, consistency, and reliability. This fourth ITIL lifecycle phase deals with the day-to-day management, operation, and maintenance of IT services. Here is the culmination of the activities that occur under Service Strategy, Service Design, and Service Transition. And it is here in operations that the tangible value of IT service delivery and service quality is practically realized.

Five processes are defined for this phase. They are:
- Event Management
- Incident Management
- Problem Management
- Request Fulfilment
- Access Management

There are also four functions defined for this phase:
Service Desk
Technical Management
Application Management
IT Operations Management

Event Management. In the domain of ITIL, an event is any change of state with regard to a service or a service component. Many events naturally occur within an IT environment. Some may be ignored. Some may simply be noted and logged. Others require intervention and attention. Incidents and problems are events that require such intervention and attention. The goal of ITIL's Event Management process is to ensure that events in the operational environment are properly tracked, assessed, and managed as necessary. A key activity here is event filtering. An effective Event Management program will filter those events that need attention away from those that do not require attention. This way, Event Management provides a point of triage so that support teams may focus on those incidents and problems that should be addressed in priority order. Event Management is a process usually managed by IT Operation teams.

Process scope:
- Detecting and filtering events
- Classifying and correlating events
- Triggering response actions
- Reviewing response effectiveness
- Closing event tickets

Incident Management. ITIL defines an incident as an event that causes an interruption to an IT service or degrades the quality of that service. An incident may also be an event that has the *potential* to do either. The purpose of Incident Management is to ensure that service interruptions are minimized through proactive and reactive management and response mechanisms. For two reasons Incident Management is closely associated with the Service Desk. First, incidents are usually experienced by users, and so the first course of action is to contact the Service Desk. Second, incidents typically require prompt attention, and the support staff at the Service Desk are prepared to provide that attention. The aim of Incident Management is not to correct what may be the underlying cause of the trouble - that is the purpose of Problem Management. The purpose of Incident Management is to simply return the normal state of IT operation to the user as quickly as possible, in the most expedient manner possible.

Process scope:
- Identifying and registering incidents
- Classifying and prioritizing incidents
- Investigating and diagnosing incidents
- Escalating incidents as necessary
- Resolving incidents
- Closing incident tickets

NOTE: Incident Management is covered in detail in Chapter 12 of this book.

Problem Management. In ITIL terms, a problem is the source of one or more incidents, or a set of related incidents. Because problems arise from endemic defects in the environment, the purpose of Problem Management is to ensure that the underlying root causes of service disruptions are identified and addressed as necessary. The goal is to remove problems so that incidents do not recur. Problems can be addressed in two ways. A permanent fix – a correction – can be applied. When this is not technically practical or economically feasible, a workaround – a patch – can be set into place. When compared to Incident Management (an urgent real-time process), Problem Management can be thought of as a process that is done at a more considered pace. The main activity here is the performance of root cause analyses (RCA) to identify the source of the problem and then propose alternative solutions. This typically requires careful investigation and diagnosis, and may require the participation of a broad spectrum of stakeholders.

Process scope:
- Detecting and registering problems
- Classifying and prioritizing problems
- Investigating and diagnosing problems
- Establishing workarounds
- Implementing resolutions
- Closing problem tickets

NOTE: Problem Management is covered in detail in Chapter 13 of this book.

Request Fulfillment. Like Incident Management, Request Fulfillment is a key customer-facing process under Service Operation. This process is intended to provide the user community with a mechanism for submitting requests for service to IT support teams. These requests are typically of such a nature that they may (but not necessarily always) circumvent the change control process. In this light they are usually considered 'standard changes,' many of which are pre-approved. Request Fulfillment is responsible for providing some form of menu system so that users may self-submit service requests. Fulfillment teams (often members of the Service Desk) are responsible for tracking current request tickets, coordinating any financial authorizations associated with a request, and obtaining formal request approvals. They are then responsible for fulfilling the requests, verifying fulfillment as being successful, and finally, closing out completed request tickets.

Process scope:
- Providing an end-user menu system
- Coordinating financial authorizations
- Fulfilling requests
- Closing request tickets

Access Management. This process is designed to provide customers with appropriate, authorized, and controlled access to services, systems, system components, and data. Access Management is often included as a responsibility under Request Fulfillment, but it carries enough operational significance for ITIL to treat it independently. Access Management is strongly related to the ITIL design process, Information Security Management. Information Security Management sets the strategic approach and operational boundaries for systems, data, and users, and Access Management provides the tactical implementation of that approach. Access Management deals with managing access requests, verifying the appropriateness of such requests, granting rights and setting up security profiles, monitoring access status, monitoring user traffic, and modifying rights as appropriate for changing business conditions.

Process scope:
- Managing access requests
- Verifying access need
- Granting rights
- Monitoring access status
- Tracking access traffic
- Modifying access profiles as required

Service Desk. The Service Desk exists to provide a primary point of contact to the customer community for users seeking technical support, status, and advice. This function serves, in many ways, as the 'face' of Service Management. It is here that customers most often engage with IT personnel. For this reason the Service Desk performs not only a valuable technical support function but also has a significant impact on customer satisfaction levels. Service Desk teams own two main customer-facing responsibilities and two back-end responsibilities. The customer-facing responsibilities include Incident Management and Request Fulfillment. The back-end duties include ticket escalation (when needed) to Tier 2 and Tier 3 teams, and participating in Problem Management activities.

Functional scope:
- Managing incidents
- Managing service requests
- Escalating to specialist teams
- Participating in problem resolution

NOTE: Service Desk is covered in detail in Chapter 14 of this book.

Technical Management. Technical Management is the specialist technical function for IT infrastructure. It is a supporting function to other processes, both in Infrastructure Management and Service Management, providing: research and evaluation, market intelligence (particularly for design and planning and capacity management), proof of concept and pilot engineering, specialist technical expertise (particularly to operations and problem management), creation of documentation (eg for the operational documentation library or known error database).

Functional scope:
- Technical support for IT infrastructure
- Provides specialist expertise and insight on wide range of IT infrastructure issues
- Market intelligence relating to technical aspects
- Responsible for producing technical documentation

Application Management. This function covers a set of best practices to improve the overall quality of IT software development and support through the life cycle of software development projects, with particular attention to gathering and defining requirements that meet business objectives.

Functional scope:
- IT software development support
- Gathering and defining business requirements
- IT software lifecycle support

IT Operations Management. The focus of IT Operations Management is to provide for day-to-day management and maintenance of the IT infrastructure. IT Operations Management resources make up the teams who provide this routine maintenance. These teams typically participate in the Event Management, Incident Management, and Problem Management processes. In terms of regular duties they are responsible for scheduling and running jobs, providing print reports and data outputs, making backups and, when needed, performing restore operations.

Functional scope:
- Scheduling jobs
- Providing print and output
- Performing backups
- Performing restores

Continual Service Improvement

The Continual Service Improvement lifecycle phase provides processes intended to position the organization so that it can develop an ongoing focus on Service Management improvement. Note that this fifth phase in the ITIL service lifecycle is labeled 'Continual'. 'Continual' is different from 'continuous.' Continual Service Improvement is a regular but periodic activity under ITIL and it lies at the philosophic heart of the framework. The idea here is to make conscientious efforts to refine and improve service delivery and service quality over time, and to make these efforts a routine part of how the organization conducts business. With any process program like ITIL this concept of improvement is key. Improved services and Service Management techniques lead to more productive and efficient services. That translates into better support for the business, heightened customer satisfaction levels, and more assured market success.

Four processes are defined for this phase. They are:
- Service Review
- Process Evaluation
- Definition of CSI Initiatives
- Monitoring of CSI Initiatives

Service Review. This process exists to establish a focus on continual improvement across the entire IT organization. This focus includes the service mix, service design, service performance (delivery and quality), and the assets that govern Service Management. Improvement begins with understanding what is essential to business success and this begins with identification of critical success factors. From these a key set is selected and the IT organization begins to measure how it performs. Over time this measurement data is used to make objective and quantifiable judgments as to where services and processes are strong and where opportunities for improvement exist. Once that is understood, IT management can take action – refining, enhancing, maybe even trimming. By following this process in controlled incremental steps, the IT Service Management program should get stronger and stronger over time.

Process scope:
- Establishing improvement plans
- Monitoring service performance and management data
- Analyzing service performance and management data
- Identifying opportunities for improvement
- Implementing improvements
- Assessing improvement effectiveness

NOTE: Service Review is covered in detail in Chapter 15 of this book.

Process Evaluation The objective of this process is to evaluate processes on a regular basis. This includes identifying areas where the targeted process metrics are not reached, and conducting regular benchmarks, audits, maturity assessments and reviews.

Process scope:
- Ongoing evaluation of processes
- Benchmarking and maturity assessments
- Identifying problem areas where target performance is not reached
- Ongoing review of processes

Definition of CSI Initiatives. The objective of this process is to define specific initiatives aimed at improving services and processes, based on the results of service reviews and process evaluations. The resulting initiatives are either internal initiatives pursued by the service provider on their own behalf, or initiatives that require the customer's cooperation.

Process scope:
- Definition of CSI initiatives that are:
  - Internal to the service provider
  - Initiatives requiring customer input

Monitoring of CSI Initiatives. The objective of this process is to verify if improvement initiatives are proceeding according to plan, and to introduce corrective measures where necessary.

Process scope:
- Verifying progress of improvement initiatives
- Introducing corrective measures if required

Service Reporting is a supporting activity. The purpose of this activity is to provide the means to report on service and Service Management performance. Service Reporting is subordinate to Service Improvement. As the organization begins to measure the performance of its IT services and the effectiveness of IT Service Management activities, it will want to share analyses of this data with key stakeholders across the organization and selected customer groups. This is accomplished through Service Reporting. The stakeholders, in the context of their experience, expertise, and responsibility, can use the reports as a foundation for generating ideas and strategies for IT Service Management improvement.

Activity scope:
- Developing performance and improvement reports
- Distributing performance and improvement reports
- Analyzing performance and improvement reports
- Selecting opportunities for improvement
- Planning improvement implementations

NOTE: Service Reporting is covered in detail in Chapter 15 of this book.

1.3. Core components of IT Service Management

As can be seen from the overview above, ITIL covers a wide field of information and offers a broad range of best practices. This volume of information leads us to the first consideration one encounters when beginning an ITIL-based Service Management initiative. This consideration is: what parts of ITIL should be adopted first? There are two general answers to that question, one practical, one practiced.

The practical answer is simple and is endorsed by many practitioners in the field. It is this: implement those components of ITIL that will serve your organization best.

The practiced answer is a little more involved (but equally recognized): implement those components of ITIL-based practices that will serve your organization best in the long term. Include some 'quick wins' to encourage support for the journey to the long-term goals.

Both points of view start from the same mark - that is, ITIL is in place to help IT organizations improve their abilities to deliver high quality IT services. Results in this regard are the only things that count. Comprehensiveness and other such factors must take a back seat to that end. But the practiced view extends this, and as it does so it asks something specific of the organization. With the practiced view there is the understanding that adopting ITIL as a way to manage an IT infrastructure necessarily requires a long-term commitment. And so creating such a program should be begun in a way that sets a solid foundation in place, one that will support that long-term commitment.

Here we come to the topic of 'key processes', the subtitle of this book.

When implementing an ITIL–based program, one designed for the long term, there are certain processes that ought to be considered first. These processes have demonstrated their effectiveness in the short term for strengthening operational control, and they have demonstrated their effectiveness in the long term for establishing a sound base upon which a program might grow.

This book promotes the practiced view, and in doing so focuses on areas common to both ITIL V3 and its more formalized companion ISO/IEC 20000. For the sake of convenience these areas might be grouped into six mini-categories: core processes related to relationship, service design, control, release, resolution, and improvement.[2]

Core Relationship Processes are the processes that act as the 'face of the service provider' and assures that at a strategic level the service provider understands the business and its current and future needs, understands the capabilities and restraints

---

[2] These are not formal ITIL categories, but neither are they arbitrary. These reflect the breakdown used by the ISO/IEC 20000 standard to group its IT Service Management processes.

and finally understands the responsibilities and obligations. One key process is included here:
- Business Relationship Management

Core design processes are those processes essential for planning, structuring, developing, and managing IT services. It is here that consideration is given to such factors as capacity, availability, security, and continuity, addressed both from the viewpoint of performance expectations (defined service levels) and operational integrity. Five key processes are included here:
- Service Level Management
- Capacity Management
- Availability Management
- Information Security Management
- IT Service Continuity Management

Core control processes are those processes essential for protecting the integrity of IT services across the full lifecycle. The scope of this area is two-fold: to manage the activities around which IT services are developed over time, and then to control configurations in operational service to ensure predictable and manageable performance. Two key processes are identified here:
- Change Management
- Service Asset and Configuration Management

The single core release process is an extension of the control processes and is used to ensure that transitioning services from development into operation is handled in a manner that is planned and coordinated, poses little risk to environmental integrity, and has minimal impact to ongoing service delivery. The single key process here is:
- Release and Deployment Management

Core resolution processes are the processes designed to protect users' ability to access those IT services essential for the work of the business. It is here that service interruptions are mitigated, environmental improvements are identified, and – perhaps most significantly – it is here that customer interactions tend to be high. Two key processes and a single function are identified for this process:
- Incident Management
- Problem Management, with
- Service Desk

Core improvement processes are those processes essential for the growth and development not of IT services *per se* but rather of the governing Service Management program. As with any process-based management framework ITIL carries with it an underlying theme of continual improvement. For IT Service Management to realize its full potential in the long run, management must be committed to the program's ongoing development and growth. Just as IT services need to change and evolve over

time in order to meet changing conditions, so too should the methods for managing those services. One key proces is identified here:
- Service Management and Service Improvement

With these core components now identified, let's take a strategic look at the global considerations most organizations will be likely to face when they begin an ITIL adoption effort.

2. Steps towards implementing an ITIL-based IT Service Management program

In the previous chapter we took a high-level look at the scope of ITIL V3, with all of its major processes and functions. In the following chapters we will look at the core ITIL components that usually serve as the foundation for an IT Service Management program. In this chapter we'll take a brief pause from our examination of ITIL's contents and focus on some incremental steps that organizations might consider when they are setting up an IT Service Management program for the first time. These steps are important to consider for three reasons. Implementing an IT Service Management program will require the organization to provide focused resources and assets over a span of time; this will require managerial control and oversight. Then, if the implementation program is not approached in an ordered way, the risks of program failure will rise. And because the resulting program will be a reflection of the organization's culture, it is important that it is carefully designed and implemented in a way that both supports and enhances that culture.

But perhaps the most important reason, above those three, is simply this: implementing an ITIL-based IT Service Management program is an exercise in organizational change, and change is a challenge for any organization, whether it is large or small, mature or immature. Rolling your program through a series of ordered steps is a way to control how change is introduced into the organization. It provides a series of guideposts and checkpoints along the way to ensure that your program, as you build, provides an effective and valuable contribution to the mission of the company.

The nine implementation steps – in their generally accepted order – are:
- Know the model
- Appreciate the value
- Obtain commitment
- Select the scope
- Assess the organization
- Create your ITIL-based IT Service Management program
- Implement the program
- Establish a service-based organization
- Support the program

Here is a brief description of each.

2.1. Know the model

Curiously enough, this first step is sometimes overlooked when an organization sets out to adopt ITIL. The feeling is (and this typically comes from senior management) that someone else can be appointed to get into the nuts and bolts of the task. That is a misleading position to take. ITIL and IT Service Management are not *technical* frameworks as is often thought; they are *managerial* frameworks. They require management to think and act in new ways, much more so than technical teams. And so it is important (even a prerequisite) that your managers understand what ITIL is, what falls under its scope, and how it is structured. They do not need to become experts, but they will need to become comfortable with the model. Without this level of comfort they may have difficulty when they are called on to contribute to the shape and purpose of the program.

2.2. Appreciate the value

Here is another step that is often neglected in IT organizations. Many times an ITIL program (or any other process management initiative for that matter) is initiated by executive command, without an underlying appreciation for why, in tangible terms, such a program might be good for the company. In the absence of this appreciation it becomes difficult to establish the levels of commitment and energy necessary to move such an initiative from concept to execution. It also makes it hard to shape the program if you begin without knowing what it can do for you. ITIL enjoys now a pre-eminent international reputation as the de facto infrastructure management system of choice. However, impressive as that is, it does not tell you much about why your IT organization should adopt it. This is something that you and your managers will need to figure out on your own, because every organization is different and seeks different combinations of business benefits. Toward this end it is helpful to become familiar with how other companies have used ITIL and to gain a picture of how a process-centric approach to IT management can benefit your business customers. It is also helpful to begin thinking about your program's expected return on investment (ROI): what areas are you looking to improve, where do you need to get better? How will those improvements help to achieve the mission of the organization? How will ITIL be able to help in those areas? Without faith that ITIL can indeed bring you the competitive advantages you seek, no amount of energy expenditure will turn out a successful program.

2.3. Obtain commitment

Now that the organization is oriented to the purpose and scope of ITIL and you have identified how it can help your organization, you can work to establish executive commitment. Such commitment is the cornerstone of any ITIL-based initiative; without it no such initiative should be considered. Executive commitment over the long term is required for the success of all programs like this, but it is particularly important early on. Senior business management (where appropriate) and senior IT management should see the value of such a program and understand clearly how its use will help realize business goals. Then two types of commitment should materialize. The first comes in the form of resources; a commitment here is an inescapable aspect of setting up an ITIL program. You are, after all, making an investment in the future state of the company. The size of that investment will naturally vary from IT organization to IT organization but the list of considerations remains fairly constant. You will need funding, facilities, and human resources. These must then be organized into a coordinated force. This brings us to the second type of commitment: the creation of a formal, chartered project. In the same way that strategic and significant IT projects within the IT organization are handled as controlled projects, so too should the ITIL-based effort be treated as a formal project within the organization, with the aim to embed initial best practices. It should be carefully planned with identified deliverables, milestones, and expected outcomes; it should be managed through a formal project management methodology; and it should be tracked, controlled and monitored, reported on, and held accountable to senior management.

2.4. Establish a service-based organization

This step may represent the biggest challenge for IT organizations, and the topic cannot be fully addressed in a couple of paragraphs. At the same time, however, it is important to note, because treating IT as a set of integrated services lies at the heart of ITIL. We touched on this theme in the Introduction and Chapter 1 of this book, so we will just briefly revisit it here. Managing IT as a service often requires an IT organization to willingly make a cultural shift, moving away from a component-based, product-oriented view of IT. This can be a tough shift to make; after all, infrastructure technicians and analysts can spend most of their time looking at components. But in a way that is beside the point. What ITIL strives for is to have *management* view things differently.

Considering the purchase and maintenance of a car might make a good analogy. Any car is a collection of complex systems: ignition system, cooling system, sound system, transmission system, etc. Owners of cars certainly care about these systems but usually are not particularly concerned with what individual parts are required to make up each system. They just want the cars to start, to not run hot, and to shift smoothly. A good car manufacturer will work to recognize its customers' desires and needs and supply cars designed to meet both. They will then warrant such performance, and provide qualified technical support when service is needed. That is the approach ITIL would like to see with IT organizations. How you achieve that will depend largely on your culture, on your industry, and on the customer base you serve. But you will certainly want to provide an organizational design that focuses on the customer-IT relationship. This includes identifying those services you do provide and ensuring their innate capabilities, establishing service level agreements (SLAs) with customers about expected performance, and appointing service managers to ensure that service quality and delivery consistently meet performance expectations.

2.5. Select the program's scope

Once you are able to view your IT organization as a service-based organization you will want to select the scope of your ITIL program, and then decide which parts of the service mix you will manage under ITIL recommendations. The scope should reflect the business and technical needs of the organization in light of the resources available to the initiative. Decide which of the core ITIL processes you will adopt first (they are described in the following chapters of this book). Strike a balance between need and resources; seek out high value activities first; work to identify opportunities for quick wins and visible returns. To do this you should engage with those stakeholders who will be most affected by the scope you are working to select. Communicate to them the purpose, goals, and shape of the program; ask for their input and assistance. And let them know that the program scope can always be adjusted later if needed.

2.6. Assess the organization

Here is what you have done so far. You have learned about the scope and focus of ITIL. You see value in what it can do for your organization. You have received executive commitment to sponsor a program initiative. You have added a Service Management component to your organizational design. And you have selected the scope of your program. Now it is time for a *gap analysis*. A gap analysis is an assessment that compares ITIL practices with those practices you are currently performing. In process terms you are comparing the 'as-is' to the 'to-be' state. The purpose is to identify any gaps that exist, which will need to be filled in – accounted for, created – in order to achieve ITIL best practice. You will want to look at your current policies, processes, procedures, work products, and job roles; not just processes but also people-aspects and technology aspects. Note your strengths and weaknesses; then use the weaknesses as the basis for creating a Program Completion Plan. This is the plan to fill the gaps. Obtain executive commitment to the Completion Plan and then execute it.

2.7. Create your ITIL-based IT Service Management program

This is one of the major efforts in a new IT Service Management initiative. It is with this step that you create your program, and in doing this you create the program's *assets*. The major objective of this book is to assist you with this step, to describe what kinds of assets you might need and describe how they might be structured. These assets include all those things that will make up your program. This includes policies, processes, procedures, checklists, forms, templates, work instructions and so on.

Reference the individual chapters in this book for recommended program components. This will help you decide what range of assets is right for your organization.

In creating your program you may decide that you need to acquire (or perhaps reconfigure) some support tools. Tools such as a configuration management database system (CMDB) and an incident tracking system are typically employed in an ITIL program. In light of this you will need to identify what kinds of tools you need, evaluate available options, acquire the right products, and then configure them to your needs. You will want to make sure that your tools and processes are aligned to work well together, to complement and support one another. Once the tools are configured you will want to make sure that your staff members are trained in their use and comfortable with their operation.

2.8. Implement the program

As a general rule, when an organization's ITIL-based program falls short of expected performance it is usually because management paid too little attention to implementation. It is curious that many organizations willing to invest heavily in program completion seem to lose interest at implementation and pay the effort little attention. The better approach of course is to pay proper attention to this effort. It is absolutely essential to program success, both short-term and long-term. Toward this end management should strive to make implementation a focused and visible activity. It should be treated as a formal activity, and a high-end one at that. It should be thoroughly planned and managed in a formal way, and ensure that the right set of assets is in place and ready for deployment. During implementation executive management should seek regular feedback from users and line managers about how the rollout is proceeding. Central to an effective deployment is attention paid to carefully training users in the purpose, scope, and use of the program. This is a cornerstone implementation activity, the goal of which is to help individuals see where they fit into the program and what responsibilities they will be accountable for. When users are comfortable with their areas of activity, program effectiveness can be maximized. To support this the organization should supplement training with coaching and mentoring. Mentors can help people to further adopt the program, establish its use, and promote its institutionalization.

2.9. Support program use

Implementing a Service Management program based on ITIL is not a finite initiative. It is an ongoing way of doing business; it is an evolutionary process of growth and development. Management's job does not end with a successful deployment; in fact this is really where it begins. Management's real job is to promote (and ensure) the ongoing use of the program in support of IT and business missions. This involves three things: working to see that the program becomes institutionalized over time, periodically assessing the program to gain insight into performance and achievement of best practice, and then initiating a continual improvement capability across organizational teams.

Institutionalization

Institutionalization occurs when the activities of the ITIL program have become embedded into the corporate culture; that is, they have become the accepted way of doing business; they have become habit. This is the ultimate achievement of any process program and the end state you should desire for your program. And so, as an extension of implementation, you should work to embed the program activities into the other daily routines of IT activities. You should also promote the concept that the ITIL/IT Service Management program really is an extension of the organization's culture; after all, it has been based on what is important to the company in terms of managing IT services. It is helpful to understand that institutionalization takes time, so remember to give the program the time and attention it needs to become the normal way of doing business for the company.

Assessment

Another aspect of program support is the periodic assessing of the design and operation teams. The purpose of this quality assurance activity is two-fold. First, it gauges how effectively the program is working in light of the IT mission and its goals. Second, it gauges how well teams are using the program; that is, how readily they are operating within the boundaries of policies and standards. Assessment is a way for senior management to gain objective insight into program performance; assessments should be seen as an improvement and coaching exercise. Assessment results should be shared with relevant stakeholders and used as a way to move the program forward. Performance and quality issues should be addressed in a positive manner and assessment trends tracked over time to measure how well the program is moving toward institutionalization.

Continual improvement

Continual improvement is at the center of any ITIL-based program. It is how the program is managed over time. The idea with continual improvement is to always have an eye open for how your IT organization is operating, and to strive to raise that performance level when technology or market needs present viable opportunities. Management should ensure that the organization conscientiously solicits improvement advice from customers, from service users, from IT managers, and from technology staff. They should also ensure that measures of program performance are collected on a regular basis, and then they should use all this information to assess how the IT organization can become better at what it does. As needed, the IT organization can then periodically re-align its Service Management focus with evolving business goals and objectives, then plan and implement improvements so the program becomes what its potential promises: a valuable organizational asset.

2.10. The ongoing care and maintenance of your program: Plan-Do-Check-Act

In the process improvement industry there is an iterative development method known as PDCA, Plan-Do-Check-Act, which was made popular by Edwards Deming (though he always referred to it as the Shewart Cycle after the quality expert, Walter Shewart). The cycle of PDCA helps to improve a process over time through a series of four discrete steps. Once a program (such as ITIL-based IT Service Management) is in place in an organization, PDCA can be used as a means to manage the program's lifecycle. The ISO/IEC 20000 specification, the official IT Service Management standard and closely related to ITIL, specifies PDCA as a means to manage ITSM programs, so this is a good place to take a quick look at it. (For more on this topic, see Chapter 15, Service Improvement.)

PLAN: Plan Service Management
The first step in managing an ITIL-based IT Service Management program is to develop a plan by which it will be managed. In other words, approach the program's management in a controlled way. This is typically realized by what's known as a Service Improvement Plan (SIP) but it can take any form that seems best for your organization. The purpose of this step is to plan the implementation and delivery of Service Management over the course of a set period (usually annually). The plan defines the scope of the Service Management program; establishes the objectives and requirements that are to be achieved by Service Management; identifies the processes that are to be executed in support of the program; identifies the various management roles and responsibilities, including the senior executive ownership and service process owners. The plan also details the interfaces between Service Management processes and the manner in which the service activities are to be coordinated. Budgets, timelines, deliverables, communication routes, and assigned resources are all also specified in the plan. Once in place and approved, the plan is used as the master tool by which the program is managed.

DO: Implement Service Management
The purpose of the 'do' step is to implement the Sservice Management objectives and plan. The service provider conducts all the oversight activities necessary to ensure that the Service Management program becomes and remains an active organizational asset, one that supports the business and IT missions of the organization. This includes allocating funds and budgets; assigning and provisioning roles and responsibilities; documenting and maintaining policies, plans, procedures and definitions for the sets of ITIL processes; identifying and mitigating service risks; managing teams and recruiting and developing appropriate staff; managing facilities and budget outlays; managing specialized teams including Service Desk and operations staff; and reporting progress against the plans. 'Do' can be thought of as the day-to-day activities required to keep the Service Management program running (as opposed to the services themselves).

CHECK: Monitor, measure, and review

With 'check' the organization does three things. It periodically monitors the sustained performance of the Service Management program against plan objectives. It measures specific attributes of performance in both a quantitative and qualitative way. And it ensures that nonconformance issues are dealt with in a corrective way. All three of these are commonly addressed through a Process Quality Assurance function in which technical and managerial teams and activities are assessed according to a set schedule. The assessment program is a planned activity and takes into consideration the status and importance of the processes and areas to be assessed, as well as the results of previous assessments. The objectives of Service Management reviews and assessments are documented together with any identified remedial actions. Any significant areas of concern or incompatibility are then communicated to relevant stakeholders.

ACT: Work to continually improve

With 'act' the organization sets into place the capabilities needed to identify and coordinate improvements to its service set. This domain includes service features, service delivery quality, and Service Management effectiveness. To do this, the organization sets a program in place where it periodically, on a regular basis, assesses data collected in the 'check' phase above. Using this to establish a performance baseline and benchmark, the organization consults with relevant parties to solicit inputs about improvements from all the Service Management process areas. From this input the organization then identifies a series of potential improvement opportunities and assigns to them targets for quality, costs, resource utilization, ROI, etc. The next step is to select a set of improvements to implement. This is done through improvement planning, deployment, and verification. The effectiveness of the improvements is measured, assessed, and reported on. The process then starts over.

The cycle of Plan-Do-Check-Act combines with the nine initial implementation steps described at the start of this chapter to give you a managed approach for initiating, creating, deploying, and maintaining an ITIL-based IT Service Management program. Finally, here is a brief series of practical tips...

2.11. Some practical tips

In addition to the nine implementation steps described above and the quick review of Plan-Do-Check-Act there are some practical tips you may wish to consider that can help make your program as successful as it might be. These tips are based on on-the-job lessons learned, the result of working on a variety of ITIL projects, some large, and some small, but all requiring each organization to adopt new practices and, to one extent or another, embrace change. Here are eight readily applicable tips.

Keep it light at first. Your initial program does not need to address every aspect of ITIL or IT Service Management right out of the gate. Keep it light in the beginning and then grow it over time. You will find with this approach that your people will be able to adopt components quicker, use them appropriately, and learn from experience in which direction growth should proceed.

Put the organization's values into the program. Build your program so that it reflects and supports what is important to the organization. Work with senior management early on in order to determine this. When your ITIL-based program is able to demonstrably move business and IT missions forward you will find that management will back the program's continued growth and development.

Commit to ongoing training and mentoring. Over time your program will change and it is highly likely that your people may change, too. That is why it is important to embed the element of training/mentoring into the regimen of program management. By providing a continual resource of education you can ensure that people remain comfortable working within the program as the program's components change, as job roles change, and as new people come on board.

Periodically review performance. This is a tip for senior IT management. These people should periodically meet and review the program's performance and effectiveness. This review should be conducted from two perspectives: understanding how to refine the program to make it more effective and understanding how to shape the program so that it remains at the service of changing IT and business missions.

Reward adoption. IT Service Management may be an executive responsibility but it will not prove effective without adoption by your various IT team members. Performance may be the single most important factor in program success. Management needs to be aware of this and conscientiously promote adoption. This should include rewarding people and teams who contribute an early effort to make the program successful. The rewards need not be extravagant but they should be visible and valuable. When such signs of commitment are clear others will join in the effort.

Keep the message alive. This has to do with on-going commitment. It is important that senior IT management continues to promote the program after it is up and running. This will be a reminder to the organization that the program is still an important and valuable management asset. Without such communication it is possible that the program's operation may slip under the radar and dissipate over time. By keeping the message alive the program will be able to remain in the forefront of management considerations, and thus developed with focused attention.

Welcome change. There are two points to consider here. The first is to remember that your ITIL –based program will by necessity change with time – it will change as you refine it and add to it, and it will change to remain aligned with IT and business missions. And so you should welcome change into the program. It is a natural element to any process improvement initiative. At the same time it is wise to avoid constant change and flux; too much of that and your people may have a hard time fixing on a solid baseline, one they can become comfortable using. Instead, periodic, planned change is the best way to grow and develop a program.

Be patient. The ultimate goal for any ITIL-based IT Service Management program is that it becomes embedded; it becomes habitual within the organization. But understand that this will not happen overnight. It takes time and focused attention. So be patient, especially here at the outset of the journey. Give it time and give it the attention it deserves and your program will be successful.

The ITIL components described above constitute the core of an IT Service Management program. And they make up the heart of this book. At this point we can move deeper into the model, looking at these core components individually, with a view to how each might be effectively implemented in an IT organization. Let's begin this with a look at a key strategic ITIL consideration, one that will by necessity influence the shape and tone of any implementation effort. This is Business Relationship Management.

2.12. Implementation checklist

The material presented in this book covers a range of information concerning aspects of an ITIL-based Service Management program. Most of this material is focused on implementation. The following table extends this a step further. It presents a list of activities that may be helpful when you move to set up such a program in your IT organization. These activities take you from initiating the effort to maintaining adoption. And while the steps are presented in something of a chronological order there is no rule that says they have to be executed in this order.

Table 2.1 Implementation checklist for Service Management

Initiate	Understand the organization's need for a Service Management program.
	Understand the value an ITIL-based program will bring to the organization; document this value.
	Build the business case for a Service Management program.
	Document Critical Success Factors (CSFs) and performance targets for the program.
	Seek and acquire IT management approval of this material.
	Seek and acquire business management approval of this material.
	Seek and acquire executive commitment to the Service Management program.
	Acquire necessary program resources (funding, personnel, tools, etc.).
	Establish the program's strategic goals and objectives.
	Establish the program's executive policy.
Assign	Work with HR to establish Service Management process owner job descriptions.
	Adopt the job descriptions as official.
	Appoint Service Management process owners.
	Provision the positions as necessary.
Assess	Based on ITIL's practice recommendations, select the scope of Service Management for your program.
	Perform a Gap Analysis against this scope: • Assess the organization's existing processes against ITIL recommendations. • Assess personnel knowledge and skill sets. • Assess existing artifacts and work products. • Analyze and communicate the results of the Gap Analysis.

Plan and execute	Establish a Program Completion Plan to fill identified gaps. Acquire organization approval of the plan. Execute the plan.
	Establish Service Management policies. Establish Service Management process program assets. Determine methods to develop business service requirements, technical service requirements, and service component requirements. Develop service design, transition, and operation guidelines. Define Service Management work products. Establish a Process Asset Library (PAL). Place program assets under version control.
	Establish program measures – Key Performance Indicators (KPIs). Define collection and analysis techniques. Document reporting and distribution requirements. Identify and implement service monitoring tools and techniques.
	Establish Service Knowledge Management System (SKMS) requirements. Evaluate available SKMS solutions. Select an SKMS solution. Configure the SKMS solution. Implement the SKMS solution. Train personnel on the purpose and use of the SKMS system.
Support	Develop collaboration guidelines with management teams. Develop collaboration guidelines with IT technical teams. Develop collaboration guidelines with user communities.
Implement	Train relevant personnel on the use of the program. Implement the program across relevant organizational groups. Mentor and coach as necessary.
	Periodically assess the program for operational performance. Periodically assess the program for process performance. Report assessment results to management.
	Establish Service-related Service Level Agreements (SLAs) with customer groups. Establish Operational Level Agreements (OLAs) with support teams. Establish Underpinning Contracts (UCs) with third party providers.
Measure	As planned, collect program performance measures. Analyze program performance measures. Interpret program performance measures. Report on Service Management program effectiveness.
Improve	Periodically assess program performance to identify improvement opportunities. Elicit improvement opportunities from staff and customers. Select improvements. Design and implement improvements. Monitor program performance.

3. Business Relationship Management

Here in Chapter Three we begin our *pro forma* look at the processes that make up the core components of ITIL. And odd though it may seem, we begin with a look at Business Relationship Management, a process that is not even in ITIL until the release of the 2011 edition.

Business Relationship Management is a process originally identified for the ISO/IEC 20000 standard. This is the standard that guides implementation of IT Service Management programs for organizations that may wish to have their achievement officially certified. ISO/IEC 20000 and ITIL V3 are very closely aligned, with the major difference being that ITIL contains a larger set of Service Management processes. The practices ISO requires for Business Relationship Management are actually included, although a little less specifically, as ITIL recommendations for Service Level Management. So, if you implement Service Level Management (see Chapter 4) you will automatically account for most of Business Relationship Management. But the real reason we include Business Relationship Management as ISO describes it is because of its explicit focus on the IT-customer relationship. ITIL, as a mechanism for IT Service Management, shares this focus. ITIL's aim is for IT stakeholders and business stakeholders to collaborate so as to form a tight-knit, integrated partnership. The view is that this is the best way to harness technology considerations to the overall mission of the business. Borrowing the ISO process simply lets us carry this view more clearly to the surface.

Business Relationship Management is an oversight role within IT Service Management that sees the relationship between the business and IT as an integrated, on-going partnership, one based on communication, cooperation, and collaboration. The purpose of this process is to establish and maintain a beneficial, bilateral relationship between the service provider and the customer, one based on an understanding of the customer's business drivers.

There are three aspects to Business Relationship Management: planning, interfacing, and evaluating.

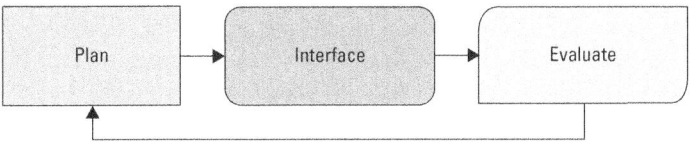

Figure 3.1 Typical Business Relationship Management process flow

The Business Relationship Management process is a continuous and ongoing cycle of planning, interfacing with the customer, evaluating performance and satisfaction levels, and then adjusting plans and activities as necessary.

3.1. Business Relationship Management activities

The Business Relationship Management process consists of a set of activities that continually cycle through and around. The main purpose of this process is to set into place a method for working and, especially, communicating with the customer. When faced with this responsibility, many IT organizations take an *ad hoc* approach, mistakenly assuming that the job is personality-driven and not amenable to formal controls, any degree of formal controls.[3] Personality is important, and social ability is a desired trait in any employee in any organization. But Business Relationship Management aims to instill a quality of social ability at the organizational level, such that it becomes a shared organizational trait and an institutionalized organizational capability. This process asks you to move through three general tasks. The first is to establish in your IT organization the management tools that will frame how you interact with customers. Next, you interact, placing an emphasis on communication, service performance, and customer satisfaction. Then you evaluate the strength of the relationship and adjust anything that needs adjusting to help the relationship grow stronger. A description of each of these activities follows.

1. Planning

The planning activity for Business Relationship Management might be better expressed as 'preparation.' It is here through a series of eight steps that you set your approach in place, equipping the program with assets and artifacts useful for dynamically managing the relationship in a controlled but flexible way. These are the eight steps:

- *Appoint a Technical Account Manager.* This is the role that carries out the bulk of the relationship management activities. The Technical Account Manager is the person (or the team) who liaises between the customer and technical teams. This manager is responsible for coordinating communications, setting agendas, facilitating discussions, sharing and interpreting information, resolving issues, and the myriad other activities that come with representing an IT service provider.
- *Identify key customer stakeholders.* These stakeholders are the functional counterparts of the Technical Account Manager. These are the customer representatives with whom the account manager will mainly work. They are the key points of contact for the business, and represent business interests and objectives in the relationship.
- *Acquire an understanding of the customer's business mission and market drivers.* In order for the service provider to deliver the right type and mix of IT services, it needs to have an appreciation of the customer's business mission and market drivers.

---

[3] When technology people resist process the reason they typically give to defend their position is that technology work – whatever job may be the subject of the discussion – is best managed at the individual level.

This is a distinguishing feature of IT Service Management: it is an obligation on the part of the provider to learn what it can about its customer base, learn what is important to that customer base, and only from that vantage point shape a service offering.

- *Establish and maintain a Communications Plan with the customer.* This plan is the central tool for managing the business relationship process. It describes the communication approach the IT organization will take for initiating, conducting, acting upon, and evaluating customer communications. The plan will typically cover approaches both for formal and informal communications. The plan will define and document the frequencies of communication venues, types of meetings, communication methods, stakeholders and resources. It is usually authored by the account manager, but should be reviewed and approved with input from the customer stakeholders. This plan will shape how the relationship is managed and developed over time.

- *Establish a formal complaint (and compliment) process.* With this step the organization establishes a process whereby customers can submit complaints (and compliments) to senior IT management. As with all businesses (product or service) when a route is readily available for customers to register complaints and those complaints are promptly addressed, the 'blame' aspect of the issue tends to diminish. When routes are cumbersome or complaints disregarded even small issues can quickly escalate into large ones. The complaint process, then, is one way to demonstrate an IT organization's proactive commitment to customer satisfaction. The process should be closely allied with the customer satisfaction support process below.

- *Establish formal customer satisfaction metrics.* One of the key jobs of technical account management is to keep a finger on the pulse of customer satisfaction. As has been stated earlier and will be repeated throughout this book, customer satisfaction is a core concern of any ITIL-based IT Service Management program. For this reason the organization should regularly measure customer satisfaction. This is typically done through the use of one or more metrics, the most common being surveys. In a typical setup the IT organization might send a satisfaction survey to (as an example) every tenth caller to the Service Desk; then the IT organization might send a survey to everyone on the business side once a year. The pattern you decide to implement will naturally depend on your own needs and those of your customer; the key is to devise metrics that adequately capture a qualitative picture of your performance as perceived through your customers' eyes.

- *Establish formal customer satisfaction support processes.* The customer satisfaction support process takes advantage of the information that comes from the use of the metrics described above. The process typically covers the following activities: when to issue metrics, how the data will be collected, where the data will be stored, how the data will be processed, what reports will be produced, to whom the reports will be distributed, and what follow-up actions will be taken based on the results.

- *Establish a formal performance-delivery contract (e.g. Service Level Agreement - SLA) with the customer.* An SLA serves as an official performance contract between you and your customer. In many ways it is like a warranty; it defines the level of service the customer can expect to receive from your Service Management efforts. The SLA is a cornerstone relationship artifact. It is at the center of most

IT Service Management programs and the success you have in realizing its performance targets goes a long way to shaping how successful the relationship is. (For a detailed discussion on this topic, see Chapter 4.)

With these assets in place, the *pro forma* work of the Business Relationship Management program now begins.

2. Interfacing

The bulk of the work of Business Relationship Management goes into interfacing with the customer. Here the Business Relationship Management Plan is executed in all its detail. The key to this activity is that the relationship is 'controlled,' not in a way that would be seen as restrictive or binding, but rather in a way that promotes collaboration, flexibility, and responsiveness. Naturally the key technique of interfacing is face-to-face communication.

- *Communicating.* It is with this step that the Technical Account Manager (see the *Roles* section in this chapter) meets regularly with customer stakeholders to discuss service delivery, performance, and quality. Issues and concerns are addressed. Current and planned activities are discussed. General progress is assessed and mapped. Two forms of follow-up tend to come from these meetings. The first are documented meeting minutes. These minutes are captured, put in writing, and then distributed to relevant stakeholders for two reasons. They give stakeholders a chance to verify the documented information and they are the basis for follow-on actions. They are in a very real sense a diary of the provider-customer relationship. For tactical action items that affect the contract, the Technical Account Manager will use change control to make sure they are managed and addressed. Action items that do not affect the contract will be handled outside change control but are nevertheless addressed. When action items that come from customer contact are managed through to closure the indication is that communication channels are working effectively.
- *Measuring service performance.* Providing information is the purpose of communicating. With this step service performance is measured in order to produce information. In the following chapter we will look at Service Level Management. Under Service Level Management the IT organization works with the customer to develop SLAs. These SLAs set performance targets relative to the services being delivered. One of the jobs of the Technical Account Manager is to ensure that service performance metrics are indeed being captured and that performance reports are being made available on a regular basis to the customer. It is the analysis of this information that largely sets the tone of the provider-customer relationship, and the approach taken to Business Relationship Management.
- *Tracking customer satisfaction.* This third step prompts the Technical Account Manager (in practice, all of senior IT management) to conscientiously track customer satisfaction levels. Using the complaint process, the satisfaction support process, and the metrics, customer satisfaction levels will be measured and assessed over time. Satisfaction level targets should be in place against which results can be compared. The job here is to monitor customer satisfaction levels; if they fall below an acceptable range, the Technical Account Manager works with IT teams and the

customer to identify ways through which the customer satisfaction levels can rise to where they ought to be.

3. Evaluating
Periodically the organization's relationship managers should evaluate how their relationship management practices are performing. Three qualities are typically assessed; the first is service performance. The organization evaluates service performance levels compared to contracted levels. An analysis of service level agreements compared with performance is helpful. A healthy indicator is the achievement of performance targets. The second quality is an assessment of customer satisfaction levels. If customer satisfaction is up to expectations relationship practices can be seen as effective. If customer satisfaction levels are low, or disproportionate with service level performance, the relationship practices may require deeper scrutiny. The third quality is contractual performance (above and beyond SLAs); in short, the assessment here is of value. A robust indication of sound Business Relationship Management is when you can manage a balanced blend of high quality service delivery, high (or at least stable) levels of customer satisfaction, and adequate return on investment. This indicates a nicely balanced relationship. But because the values of these three qualities are prone to flux over time the activity of evaluation needs to be a regular one. If the results are what you intended, then your practices are probably in good shape. If they are not, you and your team should consider recommendations for improvements so that the relationship practices can bring you and your customers into a closer, more effective and equitable partnership.

3.2. Process inputs and outputs

The Business Relationship Management process is not a stop-and-go workflow as might be seen with many other processes. Rather it is one that is continually in motion, flowing and adjusting to changing conditions. As long as an IT organization has customers it will be engaged in Business Relationship Management, which makes it difficult to discuss inputs and outputs, entry and exit criteria, as if there were concrete starting and stopping points, internal and external. However, since we use this format throughout the rest of the book where the processes are more formalized and structured, we will follow it here.

Entry criteria
The entry criterion for the Business Relationship Management process is simple: it begins whenever an IT organization engages in a business relationship with a customer and vice versa.

NOTE: It is helpful to note here that while Business Relationship Management is an ongoing activity, its more formal components may be initiated at certain milestones in the relationship. Often this happens on an annual or semi-annual basis, depending on the form and structure of the organization's contract, when contracts or agreements may be renegotiated and when performance may be assessed.

Inputs

Inputs into the process can come from a variety of sources, individually or in combination. These inputs can include:
- Existing or proposed contracts
- Existing or proposed communications plans
- Strategic plans (business and technical)
- To-date SLA performance metrics
- Customer satisfaction levels and customer complaints

Exit criteria

Because the relationship management process is never complete (unless a contract is being closed) there are no hard exit criteria. But at certain relationship milestones there may be formal review and assessment activities. If so, the exit criteria may include the following:
- New agreements established for future communication, collaboration, and service performance expectations.

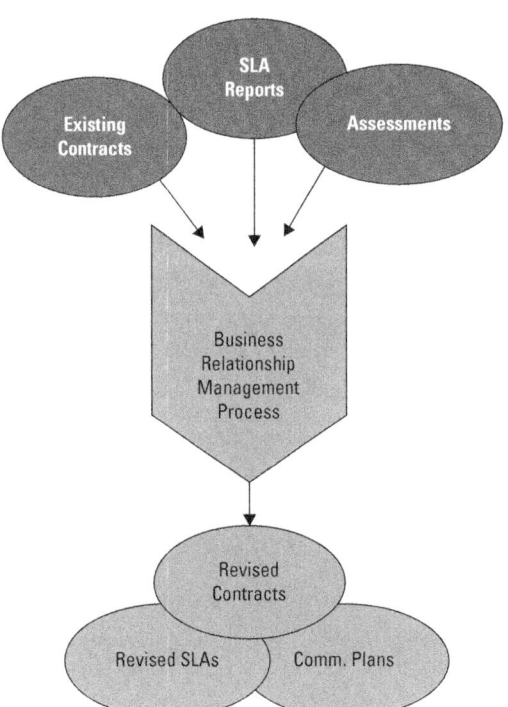

Figure 3.2 Inputs and outputs for Business Relationship Management

Outputs

The Business Relationship Management process, once formal activities have concluded, may produce a set of work products in support of the procedural activities. At a minimum the set will usually include the following artifacts:
- Performance assessments
- Renegotiated contracts
- Renegotiated service level agreements
- New or refreshed communication plans

3.3. Processes related to Business Relationship Management

Every aspect of an IT Service Management program is related to Business Relationship Management. It is the job of Technical Account Management to ensure that services, systems, data, and processes are configured in such a way that they reliably met the needs of the customer. If service delivery or quality drift from this goal it is the responsibility of Technical Account Management to ensure that the affected capabilities, whatever they may be, are restored to appropriate levels as quickly as possible. Two core processes are directly relevant to Business Relationship Management:
- Service Level Management is a process whose work products (SLAs) must often account for Business Relationship Management commitments (and vice versa).
- Service Improvement activities are often initiated through Business Relationship Management communication channels and insight.

Service Level Management

Because of its importance in shaping a cooperative, collaborative provider-customer environment, Business Relationship Management is commonly included as a major driver in the shaping and structuring of SLAs. The SLAs inevitably include targets for service delivery and service quality, and these targets need to be balanced and realistic. The Technical Account Manager is usually responsible for negotiating these targets, which means that it is important for Technical Account Managers to work closely with Service Level Managers to negotiate appropriate performance targets with customers. Once SLAs have been agreed, it is also important that they continue to work with Service Level Managers to periodically assess and evaluate the organization's performance in terms of delivering services.

In summary:
- Relationship practices and insight have direct bearing on overall service quality, and thus on the customer's perception of IT's value to the business.
- SLAs should set realistic service performance expectations.
- Effective management practices are essential for supporting IT's effort to create strong and cooperative business relationships.

Service Improvement

Service Improvement is an umbrella activity for all aspects of an IT Service Management program, with particular emphasis on relationship management practices. With Business Relationship Management, improvement work falls into two broad categories. The first is technical: Technical Account Managers work with business stakeholders to investigate ways in which service policies, plans, designs, and tactics can be enhanced. The second category is procedural support. Management teams (along with process owners) work to identify improvement opportunities that can be applied to the program, processes, procedures, monitoring tools, and measurements.

In summary:
- A key responsibility of Business Relationship Management is to work with customers to continually investigate and identify ways in which service designs and operating performance can be improved.
- Improvements should not be confined just to the technical arena; Business Relationship Management teams should seek improvements in relationship techniques, management processes, monitoring tools, and measurements.

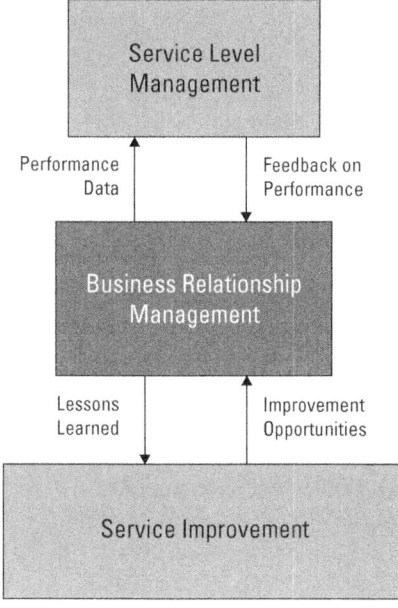

Figure 3.3 Processes related to Business Relationship Management

3.4. Tools and techniques

Business Relationship Management is the area that requires, more than any others, a strong set of 'soft' skills, those that effectively promote successful interpersonal relationships. Whole books have been written on this topic, of course; as a summary, we identify here three techniques that are typically seen as essential for relationship programs. Strong customer communication procedures are needed to establish a partnership based on trust, reliability, and commitment. A balanced approach to contract management is required in order to protect and realize initial agreements and expectations. And an effective Service Level Management program is needed in order to track progress against contractual obligations over time. These three techniques are described below.

Strong customer relationships	Business Relationship Management requires firm agreement between the customer and IT management on specific areas of operational performance and focus. IT management and business management must work to forge a close relationship so that IT objectives and business objectives can merge and complement one another, as closely as practical. IT management and business management should strive to work in a committed partnership to refine and improve services over time.
A balanced approach to contract management	In order to capture delivery and performance expectations the organization should have a sound contract in place, one that mutually balances the needs of both the customer and the IT organization. The organization should have established mechanisms for monitoring and reviewing contract performance over time. **NOTE:** This is closely linked to the Service Level Management program (see Chapter 4).
An effective Service Level Management program	To manage the expectations of both parties, and to adequately focus resources, IT management should implement a sound Service Level Management program. This program should include commitments to levels of service delivery, service performance, and service quality. For more on this, see Chapter 4.

3.5. Key Performance Indicators

Measuring Business Relationship Management performance can be tricky for two reasons. Its success is intertwined with the success of the IT Service Management program as a whole. Plus, its focus on 'soft skills' makes its results difficult to quantify. However, there are some key performance indicators (KPIs) that you might wish to consider, at least from a strategic level, to help you assess how well your relationship management efforts are working. Here are four metrics that are readily available in most ITIL-based programs.

SLA performance measures
In Chapter 4 we shall look at Service Level Management and at how SLAs are used to measure and report on IT performance. These measures indicate how well IT teams are meeting contractual obligations, and as KPIs these measures deliver good value. So SLA metrics are at the top of the list of KPIs for Business Relationship Management. Business Relationship Management performance is closely linked to SLA performance and ITIL's Service Level Management process. The KPIs defined for Service Level Management are just as valid and useful for Business Relationship Management and should be so applied if they provide value for your organization. For more on this topic, see the next chapter.

Number and types of customer complaints

This is a count of the total number by type of customer complaints (and compliments may be included) for a given period of time. This data can be useful for acquiring a qualitative understanding of the customer's view of IT strengths and weaknesses, and thus help identify potential modifications to strengthen relationships in the future. We mention the importance that ITIL places on customer satisfaction many times in this book. It can even be argued that achieving a high level of satisfaction is more important that an equal level of technical competence. The push behind this KPI is to not forget the criticality of this 'soft' aspect when evolving an IT Service Management program.

Number and types of contract modifications

This count offers an analysis of contract activity over time. Lots of activity from either party to the contract may indicate that a poor initial contract has been set into place, or that a formerly balanced contract has skewed off track over time. It may also indicate a business or technical environment that is too fluid. Tracking and analyzing the reasons and the sources of contract and SLA modifications can give IT management insight into what kind of relationship exists between the provider and customer, and why – from an IT perspective – the existing relationship may be unsatisfactory. A key part of Business Relationship Management is to work to establish balanced agreements. A significant volume of activity here may indicate a need to take a corrective look at Business Relationship Management practices.

Profitability of performance

This is a breakdown, for a given period of time, of the cost of fulfilling contract obligations at current performance levels versus income. In other words, it's a look at profitability. This data helps establish a picture as to how well balanced the contract is, and how well balanced the customer-IT relationship is. If profitability is high yet the customer is dissatisfied the relationship cannot be considered to be in good shape. The same point applies if the customer is delighted with service but operations are losing money. Steady monitoring of this indicator (which most professional business organizations will already be doing) is a way to keep the relationship in balance, to make sure that both parties enjoy benefits from the association.

3.6. Critical Success Factors

Because Business Relationship Management operates at such a high level across the enterprise the Critical Success Factors (CSFs) that indicate it to be successful are at an equally high level. But because this process is so integrated with every other aspect of an IT Service Management program and so intertwined it is often hard to clearly distinguish earned success from borrowed success. Nevertheless, if an IT service engagement is meeting its contractual obligations, is realizing its SLA targets, and has achieved positive customer satisfaction levels then that relationship and the way that relationship is being managed can be called a success. Here is a brief description of these three success factors.

Contractual obligations are being met

You will know that your Business Relationship Management program is doing its job, and perhaps more than its job, when you can demonstrate that contractual obligations are being met. That is not to discount the value of the shop-floor work that needs to be realized in order to reach this position but it illustrates the importance of attending to relationships. Without effective relationship management it would be difficult to operate under a balanced contract that is capable of being realized. A key task of Business Relationship Management is to help set balanced contracts and SLAs in place. Once a contract is underway it is the job of the Business Relationship Manager to interface with the customer, to communicate the status of activities and functional needs in an open and clear manner. When things go wrong, the manager's job is to work with the customer to mitigate poor performance and set corrective actions in place so that performance improves. And since this may require the effort of the whole IT staff it is safe to say that the entire IT organization is involved in Business Relationship Management. When the customer is happy, when obligations are being fulfilled, and when IT domains are operating at a profit, these are all indicators that the relationship is in good shape and the program is a success.

SLA targets are being met

Hand in hand with meeting the spirit and letter of the contract is meeting SLA performance targets. When SLA targets are being met you have an indicator that Business Relationship Management efforts are effective. There is a reciprocal relationship here. When performance levels are high and expectations are being met, customers tend to relax; it becomes easier to build strong relationships. At the same time, when performance levels are low and the going gets tough, the Business Relationship Manager's job becomes all the more important. It is at this time that a plea for patience or a cooperative renegotiation might be called for. Effective relationship management can contribute significantly to aligning or re-aligning an IT organization to the needs of its customer, in such a way that both parties feel they are collaborating toward success. And when that success is realized both can share the credit.

Customer satisfaction targets are being met

A well-regulated Business Relationship Management program will deliver consistent and expected levels of customer satisfaction. To promote a long-term relationship, meeting satisfaction targets is as important as service delivery and service quality. It may appear to be a 'soft' factor – and in many ways it is – but the softness should not be underrated. The customers' affinity for you as a provider, the degree to which they rely and count on you – that is directly derived from relationship management. This power of cementing and sustaining relationships, even through tough times, is worth noting. When well directed and well apportioned it promotes strong ties and mutually beneficial working environments.

3.7. Business Relationship Management roles

Managing business relationships in the domain of IT service provisioning requires a unique (and some may say, rare) blend of technical and 'soft' skills. The technical skills are needed so that Business Relationship Managers can competently and clearly communicate information about the operation and needs of the enterprise's infrastructure. The soft skills are needed because they help instill perceptions of trust, competency, commitment, and reliability – traits that are integral to establishing and maintaining strong relationships. The following three roles are usually accounted for in some way in a Business Relationship Management program. As with other ITIL processes, and depending on the size and focus of the organization, these roles may be full time or part time; combined or shared by multiple individuals. View the job titles and responsibilities described below as starting points for developing your own job descriptions.

Business Relationship Management Process Owner

The Business Relationship Management Process Owner is the person responsible for the use and performance of the activities associated with the Business Relationship Management program. Most commonly (at least in small-to-medium sized IT organizations) this person is the same as the Technical Account Manager, but this is not essential. The Business Relationship Management Process Owner champions the purpose and goals of Business Relationship Management within the organization and ensures that the program remains in a state of operational effectiveness, one that will contribute to the overall IT and business missions of the company. To summarize, the Business Relationship Management Process Owner is responsible for:

- Developing and documenting the Business Relationship Management program
- Implementing the program across relevant teams
- Coordinating program training and mentoring
- Monitoring ongoing program use
- Measuring program performance over time
- Requesting and coordinating program improvements

Technical Account Manager (Business Relationship Manager)

Sometimes this role is called Relationship Manager but whatever its label the responsibilities are the same. The Technical Account Manager is the chief point of contact, the primary liaison between the IT service provider and the customer, whether the provider is internal to the organization or an outside vendor. Technical Account Managers facilitate and shape the customer relationship. These people (and a large IT organization may have multiple Technical Account Managers) may be charged with negotiating contracts, negotiating SLAs, establishing communication plans, executing the plans, coordinating formal interactions, managing follow-on activities, and addressing customer satisfaction levels. To summarize, the Technical Account Manager is responsible for:

- Facilitating contract negotiations
- Facilitating SLA negotiations
- Planning and coordinating regular relationship meetings
- Facilitating business relationship meetings
- Ensuring the proper assessment of current service performance and process performance data
- Establishing and maintaining a communications plan
- Reporting relationship-related activities and actions to customer management and senior IT management

A note on service providers

In general there are two broad types of IT service providers – those internal to an organization (a business unit) and those external to the organization (contracted provider). When most people think of a Technical Account Manager they tend to associate the role as belonging to an outside vendor. They see it as similar to an advertising agency's account manager. And that is the correct view. The error comes with assuming that the role applies only to outside vendors. The liaison, communication, planning, and facilitation responsibilities charged to the Technical Account Manager's job are just as applicable to an internal IT organization as they are to an outside party.

NOTE: In most ITSM programs, the role of Technical Account Manager is closely allied with that of Service Level Manager. For more on this, see Chapter 4: Service Level Management.

Human Resource considerations

The following are some typical traits that Human Resource staff may want to take into consideration when they are providing personnel, tools, and other resources for a Business Relationship Management program.

- *Managerial experience and background:* Technical Account Managers should have an adequate technical background to be able to facilitate and comment on the viability of potential service delivery, performance, and quality characteristics the customer might require. They should have experience of organizing and mobilizing business management and IT management for contract negotiations, performance reviews, assessments, and improvement/adjustment activities. Technical Account Managers should have strong experience in people management, and contract management, as well as team organization and facilitation.
- *Comfort working in a process-centric environment:* Business Relationship Management staff should be comfortable working in a process-centric environment, and should be open to learning about the organization's program and contributing to its ordered growth.

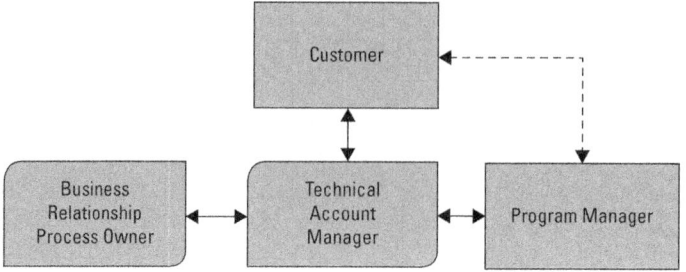

Figure 3.4 Business Relationship Management roles

3.8. Benefits of effective Business Relationship Management

Here we list and discuss the benefits an organization can expect to realize when it implements an effective Business Relationship Management program.

Higher customer satisfaction levels

The core customer activities of Business Relationship Management are communications and interpretation: communicating IT status and progress, and presenting this information in terms relevant to the business. The goal of these activities – in fact, at the heart of ITIL – is for the provider and customer to forge a close partnership. The conscientious application of communication and interpretation are key to making this happen. When such a partnership forms, both sides move closer to being one team, an integrated entity; and in line with this, customer satisfaction levels tend to rise. Shared objectives and a sense of shared mission go a long way toward overcoming operational issues.

Equitable contractual relationships

It is common in technology industries for the customer to set out most of the terms when it comes to negotiating contracts, particularly when the IT organization is in-house. The inclination is a natural one; the customer knows what it wants, after all. And often the provider feels inclined to accept such terms as proof of its willingness to serve. Unfortunately, what can result from this lopsided approach are unbalanced contracts and perhaps unrealistic SLAs. This can be avoided with an effective Business Relationship Management program, which will benefit the customer as much as it will the provider. There may be hurdles getting such a program up and running (see the *Considerations and Challenges* section below) but when negotiation exists in a give-and-take atmosphere, with business expertise blending with IT expertise, the output can be seen in contracts with manageable scopes and SLAs with rational, achievable targets.

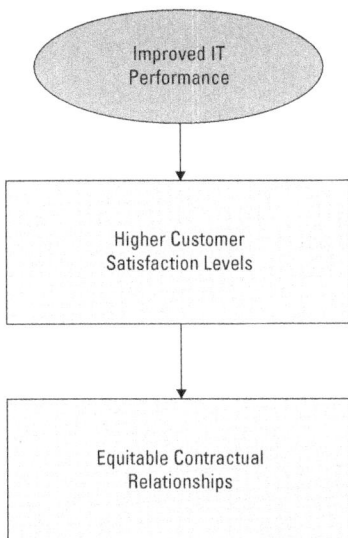

Figure 3.5 Benefits of effective Business Relationship Management

3.9. Implementation challenges and considerations

The spirit of ITIL as a framework for implementing IT Service Management is most visibly expressed through the practices of Business Relationship Management. This is the role where IT interfaces directly with the customer, and so this is the role in which ITIL's focus on partnership and customer satisfaction is most directly expressed. The benefits of a sound Business Relationship Management program, as described above, are notable. However, there are challenges and considerations to explore as you work to implement such a program. The chief challenge is to collaborate with the customer while maintaining what are (and will probably continue to be) formal boundaries. Below are three common challenges that fall into this general domain.

Establishing a collaborative customer-IT partnership

This goal lies at the heart of Business Relationship Management, yet it can be a difficult thing to achieve because of the historical divide between IT and the business. Add to that an organization's natural instinct toward protective positioning and an us-versus-them culture can easily arise. The challenge is to move through that and push toward collaboration. That spirit is essential to support a view of IT as a deliverer of specialized business services. For the provider-receiver relationship to be as successful as it might be, cooperation and participation are required on both sides of the fence – with the idea being to remove the fence. For its part, IT management should work to understand its customer's business needs, engage with the customer to determine an optimum service mix, and then frame the technical offerings in business terms. Both parties should then be actively involved in monitoring service delivery and service quality, with adjustments made in a bilateral way as needed. To support this, senior

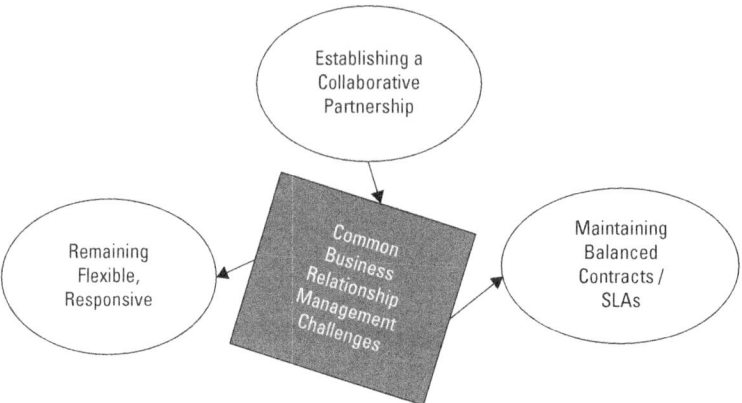

Figure 3.6 Business Relationship Management implementation challenges and considerations

business management and senior IT management should regularly communicate to the organization the importance of an on-going and open partnership.

Maintaining balanced contracts and SLAs

This is, historically, another difficult objective to achieve, at least quickly; but it is very important to long-term and beneficial business-IT relationships. The traditional tendency on both sides is to tip contractual and performance obligations to one side's favor, therefore lessening risk and perhaps increasing profitability/value. But rational as this approach might seem (and it is an entrenched tactic in the business world) it places parties in a defensive position. A better approach is to strive for balance when it comes to contracts and SLAs. This balance should be based in realistic expectations and shared obligations for realizing those expectations across parties. Getting to that stage will take work, of course, but it can be achieved with the help of frequent, open communications and a willingness to be responsive and flexible. The hurdle is getting to this state; once there, maintaining balance becomes a much more manageable task.

Remaining flexible and responsive

Even though contracts and SLAs need to be set into place and honored, the IT organization should realize that even the best of customers may not understand the intricacies of delivering IT services. On the same level IT stakeholders may not grasp all the nuances of business drivers. So it is possible, indeed likely, that over time the state and structure of the IT-business relationship will need to be adjusted. As with any relationship, flexibility and responsiveness are key. One of the central challenges in Business Relationship Management is remaining flexible and responsive in the midst of what may be a detailed contractual relationship. Toward this end technical account managers should strive to perform 'between the lines' while honoring formal commitments. Regular communication and status accounting will help in this area. When both sides share a common understanding of how the relationship is performing it becomes much easier to understand (and agree to) what will make the relationship more productive.

3.10. Typical assets and artifacts of a Business Relationship Management program

A set of documented assets and artifacts will need to be created to support your Business Relationship Management program. **Assets** are the program materials that guide how the program is governed and run. **Artifacts** are the work products that emerge when management teams engage in program activities. A list of some common assets and artifacts that you would find in a typical Business Relationship Management program is provided below. This list is typical, but not exhaustive; your program may only require some of these items, and you may wish to create others not described here.

Business Relationship Management policy
This is an executive policy that stipulates the goals and objectives of the Business Relationship Management program. The policy, which ideally should be no longer than a few pages, documents at a high level the purpose of the program, the resources available to the program, the chief responsibilities of the program (customer expectations, customer complaints, etc.), quality targets, reporting hierarchies, and program measures. Endorsed by executive management, the policy is a demonstration of organizational commitment to the value and importance of the Business Relationship Management program.

Business Relationship Management process
This is a process that documents the various procedural activities associated with Business Relationship Management across the organization. In the *Activities* section of this chapter we looked at the high level structure of such a process. Planning is used to set the Business Relationship Management Plan in place. Interfacing covers the execution of the plan. Evaluation focuses on measuring effectiveness and adjusting as necessary. A sound process will also cover procedures for requesting customer feedback in the form of complaints, compliments, and suggestions; a procedure for measuring customer satisfaction; and a procedure for escalating customer complaints to senior management levels.

Business Management Communications Plan template
This template provides the organization with a framework for creating a Business Relationship Communications Plan, a guide for how the IT provider and customer will interact on a routine basis. Templates like this are structured in outline form with sections and topics that need to be addressed. The following are typically included: goals and purpose of business communications, scope, types and modes of formal communications, customer contacts and IT counterparts, roles and responsibilities, schedules of planned communication events, communication protocols, required communication reports, and communication metrics.

Business Management Communications Plan

This is the actual plan that emerges from your use of the template above. As with any plan, producing this one follows a well-worn path. The plan is first drafted, then reviewed by relevant stakeholders, refined as necessary, and finalized. When approved the plan is placed under version control and used as the chief tool for managing the provider-customer relationship.

Customer satisfaction measurement system

Monitoring customer satisfaction is a major part of Business Relationship Management. It is also a major part of Service Level Management, a topic we cover in the next chapter. Customer Satisfaction Levels should be periodically measured and you will need some manner of system to do this. The most common one is a customer satisfaction survey, but there are other methods, too. Interviews, user groups, workshops, and focus groups all can be effective. The goal is to have an approach you can rely on to assess satisfaction levels so that resulting data can be used to determine how those levels may be sustained or, as is most often the case, elevated.

Organizational chart

This is a chart that shows the structural make-up of the Business Relationship Management operation. As with other organizational charts, its purpose is to identify teams, team relationships, and hierarchical flows. The shape of this chart will naturally depend on the general shape of your organization, and your approach to managing the provider-customer relationship. Most charts of this sort tend to be fairly simple. A box for the customer is shown at the top of the chart. A line extends down to the box for the Technical Account Manager/Business Relationship Manager. From this box a dotted line may extend across to a parallel spot for the Business Relationship Management Process Owner (if there is one separate from the Business Relationship Manager). There may be a solid line moving in the opposite direction from the Business Relationship Manager to the Program Manager. A line moves down from the Program Manager box to a series of boxes for Service Managers, and dotted lines may be used to connect Service Managers tangentially to the Release Manager.

Roles and responsibilities matrix

This matrix is an extension of the organizational chart. It describes the various roles and responsibilities the organization has assigned to support the Business Relationship Management program. The roles typically include such roles as Business Relationship Manager Process Owner, Technical Account Manager (or Business Relationship Manager), Program Manager, Service Manager, and Primary Customer Contact. Along with the job role definitions there will be descriptions of the responsibilities each role should account for, and references to how roles interrelate and communicate. The matrix might take one of several forms: a spreadsheet, a series of database records, or a version-controlled text document. Ownership of this artifact is usually shared between senior IT management and Human Resource management.

4. Service Level Management

One of the distinguishing features of an IT Service Management program is the central use of the Service Level Agreement (SLA). An SLA is an agreement reached between IT management and its customers that stipulates the level of performance IT will deliver for each of its services.

As an example, if email is a service offered by IT, an SLA might state that this service should be capable of supporting 300 concurrent users, that it should be available 99.5% of the time on a 24x7 clock, and that in the event of a system failure it is fully restored within one hour. Those three targets are known as service level requirements. IT's job then is to shape and direct its resources so that those targets can be met. This shaping and directing is known at its foundation as IT Service Level Management.

ITIL's Service Level Management process is in place so that organizations can establish effective SLAs, use them to direct management activity, and derive from them a clear picture of overall IT performance. A core concept within ITIL is that IT exists to further the missions and success of the business; this means that IT is accountable for demonstrating its value to the business. The activities within Service Level Management are designed to help do that. The performance targets within SLAs provide one window into demonstrating this value.

ITIL states the purpose of Service Level Management as follows:

"To negotiate, agree upon, and document expected levels of quality regarding service delivery and service performance, the result being a Service Level Agreement, a technique for providing a service warranty."[1]

The term 'warranty' is important. A warranty provides for a certain minimum level of suitability. These levels will vary from customer to customer, and also from service to service. One of IT management's main tasks is to understand what levels of performance its specific mix of services can support and work with its customers to understand what levels of performance it needs to deliver. This brings us to the goal ITIL states for Service Level Management:

"...To ensure that an agreed-upon level of service is provided for all current IT services, and that future services are delivered according to agreed-upon and achievable targets."[2]

"For all current IT services" covers the full service spectrum. No IT service should be deployed within an organization without an accepted service level in place. "Agreed-

---
1 Foundation of ITIL. (2007) Van Haren Publishing.
2 Ibid.

upon and achievable targets" means that the levels of service defined in an SLA should be mutually agreed to by both IT and business parties, and that they should reflect practical, realistic, and achievable goals. (Unrealistic or poorly defined expectations will only result in hazy, vague agreements that are difficult to measure, manage, and improve upon.)

4.1. Service Level Management work products

A Service Level Management program will tend to produce five major work products. The first four represent contracts of cooperation. The fifth is an indicator of the success of those contracts. The five are:
- Service Level Requirements (SLRs)
- Service Level Agreements (SLAs)
- Operational Level Agreements (OLAs)
- Underpinning Contracts (UCs)
- Customer satisfaction data

These work products are described briefly below.

Service Level Requirements (SLRs)
SLRs take an SLA down to its most detailed level. These are the performance thresholds an individual service needs to meet in order to be deemed acceptable. Every service should have its own particular set of SLRs; some may have many, some a few. SLRs usually deal with a blend of considerations such as capacity, availability, sustainability, usability, maintainability, security, and continuity.

Service Level Agreements (SLAs)
SLAs are the essential tool for establishing contracts of agreement between IT and the business. The SLAs contain the SLRs specified for each service. They are official documents that, when agreed-upon, are placed under formal change control. The aim of Service Level Management is to ensure that SLAs are established in a practical manner, with practical goals, and maintained over time to evolve with the changing needs of business and technical missions.

Operational Level Agreements (OLAs)
OLAs are similar to SLAs, but internal to the IT organization; the key difference is that they are not legally binding and are just agreements between internal departments and IT. OLAs are set up between technical support teams to help meet SLA targets. OLAs guide how IT teams will cooperate and collaborate to ensure that services are delivered in a consistent, reliable manner. OLAs also establish guidelines for how teams will interact if services are interrupted.

Underpinning Contracts (UCs)

UCs are similar to OLAs, but they involve external providers. UCs are legally binding, unlike OLAs; because they are formal contracts UCs are very specific, whereas OLAs may not be. Most IT organizations rely periodically on the assistance of outside support parties when it comes to managing and maintaining the infrastructure. UCs are set up between technical support teams and these providers to help meet OLA and SLA targets. They guide how the providers will cooperate and collaborate with each other and interrelate with teams to ensure that services are delivered in a consistent, reliable manner.

Customer satisfaction data

The final main work product of Service Level Management is customer satisfaction data. The SLA described above sets a series of quantifiable targets that can be measured and reported on to produce a picture of IT performance. To complement this, ITIL recommends that service level managers also work to collect *qualitative* performance indicators. This is the intention of collecting customer satisfaction data. This data presents IT management with a view of the business' perception of the value IT is bringing to the business. It is an important factor in thinking through continual improvement issues.

Let's begin a fuller discussion of Service Level Management with a look at the overall process as ITIL describes it.

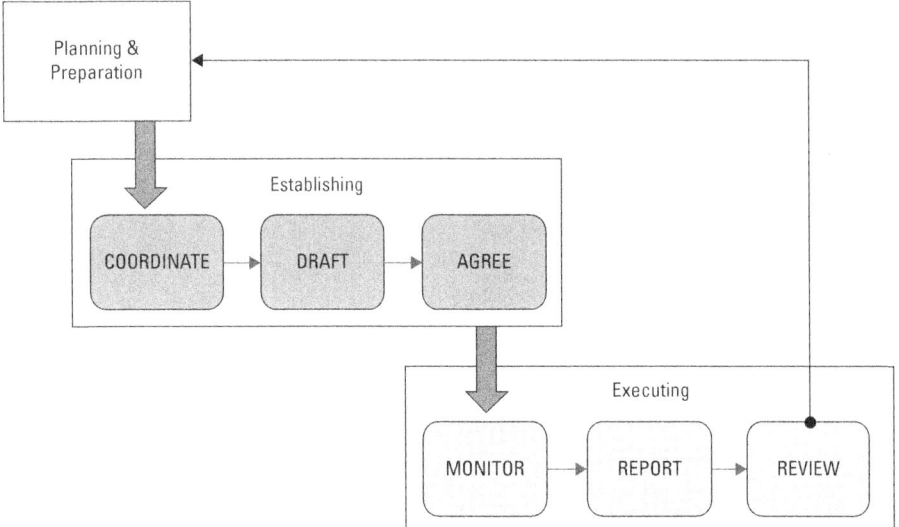

Figure 4.1 Typical Service Level Management process flow

4.2. Service Level Management activities

The Service Level Management process consists of a series of eight general activities for planning, establishing and executing service level agreements. The activities are described in a general way because each one is actually comprised of a set of sub-activities. Taken as a whole, the process leads the organization through the steps needed to prepare for managing service levels on through the actions required to monitor services in production and report on their performance. The eight general steps in the process are:
- Planning
- Coordinating
- Drafting
- Agreeing
- Monitoring
- Reporting
- Reviewing
- Improving

In the following sections we'll take a brief look at each.

1. Planning
In order for an organization to be able to manage its services it has to know what its service set is, how well that set performs, and how that set can be best monitored and measured. This is the objective of planning. The organization plans how it will manage service levels and determines the overall shape and direction of the Service Level Management program. Five sub-activities are typically recommended.

Baseline services descriptions. The first planning step is to document descriptions of all those IT services the IT organization will support. This includes descriptions of business services, technical services, and service components. These descriptions can then become the official baseline for information about service features, functions, and capabilities. The SLAs that will emerge later on in this process should use these descriptions as the basis for negotiations.

NOTE: This activity of producing baseline service descriptions is often included in the ITIL process known as Service Catalogue Management. These descriptions, in effect, constitute the Service Catalogue. Service Catalogue Management is not included in the scope of this book, so this activity has been included here under Service Level Management.

Design the SLA framework. The next step is to design the SLA framework. This is simply a determination of how SLAs will be structured. There are many ways to do this. You might, for example, wish to create individual SLAs for each IT service you offer. You might wish to have an SLA that covers all services delivered to a particular customer group. Then again, you might wish to have a single SLA for an entire organization. The options are open, and the best way to decide on the right framework is to look at your organizational structure and culture and confer with your customer on their operational preferences.

Determine service delivery and performance ranges. SLAs will set formal expectations of service performance into place. Factors such as availability, response times, service intervals, capacity, and so on will be defined against specific operational thresholds. Performance is then expected to fall within these thresholds. In order to negotiate these performance factors in a practical and realistic manner, the organization will need to know precisely how its services can perform; and what delivery and performance ranges they are capable of meeting. The organization should work to determine this technical information and then use it as a reference for later negotiations.

Determine appropriate service measures. With service descriptions set and with performance ranges understood, the organization can now determine the best way to monitor and report on service performance. Here the organization documents the service measures that may be appropriately used to gauge service delivery and service quality levels. The organization should also determine the types, frequencies, and audiences of the service reports that will be distributed to present the measures. And the organization might also determine some potential SLA performance contingencies, possible corrective actions to be invoked if SLA targets fall short of or exceed expectations (e.g. penalties, rewards, etc.).

Determine SLA, review, and revision guidelines. Finally the organization should establish templates that can be used to create SLAs, and then attach to these templates the guidelines and procedures for how agreements will be reached, how often they should be reviewed, and under what conditions they might be revised.

Service Level Management requires a variety of inputs so that management tactics may be set in line with organizational priorities and objectives. The set of inputs covers a range of considerations, from the structure of SLAs to performance contingencies if SLA targets are not met.

2. Coordinating

This second step in the process takes advantage of the sub-activities in Step 1. The work of planning is put into action. The coordinating step brings IT management and the customer together to negotiate the SLA (or SLAs). There are two sub-activities: the first is to identify the right sets of stakeholders and the second is to negotiate service performance characteristics.

Identify key stakeholders. SLAs need to be negotiated from the highest levels of IT management and business management as is practical. In this sub-activity the organization works to identify the appropriate business stakeholders for whom service delivery and quality are of primary concern, and those IT stakeholders for whom service delivery and quality are a primary job responsibility. These are the parties in the best position to negotiate service levels.

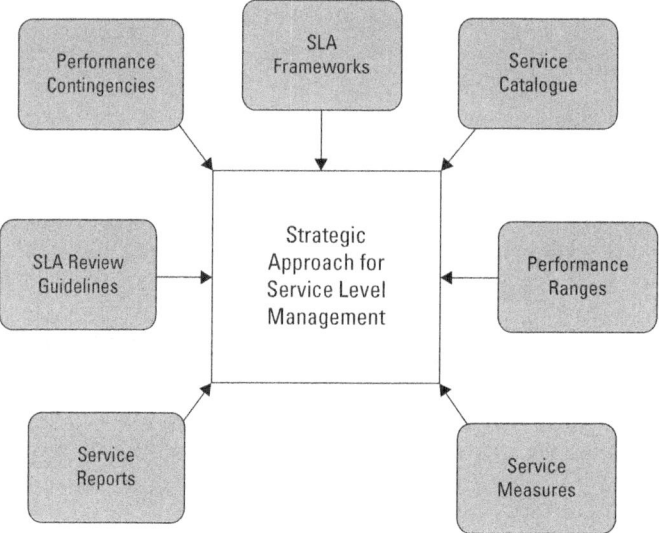

Figure 4.2 The range of inputs for planning Service Level Management activities

Negotiate SLAs. With the appropriate stakeholders identified, the parties can now meet to negotiate the contents of the SLA. There is no fixed set of considerations that needs to go into any SLAs; this is for the parties to decide. They will usually include agreed support hours, availability, Service Level targets, points of contact etc. – these are all basics to be found in any SLA. Typically the following sets of considerations are included in the negotiations:

- Service operation goals – establish the operational goals that services are required to achieve.
- SLRs – establish the SLRs that each service is required to meet.
- Service measures – identify the measures that will be collected for each service.
- Service level reporting frequencies and mechanisms – identify the frequency and content of service level reporting.
- SLA performance contingencies – identify any rewards or penalties for over- or under-performance in the SLA.
- SLA agreement, review, and revision periods – determine how often SLAs will be reviewed and under what conditions they might be revised.

Negotiate Operational Level Agreements. With SLAs in place and performance targets known, IT management can now work with internal service and support teams to negotiate OLAs:

- Support service response time – establish time limits for responding to and resolving service incidents and problems.
- Escalation guidelines – establish guidelines for escalating issue ownership to specialized teams. (See Chapter 13.)

- Documentation guides – identify documentation that needs to be developed in support of service-related activities.

Negotiate Underpinning Contracts. With OLAs in place and inter-team collaboration paths established, IT management can now work with external providers to negotiate UCs:

- Support service response times – establish time limits for responding to and resolving service incidents and problems that require external support.
- Escalation guidelines – establish guidelines for responding to issues escalated to outside parties.
- Documentation guides – identify documentation that needs to be developed in support of Service Management activities.

Note that in practice this sequence of negotiating SLAs, OLAs and UCs is not always so straightforward. It may be necessary to negotiate the UC first, for example.

3. Drafting

With negotiations complete, and (assumed) successful, the responsible party (this can be IT management or the customer, or a combination of both) takes the agreed-upon information and drafts the SLA.

4. Agreeing

With a draft SLA in place, the next step is for both parties to reconvene so that they can formally agree to the SLA and begin to work toward its goals. There are three sub-activities for this fourth step.

Convene key stakeholders. IT and business stakeholders reconvene to review the draft SLA, comment on its contents, and make any revisions that may be necessary.

Commit to the SLA. In some formal manner (e.g. via signatures) IT management and business management commit to the contents of the SLA, signifying adoption by both parties.

Control the SLA. Once adopted, the SLA is placed under formal change control, as is common with any contractual document.

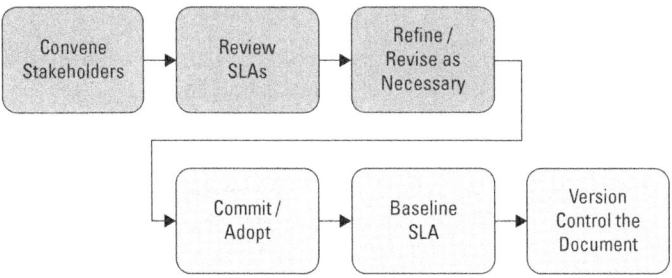

Figure 4.3 Coordinating, drafting, and agreeing as part of Service Level Management

5. Monitoring

With the SLA now in place, the organization can begin to measure its performance against the service level requirements. This involves two sub-activities: monitoring performance and collecting performance data.

Monitor service delivery and service quality levels. When services are in 'live' operation, operation teams track performance in terms of service delivery and service quality over time, using whatever mix of monitoring tools and techniques is most suitable. These teams can then compare running performance to SLA targets, and control or adjust performance in real time as necessary.

Record and collect service data. The operation teams record and collect service quality and service performance data so that it may be analyzed and then released in service reports.

6. Reporting

This sixth step verifies established SLA performance targets. On a fixed timeline, the organization amasses service performance data and uses it as a basis to prepare and release SLA performance reports. Two sub-activities occur here:

Analyze service data. Service level managers store, process, and analyze the collected data. The results are then formatted for presentation.

Distribute reports for review. Service level managers distribute the SLA performance reports to designated IT managers and customer stakeholders.

7. Reviewing

This seventh step is a key activity in the overall Service Level Management process. At set intervals (as required, e.g. monthly or quarterly), IT managers and key customer stakeholders convene to review the SLA reports and discuss the performance of the IT organization in relation to the customer's business needs. This involves two sub-activities.

Review results with IT and business management. IT management and business management review the performance of the IT organization against what was specified in the SLA. Based on the review, both parties work to determine any required follow-on or corrective actions.

Revise SLAs as necessary. As an optional step, the parties may agree to adjust or revise the SLA to realign expectations with new or changed business or technology conditions.

Once agreed-upon SLAs have been set into place, they are executed (Figure 4.4). This includes monitoring service performance in the live operational environment, analyzing performance data, creating service reports, and then providing these reports for IT management and customer stakeholders to review.

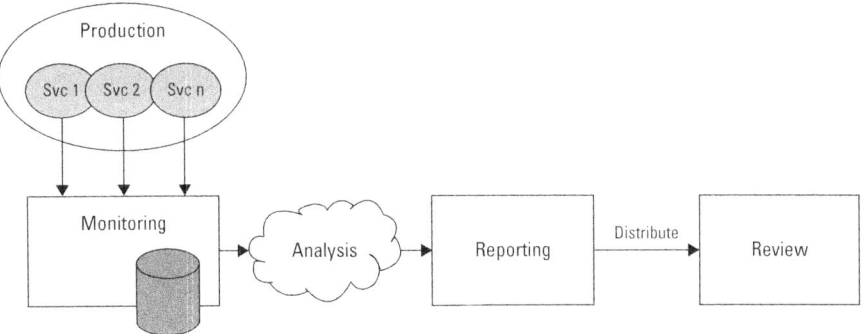

Figure 4.4 Executing the Service Level Management program

8. Improving customer satisfaction

This final step in the process represents an essential and ongoing activity for Service Level Management. It is a key consideration for any effective Service Level Management program. The objective is for the organization to set into place mechanisms for measuring and assessing customer satisfaction. In Step 5 above, the IT organization monitors and measures service performance levels. This gives a *quantitative* picture of service delivery and service quality levels. Here in Step 8 the organization is complementing this picture with a *qualitative* look at delivery and quality. Here we get the customer's perceptions of how well the IT organization is meeting its mission. The assumption under ITIL is that robust business relationships cannot be initiated and developed if customer satisfaction levels are low. Low satisfaction levels may not have a direct, causative relationship to service measures, but in all likelihood low satisfaction levels probably indicate systemic operational issues somewhere across the enterprise.

Two sub-activities are included under Step 8:
- Regularly measure customer satisfaction
- Implement improvements and refinements to increase customer satisfaction levels

Regularly measure customer satisfaction. The organization sets into place a program to regularly measure customer satisfaction levels. There is a variety of ways to do this: for example, management can host customer workshops and feedback sessions; suggestion boxes can be set into place; surveys can be sent out to specific business units or user groups. Choose the best blend of techniques for your IT organization, ones that also fit well with your customer's needs. Whichever mix you select, there are two types of satisfaction efforts that are most commonly employed with ITIL-based Service Level Management programs:

> Selective – The IT organization measures customer satisfaction on a selective basis, usually through some form of event drive mechanism.
> Example: The Service Desk sends a brief satisfaction survey to every tenth user who places a technical support call to the Service Desk.

Global – Periodically (perhaps once or twice a year) the IT organization measures satisfaction levels across as much of the entire customer base as possible.
Example: IT management works with business management to send an annual satisfaction survey via email to every employee stationed at customer headquarters.

Implement improvements and refinements to increase customer satisfaction levels. The organization incorporates the customer satisfaction data into its continual improvement efforts, sets targets for where satisfaction levels ought to be, and then makes refinements and improvement to its services and Service Management techniques in order to reach those levels.

4.3. Process inputs and outputs

The Service Level Management process begins with a need and ends with an agreement. The need is a customer-driven condition that centers on the levels of service a particular organization requires in order to pursue its business lines. The agreement is the common understanding between the business and the IT provider that defines service levels in ways that are both measurable and accountable. At the heart of the process is the work that goes into establishing this common understanding, negotiating its boundaries, and agreeing to the methods by which its performance will be monitored. The Service Level Management process is triggered when certain entry criteria are met and when certain inputs become available. The process concludes when exit conditions are met and when certain work products have been produced. Let's take a quick look at all four of these areas.

Entry criteria
The Service Level Management process is typically set into motion when one of two criteria are met:
- A new IT contract is set into place (or a re-negotiation period arrives) thus requiring business management and IT management to establish performance expectations; or
- A new or enhanced IT service, or set of services, is ready to be designed thus requiring business management and IT management to establish performance expectations.

Inputs
Multiple inputs can drive the Service Level Management process. Examples of some of these include:
- Strategic business goals, plans, and objectives
- Existing SLAs (as well as OLAs and UCs)
- Business process requirements
- Regulatory, statutory, and legislative mandates
- Existing service level requirements
- Past performance reports and analyses
- Customer satisfaction data

Exit criteria
The process typically closes when the following three criteria are met:
- An agreed-upon baseline SLA has been established.
- Services are ready to be delivered in line with SLA performance targets.
- Monitoring and measurement activities have been accounted for.

Outputs
The Service Level Management process is designed to culminate in the production of a single major artifact:
- Baseline SLA

Note: In addition to the baseline SLA, the process also drives the production of other secondary artifacts, these being produced in response to service operation activities. Sometimes they are grouped into a Service Level Management program; other times they are included in the ITIL process known as Monitoring and Control. These usually include:
- Service performance metrics (raw data)
- Service performance reports (e.g. monthly SLA reports)
- Service performance action plans

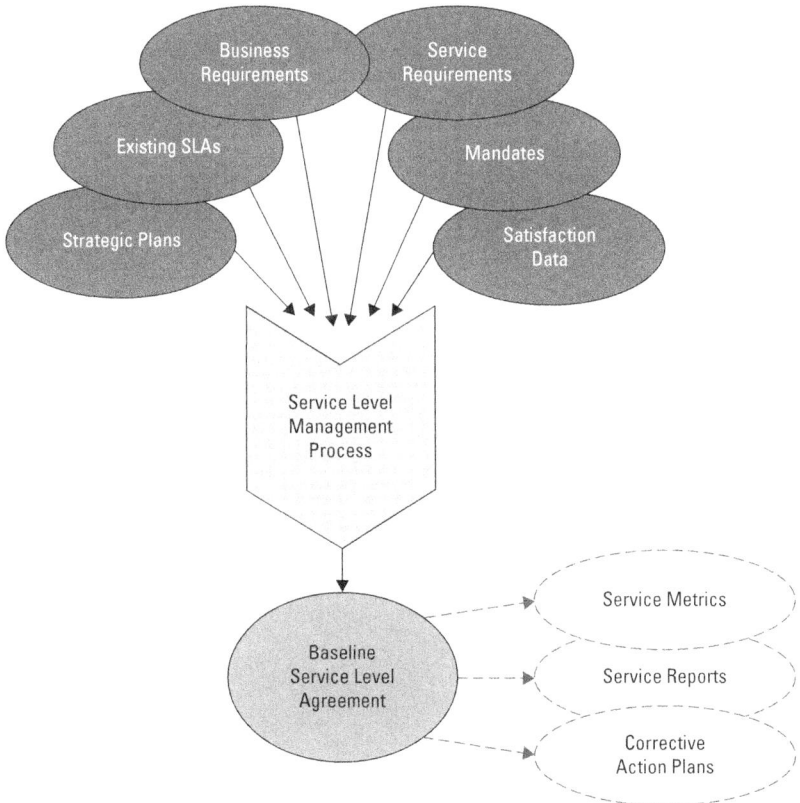

Figure 4.5 Inputs and outputs of a typical Service Level Management process

4.4. Processes related to Service Level Management

The important thing to remember about Service Level Management is that every other ITIL process is related to it. Design processes such as Availability Management, Capacity Management, Information Security Management, and IT Continuity Management are used to embed the features and functions that define service performance into services. Key aspects of this performance are then monitored and measured as part of a Service Level Management program. Transition processes such as Change Management, Configuration Management, and Release Management are used to adjust and evolve the environment in a planned and orderly way, which needs to meet the requirements of SLAs. And Service Operation processes such as Incident Management and Problem Management are used to manage the environment's ongoing use and integrity, in ways that find direct counterparts in service level requirements.

The relationships described here are not tangential, nor are they merely complementary. They are direct and linked through very real dependencies. In this way, Service Level Management might be seen as the hub that supports the spokes of a wheel. Service Level Management, at the center, contains the customer's expectations concerning service performance, quantifies the manner in which delivery and quality will be measured and then extends these controls to the sets of services and the service management practices that support those services.

However, if only one process could be cited as specially related to Service Level Management, it would have to be Service Improvement. We will take a look at that briefly now.

Service Improvement

Measures of SLA performance provide direct input into service improvement activities. The measures help identify areas of strength and areas of weakness across the organization, and thus opportunities for improvement. Likewise, continual service improvement activities provide the organization with a way to revise service designs or operation parameters in order to better meet SLA targets (or to better negotiate future SLAs). Service Level Management can be viewed as the provider for the mechanisms used to establish delivery and quality objectives. It is a *strategic* process. Service Improvement can be seen as the provider of the mechanisms for improvement planning and improvement actions. It is the *tactical* counterpart to Service Level Management. Together the two processes provide the forward momentum that drives all Design, Transition, and Operation processes into the future. (For more on this topic, see Chapter 16.)

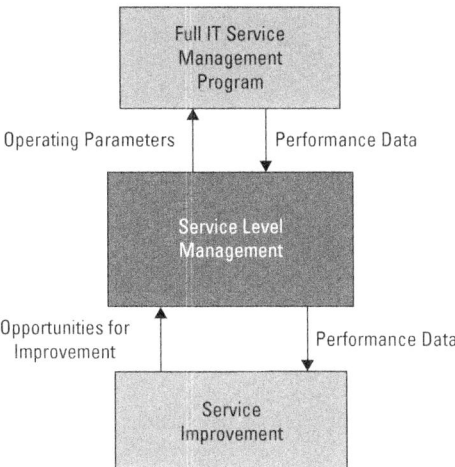

Figure 4.6 Processes related to Service Level Management

In summary:
- Service Level Management provides measures of critical performance in key areas of service delivery and service quality. Such measures provide data that is useful for undertaking the improvement analyses key to continual improvement objectives.
- Service Improvement seeks to identify opportunities to strengthen the environment so that both service performance and customer satisfaction levels may rise – two core considerations of Service Level Management.

The cycles of improvement planning and service level negotiation co-exist with one another; the outputs of one activity provide inputs for the other.

4.5. Tools and techniques

Service Level Management is not a technical process in the sense that, say, Availability Management or Capacity Management might be considered technical processes. As noted earlier in this chapter, Service Level Management is more of a strategic process, one designed to provide the operating boundaries for later technical work. This means that organizations tend not to employ a myriad of technical aids to support such a program. The required skills here tend to be softer. There are, however, a few tools and techniques that are commonly used, in areas that deal with the two major responsibilities associated with Service Level management, performance negotiation and data collection. Here are brief descriptions of four of these common tools and techniques.

Table 4.1 Tools and techniques for Service Level Management

Negotiation guidelines	In order for a Service Level Management program to be successful (in fact, for an IT Service Management program to be successful), IT management must be able to negotiate with the business in an effective manner. The key is to understand service ranges that can be supported without placing the IT organization in an untenable position where it cannot deliver the required performance. In support of this the organization should provide its service level managers with a formal approach to customer negotiations. Such guidelines will help ensure that IT staff propose management objectives that consistently adhere to practical operational objectives while, at the same time, recognizing the business's focus, priorities, and position in the marketplace.
Appropriate production monitoring and control tools	In order for service performance to be accurately tracked against SLAs, the operational environment should have in place the proper sets of tools for monitoring and measuring this performance. In support of a Service Level Management program the environment should be configured with the capability to read, capture, and store performance on a fixed and controlled basis – one that aligns with service level requirements.
Customer satisfaction collection and measurement instruments	Measuring customer satisfaction levels is central to Service Level Management. In fact, measuring satisfaction is just as important as measuring service performance and quality. For this activity the organization should consider implementing tools such as surveys, customer workshops, user advocacy groups, etc. Then the organization should employ techniques for eliciting, collecting, storing, analyzing, and reporting on this satisfaction data.
Performance analytic and trend techniques	Analytic techniques (basic or sophisticated) should be applied to service data and customer satisfaction data over time as a way to develop performance baselines and models. The baselines can be used to establish historical trends of service and Service Management performance. From these trends, models can be created to predict performance levels into the future. Baselines and models are extremely helpful in planning and managing service level-related activities.

4.6. Critical Success Factors

The KPIs contained in the next section are in place to help collect the kinds of measures that can be used to gauge the effectiveness of a Service Level Management program. They capture data about service performance, customer satisfaction, and operating costs. When analyzed, what emerges is an overall picture not only of Service Level Management performance but of IT Service Management performance as a whole. At this point we are at the pinnacle of IT management considerations. The following three critical success factors flow from the KPIs below and can be used by management to determine, at this high level, how effective the program is proving itself to be.

SLA targets met
Over time a Service Level Management program will provide the organization with a baseline history of service performance measures. These measures will reveal the overall effectiveness of the program in terms of service delivery and service quality. If SLA targets are being met this is a validation that the program is working as intended.

If targets are being consistently missed this is most likely an indication of one of two conditions: either the organization is underperforming in terms of delivery or quality, or the SLA targets have been negotiated at levels that are too high. Both conditions call for intervening actions on the part of IT management and the customer. For these reasons IT management needs to keep a watchful eye on SLA performance. They are the single most important success factors for service level management and for programmatic operations as well.

Customer satisfaction levels met

In the domain of ITIL, customer satisfaction is just as important as service delivery and service quality. The first will always falter in the absence of the latter two, and the latter are meaningless is the absence of the first. While SLA targets provide a quantitative picture of service performance, customer satisfaction levels provide a qualitative picture. Most SLAs will include customer satisfaction targets. If these targets are consistently met, this is further validation that the Service Level Management program is performing well. Poor or low satisfaction levels usually indicate organizational problems similar to that of missed SLA targets: either service performance is indeed weak or – for whatever reason – it is perceived as weak. If performance is demonstrably strong but satisfaction levels are low, the reason may simply be one of poor communications – a support staff that is focusing on technical issues while forgetting to involve the client. The importance of the business relationship in this light should never be underestimated in an ITIL program. Because the subjective nature of customer satisfaction can have a powerful impact on perceptions of IT's value to the business, IT management should keep a watchful eye on this data; again, this is an important success factor for service level management and for programmatic operations as well.

Targeted performance is delivering profitability

This final success factor is often overlooked when Service Level Management programs are being implemented. The measure is a basic one and is positioned prominently at the heart of any business. It is simply this: What is the profitability of the operation? In other words, is the operation making business sense? The measures collected here are used to verify that the costs associated with current levels of performance are producing a surplus and not a deficit.[3] The Service Management program is operating in the black, not in the red. It hardly matters if service levels and satisfaction levels are high if the program operates at a loss. Such a situation is not sustainable for any length of time. The raison d'être for any business to be in business is growth driven by profitability. And an IT organization, though it is many things, is first and foremost a business, so business success is a primary requirement for any IT Service Management program to be called successful.

---

3   The profit/loss here is usually measured financially, but it is not solely financial. Good will, market leadership, technological advancement, and other factors might be just as important to an organization.

4.7. Key Performance Indicators

Service Level Management is in many ways one big set of KPIs. It is these KPIs that normally form the basis of SLAs. Usually they are originally identified as service requirements and then negotiated and agreed upon in SLAs. Because these KPIs are integrally embedded in the program itself (and reflective of other Service Management processes) there is not a significant need for an independent set of measures. Here you may wish to consider the following three KPIs as they present an overall picture of how well the Service Level Management program is operating in general, and they link directly to the three critical success factors above.

Acceptable SLA trends over time

The SLA reports that are produced as part of the Service Level Management program contain measures of service performance and quality; the data contained in these reports provides primary input and insight into program performance. The goal the organization wishes to achieve, of course, is to continually meet SLA performance targets. By creating performance trends over time, IT management can move toward a proactive position. Data amassed over time can be used to generate performance baselines and models. The baselines capture historical performance levels; the models can be used to predict future performance. IT management can use these two together to adjust and refine service levels so that targets are more effectively managed and results are more accurately predicted.

Acceptable customer satisfaction trends over time

As with SLA reports, customer satisfaction reports are produced as part of a Service Level Management program. The reports contain measures that indicate how satisfied customers are with the service mix being delivered, with levels of service quality and service performance, and with operational support activities. Just as with the quantitative data in SLA reports, the qualitative data contained in satisfaction reports can provide a primary source of insight into Service Level Management performance. As with quantitative performance measures, the organization would like to see qualitative satisfaction trends that meet management and customer expectations. Baselines and predictive models can be implemented to foster trend lines in the right direction for this area too.

IT operating cost analyses

Traditional operating cost analyses are a valuable KPI because they can be compared with SLA performance targets and customer satisfaction levels in order to gauge overall operational effectiveness. The picture that management should be looking for here is one of balance. Is the amount of resources that are being expended to achieve current service levels and satisfaction levels proportional to the business benefits being derived (e.g. profits, good will)? Analyses of this type are fairly routine accounting practice. It is mentioned here because it is a beneficial move to bring this kind of assessment out of the exclusive domain of Financial Management and into the realm of Service Level Management.

4.8. Service Level Management roles

Four roles are primarily associated with a Service Level Management program. Because of the nature of this process (setting business-critical goals and tactical targets) these roles are all associated with IT management. The roles are process owner, Service Level Manager, Service Manager(s), and senior IT management. As with other ITL processes, and depending on the size and focus of the organization, these roles – as they are assigned to Service Level Management duties – may be full time or part time; combined or shared by multiple individuals. View the job titles and responsibilities described below as starting points for your own approach to these roles.

Service Level Management Process Owner
The Service Level Management Process Owner is the person (or persons) in the organization responsible for the development, deployment, and ongoing use of the Service Level Management program. It is common in many IT organizations that this process owner is also the same as the Service Level Manager, but this is not essential. The process owner champions the purpose and goals of Service Level Management, ensures that the program remains in a state of operational effectiveness, and interfaces with senior IT management and business representatives to facilitate program adjustments and improvements. To summarize, the Service Level Management Process Owner is responsible for:
- Developing and documenting the Service Level Management program
- Implementing the program across relevant teams
- Coordinating program training and mentoring
- Monitoring ongoing program use
- Measuring program performance over time
- Requesting and coordinating program improvements

Service Level Manager
The Service Level Manager is responsible for the ongoing operation of the Service Level Management program. Some organizations employ a single Service Level Manager; others have multiple managers spread across services. Either way the job role remains the same. The Service Level Manager is the person who facilitates the development, negotiation, and adoption of SLAs, OLAs, and UCs. Once these artifacts are in place the Service Level Manager is charged with the regular collection of performance measures, creation of performance reports, facilitating performance reviews with IT managers and customers, and negotiating corrective actions when performance targets are not being met. To summarize, the Service Level Manager is responsible for:
- Coordinating SLA, OLA, and UC content and development
- Coordinating SLA/OLA/UC negotiations
- Controlling baseline SLAs/OLAs/UCs
- Ensuring that SLA/OLA/UC performance is measured, captured, stored, and analyzed
- Capturing and monitoring customer satisfaction levels

- Creating and issuing SLA/OLA/UC performance reports
- Reviewing performance with IT management and customer stakeholders
- Identifing opportunities for service improvement

Service managers

Service Managers should participate in the Service Level Management process because they are the roles responsible for the services being delivered and managed. They represent the users of the service and the business to IT, and ensure the performance of the service is applicable. SLAs, OLAs, and UCs are all directly linked to specific services. Service Managers should possess the insight into the characteristics of these services necessary to negotiate performance and quality targets, and provide measurement collection and analysis techniques. These managers should work hand-in-hand with the Service Level Manager to ensure that performance reports are produced and discussed with senior management and the customer on a regular basis. To summarize for this domain, Service Managers are responsible for:

- Providing service performance input to Service Level Management
- Participating in SLA/OLA/UC negotiations
- Coordinating team activities in order to meet SLA/OLA/UC targets
- Working with Service Level Management to adjust services as necessary to meet agreed-upon targets

Senior business and IT management

Senior managers from both the business and the IT organization need to be involved in Service Level Management activities. After all, SLAs set the tone and expectations for all IT activities that follow. The decisions made here will have significant impacts from both business and IT perspectives. This means that senior management's roles here fall into two categories. First, they should participate in negotiations to define SLAs, OLAs, and UCs. Next, once the SLAs, OLAs, and UCs are in place they need to provide the operational resources to realize the goals of each. To summarize in this domain, Senior IT Managers are responsible for:

- Participating in SLA/OLA/UC negotiations
- Providing resources required to meet SLA/OLA/UC targets

Human Resource considerations

The following are some typical traits that human resource staff may want to take into consideration when they are providing personnel, tools, and other resources for a Service Level Management program.

Technical experience and background. Service Level Managers should have an adequate technical background, one that reflects the configuration of the infrastructure being supported. Service Levels Managers should also have a solid understanding of the capabilities that the services mix is able to deliver and the performance ranges that can be expected and reasonably delivered.

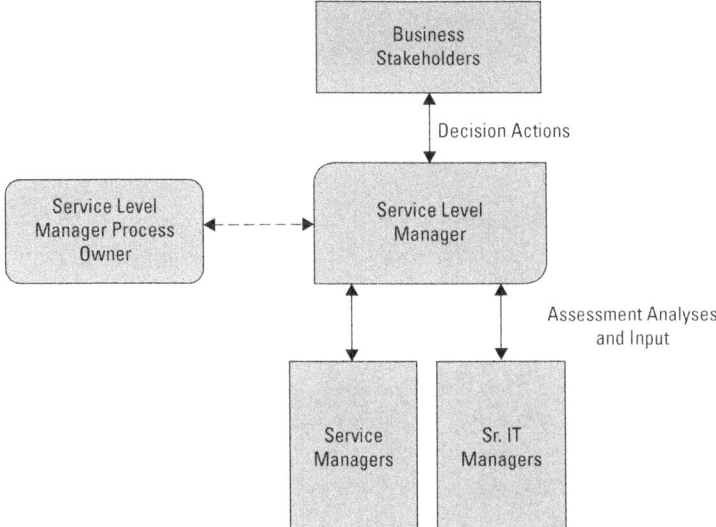

Figure 4.7 Service Level Management role relationships

Negotiation, account management, and team building skills. Service Level Managers should possess a set of skills that gives them the ability to negotiate effectively, build strong business relationships, communicate at a professional level, and align technical teams with service and business needs.

4.9. Benefits of effective Service Level Management

Effective Service Level Management will show multiple benefits across an IT organization. Design, transition, operation, and improvement teams will all be able to use the agreements established in the program as 'sounding boards' against which plans and activities can be evaluated. There are also benefits that support the customer-provider relationship. They bolster the organization's ability to deliver and manage IT services in ways that are transparent, cooperative, and collaborative. The top three benefits in this domain have to do with reliability, predictability, and customer satisfaction.

Predictable service delivery
The artifacts that emerge from a sound Service Level Management program (SLAs, OLAs, UCs) allow an organization to establish shared performance expectations across its various operating domains. Through these expectations the organization is better able to identify the mix of resources it will need to meet delivery and quality targets. The organization is also better positioned to set in place the kinds of environmental tools needed to monitor and control service performance. These shared expectations will also promote stronger communications between the service provider and the customer base. The parameters agreed upon in SLAs, OLAs, and UCs set the baseline for what constitutes acceptable performance, and it is

these parameters that can be referenced when stakeholders meet to discuss service efficiency and effectiveness. Out of all of this should emerge a predictable service delivery environment – not one that is necessarily perfect, but one whose operating characteristics can be reliably anticipated and thus one that can be intelligently managed and refined over time.

Reliable planning and forecasting

In organizations that lack a formal or sound Service Level Management program, planning and forecasting become difficult for several reasons. For one, there is likely to be a weak understanding of service capabilities, and so performance targets become soft. Second, the amount of data shared between IT management and the customer is probably minimal at best. Both traits will reduce an organization's ability to plan service delivery activities and forecast service performance trends. However, when a robust Service Level Management program is in place, performance targets and quality levels can be explicitly defined, discussed and reviewed, and collaboratively agreed upon. With common agreements in place the activities involved with meeting the service levels become much more straightforward; tactical goals and objectives exist. At the same time, efforts to forecast future performance and management needs become much more reliable. The data collection and analysis techniques that support the program's various agreements allow the organization to establish historical baselines of past performance, baselines that will, with adequate time, develop into trend lines. The organization can then use these trend lines to develop models that can be used to predict likely future performance.

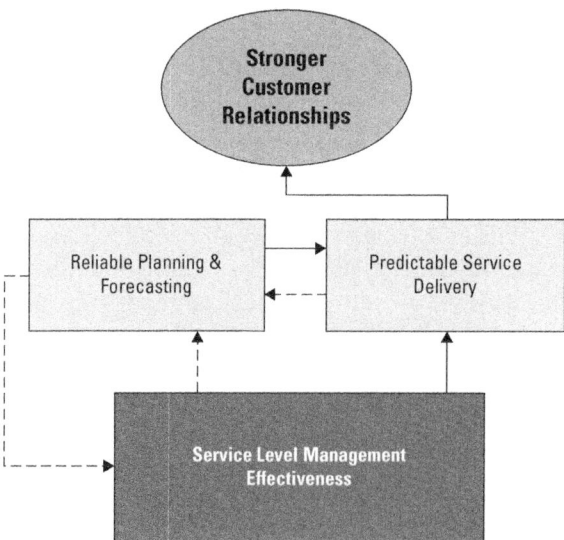

Figure 4.8 Potential benefits of a Service Level Management program

Stronger customer relationships

Service Level Management exists almost exclusively to protect customer satisfaction levels. The core strategy of this process is to define precisely what the term 'acceptable performance' means. With such a standard in place, service delivery and service quality can be objectively measured and assessed. And when such a standard is developed jointly by the service provider working with the service consumer, expectations become shared and service levels – in a very real way – become co-owned. This is the foundation of that partnership that ITIL wants to see formed between IT and the business. When Service Management is conducted in this open, communicative, and collaborative manner, customer satisfaction levels almost always tend to rise. Customer relationships usually become stronger. This inevitably results in stronger performance results in terms of IT services and overall business success as well.

4.10. Implementation challenges and considerations

There are two keys to succeeding at Service Level Management. The first is understanding the range of service performance that your organization can reliably commit to, and the second is negotiating service levels with the customer that can be consistently delivered. These two are probably fairly obvious, but unfortunately they are quite often neglected or are only partially realized. The major challenges and considerations to implementing a Service Level Management program can arise from these deficits.

Understanding service performance ranges

This is very important knowledge to possess but it can be difficult to achieve. In order for a Service Level Management program to be effective, IT management must be able to articulate just what levels of service performance its teams can dependably deliver. It needs to understand each service's capacity levels, availability levels, security functions, continuity parameters, and so on. This picture of service performance should be readily accessible, but in many organizations it simply is not the case. Often the best that management can offer are performance generalities, or vague expectations. And this can lead to one of two reduced outcomes. Management may be required to accept the customer's performance marks, especially if the customer has taken the time to formulate them precisely. Or vague expectations become the foundation of an agreement, and that can lead later to mismatched expectations and disputes. It is better, of course, for IT management to know in depth its service set, how its offering are configured, what performance levels it can deliver. This requires a thorough understanding of each service and the service components used to shape each service. Management's role here should be to empower the organization to acquire this knowledge state and use it as a basis for service level negotiations.

Negotiating equitable performance targets

Negotiating with customers can be a tricky business. Sometimes parties adopt a defensive posture and are inclined to take inflexible positions. Sometimes they prove too eager to please and over-promise or over-commit. Because of the competitive nature of business both sides of the table may often feel compelled to look out solely for their own interests, and probably feel that the other party, while perhaps not predatory, probably does not have its interests front and center in their minds. The results of these kinds of us-versus-them perceptions are often us-versus-them contracts, contracts negotiated from a 'trench' mentality and then stipulated with whatever blend of off-balance clauses. These kinds of contracts rarely serve either party well. There is a better approach. Service Level Management will become much more effective when agreements can be negotiated in a more open and informed manner, with the goal being not to get whatever one can but to seek equitable performance targets. Customers naturally want their service needs to be met and at the same time should wish to ensure that these needs are practical and sensible. IT management should likewise want to set delivery and quality expectations within ranges they feel comfortable committing to and at a fair price. When these two desires meet what can be formed is a balanced and practical SLA. Such a negotiating approach is essential to any effective Service Level Management program.

Focusing on customer satisfaction

IT people, being technical people on the whole, have a natural tendency to frame operational success in terms of technical achievement. Business people, on the other hand, may care little for technicalities. Their interests, when it comes to technology, more probably lie in operational ease. That presents something of a dichotomy. By focusing on technical efficiencies in a top-heavy way, IT teams may be unwillingly neglecting the softer side of service delivery: promoting customer satisfaction. Such an expression may in fact appear contradictory to IT teams: "If we're doing our behind-the-scenes jobs well, shouldn't the customer be automatically satisfied?" The answer is, not necessarily so. Appreciating this position can be a real challenge for Service Level Management programs, but it is not difficult to appreciate. Ensuring technical stability across the infrastructure is certainly a major responsibility for service management teams, but in the absence of regular and open customer communications it loses some of its value. High (or at least rising) customer satisfaction levels are essential when it comes to perceptions of success and nothing affects satisfaction levels as much as regular and open communication. That is why it is important that IT management encourages its teams – from service managers on down – to engage with the customer as enthusiastically and productively as possible. Where satisfaction levels are high, business appreciation for IT's value tends to rise. In fact, high satisfaction levels can result in IT success even when there are service performance, delivery or quality issues.

Maintaining strong business relationships

This may be a holdover from the days (waning but still somewhat present) when there was a wall between IT operations and the business: technical people seem to have a predisposition not to want to engage with business people. This hesitation is probably driven by several workplace fears: the fear of unintentionally acquiring more (perhaps nonessential) work, the fear of having to explain positions which may not be appreciated, the fear of conflicting missions and objectives. These kinds of fears breed little more than an appreciation of the status quo, settling for rarely more than 'good enough', and a 'don't-rock-the-boat' mentality. What needs to be understood (and it can be a challenge indeed to get this understanding across) is that successful Service Level Management – and all of IT Service Management operations– relies on establishing and maintaining strong customer relationships. It is the point of the program. The penultimate mark of success in this arena is the creation of a business-IT *partnership*, one based on shared missions, open communications, and a committed focus on business success. Maintaining robust business-IT relationships requires that IT teams work hard to understand business goals, business drivers, business services, and the organization's position in the marketplace; and then to use that knowledge to shape service delivery and service quality appropriately.

Figure 4.9 Service Level Management implementation challenges and considerations

4.11. Typical assets and artifacts of a Service Level Management program

Your Service Level Management program will require a set of program materials to cover both program assets and program artifacts. The assets provide the procedures, templates, and guides that will frame the manner in which program activities are conducted. The artifacts describe the work products that will be produced from these activities. Following is a list of some common assets and artifacts you are likely to encounter in a typical Service Level Management program. While your program may call for some of these, you will probably wish to create some items not described here. This list, while not exhaustive, is typical however and you might it useful as a starting point for designing your program.

Service Level Management policy
This is an executive policy that stipulates the goals and objectives of the Service Level Management program. The policy, which ideally should be no longer than a few pages, documents at a high level the purpose of the program, the resources available to the program, the chief responsibilities of the program, quality targets, reporting

hierarchies, and program measures. Endorsed by executive management, the policy demonstrates organizational commitment to the value and importance of the Service Level Management program.

Service performance capabilities
Service performance capabilities are technical specifications that frame the performance range that a service or set of services is able to deliver. These specifications are essential to effective service level management. They are typically used by service managers to establish service level requirements (SLRs); the SLRs then form the basis of SLAs. Without the ability to reference such specifications, IT management may under-commit or over-commit during SLA negotiations.

Negotiation guidelines
Service level negotiations can affect IT groups (and customer groups) in significant ways. To ensure that management accounts for an IT organization's primary mission and business objectives, it is helpful for the organization to provide its manager with negotiation guidelines. These guidelines set the parameters and boundaries for establishing SLAs, OLAs, and UCs with customers and customer stakeholders.

SLA / OLA / UC templates
These are templates for use by IT managers charged with developing SLAs, OLAs, and UCs. The templates define the structure, content, and presentation styles of these work products.

SLA / OLA / UC report templates
These are templates for use by IT managers charged with developing service level reports and other performance reports. The templates define the structure, content, and presentation style for each defined report.

Service Level Management reporting and distribution procedure
This is a documented procedure that describes how service level (and related) performance reports are created, how often they are generated, and to whom they are to be distributed. This procedure – and the reports – can be seen as a by-product of the SLA, OLA, and UC report templates described above. Together these artifacts provide the kind of information needed by IT management and customer groups to understand the effectiveness of service delivery and quality performance and identify opportunities for improvement.

Organizational chart
This is a chart that shows the structural make-up of the Service Level Management organization. As with other organizational charts, the purpose is to identify teams, team relationships, and hierarchical flows, and so the chart's shape will depend on the organizational units and resources you are able to apply to the program. Most organizational charts of this sort tend to be simple and basically linear. At the top, usually, there is a dotted box representing the customer. This extends down to a box for the Service Level Manager. Below this are two groups: Service Managers and

senior IT management. A dotted line from the Service Level Manager box might extend to a parallel support spot for the Service Level Management process owner (if this role is separate from the Service Level Manager).

Roles and responsibilities matrix

This matrix, an extension of the organizational chart, describes the various roles and responsibilities the organization has assigned to support Service Level Management activities. The roles typically include such positions as Service Level Management process owner, Service Level Manager, and (in tangential roles) Service Managers and senior IT management. Along with the job role definitions there should be descriptions of the responsibilities each role should account for, and references to how roles interrelate and communicate. The matrix might take one of several forms: a spreadsheet, a series of database records, or a version-controlled text document. Ownership of this artifact is usually shared between IT management and Human Resource management.

5. Capacity Management

Of all the operating qualities that an IT service can demonstrate, the two that are perhaps the most crucial to effective delivery are capacity and availability. For this reason these two ITIL processes are identified among the core components of a Service Management program. And while ITL places both of these in its Service Design phase it recognizes that the activities associated with each process span the full service lifecycle, from Strategy through to Continual Improvement. In this chapter we'll look at the factors that influence how you might implement a Capacity Management process. (For Availability Management, see the following chapter.)

Capacity Management exists as a delineated process to provide an organization with a point of focus for all capacity related issues and requirements. In any IT organization these issues and requirements may be quite diverse. The discipline of Capacity Management covers a wide range of domains. Some of the most obvious include: processor utilization, disk storage, bandwidth, transaction rates, and concurrency levels. But in mature organizations you'll find Capacity Management applied to some domains that are not so obvious: resource allocation (*Do we have the people to do this?*), scheduling (*Do we have the time to do this?*), even skill sets (*Do we have the experience to do this?*). Whatever scope you elect to include in your Capacity Management program, begin with a consideration of its intended purpose.

As ITIL defines it, the purpose of Capacity Management is:

...To provide for an organization's present and future capacity needs balanced against cost.[1]

That is a simple summation but it has broad implications. To balance cost with performance and supply with demand requires a well designed and well structured management approach. This leads to the objectives ITIL has set for this process. According to the specification, the objective of Capacity Management is:

...To set into place mechanisms to design capacity requirements and monitor capacity performance for business services, technical services, and service components.[2]

That objective shapes the content for this chapter. It also alludes to an important aspect of Capacity Management: it has its base in technology engineering; it is a technical discipline. Implementing a Capacity Management program requires an organization to bring its technical expertise together and direct its technical activities

---

[1] Foundations of ITIL (2007), Van Haren Publishing.
[2] Ibid.

to fit its management approach. This should accommodate a variety of considerations, including:

- Developing and maintaining capacity plans to manage service designs, delivery, and improvements
- Providing capacity-related guidance and advice to service managers and other organizational stakeholders
- Establishing effective capacity designs and support materials
- Assisting with the monitoring and management of capacity performance in production
- Participating in capacity-related diagnostic activities
- Assessing the impacts proposed changes may have on capacity performance
- Developing cost-justifiable capacity improvement recommendations.

To delve into these responsibilities further let's begin with a look at the activities associated with the Capacity Management process.

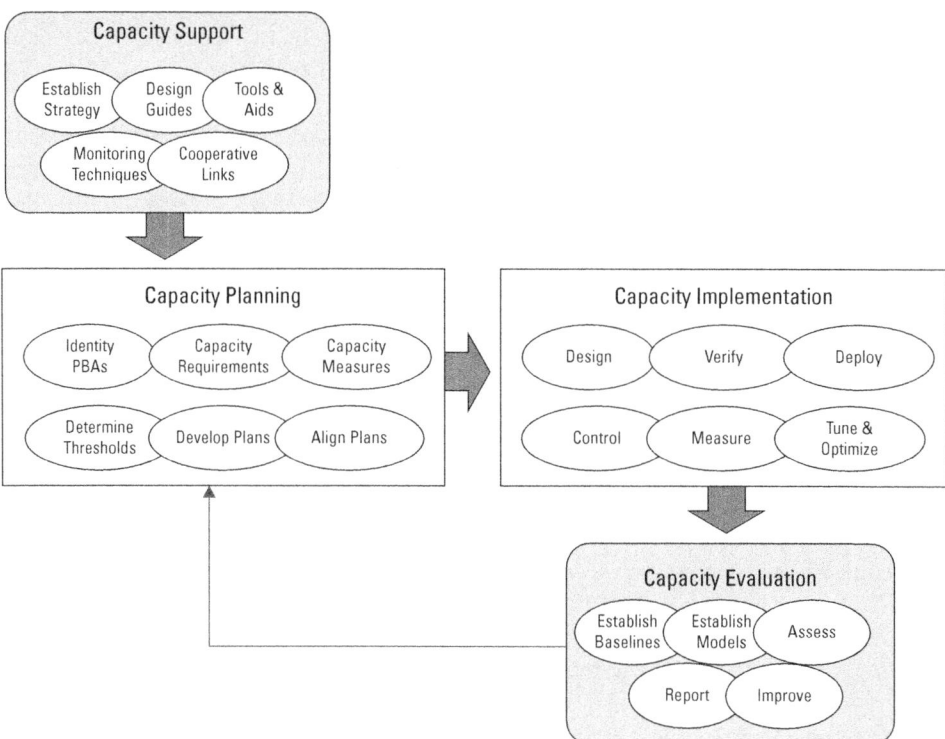

Figure 5.1 Typical Capacity Management process flow

5.1. Process activities for Capacity Management

Many variables can affect the scope and complexity of the activities associated with Capacity Management. Organization size, industry focus, the shape of the infrastructure, and market position are just a few of these factors. But whether the end result is a simple environment or a sophisticated one the stages of Capacity Management are usually the same. The process will always include the essentials of preparation, planning, designing, transitioning into live operation, monitoring, tuning, optimizing, assessing, reporting, and improving. These activities – sometimes referred to as sub-processes – can be grouped into four procedural areas. These are:
- Capacity support
- Capacity planning
- Capacity implementation
- Capacity evaluation

Here is a description of each.

1. Capacity support

Here the organization provides the resources required to operate an effective Capacity Management methodology. This stage could also be called preparation. Once the resources are in place they do not need to be recreated with each new service initiative; however, it is important to recognize that these resources are not of a static nature. As the basis for the overall Capacity Management program they will need to be reviewed with an eye toward improvement from time to time. Five activities are associated with this stage. They are outlined below.

Establish a Capacity Management strategy. Because the organization will need a cohesive, coordinated approach to Capacity Management, a strategy should be set in place, one that is defined and documented. The strategy sets the boundaries for the program – identifying the range and types of service facets that will be controlled – and establishes mechanisms for planning, designing, and managing those facets. Common types of strategies are *lead*, *lag*, and *match* strategies. With a lead strategy, the organization works to anticipate capacity needs and positions itself with an economical surplus in place. A lag strategy is just the opposite. The organization runs just short of ideal capacities, incrementing up only when absolutely required. A match strategy is just that: a one to one match, matching capacity adjustments in time with precise capacity demands. To support the strategy an executive policy covering Capacity Management roles in the organization should also be created and disseminated.

Establish Capacity Management design guidelines. These guidelines are intended to introduce consistency and control into capacity design considerations and activities. They should reflect the kinds of services your organization delivers and the infrastructure upon which they operate. The value of defining, documenting, and training your analysts in the use of these guidelines comes is three-fold: they promote a technical consistency that can be recognized and referenced by all; they provide a baseline for capturing design best practices; they provide a knowledge-base for use by new design staff and IT support.

Implement design aids and tools. Aids and tools are often required to assist capacity teams with management and support duties, such as designing, tuning, and optimizing capacity performance. Implementation of a Capacity Management Information System (CMIS) is especially important. The CMIS is a repository for information about capacity needs, requirements, design guidelines, performance data, baselines, models, and improvement data. For more on this, see page 108.

Implement capacity performance monitoring techniques. Before an organization can realistically achieve a Capacity Management program it will need to implement tools to monitor service capacity performance. Without such a toolset management becomes, at best, a reactive guessing game. It follows that because Capacity Management is a technical discipline, technology will make up a large part of its operational effectiveness. Monitoring tools specific to the services being delivered will need to be acquired, installed, and configured in production so that capacity performance can be adequately controlled and measured.

Establish cooperative links. Capacity Management, as a practiced process, needs to operate in harmony with other ITIL Service Management processes. Capacity Management particularly has strong ties to Availability Management, IT Service Continuity Management, Service Level Management, and Continual Service Improvement. To a lesser extent there are also dependencies with Change Management and Release and Deployment Management. It is important to establish connecting links and interfaces between Capacity Management activities and these other areas.

2. Capacity planning

Planning is a key aspect associated with every ITIL process. In this case, capacity planning sets the foundation for executing the Capacity Management strategy and for realizing Capacity Management objectives. There are six activities typically undertaken to ensure solid, reliable planning. These are outlined below.

Determine Patterns of Business Activity (PBAs). PBAs are trend analyses that can be used to understand capacity demand and thus strengthen capacity planning. Because business activities have a direct bearing on service performance they can particularly affect Capacity Management. It is helpful for the organization to look at its business lines in order to understand past and current performance in these areas. Such an understanding will not only help with planning; it will also help the organization as it works to establish capacity performance baselines and models.

Identify capacity requirements. A core part of capacity planning is determining a service's functional requirements. These take the form of business requirements, service (technical) requirements, and service component requirements. As part of planning these requirements should be elicited, documented, verified, and approved.

Once they are approved, they should be placed under change control and referenced as a primary design input.

Identify capacity monitoring needs. Just as an IT service will have requirements different from other services, so each service will have its own monitoring needs. And just like the requirements, these needs will have to be elicited (usually from a combination of customer and technical stakeholders), documented, verified, approved, and placed under change control. Monitoring needs should then trace back to the requirements.

Identify capacity measurement methods. Measurement methods are often grouped as part of the business requirements. The methods identify the performance metrics that will be captured for a particular service, where that data will be stored, how the data will be analyzed, and when and how that data will be presented to relevant stakeholders. Measurement methods are closely allied with monitoring techniques.

Determine capacity threshold management techniques. Once new or enhanced capacity capabilities are live in production, performance should be monitored. It is essential to frame that performance within specific boundaries to distinguish acceptable performance from unacceptable performance. For each service, performance thresholds should be defined. Along with these, response measures should also be defined and triggers for action identified when threshold limits are breached or exceeded.

Align capacity plans. Because capacity plans guide how design, implementation, and evaluation activities are accounted for, it is important to synchronize the plans with the agreements stipulated in other guiding documents, such as SLAs, OLAs, and UCs. These documents all establish requirements and expectations, and they often have a direct bearing on capacity performance, especially with regard to capacity designs. So, as capacity plans are being prepared it is important to compare them with these other documents and verify that their directions align along a common path.

3. Capacity implementation

Capacity implementation puts the capacity plan into action. It is here that the full program is deployed, and it is here that the activities most commonly associated with Capacity Management appear. Six activities in this stage move a service through the point where new features or enhancements are being prepared, through to the point where the service is being actively managed in production. The six activities are outlined below.

Design. Using the organization's design guidelines, design criteria, and the established business, technical, and component requirements, capacity capabilities are designed and then integrated into the service design.

Verify. With the design in place, the service can now be tested. This is to ensure three things. First, that performance meets all the functional and technical requirements requested by the customer. Second, that the solution operates as intended in the production (or production-like) environment. Third, that capacity performance as tested meets operational expectations. If all three of these conditions prove acceptable the solution can be made ready for deployment.

Deploy. With the design in place and verified, the solution can now be deployed to production. This is a planned activity that is coordinated with the customer and operational staff to ensure a smooth installation. Deployment includes the technical components of the solution and the documentation and specifications required to successfully operate and manage the solution. (For more on this see chapter 10, Release Management.)

Implement threshold management controls. A key part of Capacity Management is implementing the kinds of threshold controls useful for managing a live service in operation. These controls can be used to send alerts to support teams if thresholds fall out of acceptable range. They can even cue automation tools to adjust capacity performance in real time in order to avoid threshold breaches. These controls tie to the monitoring and measurement activities associated with Capacity Management.

Monitor and measure. All active operational services need to be regularly monitored. Part of the design process is to recognize performance traits that need to be monitored, then provide ports for these data feeds. With service implementation, solutions should be configured for such monitoring, which begins once the service goes live. Monitoring and measuring should be continual tasks in Capacity Management.

Tune and optimize. Monitoring and measuring provides accumulated and real-time performance data to operation teams and capacity analysts. This data can then be used by support teams to tune and optimize performance to adjust results to desired levels. Tuning and optimizing can be a real-time activity, or it can be rolled into the design stage as a planned and calculated activity.

4. Capacity evaluation

The purpose of capacity evaluation is to close the loop on Capacity Management activities. As with all other ITIL processes, Capacity Management features an embedded imperative: continual improvement. Evaluation establishes the base for analyzing performance and determining potential improvements. The assumption is that a service (or a set of services) operates in the environment in a controlled and managed way. With that in place six activities associated with evaluation can occur; they are described below.

Assess capacity performance metrics. In the implementation stage above, a service is set into production and there its performance is monitored and controlled. Monitoring includes capturing performance measures. These measures are accrued over time, and periodically it is the task of capacity analysts and capacity managers to assess this data. The data serves two purposes. As a snapshot it gives managers and analysts insight into current performance; this insight can then be used to further tune and optimize performance. The data also serves a longer-term goal: to help establish capacity performance baselines.

Establish capacity performance baselines. A baseline is a picture of past performance, typically presented as a diagrammatic trend line over time. Baselines are important because they allow analysts, managers, and customers to see how performance varies with time. Baselines of capacity performance can reveal any number of qualities, such as how effective capacity designs have been in improving performance, performance fluctuations relevant to seasonal or environmental production changes, and other kinds of associations. Baselines are an important tool also in establishing capacity performance models.

Establish capacity performance models. A model is a projection of a future state based on a valid sample of a past state. With Capacity Management, models can be used to predict future capacity performance, and thus future needs. When enough data has been accumulated, analytic techniques can be applied to push trends out into the future. One of the main purposes of the CMIS is to provide such techniques along with the baseline data on which to calculate the projections. Capacity performance modeling is of particular use to capacity planning, capacity tuning and optimizing, and for determining potential capacity improvements.

Assess the effectiveness of capacity designs. The key activity in the capacity evaluation stage is to assess the effectiveness of capacity designs. The raw performance data, the baselines, the models, and SLA targets can all be analyzed in order to determine if Capacity Management, as an organizational responsibility, is meeting its business and technical objectives. If assessments show that to be true, further enhancements might be considered; if they show that not to be the case, then management may wish to look again at the processes, tools, and activities that produced such results. This task of assessing effectiveness, as indeed with all tasks in the evaluation stage, should be an ongoing, coordinated activity.

Develop recommendations for improvement. An understanding of the current state of capacity management as an internal discipline will emerge from the assessments described above. This should lead to the final responsibility for capacity managers and analysts in the capacity lifecycle, which is to make recommendations for improving capacity performance. Recommendations may address any aspect of the program: technical innovations, monitoring changes, process adjustments, the acquisition of different skills sets, and so on. This is part of ITIL's focus on continual service improvement. (For more on this topic, see Chapter 15.)

Prepare and distribute capacity performance reports. Capacity Management should communicate the performance of its program and its services through periodic Capacity Management reports. These reports help to inform Service Managers, IT senior managers, and customer stakeholders about the program's overall effectiveness and efficiency.

The four stages of support, planning, implementation, and evaluation enable an IT organization to manage capacity in a consistent, predictable, and controlled manner. Below we look at the inputs and outputs, and the entry and exit criteria associated with the Capacity Management process.

5.2. Process inputs and outputs

Like all of ITIL's Service Design phase processes, Capacity Management operates as a cycle. Customer needs and the existing infrastructure drive how capacity requirements are established. Service design activities incorporate those requirements into IT solutions. The solutions are implemented, then transitioned into operational service. In live operation they are monitored and measured. Based on operational performance, new or enhanced capacity requirements may emerge, and the cycle begins again. The entry state for the Capacity Management process is always the same: a service – new or enhanced – is being prepared for live operation. Triggers that set this process in motion may come from a variety of inputs: customer business plans, strategic IT plans, or Requests for Change. Triggers that indicate the process is complete are also fairly stable. They include capacity designs, new performance measures of services in production, and lessons learned from Post Implementation Reviews (PIRs). Below is a summary of entry criteria, inputs, exit criteria, and outputs of the Capacity Management process.

Entry criteria
The Capacity Management process is typically set into motion when one of two events occurs:
- A new IT service is being made ready for live operation; or
- An existing production service needs to be enhanced or modified to meet new customer/IT needs.

Inputs
Inputs into the process can come from a variety of sources, individually or in combination. These inputs can include:
- Customer business plans
- Strategic IT plans
- Patterns of Business Activity (PBAs)
- Analyses of capacity baselines and models in the CMIS
- Capacity performance reports from production that drive Requests for Change for any of the following areas:
  - Business capacity requirements
  - Service capacity requirements
  - Service component capacity requirements

Exit criteria
The process is typically recognized as having been completed when three general exit conditions are met:
- A new or enhanced service has been successfully transitioned into operation, and
- Monitoring and control tools are capturing capacity performance, and
- A PIR of Capacity Management activities has been conducted.

Outputs
The Capacity Management process is designed to produce a set of work products that support the activities embedded within the process. The set typically includes the following artifacts:
- Capacity designs (new or updated)
- Capacity performance metrics (from production)
- PIR lessons-learned notes

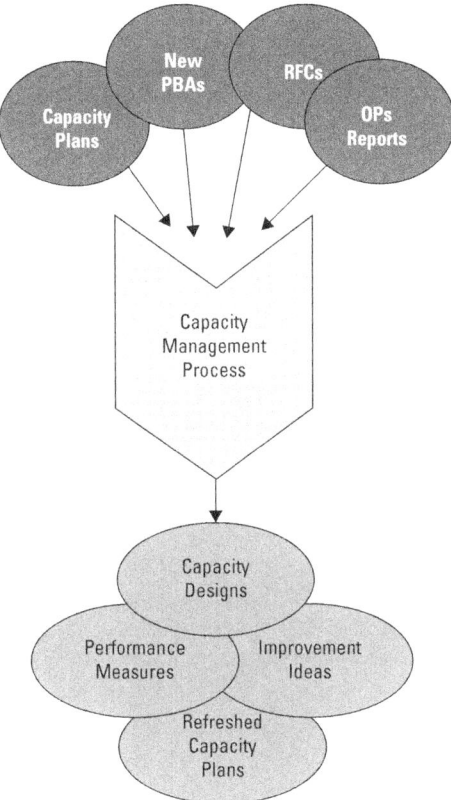

Figure 5.2 Inputs and outputs for Capacity Management

5.3. Processes related to Capacity Management

ITIL's design processes, including Capacity Management, operate in somewhat of a stand-alone mode, more so than the Service Strategy, Transition, Operation, and Improvement processes. The reason is clear. Each Design process addresses a separate facet of service performance. The considerations for each are unique. And while these processes form a whole and cohesive set when taken together, they can be implemented independently of each other. However, when it comes to Capacity Management there are two ITIL processes that have a direct bearing on how its process activities are conducted and managed. The first is Availability Management, whose functional scope tends to capitalize on capacity efficiencies. The second is Service Level Management, through which capacity performance is most often established and reported on.

Availability Management

Capacity Management and Availability Management are often regarded as sister processes. Rarely is one implemented without the other. Capacity and availability, after all, are two highly visible service performance traits. And while capacity deals with one set of technical considerations, and availability another, these considerations complement each other and thus benefit when treated as a shared domain. Capacity solutions (such as storage and throughput) directly influence how service availability performs. Capacity-related service interruptions can lead to availability interruptions. At the same time, well-considered capacity designs integrated with other service needs can add a layer of protection for availability performance.

In summary:
- The effectiveness and efficiency of capacity management solutions has a direct bearing on how a service's availability targets might be met.
- Capacity-related production issues can have significant impacts on availability performance.
- Well-considered capacity designs can provide a layer of additional protection for availability performance.

Service Level Management

Capacity performance is such a visible trait of overall service performance that it is almost always included as a target under Service Level Management. SLAs inevitably include some kind of capacity delivery and quality metrics relating to its mission-critical systems. It is essential that capacity managers work closely with Service Level Managers to negotiate customers' appropriate capacity performance targets. Once SLAs in this area have been set it is also important for capacity managers to work with Service Level Managers to track ongoing performance. Poor performance in such a visible area can be detrimental not just to other technical targets but to customer satisfaction levels as well. For these reasons, a Service Level Management program should work to integrate and support the function and shape of a Capacity Management program.

In summary:
- Capacity performance has a direct bearing on service quality, and thus on the customer's perception of IT's value to the business.
- SLAs are a key source for establishing capacity Management performance expectations.
- Effective Capacity Management supports IT's effort to create strong and cooperative relationships between IT management and business management.

Service Improvement

As a process in the Continual Service Improvement lifecycle phase, Service Improvement is an umbrella activity for all aspects of an IT Service Management program. With Capacity Management, improvement work falls into two broad categories. The first is technical. Here capacity analysts and operation teams investigate ways in which capacity designs and operational performance can be enhanced. The second category falls under support. Capacity management teams (along with the Capacity Management process owner) work to identify improvement opportunities that apply to the program's processes, procedures, monitoring tools, and measurements.

In summary:
- A key responsibility of capacity analysts is to continually investigate and identify ways in which capacity designs and operating performance can be improved.
- Capacity improvements are not confined just to the technical arena; teams should seek improvements in management processes, monitoring tools, and measurements.

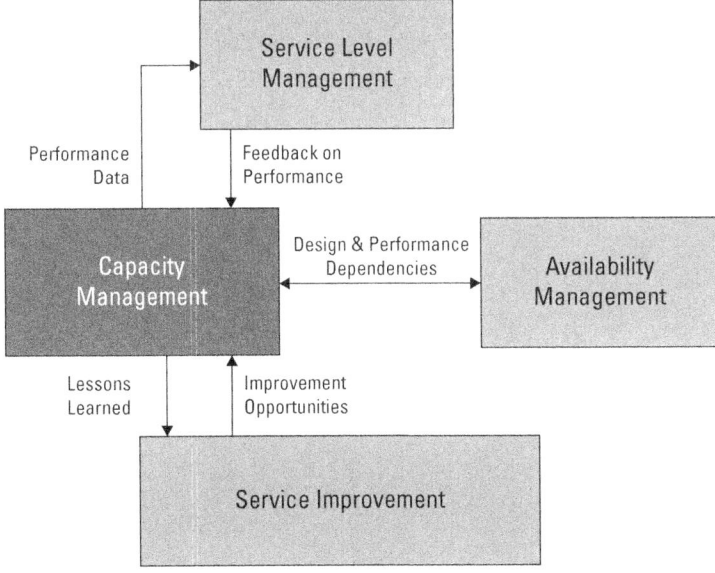

Figure 5.3 Processes related to Capacity Management

5.4. Tools and techniques

Capacity Management is a domain that occupies two functional areas. First and foremost is design activity. For this, the organization will need to provide the program with the kinds of materials to support capacity design activities, particularly design guidelines and some form of CMIS. Secondly, Capacity Management is an operational function, an operational exercise in which capacity performance is monitored, controlled, and measured in an ongoing way. To support this, the organization should provide the program with an appropriate set of monitoring tools and a strategy for collecting and analyzing performance metrics. These four techniques and tools are described below.

Table 5.1 Tools and techniques for Capacity Management

Capacity Management design guidelines	To manage the process of designing for service capacities it is important that the organization approaches this discipline in a way that promotes consistency and repeatability while focusing on performance efficiencies. Standardized service design guidelines provide for this. Capacity design guidelines can be so configured that technical teams are able to address the specific and unique needs of different business systems, technical services, and service components. Considerations usually include data storage needs, functional overhead, throughput, response times, and concurrent use. Documented design guidelines provide a measure of protection to the design process and serve as a basis for improvement and refinement over time.
Capacity Management Information System (CMIS)	The CMIS is most commonly implemented as an automated tool used to register, analyze, and present capacity performance data. The information in such a repository can be referenced by service analysts when planning capacity designs. It can be used by Service Level Managers as a source for collating capacity performance data. It can also be used by service managers and senior IT managers to establish performance baselines and models.
Operational monitoring and control tools	In order for service delivery and service quality to be adequately managed, it is essential for service capacity performance to be monitored, controlled, and measured. This requires the organization to implement and configure an appropriate suite of production monitoring tools. These tools provide recorded feedback of service performance over time. They also provide a degree of real-time control over capacity performance. And they can be configured to capture measures of this performance. These tools provide the data that are a major source of input into the CMIS. Common service traits to be monitored include: • Processor utilization • Disk space utilization • Memory utilization • Queue lengths • Transaction rates • Hit rates • Response times • Concurrency levels

Performance analytic and trending techniques	In order to manage capacity issues with existing services and to effectively plan design performance for emerging services, the organization should provide its Capacity Management program with analytic and trending techniques. These may be basic or sophisticated, depending on the needs of the IT organization. These techniques provide a way to develop performance baselines and models over time. The baselines can be used to establish historical trends of capacity performance. From these trends, models can then be created to predict where performance levels might fall in the future. Baselines and models are extremely helpful in planning and designing service capacity components.

5.5. Key Performance Indicators

As an ITIL design activity, Capacity Management is largely a technical process, so the KPIs that may be set into place to measure process activities are somewhat technical themselves. The data used to support and generate the KPIs typically come from monitoring and control efforts managed by operation teams and from metrics posted to the CMIS. These efforts produce measures that can be assessed to help determine the effectiveness of capacity planning, design, and implementation practices. Following are six examples of some typical Capacity Management key performance indicators. These do not make up a comprehensive set, nor are they right for every organization but they may give you a good idea of the kinds of KPIs your program could use.

Current capacity levels by service
A single service may have multiple capacity requirements. Each of these requirements should be expressed through some type of capacity level (e.g. terabytes, throughput, concurrent users, etc.) In order to manage and monitor capacity effectively the organization should identify and track its capacity levels. This includes capacity levels for business services, technical services, and individual service components. When it tracks this data over time, the organization can produce capacity trend lines useful for planning activities, understanding performance, and anticipating upcoming needs. The data also identifies the current capacity volumes that operations teams need to support in order to ensure smooth service delivery.

Number and types of capacity-related incidents
Measures here paint a picture of capacity performance stability and reliability. This KPI presents counts of the total number and types of incidents that occurred over a given period directly or indirectly related to capacity issues. Analyses of this data can reveal weaknesses in capacity designs or may indicate support issues that may need to be addressed by Tier 2 operations teams or perhaps Tier 3 capacity analysts.

Number and types of capacity-related problems
Measures here offer a complementary view of the incident metric above. This KPI shows another facet of capacity performance stability and reliability. It presents counts of the total number and types of problems for a given period that were directly

or indirectly associated with capacity issues, capacity problems being one of the root causes of embedded incidents. Analyses of this data can reveal issues with capacity planning, design, and development practices, highlight support issues that may need to be addressed by Tier 3 capacity analysts, and point to considerations for capacity design and capacity management improvements.

Capacity growth trends over time by service

These measures can be collected over time so that they may be used as the basis for establishing capacity performance baselines. The baselines are helpful for understanding performance levels historically. Assessments of trend directions and fluctuation can be used to make sure capacity resources (people, equipment, and funding) are appropriately and efficiently allocated.

Projected future capacity growth by service

This analysis may be used as a foundation for establishing existing capacity trend baselines. Projecting future growth is a technique that takes current baseline trends and uses predictive algorithms, extending them into a future model of likely performance. These projections are helpful for understanding where performance levels are likely to move to so that resources (again: people, equipment, and funding) may be properly allocated.

Capacity cost-per-unit by service

This is a very useful KPI but one that invariably has to be custom configured based on the shape of the organization's infrastructure. These measures delineate the costs associated with establishing capacity levels for business and IT services, and usually express this relationship in terms of capacity 'units.' A unit may be one gigabyte, or a single MIP, or ½ second of response time, a data transfer rate, or any number of other variables. The key point is for the organization to identify these variables for its service sets and then assign a unit capacity cost to each one. Once that foundation is in place, the organization can track variations to these unit costs over time. This KPI is helpful when it comes to balancing the capacity needs of the organization with financial investment requirements and limitations. It also provides a sound base for reliable capacity planning.

5.6. Critical Success Factors

A successful Capacity Management program is one in which effective capacity performance is achieved relevant to the level of investment required. Where exactly that point of balance is struck will depend on many individual organizational traits. But the bottom line rests on the idea of value: are Capacity Management activities delivering cost-effective value to the business? This goal is primary to any well-designed Capacity Management program. And it is from this principle that a program's CSFs should emerge. CSFs in this domain should seek to enlighten two functional areas: the suitability of current capacity levels and the costs involved in maintaining these levels. Below are three common CSFs that most baseline capacity programs employ in one form or another. They can be key for demonstrating the effectiveness of a Capacity Management program overall.

Current service capacity costs versus budgeted costs

This is a program analysis that compares budgeted capacity costs with actual costs. It should be an ongoing exercise, conducted on a regular basis with a frequency sufficient to allow for adjustments and redirection as conditions dictate. The measures include business capacity budgets and expenditures, service capacity budgets and expenditures, and component capacity budgets and expenditures. Data sets here are often grouped by service. These types of analyses are important for several reasons. They provide insight into how well capacity planning and design practices are proving. They give an indication of the volatility of environment and business objectives. They produce a basis for forecasting future capacity issues and needs. And they provide a picture of current performance that can be compared with existing SLAs as a way to plan subsequent Capacity Management activities and prepare upcoming budgets.

NOTE: This analysis is not intended to measure capacity performance effectiveness. It simply compares configuration with capital costs. The following CSF looks at effectiveness.

Current service capacity levels versus 'ideal' levels

Current capacity levels may or may not be in line with 'ideal' levels. Ideal levels are basically estimates of the number of capacity units needed to ensure that SLA performance targets will be met. Ideal levels will naturally vary over time. When targets are being met, the ideal can be said to synchronize with the current configurations. When targets are not being met, a capacity deficit can be said to exist; when they are being exceeded, a surplus exists. The ongoing responsibility of Capacity Management is to balance the environment so that, as far as practical, current capacity levels are synchronized with the ideal. This type of analysis is essential for understanding both current management needs (e.g. up-scaling, downscaling) and for forecasting and planning needs.

Projected service capacity needs and costs

Effective Capacity Management requires regular capacity planning, and effective planning requires reliable estimation and projection techniques. In order for a Capacity Management program to deliver its value to the IT organization, management should regularly establish capacity projections and forecasts in anticipation of changing service needs. This activity provides a running analysis that captures current Capacity Management issues (levels and costs) and projects them into the future with an eye toward balancing capacity needs with technology and business needs. As a running analysis, these results should be regularly assessed, verified, and updated.

5.7. Capacity Management roles

The following job roles are typically seen in mature Capacity Management programs. Depending on the size and focus of the organization these roles may be full-time or part-time, combined, or shared by multiple individuals.

Capacity Management Process Owner

The Capacity Management Process Owner is the person (or persons) in the organization responsible for the development, deployment, and ongoing use of the Capacity Management program. It is common in many IT organizations that this process owner is also the same as the Capacity Manager, but this is not essential. The process owner champions the purpose and goals of Capacity Management, ensures that the program remains in a state of operational effectiveness, and interfaces with senior IT management and business representatives to facilitate program adjustments and improvements. To summarize, the Capacity Management Process Owner is responsible for:
- Developing and documenting the Capacity Management program
- Implementing the program across relevant teams
- Coordinating program training and mentoring
- Monitoring ongoing program use
- Measuring program performance over time
- Requesting and coordinating program improvements

Capacity Manager

Every IT service supported by the organization should have assigned to it someone responsible for managing capacity design activities and for monitoring capacity performance in production. This position is known as the Capacity Manager. It is a technical role in that understanding, implementing, and controlling service capacities can be a complex undertaking. Capacity Managers manage a technical staff of analysts, prepare and coordinate capacity plans, oversees design and monitoring activities, and report on performance to senior IT managers and Service Level Managers. To summarize, the Capacity Manager is responsible for:
- Capacity planning and ongoing management for a specific service or set of services
- Understanding capacity needs and configurations at the business, service, and service component levels
- Reviewing, assessing, and distributing capacity analyses and reports, both up-chain and down-chain
- Coordinating design, monitoring, test, and evaluation activities relevant to service capacity management
- Working with the Capacity Management process owner to refine and develop the program in an effective manner over time

Capacity analysts

Capacity analysts are usually members of a specific service team. They work under the direction of Service Managers and Capacity Managers to design and implement Capacity Management solutions. They elicit and validate capacity requirements,

structure designs, develop and test technical solutions, assist in capacity related implementations, and provide Tier 2 or Tier 3 capacity-related support for services in production. To summarize, capacity analysts are responsible for:
- Eliciting capacity requirements, developing capacity designs, and implementing Capacity Management solutions
- Analyzing and assessing service capacity performance on a regular basis
- Investigating, diagnosing, and troubleshooting capacity related incidents and problems
- Working in close collaboration with Tier 1 and Tier 2 support staff
- Working with external third party providers as required
- Supporting change control Request for Change impact assessments

Operation support teams

Operation support teams provide production support for IT services. One aspect of this support is monitoring and reporting on service capacity performance. These support teams work with capacity analysts as needed to ensure that service delivery and service quality remain at designated levels. They also provide performance data and feedback when capacity issues need to be investigated and diagnosed. To summarize, the operation support teams are responsible for:
- Monitoring capacity performance in production
- Providing capacity performance measures to Capacity Managers and capacity analysts on a regular basis
- Working in close collaboration with capacity analysts to troubleshoot capacity-related production incidents and problems

Human Resource considerations

The following are some typical traits that Human Resource staff may want to take into consideration when they are providing personnel, tools, and other resources for a Capacity Management program.

Technical experience and background: Capacity Managers should have an adequate technical background, one that includes experience with the types of components in the current environment. They should also have experience organizing and mobilizing capacity design, implementation, and monitoring activities. They should have experience in developing plans and creating forecasts of levels and costs for the organization.

Capacity analysts should have experience eliciting capacity requirements from stakeholders, developing effective capacity designs, and deploying solutions into production. Capacity analysts should also have experience documenting capacity requirements, designs, and support material relevant to the services.

Comfort working in a process centric environment: Capacity Management staff should be comfortable working in a process-centric environment, and should be open to learning about the organization's program and contributing to its ordered growth.

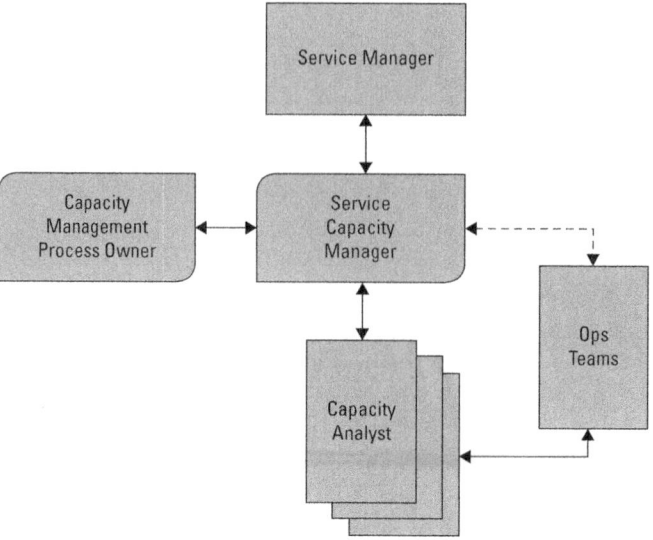

Figure 5.4 Capacity Management roles

5.8. Benefits of effective Capacity Management

An effective Capacity Management program can deliver benefits across multiple organizational areas, from strategy through design to production. In fact, capacity performance is such a significant factor in how service quality is perceived that its orderly management is a necessary priority in most IT organizations. A well designed Capacity Management program will result in smoother operational performance and reduced service interruptions. The data collected from the program can be used to bolster planning and forecasting activities. And the design techniques employed by capacity analysts can be used to refine the balance between costs, performance, and demand. The result should be overall improvements to customer service.

Well-balanced capacity cost/performance ratios

The driving objective for a Capacity Management program is to strike an effective balance between capacity performance and capacity costs. In organizations where capacity factors are not managed proactively it is common to find uneven conditions: top-heavy costs that outweigh performance benefits; deficient capacities due to poor planning; even a mix of the two due to weak forecasting. Setting the proper balance between investment and capability will always remain a technical challenge; an ITIL-based Capacity Management program is a reliable way to strive for such a balance. ITIL's emphasis on a cycle of planning, design, measurement, and evaluation promotes the view of Capacity Management as an engineering discipline that can be apportioned, controlled, and methodically refined. The use of forward-looking baselines and models supported by the program help balance capacity levels with business needs and thus produce cost-efficiencies when capacity investments or adjustments are required. Together, these can all be used to deliver capacity capabilities right-sized to the needs of the organization.

Better forecasting and planning

Because Capacity Management is an ongoing IT responsibility, the ability to effectively forecast and plan around capacity needs is essential. Without such ability Capacity Management is relegated to a reactive position in an IT organization, one that cannot be relied upon to promote high levels of service quality. Implementing a focused Capacity Management program helps the organization move this concern from a reactive to a proactive position. ITIL's recommendations for such a program includes measuring capacity design and performance efficiencies, employing a CMIS as a way to assess and evaluate performance data, developing baselines and models to project capacity needs into the future in a fact-based manner, and relying on these projections as a basis for planning. Movement down this path may well require time in order to gain momentum, but once you have amassed representative sets of data you will find your ability to forecast greatly increased. As a result, planned performance and operational benefits become much more reflective of real-world outcomes.

Well-controlled service delivery

A daily benefit of effective Capacity Management is well-controlled service delivery. The tools and procedures ITIL recommends for this process ensure that service demands are well matched to capacity configurations. The controls in the process provide for flexibility and responsiveness when capacity issues do arise. Further, the rigor placed around planning, design activities, and operational monitoring gives managers and analysts alike the level of insight needed to anticipate potential events and circumvent or diminish their negative impacts. All of this contributes to predictable and consistent service delivery.

Improved customer service

The above benefits result in a degree of service delivery transparency from balanced capacity levels, an engineered approach to forecasting and planning, and managed control of capacity performance. Taken together, this almost always translates into improved customer satisfaction levels for the IT organization.

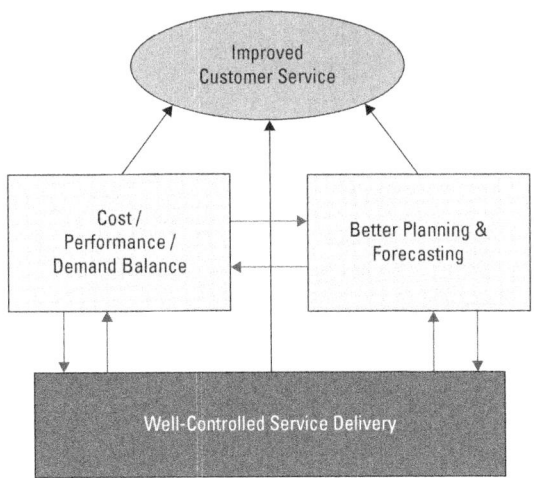

Figure 5.5 Benefits of effective Capacity Management

5.9. Implementation challenges and considerations

Together with availability, continuity, and security, capacity constitutes an essential component of service quality. The ability to control this quality is proportional to the level of Capacity Management techniques and practices the organization provides in resources. The recommendations ITIL defines for its Capacity Management process help set such techniques and practices into place. Even so, IT organizations should be aware that implementing these carries a set of challenges that may – if left unaddressed – potentially impede program performance or degrade Capacity Management effectiveness. This is especially true in IT organizations new to IT Service Management. As with the challenges associated with other ITIL design processes, it is important here that these are recognized early on so that they may be understood within the context of the culture and, to as great an extent as possible, minimized. As might be assumed, these challenges stem from the fact that managing capacities can be a technically sophisticated job. Determining capacity units, calculating capacity costs, understanding the range of capacity considerations across a diverse service mix, identifying effective capacity designs in dynamic environments – these are just a few of the tasks that need to be accounted for, and accounted for not just on an ongoing basis but on an *evolving* basis too. This calls for skilled resources, deep knowledge of the infrastructure, and access to specialized tools. And from there the challenges appear. Four of the biggest that tend to arise for this ITIL process are described below.

Determining capacity costs-per-unit
In order for a Capacity Management program to be effective as it might be, it is important that the organization understands the costs associated with this domain. Estimation, planning, design, and efficiency measures all rely on an appreciation for these costs. But acquiring such an appreciation is often challenging to do, especially in complex environments. The goal is for the organization to somehow (and this will vary from IT organization to IT organization) arrive at a capacity-cost-per-unit; that is, a sum that pinpoints what adding one unit of capacity for a specific service will cost. However, there is a range of possible capacity units. Capacity is not one thing but a set of things. Data storage, concurrency, throughput, and bandwidth are all forms of capacity, and each are expressed in their own types of units. When you see that different services naturally contain different capacity combinations the factoring of this matrix can become daunting. Organizations tend to approach the challenge in several ways. They might begin by first using a rough-order-of-magnitude to approximate costs, and then work to refine the detail of this approach over time. They might work to first understand capacity costs for only the most capacity-intensive or capacity-essential of the organization's services, then expand from there. Any number of other approaches might also be used. The aim is to actively and regularly consider cost when working to deliver service capacities. As with all baselines, once established, these cost baselines should be maintained and updated with an appropriate degree of regularity.

Validating capacity designs

Because capacity performance is critical to the overall quality of an IT service, it is essential to thoroughly test capacity performance before deploying a service into live operation. Implementing weak or faulty designs can transmit impacts across the infrastructure. All Capacity Management programs, then, should accommodate an appropriate level of testing. The challenge for this practice comes from two areas. First, many IT organizations lack (for a variety of reasons, some quite valid) the ability to mimic in the test laboratory the intricacies of the production environment. And so tests results from the laboratory may prove to be unreliable indicators of operational performance. Secondly, many IT organizations simply fail to allocate enough project time for adequate test and verification activities; the rush to production overtakes the perceived importance of testing. As a result, solutions may move into production with significant capacity issues. Removing the risks from each of these areas may be challenging for many IT organizations. Test laboratories may have to remain mere approximations of the operational environment. Test schedules may have to be squeezed in order to meet project milestones. But a well-designed Capacity Management program can address these weaknesses, even in a minimal way. This is done by openly acknowledging the conditions, identifying these as known risks in design documents and release plans, tracking the risks through development, and then thoroughly assessing them before deployment.

Establishing a Capacity Management Information System

For most mature Capacity Management programs the CMIS is the central tool used for forecasting, assessments, planning, design, management, and reporting on capacity issues and performance. But in order for a CMIS to effectively assume this role the organization needs to commit to its acquisition, configuration, and growth. This can pose a number of hurdles for any IT organization. Acquiring the right tool will call for some degree of capital investment. Configuring it to the shape and needs of the service set and infrastructure will require dedicated resources with specialized skills, as well as the time needed to get the configuration right. Most importantly, growing the CMIS so that its value to the organization will increase over time requires that the organization makes a firm commitment to its ongoing use in decision-making. Establishing and growing such a system can be a full-time job; it can be expensive; especially early on, its value might seem questionable. But the CMIS can be an important key for managing the technical complexities involved in the Capacity Management process, so each organization should attempt to balance the realistic scope of its capacity needs with the kind of CMIS it can afford to support.

Configuring effective monitoring tools

The technical nature of Capacity Management extends into the operational environment. So do the challenges. Because capacity solutions are designed to fit both the needs of the customer base and the environment, capacity performance needs to be monitored to verify that those needs are being met. This job can present its own set of challenges to an IT organization – for a variety of reasons. First, the infrastructure needs to be equipped with the right set of monitoring tools. These tools then need to be configured so that IT operations staff, support staff, and service managers have a view into how well various services and service components are operating, relevant to capacity. Such set-up and configuration requires a thorough knowledge of the environment, deep knowledge of the services operating in that environment, and a firm handle on how capacity requirements can best be translated into empirical measures. Even though most IT components today come with at least a base set of Capacity Management features and options, the trick – and thus the challenge – comes with aligning what those features and options can do with what the IT organization needs to know and what analyses the customer expects to receive.

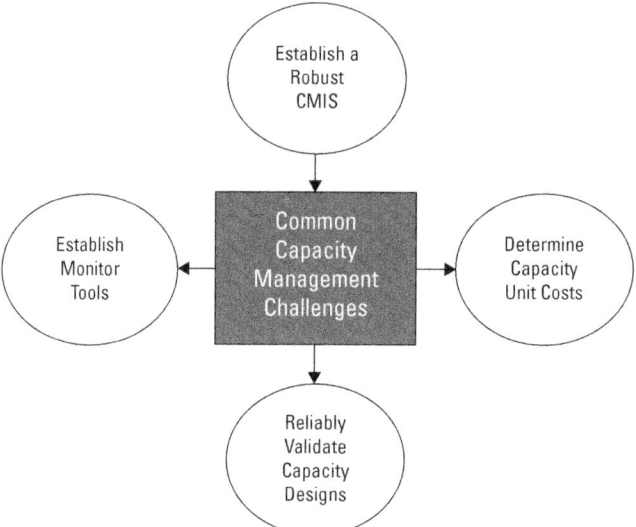

Figure 5.6 Implementation challenges and consideration for Capacity Management

5.10. Typical assets and artifacts of a Capacity Management program

A fully designed Capacity Management program requires a set of assets and artifacts that can be used to frame how program activities are run. The assets provide the procedural guides and supporting materials for the activities. The artifacts shape the work products that the Capacity Management activities produce. The following is a list of some of the more common materials that an organization is likely to employ when implementing a Capacity Management program. Your program may well require assets and artifacts not included here, but the set described below represents a typical baseline.

Capacity Management policy
This is an executive policy that states the goals and objectives of the Capacity Management program. The policy, which ideally should be no longer than a few pages, documents at a high level the purpose of the program, the resources available to the program, the chief responsibilities of the program, quality targets, reporting

hierarchies, and program measures. Endorsed by executive management, the policy is a demonstration of organizational commitment to the value and importance of the Capacity Management program.

Capacity Management plan template
This template provides a structural guide for creating the organization's Capacity Management Plan. The template outlines the contents and sections that a properly documented plan should contain. Such plans usually identify the following kinds of information:
- Purpose and scope of Capacity Management
- Resources assigned to create capacity designs and monitor capacity performance
- Capacity targets for each supported service
- Capacity measures and links to SLA targets
- Capacity monitoring techniques
- Strategies for meeting capacity targets
- Identification of Capacity Managers and key business stakeholders
- Types and frequency of capacity reporting, and report distribution channels
- Plan duration and review/revision schedule

Capacity Management plan
This is the organizational plan, based on the template above, that – once approved and adopted – stipulates how Capacity Management activities will be conducted over a set period of time.

Capacity design guidelines
These are guidelines that detail the technical, operational, and support factors that should be considered when designing capacity needs for specific services.

Capacity Management Information System (CMIS)
This is some form of automated system (selected based on the needs of the organization) that can be configured as a prime repository for storing and managing information about capacity designs, capacity deployment factors, and capacity performance measures.

Capacity monitoring procedures
These are documented procedures that detail how business capacity, service capacity, and service component capacity will be monitored in the live operational environment. These procedures typically describe the events to be associated with capacity indicators, the thresholds of acceptable performance, identification of the tools that will monitor each event, and descriptions of response activities to be invoked when thresholds are breached. These procedures usually serve as the basis for establishing OLAs between Capacity Managers and operations teams.

Capacity Management reporting and distribution procedure
This is a documented procedure that describes how capacity planning, design, and performance reports are created, how often they are generated, and to whom they

are to be distributed. This procedure – and the ensuing reports – can be seen as a by-product of the management plan described above. Together these artifacts provide for the generation of the kind of information that IT management and customer groups need to understand the effectiveness of capacity delivery and capacity performance to identify opportunities for improvement.

Service Level Agreement
Because capacity is a service trait so often linked with Service Level Management, the organization should ensure that there is a documented agreement between IT management, service managers, Capacity Managers, and the customer that stipulates the levels of performance that will be delivered concerning capacity by service.

Monitoring and control tools
The organization will need to acquire and configure a set of tools that can be used in production for monitoring capacity performance and adjusting that performance as needed.

Organizational chart
This is a chart that shows the structural make-up of the Capacity Management operation. As with other organizational charts, the purpose here is to identify teams, team relationships, and hierarchical flows, and so the chart's shape will depend on the organizational units and resources you are able to apply to the program. Most organizational charts of this sort tend to be simple and basically linear. At the top, perhaps, there is a dotted box representing the Service Managers. This extends down to a box for the Capacity Manager. Below this might be two groups: capacity analysts and operation analysts. A dotted line from the Capacity Manager box might extend to a parallel support spot for the Capacity Management process owner (if this role is separate from the Capacity Manager). This chart may be service-specific or combine a set of service offerings.

Roles and responsibilities matrix
This matrix, an extension of the organizational chart, describes the various roles and responsibilities the organization has assigned to support Capacity Management activities. The roles typically include such positions as Capacity Management process owner, Capacity Manager, capacity analysts (designers and developers), and (in tangential roles) operations analysts and senior IT management. Along with the job role definitions, there should be descriptions of the responsibilities each role should account for, and references to how different roles interrelate and communicate. The matrix might take one of several forms: a spreadsheet, a series of database records, or a version-controlled text document. Ownership of this artifact is usually shared between IT management and Human Resource management.

6. Availability Management

Availability may be the most visible of service attributes. If a user wants to access a technology device –an application, email, a printer – and it is down, that user sees a problem. More so, business may be interrupted, production might fall, frustrations can grow. In most IT organizations a significant percent of calls that come in to the Service Desk deal with issues of availability. In IT organizations that are proactively able to control the availability of their services, customer satisfaction levels tend to be high. When availability problems pepper the enterprise, customer satisfaction drops.

In this chapter we will look at the aspects of Availability Management that affect service delivery and service quality, and we will delve into the recommendations ITIL sets out for managing these aspects in a consistent and predictable manner. To begin, let's start with the purpose of the Availability Management process as ITIL states it:

"...To provide for an organization's present and future availability needs balanced against cost."[1]

That purpose statement is very much like the purpose statement for Capacity Management. It is easy to understand why. Of all the operating qualities that an IT service can demonstrate, the two that are perhaps the most crucial to effective delivery are capacity and availability. But because these two areas can be deeply technical in nature, these operating qualities, by necessity, come at a cost, sometimes at a significant cost. Balancing cost with performance (and supply with demand) requires an organization to approach availability concerns (just as it approaches capacity concerns) with a well designed and well structured management program. This leads to the objective ITIL sets for Availability Management. According to the specification, the objective is:

"...To set into place mechanisms to design availability requirements and monitor availability performance for business services, technical services, and service components."[2]

When components of the infrastructure experience operational interruptions the fallout can be significant. Downtime can mean lost productivity, lost revenues, wasted goods and materials, even industry or government fines and penalties. For these reasons designing for availability includes a variety of considerations. High availability targeting, redundancies, fault tolerance, resiliency, failover, backups,

---
1 Foundations of ITIL., (2010), Van Haren Publishing.
2 Ibid.

and continuity are all facets of this technical discipline. And the responsibilities for Availability Management teams cover a range of activities. These include:

- Developing and maintaining availability plans to manage service designs, delivery, and improvements
- Determining vital business functions (VBFs) upon which to focus availability resources
- Providing availability-related guidance and advice to service managers and other organizational stakeholders
- Establishing effective availability designs and support materials
- Assisting with the monitoring and management of availability performance in production
- Participating in availability-related diagnostic activities (service failure analyses, single point of failure analyses, etc.)
- Assessing impacts of proposed changes on availability performance
- Linking availability planning and management with IT Service Continuity planning and management
- Developing cost-justifiable availability improvement recommendations

To delve into these responsibilities further let's begin with a look at the activities associated with the Availability Management process.

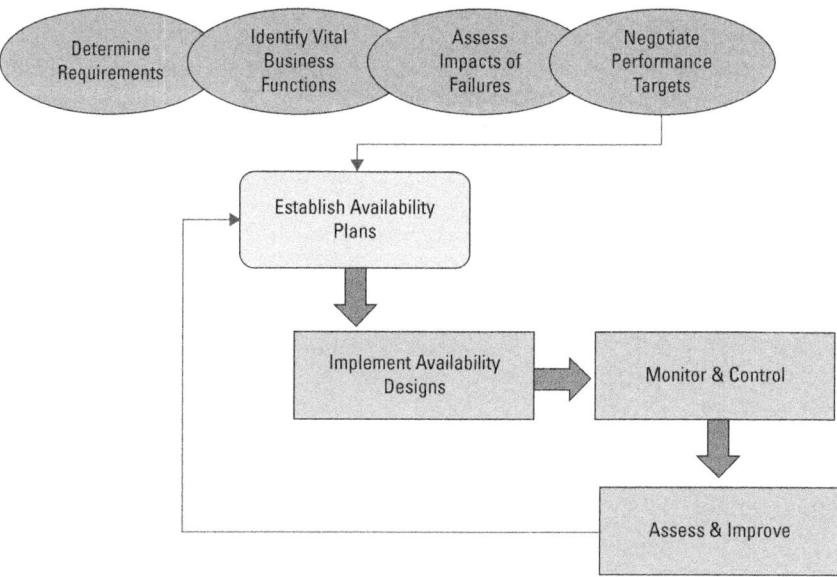

Figure 6.1 Typical Availability Management process flow

6.1. Availability Management activities

As is true with ITIL's other Service Design phase processes, Availability Management is largely technical in nature. Depending on the size and focus of an IT organization, the degree of technicality may run from fairly straightforward to very complex. But whether your organization finds itself at the straightforward end or the complex end, the steps associated with managing an Availability Management process are usually the same. There is always the need to establish requirements, understand key operating points across the infrastructure, set performance targets, set up plans to reach those targets, design to requirements, transition into production, monitor performance, assess performance, and look for improvement opportunities. For Availability Management these steps fall into eight process activities. These eight are:

- Determine availability requirements
- Identify vital business functions
- Assess the impacts of failing components
- Negotiate performance targets
- Establish availability plans
- Implement availability designs
- Monitor and control performance
- Assess and improve

Here is a description of each.

1. Determine availability requirements

Availability requirements are usually developed in a tiered structure. At the top are business requirements – the expectations the business has for the availability of each IT service. For this top tier it is important for IT management to work closely with customer stakeholders to identify and document these needs. This high level should be given focused attention. The business requirements are essential for driving out service and service component requirements; they will also in all likelihood form the basis of SLA performance targets.

Next come service availability requirements. As each service provides a specific function in a business enterprise its availability requirements will differ based on function. The elicitation and documentation process now moves to include technical teams and IT service managers. It is important to work with these stakeholders to derive realistic, informed IT service requirements and ensure they trace back to relevant business requirements. When these requirements have been captured you should validate them with your business stakeholders.

At the base of this tiered structure are the service component requirements. It is here that requirements derivation becomes the most technical. IT components (e.g. servers, routers, hubs, power supplies, printers, databases, etc.) operate within given configurations and these configurations affect availability parameters. These parameters cover how a particular device itself is configured and how it operates as a component in an integrated environment. This is where issues of redundancy, failover, backup and so on come into play. An added degree of complexity surfaces when you appreciate that a single component might be a dependent device for multiple IT services. For these service component requirements the most useful input will come from line level technical teams. You should work with these teams to derive component-capable technical requirements. Ensure that these too trace up to relevant service requirements, and then validate these with relevant service managers and senior IT management.

Once availability requirements for business services, technical services, and service components have been established and approved by IT management and business stakeholders, these baselined sets should be placed under formal change control.

2. Identify vital business functions

The focus of an Availability Management program should rest on an organization's vital business functions (VBFs). VBFs are those business and technical processes that are essential to business success. VBFs should receive top consideration when availability resources (people, technology, funding, etc) are being allocated. To support this, customer groups and service managers should work together to determine what the business VBFs are. Once identified, they should be documented and prioritized; then they should be linked to their associated business services, technical services, and service components. This will position the IT organization for analyzing crucial operational linkages to determine the impacts of failing components.

3. Assess impacts of failing components

The foundation knowledge necessary for an effective Availability Management program rests with understanding the impacts of failing components. If the functionality of a device degrades or fails altogether the end results on technical and business services need to be fully accounted for. At risk can be lost business opportunities, lost productivity, and a host of other consequences. With this in mind, technical teams should assess the environment (in light of established VBFs), analyze potential points of failure, and document the impacts that may occur if these points experience faults. Based on that, the organization should establish shelf-ready workarounds and contingency plans for such failures. The organization should also be sure to link its Availability Management strategies to IT Service Continuity Management plans and strategies. Among the variety of formal risk and impact assessment techniques that can be applied to impact assessments are:

- Failure Mode Analysis
- Service Failure Analysis (SFA)
- Component Failure Impact Analysis (CFIA)
- Fault Tree Analysis (FTA)
- Single Point of Failure Analysis (SPOF)

4. Negotiate performance targets

Service availabilities need to be measured in order to be controlled. Setting performance targets is an important step toward providing proper measures and controls. Performance targets set the thresholds that delineate acceptable service quality from the unacceptable. It is important that these targets are determined not by the IT organization alone, but in conjunction with the business. There needs to be a shared agreement over these levels because availability targets are usually included in SLAs.

Many IT organizations develop service availability targets based on a mix of the following operational characteristics:
- General availability
- Response times
- Reliability
- Serviceability
- Maintainability
- Sustainability
- Planned downtime
- Unplanned downtime

5. Establish availability plans

Availability plans should be employed as the chief tool for managing availability-related activities. Usually an organization's availability manager is responsible for developing these plans, but service managers, availability analysts, and customer stakeholders should be ready to provide input. Plans may be service specific or account for a blend of services. Availability plans typically require the following management considerations.

Identify Availability Management resources. The Availability Management Plan should identify those resources that have been allocated to support availability related duties for each supported service. These resources include people (availability managers, designers, analysts, and support staff), facilities (development and test equipment), and funding.

Identify requirements and design control techniques. Availability plans should specify how service teams will manage the integrity of availability requirements and designs. This includes how requirements and designs will be developed and documented, what review process they will be subject to, what approval process they will be subject to, and what level of change control they will be placed under.

Identify availability monitoring needs. Just as each IT service will have operating requirements different from other services, so each service will have its own monitoring needs. And just as with operating requirements, these needs will have to be elicited (usually from a combination of customer and technical stakeholders), documented, verified, approved, and placed under change control.

Identify availability measurement methods. Measurement methods are often grouped with business requirements, but wherever they are recorded they exist to identify the performance metrics that will be captured for a particular service, where that data will be stored, how the data will be analyzed, and when and how that data will be presented to stakeholders. Measurement methods are closely allied with monitoring techniques.

Identify availability threshold management techniques. Once new or enhanced availability capabilities are live in production, their performance will need to be monitored. It is important to frame that performance within specific boundaries; that is, to distinguish acceptable performance from unacceptable performance. And for each service, performance thresholds should be defined. Along with these, response measures should be defined and triggered for action when threshold limits are exceeded.

Identify Availability Management reporting practices. Availability plans should identify the management and performance reports that will be created for a service, how these will be generated, who will be responsible for their creation, to whom they will be distributed, and on what schedule they will be released.

Align availability plans. Because availability plans guide how design, implementation, and evaluation activities are accounted for across a set of services it is important for the plans to be synchronized with agreements stipulated in other guidance documents (e.g. SLAs, OLAs, and UCs). SLAs, OLAs, and UCs all establish requirements and expectations, and often have a direct influence on availability performance and designs. So, as availability plans are being prepared it is important to compare them with these other types of documents and verify that their directions align along a common path.

The process of establishing these plans includes soliciting technical and managerial content, drafting the documents, reviewing the documents with technical and business stakeholders, revising the documents as necessary based on feedback, obtaining commitment to the plans, and then managing the plans under change control.

6. Implement availability designs

Availability Management is categorized as an ITIL Service Design activity, so establishing availability designs is a key activity for this process. Each organization, however, must account for its approach to design in its own way. That approach depends on its mix of IT services, the shape of the infrastructure, and current business and IT strategies. No two organizations will be likely to use exactly the same methods, but the general boundaries and techniques of the job can be shared from IT organization to IT organization. For instance, it is helpful that IT management works to provide its architects and analysts with standardized design guidelines. These are guides specifically shaped to the needs of the enterprise. They ensure that design activities will account for all the technical and operational considerations important to the company. Next, technical teams should explicitly reference availability requirements,

VBFs, and business objectives as a basis for design decisions. They should also reference technical best practices as input into choosing availability tactics. The selection of practices and methods is broad. A sampling of the choices includes:
- Clustering
- Network load balancing
- RAID data stores
- Distributed file systems
- Queuing
- Failover
- Redundancy
- Fault tolerance
- Multi-link trunking

Once a technical solution has been developed, the task of implementation begins. Implementing designs involves verifying their suitability for use, documenting required support materials, validating a service package's readiness for production, and then deploying the package into production.

7. Monitor and measure availability performance

Availability levels are so essential to service delivery that they should be regularly monitored. Many design activities are in place to recognize those performance traits most likely to influence service quality and so provide mechanisms to monitor those traits. With each service implementation, the solution should be configured for monitoring once the service goes live. Such monitoring (and the measurements that follow) is a routine checkpoint for operation teams. As a service is monitored, performance can be evaluated. From here real-time decisions can be made about tuning and optimization. Measurement data collected over time can be fed into the Availability Management Information System (AMIS) and used as the basis for establishing availability baselines and performance models. That will lead to more effective forecasting and planning. The data will also provide the basis for availability performance reports and will provide insight into identifying opportunities for improvement.

8. Assess and improve

The final activities in the Availability Management process cycle involve assessing performance and determining opportunities for improvement. As noted above, once a service is in live operation its performance is monitored, controlled, and measured. As these measures accrue over time, it is the task of availability analysts and managers to periodically assess this data. Such data sets serve two purposes. They provide a snapshot that gives analysts and managers insight into current performance, insight that can then be used to tune and optimize availability performance. They also serve a longer-term goal: they help management establish availability baselines and models.

Out of these assessments there should emerge an understanding of the current state of Availability Management as an internal discipline. This will lead to the final responsibility in the Availability Management lifecycle. That is to make recommendations for improving overall availability performance. Recommendations may address any aspect of the program: technical innovations, monitoring changes, process adjustments, the acquisition of different tools and skills sets, and so on. This is part of ITIL's focus on continual service improvement. (For more on this, see Chapter 15.)

6.2. Process inputs and outputs

Like all of ITIL's Service Design processes, Availability Management operates as a cycle. Business needs and the shape of the IT environment drive the baseline for availability requirements. Availability designs then incorporate those requirements into service solutions. Those solutions are validated and transitioned into production. There they are monitored and measured. From assessments of these measures new or enhanced availability requirements may emerge, and the cycle begins again. The entry state for the Availability Management process always appears at the same point: a service – new or enhanced – is being made ready for production. The triggers that set the cycle into motion may come from a variety of inputs: new VBFs, business plans, strategic IT plans, Requests for Change, etc. Triggers that indicate the cycle is complete are also fairly stable. They include refreshed availability designs, new performance measures, lessons learned from PIRs, etc. Below is a summary of typical entry criteria, inputs, exit criteria, and outputs for the Availability Management process.

Entry criteria
The Availability Management process is typically set into motion when one of two events occurs:
- A new IT service is being made ready for production; or
- An existing operational service needs to be enhanced or modified to meet new customer/IT needs.

Inputs
Inputs into the process can come from a variety of sources, individually or in combination. These inputs can include:
- Customer business plans, strategic IT plans, existing availability plans
- Business forecasts
- Identification of new VBFs
- Analyses of availability baselines and models in the AMIS
- Risk assessments from SPOF, FTA, and SFA activities
- Availability performance reports that drive Requests for Change for any of the following areas:
  ○ Business availability requirements
  ○ Service availability requirements
  ○ Service component availability requirements

Exit criteria
The process is typically recognized as having been completed when three general exit conditions are met:
- A new or enhanced service has been successfully transitioned into production, and
- Monitoring and control tools are capturing availability performance, and
- A PIR of Availability Management activities has been conducted.

Outputs
Availability Management is designed to produce a set of work products that support the activities embedded within the process. At a minimum the set includes the following artifacts:
- Availability designs (new or updated)
- Availability performance metrics (from production)
- PIR lessons-learned
- Refreshed availability plans

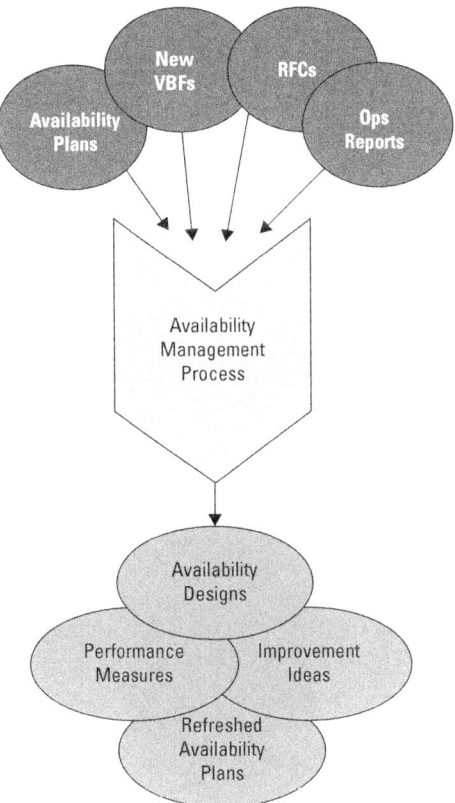

Figure 6.2 Inputs and outputs for Availability Management

6.3. Processes related to Availability Management

To some degree Availability Management can be said to operate in a stand-alone mode. The reason is clear. This process addresses a separate and distinct facet of service performance; the considerations for this area are unique. Although all of ITIL's design processes form a single, cohesive set when taken together, they can be implemented independently of each other. However, with Availability Management there are four processes that have a direct bearing on how its solution activities are executed and managed. These are IT Service Continuity Management, Capacity Management, Service Level management, and Service Improvement.

IT Service Continuity Management

Availability Management and IT Service Continuity Management are so closely integrated that the ISO/IEC 20000 Service Management standard treats them as a single process. Though this is not completely precise, when it comes to the availability of a service, Availability Management can be seen as the proactive arm of the discipline: preparing a service to meet availability expectations in production. IT Service Continuity can be seen as the reactive arm: restoring availabilities when severe interruptions occur. Availability plans and continuity plans should reference one another; availability designs drive continuity considerations, and vice versa; and analysts on either team may often be enlisted to provide support for the other team.

In summary:
- Availability Management and IT Continuity Management exist as extensions of one another; availability having a largely proactive stance, continuity having a largely reactive stance.
- Availability management strategies will have direct impacts on service continuity strategies.
- The preventive and response measures of a well-considered IT Service Continuity program can provide insight into how to approach availability design, development, and monitoring activities.

Capacity Management

Capacity Management and Availability Management are often regarded as sister processes. Rarely is one implemented without the other. Capacity and availability, after all, are two highly visible service performance traits. And while capacity deals with one set of technical considerations, and availability another, these considerations complement each other rather than compete and thus benefit when treated as a shared domain. Capacity solutions (such as storage and throughput) directly influence how service availabilities perform. Capacity-related service interruptions can lead to availability interruptions. At the same time, well-considered capacity designs integrated with other service needs can add a layer of protection for availability performance.

In summary:
- The effectiveness and efficiency of Capacity Management solutions have direct bearing on how a service's availability targets might be met.
- Capacity-related production issues can have significant impacts on availability performance.
- Well-considered capacity designs can provide an additional layer of protection for availability performance.

Service Level Management

Availability performance is such a visible trait of overall service performance that it is almost always included as a target under Service Level Management. With mission-critical systems, SLAs always include some kind of availability delivery and quality targets, so it is important that availability managers work closely with service level managers to negotiate appropriate performance targets. Once SLAs in the area have been set it is also important for the availability managers to work with service level managers in tracking ongoing performance. Poor performance in such a visible area can be detrimental not just to other technical targets but to customer satisfaction levels as well. For these reasons, a Service Level Management program should work to integrate and support the function and shape of an Availability Management program.

In summary:
- Availability performance has a direct bearing on service quality, and thus on the customer's perception of IT's value to the business.
- Service Level Agreements are the source for establishing Availability Management performance expectations.
- Effective Availability Management supports IT's efforts to create strong and cooperative relationships between IT management and business management.

Service Improvement

As a process in the Continual Service Improvement lifecycle phase, Service Improvement is an umbrella activity for all aspects of an IT Service Management program, but has particular emphasis for design processes. With Availability Management, improvement work falls into two broad categories. The first is technical: availability analysts and operation teams investigate ways in which availability designs and production performance can be enhanced. The second category falls under support. Availability Management teams (along with the Availability Management process owner) work to identify improvement opportunities that apply to the programs processes, procedures, monitoring tools, and measurements.

In summary:
- A key responsibility of availability analysts is to continually investigate and identify ways in which availability designs and operating performance can be improved.
- Program improvements are not confined just to the technical arena; teams should seek improvements in management processes, monitoring tools, and measurement techniques.

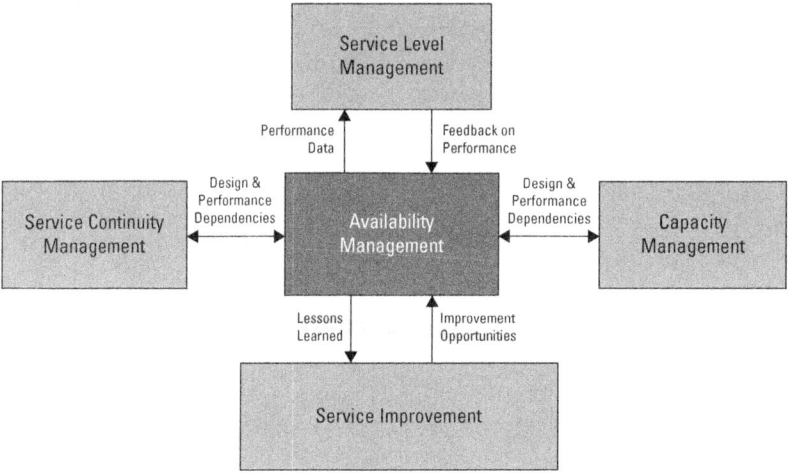

Figure 6.3 Processes related to Availability Management

6.4. Tools and techniques

Like Capacity Management (see previous chapter) Availability Management is a domain that occupies two functional areas. First and foremost it is a design activity. With this in mind, the organization should provide the program with the kinds of materials that support availability design activities, especially design guidelines and some form of AMIS. Secondly, Availability Management is a production function, an operational exercise in which performance is monitored, controlled, and measured in an ongoing way. To support this, the organization should provide the program with an appropriate set of monitoring tools and a strategy for collecting and analyzing performance metrics. These techniques and tools are described below.

Table 6.1 Tools and techniques for Availability Management

Availability Management design guidelines	To manage the process of designing for service availability it is important for the organization to approach this discipline in a way that promotes consistency and repeatability while focusing on performance efficiencies. Standardized service design guidelines provide for this. Availability design guidelines can be so configured that technical teams can address the specific and unique needs of different business systems, technical services, and service components. Considerations here usually include up-time, power support, serviceability, maintainability, reliability, VBFs, restorability, and redundancy. Documented design guidelines provide a measure of protection to the design process and serve as a basis for improvement and refinement over time.

Availability Management Information System (AMIS)	The AMIS is most commonly implemented as an automated tool used to register, analyze, and present availability performance data. The information in the repository can be referenced by service analysts when planning for availability designs. It can be used by service level managers as a source for collating performance data. It can also be used by service managers and senior IT managers to establish performance baselines and models, providing a look at past availability performance and projections of future performance.
Production monitoring and control tools	In order for service delivery and service quality to be adequately managed, it is essential that a service's availability performance is monitored, controlled, and measured. This requires the organization to implement and configure an appropriate suite of production monitoring tools. These tools provide recorded feedback of service performance over time. They also provide for a degree of real-time control over performance. And they can be configured to capture measures of this performance. These tools provide a major source of input into the AMIS. There are also risk assessment techniques that can be applied, which include: • Service Failure Analysis (SFA) • Component Failure Impact Analysis (CFIA) • Fault Tree Analysis (FTA) • Single Point of Failure Analysis (SPOF)
Performance analytic and trending techniques	In order to manage availability issues with existing services and to effectively plan design performance for emerging services, the organization should provide its Availability Management program with analytic and trending techniques. These may be basic or sophisticated, depending on the needs of the IT organization. These techniques serve as a way to develop performance baselines and models over time. The baselines can be used to establish historical trends of availability performance. From these trends, models can then be created to predict where performance levels might fall in the future. Baselines and models are extremely helpful in planning and designing service availability components. The following analyses are typically used: • VBF – Vital Business Function Analysis • Risk Assessment and Analysis • SFA – Service Failure Analysis • MTBF – Mean Time Between Failure • MTRS – Mean Time to Restore Service • MTBSI – Mean Time Between Service Interruptions • MTR – Mean Time to Repair

6.5. Key Performance Indicators

As mentioned earlier and being true for all ITIL design processes, Availability Management is largely technical in nature, so the KPIs that may be set into place to measure this process' activities are somewhat technical themselves. The data that can be used to support and generate the KPIs typically comes from monitoring and control efforts managed by operation teams and from metrics posted to the AMIS. These efforts produce measures that can be assessed to help determine the effectiveness of Availability Management planning, design, and implementation practices. The following are six examples of typical Availability Management KPIs. They do not make up a comprehensive set, nor are the right for every organization, but they should give you a good idea of the kinds of KPIs your program could benefit from.

Current availability levels by service

A single service may have multiple availability requirements. Each of these requirements should be expressed through some type of availability level. In order to manage and monitor availability effectively the organization should identify and track these levels. This includes levels for business services, technical services, and individual service components. When it tracks this data over time, the organization can produce trend lines useful for planning activities, understanding performance, and anticipating upcoming needs. The data also sheds light on the current availability volumes that operations teams have to support in order to ensure smooth service delivery.

Number and type of availability-related incidents

These measures describe availability performance, stability, and reliability. This KPI presents counts of the total number and types of incidents that occurred over a given period that were directly or indirectly related to availability issues. Analyses of this data can reveal weaknesses in designs or point to support issues that may need to be addressed by Tier 2 operations teams or perhaps Tier 3 availability analysts.

Number and type of availability-related problems

These measures offer a complementary view of the incident metric above. This KPI offers another facet of performance, stability, and reliability. It presents counts of the total number and types of problems for a given period that were directly or indirectly associated with availability issues, availability problems being at the root cause. Analyses of this data can reveal issues with availability planning, design, and development practices, highlight support issues that may need to be addressed by Tier 3 analysts, and point to considerations for design and management improvements.

Number and types of outages

This basic measure is an organized count of the number and types of service outages that occurred over a given period. Usually organized by service, the counts provide a major indicator of availability issues and delivery quality. This KPI is also important for understanding points of weakness within the infrastructure, for gaining insight into factors that appear to be in the organization's control and those that do not, and for establishing reliability trends over time.

Improvements in MTBF

In measuring Availability Management performance the organization should be interested in metrics that show increasing reliability and dependability across the enterprise. Measures that show improvements in Mean Times Between Failures (MTBF) help achieve that. When captured for business services, technical services, and service components this KPI provides a measure of system up-time and demonstrates the effectiveness of Availability Management activities.

Improvements in MTRS

Capturing measures of Mean Times to Restore Service (MTRS) provide an indicator of response effectiveness. When interruptions or outages do occur, support teams will invoke a series of actions to restore the normal state of IT service. Organizations in which times-to-restore are becoming quicker and quicker are likely to have well designed availability management practices.

Availability cost-per-unit by service

This is a very useful KPI but one that invariably has to be custom configured based on the shape of the organization's infrastructure. The measures are concerned with the costs associated with establishing availability levels for business and IT services, and usually express this relationship in terms of availability 'units.' A unit may be one gigabyte, or a single MIP, ½ second of response time, a data transfer rate, or any number of other variables. It is essential for the organization to identify these variables for its service sets and then assign a unit cost to each. Once that foundation is in place, the organization can track variations to these costs over time. This KPI is helpful when it comes to balancing the availability needs of the organization with financial investment requirements and limitations. It also provides a sound base for cost-based availability planning.

6.6. Critical Success Factors

A successful Availability Management program is one in which effective availability performance is achieved relevant to the level of investment required. Where that point of balance is struck will depend on many individual organizational traits. But the bottom line, wherever it settles, will rest on the idea of value: are Availability Management activities delivering cost-effective value to the business? This concept resides at the heart of any well-designed Availability Management program. And it is from this point that a program's critical success factors should emerge. CSFs in this domain should seek to enlighten two functional areas: the suitability of current availability levels, and the costs involved in maintaining these levels. Below are three common CSFs that most baseline Availability Management programs employ in one form or another. They can be key for demonstrating the overall effectiveness of the program.

Current service availability costs versus budgeted costs

This is a comprehensive program analysis that compares budgeted availability costs with actual costs. It should be an ongoing exercise, conducted on a regular basis with a frequency sufficient to allow for managerial adjustments and redirection as conditions dictate. The measures include business-related availability budgets and expenditure, IT service-related availability budgets and expenditure, and component-related availability budgets and expenditure. Data sets are often grouped by service. This type of analysis is important for several reasons. It provides insight into how well availability planning and design practices are proving. It gives an indication of the volatility of the environment and of business objectives. It produces a basis for forecasting future issues and needs. And it provides a picture of current performance that can be compared with existing SLAs as a way to plan subsequent availability management activities and budgets.

NOTE: This analysis is not intended to measure availability *effectiveness*. It simply compares configurations with capital costs. The following CSF looks at effectiveness.

Current service availability levels versus 'ideal' levels

Current availability levels may or may not be inline with 'ideal' levels. Ideal levels are estimates of the availability units needed to ensure SLA performance targets will be met. Ideal levels naturally vary over time. When targets are being met, the ideal can be said to synchronize with current configurations. When targets are not being met, an availability deficit can be said to exist; when they are being exceeded, a surplus. An ongoing responsibility of Availability Management is to balance the environment so that, as far as is practical, current availability levels are synchronized with the ideal. This type of analysis is essential for understanding both current management needs (e.g. up-scaling, downscaling) and future forecasting and planning directions.

Projected service availability needs and costs

Effective Availability Management requires regular planning, and planning requires reliable estimation and projection techniques. In order for an Availability Management program to deliver on its potential value, management should regularly establish availability projections and forecasts in anticipation of changing service needs. This activity provides a running analysis that captures current management issues (levels and costs) and projects them into the future with an eye toward balancing availability needs with overall technology and business needs. As a running analysis, these results should be regularly assessed, verified, and updated.

6.7. Availability Management roles

The following job roles are typically seen in mature Availability Management programs. Depending on the size and focus of an organization these roles may be full time or part time, combined, or shared by multiple individuals.

Availability Management Process Owner

The Availability Management Process Owner is the person (or persons) in the organization responsible for the development, deployment, and ongoing use of the Availability Management program. It is common in many IT organizations that this process owner is also the same as the Availability Manager, but this is not essential. The process owner champions the purpose and goals of Availability Management, ensures that the program remains in a state of operational effectiveness, and interfaces with senior IT management and business representatives to facilitate program adjustments and improvements. To summarize, the Availability Management Process Owner is responsible for:

- Developing and documenting the Availability Management program
- Implementing the program across relevant teams
- Coordinating program training and mentoring
- Monitoring ongoing program use
- Measuring program performance over time
- Soliciting and coordinating program improvements

Service Availability Manager

Every IT service supported by the organization should have assigned to it someone responsible for managing the activities associated with availability designing and for monitoring availability performance in operational service. This position is known as the Availability Manager. It is a technical role in that understanding, introducing, and controlling service capacity can be complex activities. Availability Managers oversee technical teams of analysts, prepare and coordinate availability plans, oversee design and monitoring activities, and report on performance to senior IT managers and service level managers. To summarize, the Availability Manager is responsible for:

- Availability planning and ongoing management for a specific service or set of services
- Understanding availability needs and configurations at the business, service, and service component levels
- Reviewing, assessing, and distributing availability analyses and reports, both up-chain and down-chain
- Coordinating design, monitoring, test, and evaluation activities relevant to service availability management
- Working with the Availability Management process owner to refine and develop the program in an effective manner over time
- Linking program objectives with those of IT Service Continuity Management

Availability Analysts

Availability analysts are usually members of a specific service team. They work under the direction of service managers and Availability Managers to design and implement Availability Management solutions. They elicit and validate availability requirements, structure designs, develop and test technical solutions, assist in availability-related implementations, and provide Tier 2 or Tier 3 support for services in production. To summarize, Availability Analysts are responsible for:

- Eliciting availability requirements, developing availability designs, and implementing availability management solutions
- Analyzing and assessing service availability performance on a regular basis
- Investigating, diagnosing, and troubleshooting availability-related incidents and problems
- Working in close collaboration with Tier 1 and Tier 2 support staff
- Working with external third party providers as required

Operation support teams

Operation support teams provide production support for IT services, and one aspect of this support is monitoring and reporting on service availability performance. These support teams work with Availability Analysts as needed to ensure that service delivery and service quality remain at designated levels. They also provide performance data and feedback when availability issues need to be investigated and diagnosed. To summarize, the operation support teams are responsible for:
- Monitoring availability performance in operational services
- Providing availability performance measures to service availability management and Availability Analysts on a regular basis
- Working in close collaboration with Availability Analysts to troubleshoot availability-related production incidents and problems

Human Resource considerations

The following are some typical traits that Human Resource staff may want to take into consideration when they are providing personnel, tools, and other resources for an Availability Management program.

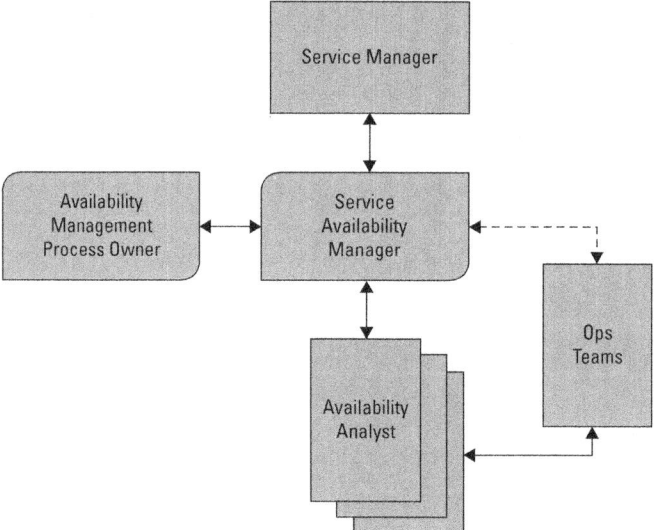

Figure 6.4 Availability Management roles

Technical experience and background: Availability Managers should have an adequate technical background, one that includes experience with the types of components in the current environment. They should also have experience of organizing and mobilizing availability design, implementation, and monitoring activities. They should have experience in developing plans and creating forecasts of levels and costs for the organization.

Availability Analysts should have experience of eliciting availability requirements from stakeholders, developing effective availability designs, and deploying solutions into production. Availability analysts should also have experience documenting availability requirements, designs, and support material relevant to the services.

Comfort working in a process centric environment: Availability Management staff should be comfortable working in a process-centric environment, and should be open to learning about the organization's program and contributing to its ordered growth.

6.8. Benefits of effective Availability Management

Implementing an effective Availability Management program can provide distinct benefits to any IT organization. Availability is such a pronounced and visible aspect to service delivery that its smooth operation and reliable performance enhances many other aspects of an IT Service Management initiative. The major root benefit is realized in higher availabilities and therefore fewer service interruptions; this should lead to a reduction in incident and problem levels. The standardized design activities the program contains should promote increased efficiencies and improve the balance between availability costs and performance. The operational data that the program amasses over time will prove valuable for planning and forecasting activities. Through all of this, service levels with regard to availability should become more predictable, more reliable, and SLA targets more achievable. And finally, from all this should come improved customer satisfaction.

Fewer service interruptions
One of the most visible indicators of a well-run IT operation is up-time: customers having access to the services they want when they want them. From this state, business runs smoothly. Availability Management works to deliver this up-time, and as up-time rises, service interruptions fall. High availability for services is a solid and quantifiable way to show the value that IT is bringing to the business, and to demonstrate IT's contribution to business success.

Well-balanced availability cost/performance ratios
The driving objective for an Availability Management program is to strike an effective balance between performance and costs. In organizations where availability factors are not managed proactively it is common to find uneven conditions: top-heavy costs that outweigh performance benefits; deficient availability due to poor planning; even a mix of the two due to weak forecasting. Setting the proper balance between investment and performance will always remain a technical challenge, because Availability Management is a technical domain. But an ITIL-based program is a reliable way to achieve such a balance. ITIL's emphasis on a cycle of planning, design, measurement, and evaluation promotes a view of Availability Management as an engineering discipline that can be apportioned, controlled, and methodically refined. The use of forward-looking baselines and models supported by the program help balance availability levels with business needs and thus produce cost-efficiencies when investments are required. Together, these can all be used to deliver availability capabilities right-sized to the needs of the organization.

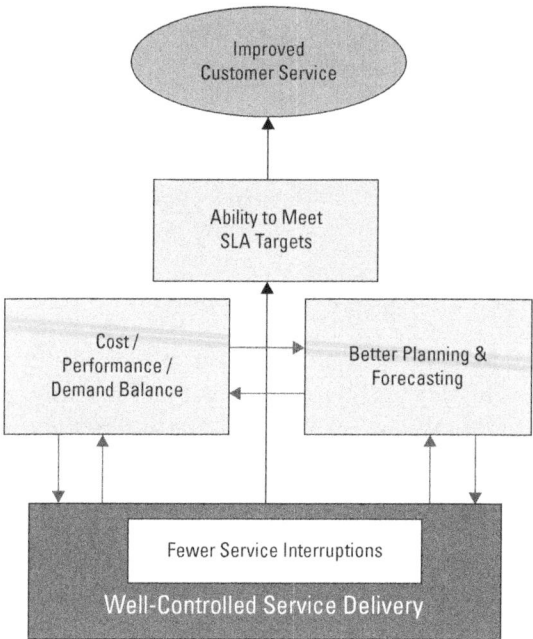

Figure 6.5 Benefits of effective Availability Management

Better forecasting and planning

Because Availability Management is an ongoing IT responsibility, the ability to effectively forecast and plan around availability needs is essential. Without such ability Availability Management is relegated to a reactive position in an IT organization. That position cannot be relied upon to promote high levels of service quality. Implementing a focused management program in this area helps the organization move from a reactive to a proactive position. ITIL's recommendations for such a program includes measuring availability design and performance efficiencies, employing an AMIS as a way to assess and evaluate performance data, developing baselines and models to project needs into the future in a fact-based way, and relying on these projections as a basis for planning. Movement down this path may well require some time in order to gain momentum. But once you have amassed representative sets of data you will find your ability to forecast greatly increased. As a result, planned performance and operational benefits from Availability Management become much more reflective of real-world outcomes.

Well-controlled SLA targets

Availability has the potential to affect so many characteristics of IT operations that an effective management program can go a long way toward helping the IT organization meet its SLA targets. Availability can influence incident rates, problem rates, capacity performance, IT continuity, even security. The tools and procedures ITIL recommends for this process ensures that service demands are well matched to environment configurations. The controls in the process provide for flexibility and responsiveness when availability issues do arise. Further, the rigor placed around planning, design activities, and production monitoring give managers and analysts alike the level of insight needed to anticipate potential events and circumvent or diminish their negative impacts. All of this contributes to predictable and consistent service delivery.

Improved customer service
The above benefits result in a degree of service delivery transparency from balanced availability levels, an engineered approach to forecasting and planning, and managed control of performance. Taken together, that almost always translates into improved customer satisfaction levels for the IT organization.

6.9. Implementation challenges and considerations

Like capacity, security, and continuity, availability is such an essential component of service quality that it practically begs to be managed by some type of formal program. The recommendations that ITIL makes for this domain can help set such a program in place. However, IT organizations should be aware that implementing Availability Management practices can pose a set of challenges that, when left unattended, carry the potential to negatively affect the program's goals and objectives. So that such impacts might be addressed and perhaps minimized, these challenges should be considered early on, when the program is being designed. As might be assumed, these challenges stem from the fact that managing availabilities can be a very technical task. Determining availability units, calculating availability costs, understanding the range of availability considerations across a diverse service mix, identifying effective designs in a dynamic environment – these are just a few of the tasks that wait to be accounted for, and accounted for not just on an ongoing basis but on an *evolving* basis too. This calls for skilled resources, deep knowledge of the infrastructure, and access to specialized tools. And from there the challenges appear. Four of the biggest that tend to arise for this ITIL process are described below.

Meeting availability demands
Services have availability requirements. Customers often have availability demands. The reason requirements may evolve into demands is simply that to customers Availability Management may appear as a transparent, benign activity, similar perhaps to keeping a machine plugged in. Such a view can easily tempt customers to expect (innocently enough) constant and uninterrupted services. Indeed, meeting a customer's availability demands is often a challenging thing to do, especially when IT environments are large or complex. What is called for here may actually have more to do with *managing* demand than meeting demand. It is here that ITIL's emphasis on maintaining strong business relationships and focusing on the IT-customer partnership shows its value. In situations where availability expectations seem to be unrealistic, misaligned, or ill-informed, it is important for IT management to work with business stakeholders to perhaps re-inform, re-align, and – as always – listen. By engaging in open and informative dialogs, both parties can work to establish realistic and achievable availability targets. When IT management shows that it is willing to accommodate, that it wants to deliver according to need, and that it will strive to get

as close to expectations as possible, customers are usually willing to compromise too, and will work to establish balanced, common expectations.

Validating availability designs

Because availability performance is critical to the overall quality of an IT service, it is essential to thoroughly test availability performance before deploying a service into production. Implementing weak or faulty designs can perpetuate impacts across the infrastructure. All Availability Management programs should accommodate an appropriate level of testing. The challenge for this practice comes from two areas. First, many IT organizations lack (for a variety of valid reasons) the ability to mimic in the test laboratory the intricacies of the production environment. And so tests results from the laboratory may prove to be unreliable indicators of production performance. Secondly, many IT organizations simply fail to allocate enough project time for adequate test and verification activities; the rush to production overtakes the perceived importance of testing. As a result, solutions may move into production with significant availability issues. Removing the risks from each of these areas may be challenging for many IT organizations. Test laboratories may have to remain mere approximations of the production environment. Test schedules may have to be squeezed in order to meet project milestones. But a well-designed Availability Management program can address these weaknesses, even in a minimal way. This is done by openly acknowledging the conditions, identifying these as known risks in design documents and release plans, tracking the risks through development, and then thoroughly assessing them before deployment.

Establishing an Availability Management Information System

For most mature Availability Management programs the AMIS is the central tool for availability forecasting, assessments, planning, designs, management, and reporting. But for the AMIS to successfully assume this key role the organization needs to commit to its acquisition, configuration, and growth. This can pose a number of hurdles for any IT organization. Acquiring the right tool will call for some degree of capital investment. Configuring it to the shape and needs of the service set and infrastructure will require dedicated resources with specialized skills, along with the time to get the configuration right. Most importantly, growing the AMIS so that its value to the organization increases over time requires that the organization makes a firm commitment to its ongoing use and its central importance to the program. It is not uncommon for IT organizations to struggle with these requirements. Establishing and growing such a system can be a full-time job; it can be expensive; especially early on, its value might seem questionable. But the AMIS can be key to managing the technical complexities involved in Availability Management decision-making, and so each organization should attempt to balance the true scope of its availability needs with the kind of AMIS it can afford to support.

Configuring effective monitoring tools

The technical nature of Availability Management extends into the operational environment, and so do the challenges. Because availability solutions are designed to fit the needs of the customer base and environment, availability performance needs to be monitored in live operation to verify that these needs are being met. This job of monitoring availability performance can present its own set of challenges to an IT organization for a variety of reasons. First, the infrastructure has to be equipped with the right set of monitoring tools. These tools then need to be configured so that IT operations staff have a view into how well, relevant to availability, various services and technical service components are operating. Such set-up and configuration requires a thorough knowledge of the environment, deep knowledge of the services operating in that environment, and a good understanding of how availability requirements can be translated into empirical measures. Even though most IT components today come with at least a base set of Availability Management features, the trick – and thus the challenge – comes with aligning what those features can do, what the IT organization needs to know, and what analyses the customer expects to see.

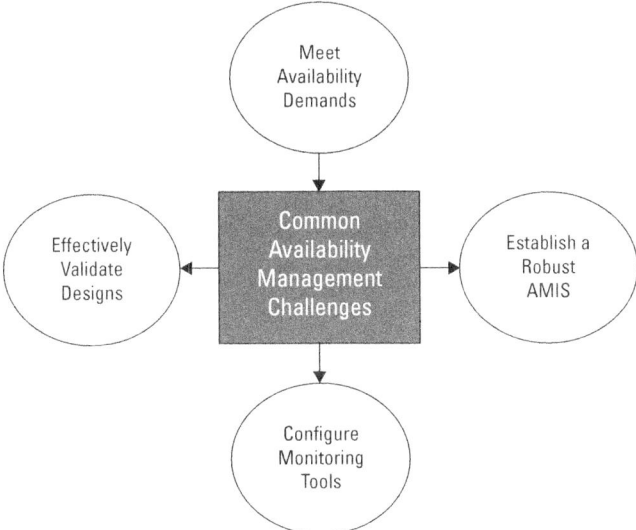

Figure 6.6 Implementation challenges and considerations for Availability Management

6.10. Typical assets and artifacts of an Availability Management program

A fully designed Availability Management program requires a set of assets and artifacts that can be used to frame how program activities are run. The assets provide the procedural guides and supporting materials for the activities. The artifacts shape the work products that the Availability Management activities produce. Following is a list of some of the more common materials that an organization is likely to employ when implementing an Availability Management program. Your program may require assets and artifacts not included here, but the set described below represents a typical baseline.

Availability Management policy
This is an executive policy that stipulates the goals and objectives of the Availability Management program. The policy, which ideally should be no longer than a few pages, documents at a high level the purpose of the program, the resources available to the program, the chief responsibilities of the program, quality targets, reporting hierarchies, and program measures. Endorsed by executive management, the policy is a demonstration of organizational commitment to the value and importance of the Availability Management program.

Availability Management plan template
This template provides a structural guide for creating the organization's Availability Management Plan. The template outlines the contents and sections that a properly documented plan should contain (see page XX). Such plans usually identify the following kinds of information: purpose and scope of Availability Management, resources assigned to create availability designs and monitor availability performance, availability targets for each supported service, availability measures and links to SLA targets, availability monitoring techniques, strategies for meeting availability targets, identification of Availability Managers and key business stakeholders, types and frequency of availability reporting, report distribution channels, and a plan duration and review/revision schedule.

Availability Management Plan
This is the organizational plan, based on the template above, that – once approved and adopted – specifies how Availability Management activities will be conducted over a set period of time.

Availability design guidelines
These are guidelines that detail the technical, operational, and support factors that should be considered when designing availability needs for specific services.

Availability Management Information System (AMIS)
This is some form of automated system (selected based on the needs of the organization) that can be configured as a prime repository for storing and managing information about availability designs, availability deployment factors, and availability performance measures.

Availability monitoring procedures
These are documented procedures that detail how business availabilities, service availabilities, and service component availabilities will be monitored in the operational environment. These procedures typically describe the events to be associated with availability indicators, the thresholds of acceptable performance, identification of the tools that will monitor each event, and descriptions of response activities to be invoked when thresholds are exceeded. These procedures usually serve as the basis for establishing OLAs between Availability Managers and operations teams.

Availability Management Measurement Plan template
This template provides a structural guide for creating the organization's Availability Management Measurement Plan. The template outlines the contents and sections that a properly documented plan should contain (see page XX). Such plans usually identify the following kinds of information: Purpose and scope of measuring Availability Management performance; resources assigned to establish metrics and performance reports; a description of each availability measure, how the data is to be collected, where the data is to be stored, and how data sets are to be analyzed. The plan also documents the type and format of measurement reports and also identifies stakeholders for receiving reports. Measures should be taken not only of availability performance in operational service but also of planning, design, and deployment activities.

Availability Management Measurement Plan
This is the organizational plan, based on the template above, that – once approved and adopted – specifies how availability measurement activities will be conducted over a set period of time.

Availability Management reporting and distribution procedure
This is a documented procedure that describes how availability planning, design, and performance reports are created, how often they are generated, and to whom they are to be distributed. This procedure – and the ensuing reports – can be seen as a by-product of the measurement plan described above. Together these artifacts provide for the generation of the kind of information IT management and customer groups need to understand the effectiveness of availability delivery and availability performance in order to identify opportunities for improvement.

Service Level Agreement
Because availability is a service trait so often linked with Service Level Management, the organization should ensure that there is a documented agreement between IT management, service managers, Availability Managers, and the customer that specifies the levels of performance that will be delivered concerning availability by service.

Monitoring and control tools
The organization will need to acquire and configure a set of tools that can be used in operational service for monitoring availability performance and adjusting that performance as needed.

Organizational chart
This is a chart that shows the structural make-up of the Availability Management operation. As with other organizational charts, the purpose is to identify teams, team relationships, and hierarchical flows, and so the chart's shape will depend on the organizational units and resources you are able to apply to the program. Most organizational charts of this sort are simple and basically linear. At the top, perhaps, there is a dotted box representing the Service Managers. This extends down to a box

for the Availability Manager. Below this might be two groups: availability analysts and operation analysts. A dotted line from the Availability Manager box might extend to a parallel support spot for the Availability Management process owner (if this role is separate from the Availability Manager). This chart may be service-specific or combine a set of service offerings.

Roles and responsibilities matrix

This matrix, an extension of the organizational chart, describes the various roles and responsibilities the organization has assigned to support Availability Management activities. The roles typically include such positions as Availability Management process owner, Availability Manager, availability analysts (designers and developers), and (in tangential roles) operations analysts and senior IT management. Along with the job role definitions there should be descriptions of the responsibilities each role should account for, and references to how different roles interrelate and communicate. The matrix might take one of several forms: a spreadsheet, a series of database records, or a version-controlled text document. Ownership of this artifact is usually shared between IT management and Human Resource management.

7. IT Service Continuity Management

IT disasters typically arrive unannounced, and often through the simplest of entry points. The launch in 1996 of the European Space Agency's Ariane 5 rocket is a good example. Thirty-six seconds into its maiden flight the computerized guidance system tried to interpret the rocket's sideways velocity – by converting a 64-bit string of data into 16-bit format. But the number was too big and an overflow error occurred. Just as it was programmed to do, the computer shut itself down, but not before turning control over to a backup system. The only problem was that the backup used exactly the same software as the prime system and so naturally the same overflow error occurred. The backup then shut itself down. Without a working guidance system there was nothing for the mission controllers to do. They blew Ariane 5 up. On board had been a set of four scientific satellites valued at £240 million. Ariane 5 itself was valued at slightly more, £8 billion.[1]

A less explosive but no doubt just as frustrating event happened in 2006 with the design and assembly of the Airbus A380, one of the world's largest aircraft. The component parts were coming together in two locations: French Dassault Aviation in Paris and a factory in Hamburg. The event was triggered by a simple difference in software versions. The CATIA design/assembly software used by Hamburg was slightly older than that used in Paris. As a result, when the two halves of the plane were brought together to be joined up, the wiring in one did not match the wiring in the other. The extensive cabling could not be made to meet up without being re-engineered. No cost figures were released on the error but that one glitch was enough to knock the project a year behind schedule.[2]

Those are two big and probably untypical examples of IT continuity problems. But they serve to illustrate a point. When technology malfunctions or when some destructive agent intervenes in operations, the results can have serious impacts on the ability to conduct business. Natural disasters such as tornadoes, floods, blizzards, earthquakes and fire can have devastating effects. Environmental disasters such as pollution and hazardous materials spills can be equally harmful. Plus there can be communications, transportation, safety, and service sector failures, not to mention sabotage, cyber attacks and hacker activity, and even simple innocent accidents.

That is a lot to account for, and it points to the scope and importance of IT Service Continuity Management. Perhaps the most recognizable domain of this process is disaster recovery– it is certainly the most visible – but effective continuity management requires more than just effective response. It requires that the organization position

---
1 "Top 10 IT Disasters of All Time." Barker, Colin. ZDNetUK. November 27, 2007.
2 Ibid.

itself to understand what kinds of *force majeure* events it may be prone to and, as much as possible, insulate itself against the impacts of those events.

Here is the ITIL V3 definition for IT Service Continuity Management:

"...To support the overall business continuity process by ensuring that the required IT technical and service facilities (including computer systems, networks, applications, data repositories, telecommunications, environment, technical support and service desk etc.) can be resumed within required and agreed-upon business timescales."[3]

The focus as noted above is to see IT Service Continuity Management as an extension of business continuity, with the assumption being (as it is throughout ITIL) that while IT services and facilities are down business processes will not be able to run effectively. And so the preeminent job of IT Service Continuity Management is to provide this restore-and-run capability is as an effective a manner as possible. Toward that, ITIL states the purpose of IT Service Continuity Management as:

"...To set into place mechanisms to address force majeure events, and to do so in a way that promotes event avoidance, minimizes event impacts, and restores essential services as quickly as practical."[4]

Service Continuity Management deals with those events the organization considers disasters. In this light, this process can be seen as linked to Incident Management and Problem Management – its job is to step in and mitigate when major disruptive events occur. It can also be seen as being linked to Availability Management in that its job is to ensure that the availability of IT services and facilities are protected from serious interruption, and that in the event of such an interruption restoration is accomplished quickly.

Because the role Service Continuity Management plays is so important to the IT organization and the business at large, the scope of its domain is necessarily broad. There are a variety of considerations that need to be addressed when continuity strategies and tactics are being set into place, either for a single service or a collection of services. These considerations include:
- Identifying critical and essential business functionality
- Mapping the geographical distribution of IT services, facilities, and resources
- Documenting the sensitivity (e.g. statutory, regulatory) of at-risk systems and data
- Understanding current backup and restore practices and capabilities
- Understanding redundancy capabilities and limitations
- Mapping infrastructure configurations and dependencies
- Documenting IT service mix configurations and dependencies
- Identifying and rating potential continuity threats
- Documenting methods of testing continuity preparedness

---

[3] Foundations of ITIL. (2010). Van Haren Publishing.
[4] Ibid.

To delve into these considerations further let's begin with a look at the activities associated with the IT Service Continuity Management process.

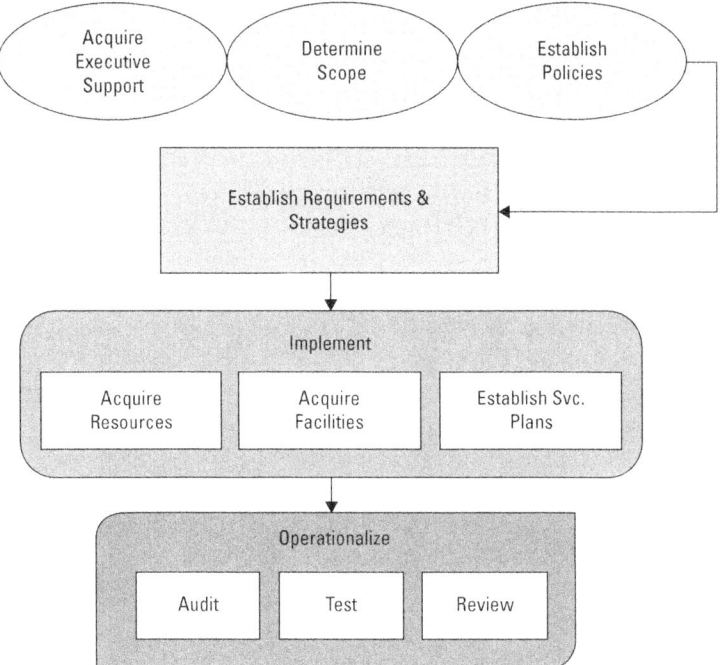

Figure 7.1 Typical IT Service Continuity Management process flow

7.1. IT Service Continuity Management activities

The IT Service Continuity Management process consists of a series of four general activities for program establishment, strategy development, roll-out, and operationalization. For each of these general activities there are a series of sub-practices. Taken as a whole, the process leads the organization through the steps needed to establish a continuity capability across the enterprise through the actions required to test and evaluate these capabilities in production. The four general steps in the process are:
- Initiation
- Requirements and strategy
- Implementation
- Operationalization

In the following sections we'll take a brief look at each.

1. Initiation
With this first step the organization moves to establish service continuity as an official capability across the enterprise. The activities that occur under initiation are very similar to what you might encounter during the initiation phase of any IT

development project, or in the initiation phase of project management frameworks such as PMBOK or PRINCE2. Here the objective is to charter the initiative so that it is recognized as an official effort and sponsored appropriately. The three sub-practices that distinguish this activity are in place to cement executive involvement, bind the scope of the program, and set out strategic program directives.

Set executive focus. From a technical standpoint, IT Service Continuity Management may not be more important than any other ITIL design process but it carries with it such all-encompassing impact across an organization that executive involvement needs to be particularly emphasized. Continuity strategies are likely to touch every facet of the IT infrastructure: services, systems, service components, and data. They are also likely to reach across multiple domains, both business and technical. The reach across business domains is due to the fact that IT continuity is a direct component of business continuity and thus has the potential to affect how domains such as accounting, marketing, and shipping and receiving construct their business processes.

Determine scope. Determining the scope of the continuity program helps the organization to identify essential functionalities, those that need to be preserved in the event of a severe disruption. For this step IT management should work with business and technical stakeholders to review the current mix of services and select those that will be included in the program. Constraining scope at this point is important from a practical standpoint: maintaining continuity requires focused resources and in most IT organizations these resources are limited. By limiting the scope the organization is able to match capacity with essential need and thus plan accordingly.

Establish continuity policies. Based on the scope of the program, the organization can now establish a set of executive policies concerning IT continuity. The policies document the priorities of the program and identify the resources that have been allocated to its ongoing operation. The organization can use this policy as a base for building the rest of the program.

2. Requirements and strategy

With the program initiated and its scope established the organization can now set its approach to IT Service Continuity Management in place. The end goal is to develop and deploy an IT Service Continuity Management Plan. To do this, the program's strategic approach to IT Service Continuity Management needs to be derived from the organization's IT service continuity requirements. A key practice for this is to conduct business impact analyses (BIAs).

Conduct BIAs. A BIA is an assessment of a service or set of services with the intention of understanding that service's impact on business missions and processes. Understanding those impacts provides the organization with the background it needs to set continuity tactics in place. The following are typical considerations for conducting a BIA.

Table 7.1 Considerations for conducting a BIA

Essential business activity	For each business and technical service, identify the delivered business activities. Ensure that these activities correlate to the organization's business missions and marketplace objectives.
Prioritize	Prioritize the business and technical services in terms of business missions and marketplace objectives.
Disruption impacts	For each business and technical service, identify the range of disruptions that may occur and the impacts those disruptions would have on related business activities.
Revenue losses	Establish a standardized scale and for each identified disruption assign a value for the potential loss of revenue if the event occurs.
Additional expenses	Identify any other incidental, tangential, or auxiliary expenses that might be incurred if the disruption occurs.
Intangible losses	Identify the intangible losses that might be suffered if a continuity disruption occurs. Intangible losses include such things as goodwill, reputation and missed opportunity.
Insurance requirements	Identify the insurance requirements that need to be met for each service so that fiduciary responsibility may be upheld, loss may be minimized and recovery options may be realized to their full potential.
Dependencies	Once the business impact characteristics of the service mix have become known the organization should work to identify dependencies among services. This will help delineate structured paths for continuity plans and reveal points where options can be shared and exploited. It will also help with the ranking activity below.
Ranking	With the impact analysis complete the organization should now rank its business and technical services according to the continuity criticality of each.

Perform risk/recovery assessments. Results from the BIAs will give the organization a basis for identifying where impacts are most critical. This will point to where continuity efforts should be focused. At this point the organization should look closer at high impact areas and perform assessments as to how these impacts can be avoided or mitigated. Toward this, three practices are recommended.

- Assess each impact area and produce risk estimates as to how likely it is a disruption might occur and what the causes of such a disruption might be.
- For each potential cause define, design, and implement risk reduction measures.
- For each potential cause define, design, and document IT recovery options.

Establish IT Service Continuity Plans. At this point the information needed to go into an IT Service Continuity Plan should be in place. Services have been identified and prioritized; business impacts are understood; risks have been documented; mitigation steps have been taken; and recovery options have been established. All of this detail should be collected and collated in an organizational IT Service Continuity Management Plan. It is also helpful for the plan to contain continuity contacts by service and a schedule of targeted continuity tests. Once drafted, the plan should be reviewed by senior IT management and key business stakeholders, approved as appropriate, and then managed under formal change control.

3. Implementation

The implementation step for this process is straightforward. You simply take action on the plan you have developed: the organization puts its IT Service Continuity Plan into effect. Risk reduction techniques are set in place. Monitoring tools are configured and turned on. Recovery capabilities are placed at the ready. As direct as implementation is, it does require two significant efforts. First, before the plan can be put into action the organization will need to acquire the facilities and resources required by that plan. Resources include those tools and products that support risk reduction and service recovery. Introducing them may involve entering into agreements with third party providers. Facilities include the operational spaces and equipment required for continuity staff to carry out their duties. That leads to the second effort. Here the organization will need to assign continuity management responsibilities to appropriate stakeholders, training them in their duties and then mentoring them on the shop floor until they are proficient in their roles.

The directness of implementation can be compounded by a single characteristic: implementation potentially requires a noticeable investment. Depending on the shape and size of the infrastructure, the goals and scope of the continuity strategy, and the customer bases the IT organization serves, the provision of teams and resources may require a significant outlay.

4. Operationalization

Operating the continuity program is actually an exercise in evaluating readiness. This is a periodic, repeating activity for IT Service Continuity Management. Here management looks at the program's performance in order to determine its effectiveness. In some organizations and within some process frameworks (such as CMMI) this activity is grouped under Quality Assurance. And it does in fact have a process quality focus to it. The purpose of evaluation is really three-fold: perform assessments to verify that continuity policies and practices are being followed, test continuity capabilities in order to validate they are operating as intended, and determine any adjustments or revisions that may be required to improve program performance.

Conduct continuity assessments. Assessments are spot checks on on-going continuity preparedness. In essence an assessment is an evaluation of readiness; that is, a gauge of how well continuity teams are executing the organization's policies and practices. Assessments usually involve the review of process activities, inspections of work products, and interviews with team members. The results are then recorded and presented to the teams as well as to IT management. Based on the results, corrective actions (or congratulations) – to the program or to the people – may be recommended.

Test continuity capabilities. Just as assessments reveal procedural preparedness, continuity tests demonstrate functional preparedness. The purpose of testing is to mimic disruptive events that may potentially affect the enterprise in a harmless way. Tests should be complete (moving through a full service chain) and reflect real-world variety and sophistication. Test cycles should be competently planned and scripted, with their executions carefully monitored. Results should be distributed to relevant stakeholders and used as the basis for identifying possible procedural or environmental improvements.

Review and revise. Based on the results of performance assessments and continuity testing, the organization may elect to review requirements and strategies in light of industry practices and lessons learned and perhaps revise the requirements and strategies as needed.

7.2. Process inputs and outputs

IT Service Continuity Management is a process that takes two continual paths. The first is one of planning. Since the factors that affect continuity performance are themselves dynamic (natural disasters, environmental failures, security breaches, etc.) there is a need to regularly assess the organization's strategic position when it comes to preparedness and response tactics. The next is one of execution, which mainly centers on the development and implementation of new continuity requirements and the periodic testing of the resulting solutions. The entry state for the IT Service Continuity Management process is always predicated on one of two conditions: either a service – new or enhanced – is being made ready for production or the time has arrived to refresh continuity plans. The triggers that set the process in motion may come from a variety of inputs: new requirements, continuity test results, industry trends, emerging threats, etc. Triggers that indicate the process is complete are also fairly stable. They include new continuity strategies and solutions, refreshed continuity plans, new performance measures of services in operation, and lessons learned from PIRs. Below is a summary of common entry criteria, inputs, exit criteria, and outputs of the IT Service Continuity Management process.

Entry criteria
The IT Service Continuity Management process is typically set into motion when one of three events occurs:
- A new IT service is being created for production (or)
- An existing operational service needs to be enhanced or modified (or)
- Service Continuity re-planning is due.

Inputs
Inputs into the process can come from a variety of sources, individually or in combination. These inputs can include:
- Business forecasts
- Existing IT Service Continuity Management Plans
- Analyses from service continuity tests
- Industry trends, emerging threats
- Continuity performance reports from production that drive Requests for Change for any of the following areas:

- Business continuity requirements
- Service continuity requirements
- Service component continuity requirements

Exit criteria

The process is typically recognized as having been completed when three general exit conditions are met:
- A service has been successfully transitioned into operation.
- Monitoring and control tools (typically realized as continuity tests) are capturing service continuity performance.
- The IT Service Continuity Management Plan has been tested and refreshed.

Outputs

The IT Service Continuity Management process, once it has run its course, will produce a set of work products that supports its procedural activities. At a minimum the set should includes the following artifacts:
- Service continuity designs
- Service continuity performance metrics
- PIR assessment notes
- Refreshed IT Service Continuity Management Plans

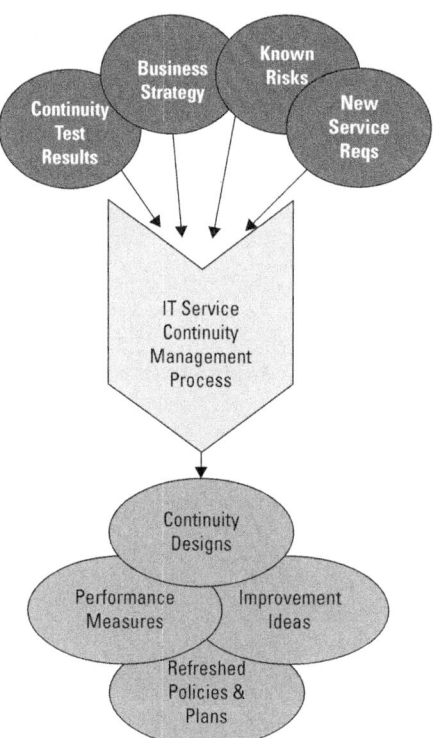

Figure 7.2 Inputs and outputs for IT Service Continuity Management

7.3. Processes related to IT Service Continuity Management

In a sense every aspect of an IT Service Management program is related to IT Service Continuity Management. It is the job of continuity management to ensure that services, systems, data, and processes are configured in such a way that they are, as far as possible, protected from loss or corruption. If a major event occurs it is the responsibility of IT Service Continuity Management to ensure that the affected capabilities, whatever they may be, can be returned to service as quickly and as fully as possible. There are, however, three core processes that have a more direct bearing on IT Service Continuity Management. Availability Management works as an extension of continuity, or better perhaps, a preamble. Information Security Management is a process whose preparations and responses may call continuity management into action. And Service Level Management is a process whose work products (SLAs) must often account for IT Service Continuity Management performance.

Availability Management
Availability Management and IT Service Continuity Management are so closely allied that one can be said to be a direct extension of the other. Both are founded on the mission to ensure that IT services are available to customers when they are needed. With Availability Management this mission is largely proactive: delivering adequate availabilities. With IT Service Continuity Management it is largely (through major events) reactive: restoring service when severe interruptions occur. Availability requirements, strategies, and designs affect the framework around which continuity plans and capabilities can be structured, and vice versa. Availability incidents or problems may call continuity plans into action. Improvement assessments relevant to IT Service Continuity Management should reference the current state of Availability Management. And finally, adjustments or improvements to Availability Management procedures and work products should be communicated to service continuity managers so they may be taken into account.

In summary:
- IT Service Continuity Management and Availability Management share very similar organizational missions.
- Availability requirements, strategies, and designs affect the framework around which continuity plans and capabilities are structured.
- Availability incidents or problems may call continuity responses into action.
- Improvement assessments relevant to IT Service Continuity Management should reference the current state of Availability Management.
- Adjustments or improvements to Availability Management should be communicated to service continuity managers.

Information Security Management

Information Security Management is linked to IT Service Continuity Management because security issues, particularly severe ones, can call continuity actions into play. So, with both processes, considerations apply one for another. Continuity strategies and tactics that deal with prevention and recovery need to support Information Security requirements and configurations. Disaster plans and continuity tests need to include security management as part of their scope. And when security methods or models are adjusted or improved, Information Security Management must be sure to communicate such changes to IT Service Continuity Management so the new configurations may be absorbed into their plans and methods.

In summary:
- The protection and response strategies inherent in IT Service Continuity Management need to support security requirements and configurations.
- Existing threats and vulnerabilities need to be accounted for in continuity plans and tests.
- Operational incidents or problems related to security have the potential to call disaster recovery and other continuity methods into action.
- Changes and improvements made to security methods and models need to be communicated to IT Service Continuity Management stakeholders.

Service Level Management

Because of its importance in risk reduction and risk mitigation, IT Service Continuity Management is commonly included among those processes whose performance is tracked under SLAs. These SLAs always include some targets for continuity capabilities, such as time to restore, effectiveness of prevention, depth of essential services, etc. Because continuity assurance is essential to any business, it is important for IT continuity managers to work closely with Service Level Managers to negotiate appropriate performance targets with customers. Once SLAs have been agreed to it is also important that continuity teams work with service level managers to periodically assess and evaluate continuity performance through testing. Poor performance in such a critical aspect could place not only the IT infrastructure at risk, but the business enterprise as well. For these reasons, a Service Level Management program should work to integrate and support the function and shape of an IT Service Continuity Management program.

In summary:
- Service continuity designs and methods have direct bearing on overall service quality, and thus on the customer's perception of IT's value to the business.
- SLAs should realistically set continuity management performance expectations.
- Effective IT Service Continuity Management is essential for supporting IT's effort to create strong and cooperative business relationships.

Service Improvement

Service Improvement is an umbrella activity for all aspects of an IT Service Management program and it is used with particular emphasis on ITIL design processes. With IT Service Continuity Management, improvement work falls into two broad categories. The first is technical. Here continuity analysts and operation teams investigate ways in which continuity policies, plans, designs, and tactics can be enhanced. The second category falls under procedural support. Continuity management teams (along with the IT Service Continuity Management process owner) work to identify improvement opportunities that can be applied to the program's processes, procedures, monitoring tools, and measurements.

In summary:
- A key responsibility of capacity analysts is to continually investigate and identify ways in which continuity designs and operating performance can be improved.
- Continuity improvements are not confined just to the technical arena; teams should seek improvements in management processes, monitoring tools, and measurements.

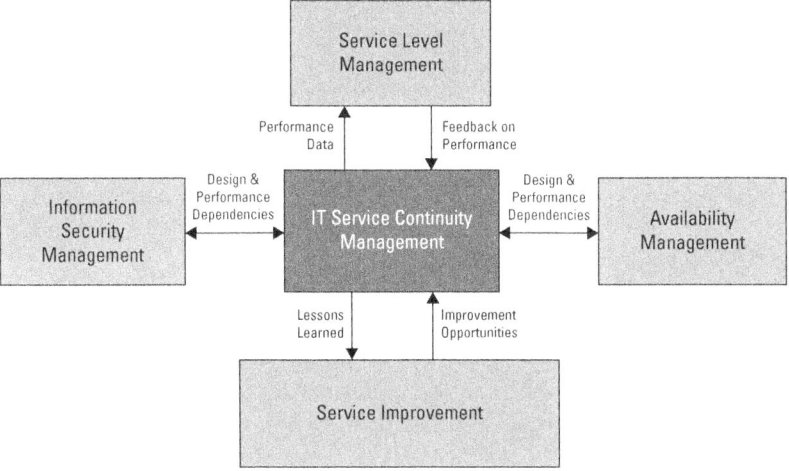

Figure 7.3 Processes related to IT Continuity Management

7.4. Tools and techniques

Continuity management requires a range of operational considerations. Options in terms of strategies abound and are well known. Tools and techniques for this domain are well established, too. The issues come from selecting those best suited to your operational needs, and doing so in a cost effective manner. Below are some common tools and techniques used in basic IT Service Continuity Management programs.

Table 7.2 Tools and techniques for IT Service Continuity Management

Operational redundancies and replicate facilities	In order to ensure on-going service continuity many organizations embed operational redundancy into their infrastructures. This redundancy includes such things as mirrored servers, failover systems and spare parts. Many organizations also invest in replicate facilities. This includes things like emergency operation centers, alternative support sites etc.
Off-site storage	Another service continuity technique is off-site storage – where key operational components are backed up and then removed to a remote location that is protected from certain kinds of catastrophic events. Off-site storage is typically used for the following kinds of IT assets: paper contracts specifications and documentation; data back-ups; software and system back-ups.
All-terrain equipment	In certain environments prone to potential continuity issues (e.g. war zones and scientific explorations) many organizations invest in what is becoming known as all-terrain equipment. All-terrain equipment includes IT assets that are made to withstand harsh environments and harsh treatments. Laptops with specialized shock-mount casings are examples of all-terrain equipment.
Disaster recovery routines	In order to guard against continuity-threatening events many organizations ensure that their CMDBs have maintained version histories of key data core software and technical documentation. This gives the organization the ability to restore a snapshot of operations to a great extent at any given point in time. To protect the CMDB and the rest of the 'soft' environment organizations practice the regular routine of making backups of key assets and then storing those backups in case a later restore is needed.

7.5. Key Performance Indicators

The KPIs that support an IT Service Continuity Management program are similar in nature to the KPIs that support Availability Management. The measures are in place to capture two basic operational states: the nature of system failures and the effectiveness of restarts. Those states represent the essence of service continuity's mission. Understanding the nature of failures will lead over time to better response mechanisms and perhaps (through Problem Management) to corrective actions in the environment. Understanding restart effectiveness will have its own benefits: greater operational integrity and less operational risk. The KPIs used to measure these states typically apply to the full scope of IT service delivery – business services, technical services, and service components. The following is a description of eight common key performance indicators often found in baseline IT Service Continuity Management programs.

Number and types of business service failures per period

These measures break down by type the number of business service failures that have occurred over a given period of time. This information provides an indication of the stability of the enterprise from a business perspective, a perspective that is highly customer-centric. Service failures at this level have a direct impact on users' ability to move through business processes. And it is these types of failures that most often qualify, in the customer's mind, as 'disasters.' These measures also provide an indication of how effective the proactive aspects of the IT Service Continuity Management program are: that is, how well the program is able to prevent or at least minimize the impact of systemic business service interruptions.

Number and types of technical service failures per period

These measures break down by type the number of technical service failures that have occurred over a given period of time. This information provides an indication of the stability of the infrastructure from a technical perspective, a perspective that here is somewhat removed from business domains but nevertheless carries the risk for affecting those domains. These types of failures, when recognized by operations teams early enough, can often be significantly mitigated. If neglected or missed they can lead to business failures. Measures of technical service failures can also provide an indication of how effective the proactive aspects of the IT Service Continuity Management program are.

Number and types of component failures per period

These measures break down by type the number of service component failures that have occurred over a given period of time. This information provides an indication of the stability of the infrastructure from a device perspective. This is a perspective that is shaped by equipment reliability and architectural redundancies. In a robust environment, component failures need not inevitably lead to service interruptions. They have the potential to be addressed automatically (e.g. failovers) as well as by operations teams. These measures, when compared to technical and business service failure rates, provide a strong indication of how effective the proactive aspects of the IT Service Continuity Management program are. They also provide insight into aspects of Incident Management, Problem Management, and Availability Management activities.

Mean Time-to-Restore service failure by event

These measures track the amount of downtime for each business and technical service failure and record the time taken to restore the failed service to full operational capability. Naturally the longer a service is down, the more impact it may have on business processes. It is also logical to link the amount of downtime with the complexity or breadth of a failure. It is helpful with this KPI to calculate averages by event type and/or service type. With an effective IT Service Continuity Management program, the trend the organization hopes to see in this area is that downtimes are diminishing, that MTRs are shrinking. This is an indication that restoration activities are well conceived and responsibly executed.

Mean-Time-Between-Failure by business service

These measures track MTBFs for in-production business services. The data collected here can be used to assess the overall stability and reliability of business services. Stability and reliability indicators filter down, by extension, to supporting technical services and service components. The trend the organization will be hoping to see is that mean times are expanding; that is, failures are becoming less and less common over time. The implication with such a trend is that continuity strategies and architectural designs (redundancy, serviceability, etc.) are effectively conceived and well implemented.

Mean-Time-Between-Failure by technical service

These measures track MTBFs by technical services. The data collected here can be used to assess the overall stability and reliability of the infrastructure at the system level. Stability and reliability indicators filter down, by extension, to service components. As with the business service measure above, the trend the organization will be looking for here is to see mean times expanding; that is, technical service failures are becoming less and less common. The implication with such a trend is that continuity strategies and architectural designs (technical solutions, system integrations, interoperability, etc.) are effectively conceived and well implemented.

Mean-Time-Between-Failure by component type

These measures track MTBFs by individual service components. The data collected here can be used to assess the overall stability and reliability of the equipment that makes up the infrastructure. Over time this information can be used to pinpoint weak or unreliable brands, shape purchasing decisions, negotiate warranties, and configure support teams. As with the business and technical service measure above, the trend the organization will be looking for here is to see that mean times are expanding. This is another indication that continuity strategies and equipment selections are effectively conceived and well implemented.

7.6. Critical Success Factors

It is probably too bold to define an effective IT Service Continuity Management program as one in which no failures occur. To expect such a state, given the complexity and reach of most IT infrastructures, is not really practical. A better definition might be a program that is able to manage failures within agreed-upon timeframes and to the least detriment of the business. Establishing CSFs for a process program like IT Service Continuity Management is one way to direct it toward delivering a positive return-on-investment, to shape it so that it furthers both IT missions and business objectives. The following are three example CSFs that can be helpful in measuring the effectiveness of an IT Service Continuity Management program. These examples make use of the KPIs described above and give management an empirical picture of continuity performance. Here is a description of each.

Percent of service restores that met SLA targets

This is a set of measures by service that breaks down the number of service restores (business and technical) that were undertaken for a given period and that met the restore-to-service time targets as set in SLAs. These measures should also capture the percent of restore efforts that fell outside the agreed-upon targets. These measures help the organization understand how well their continuity response teams, plans, and tactics are working within the organization. By definition, if the organization is able to consistently meet or exceed these expectations, the IT Service Continuity

Management program is a success, so this might be considered – as with other SLA targets – the chief success factor to strive for.

Number and types of failures over time
This is a set of measures by service that breaks down for a given period the number and types of failures the organization experienced. These measures help the organization understand the overall reliability and stability of the environment. Through this data, management can identify areas of solidity and areas of weakness – and then move to set corrective or improvement actions into place. This information also helps management appreciate the overall effectiveness of the IT Service Continuity Management program itself. Since part of such a program is implementing preventive measures – protections against *force majeure* events – the rolling rate of failures will provide a glimpse into the suitability of these measures. (The KPIs described in the previous section will help collate these metrics.)

NOTE: If the IT organization has a practical way of doing so, it is beneficial to associate a cost with each failure event that occurred.

Number and types of non-impact service failures
These are measures of the number and types of service failures that were handled in such a progressive way that the failures achieved no significant impact on business service delivery or quality. These measures help demonstrate the effectiveness of the IT Service Continuity Management program. Failures cannot be completely avoided, yet a good continuity program will feature the kinds of alert mechanisms, diagnostic techniques, and response activities that minimize the impacts of failures, often to negligible degree. The trend the organization hopes to see with these measures is that the percentage of non-impact failures – in relation to impact failures – is increasing. That is the mark of not only a successful IT Service Continuity Management program but of a successful IT Service Management program as well.

7.7. IT Service Continuity Management roles

The following job roles are typically seen in mature IT Service Continuity Management programs. Depending on the size and focus of an organization these roles may be full-time or part-time, combined, or shared by multiple individuals.

IT Service Continuity Management Process Owner
The Service Continuity Management Process Owner is the person (or persons) in the organization responsible for the development, deployment, and ongoing use of the IT Service Continuity Management program. It is common in many IT organizations that this process owner is the same person as the Service Continuity Manager, but this is not essential. The process owner champions the purpose and goals of IT Service Continuity Management, ensures that the program remains in a state of operational effectiveness, and interfaces with senior IT management and business representatives

to facilitate program adjustments and improvements. To summarize, the IT Service Continuity Management Process Owner is responsible for:
- Developing and documenting the IT Service Continuity Management program
- Implementing the program across relevant teams
- Coordinating program training and mentoring
- Monitoring ongoing program use
- Measuring program performance over time
- Reporting on program effectiveness over time
- Soliciting and coordinating program improvements

Service Continuity Manager

Every IT service supported by the organization should have assigned to it someone responsible for managing the activities associated with continuity preparedness and response actions. This position is typically known as the Service Continuity Manager, although the role commonly goes by other names, including disaster recovery specialist and service assurance analyst. It is a technical role in that understanding, implementing, and controlling service continuity capabilities tend to be complex activities. Service Continuity Managers manage a technical staff of analysts, prepare and coordinate continuity plans, oversee design, monitoring, and test activities, and report on continuity performance to senior IT managers, service level managers, and the customer. To summarize, the Service Continuity Manager is responsible for:
- Establishing, maintaining, and monitoring strategic IT Service Continuity Management plans
- Coordinating the definition, management, and control of service continuity requirements
- Planning and coordinating continuity preparation and test activities
- Analyzing and distributing continuity test results
- Collaborating with Availability Management, Capacity Management, and Security Management, and Service Level Management teams
- Participating in Change Management activities
- Gathering program measurements and releasing program performance reports
- Facilitating continuity-related PIRs
- Identifying continuity improvement opportunities

Service Continuity Analyst

Service Continuity Analysts may be members of a specific service team but in most organizations they work at the enterprise level and account for multiple or sets of services. They work under the direction of senior IT management and service managers to design, implement, and test continuity solutions. These solutions cover protective measures to reduce the likelihood of service interruptions and recovery measures to mitigate the impact of interruptions should they occur. They are responsible for eliciting and validating continuity requirements, structuring solution designs, assisting in continuity related implementations, providing Tier 2 or Tier 3 support for continuity-related production issues, periodically testing protective and recovery strategies, and providing assessments and advice to change control stakeholders. To summarize, Service Continuity Analysts are responsible for:

- Providing input into IT service continuity strategies and plans
- Eliciting, documenting, and managing IT service continuity requirements
- Establishing and maintaining continuity designs
- Monitoring service continuity performance over time
- Executing periodic service continuity tests
- Providing Tier 2 and Tier 3 continuity technical support
- Assessing test results and reporting on continuity effectiveness
- Providing continuity assessments and advice relevant to change control activities
- Participating in continuity-related PIRs

Human Resource considerations

The following are some typical traits that Human Resource staff may want to take into consideration when they are providing personnel, tools, and other resources for an IT Service Continuity Management program.

Experience and background: Service Continuity Managers should have experience that includes technical awareness of interoperability and dependencies across the infrastructure, sound knowledge of disaster recovery techniques, sound knowledge of event prevention and protection techniques, good coordination and collaboration skills, sound planning skills, and the ability to interface effectively across functional teams.

Service Continuity Analysts should have the right level of technical experience in the areas of availability, capacity, redundancy, fail-over, back up and restores, and experience supporting continuity solutions installed in specific environments

Comfort working in a process centric environment: IT Service Continuity management and staff should be comfortable working in a process-centric environment, and should be open to learning about the organization's program and contributing to its ordered growth

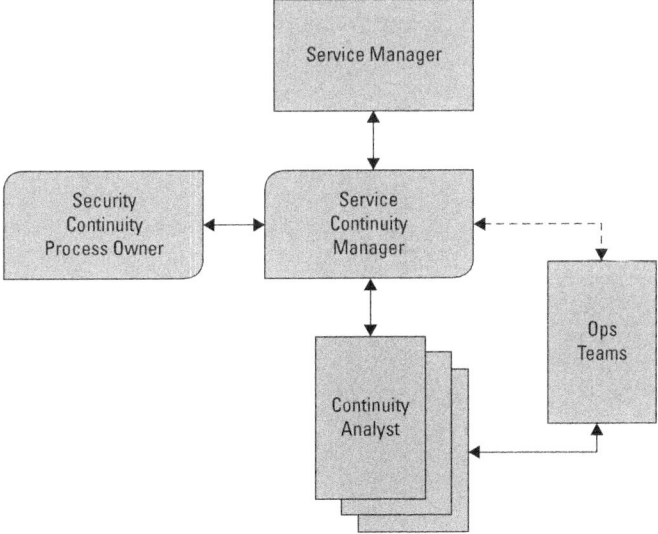

Figure 7.4 IT Service Continuity Management roles

7.8. Benefits of effective IT Service Continuity Management

Ensuring IT continuity is a major responsibility of senior IT management. Indeed, one of the common themes running through all of ITIL is the essential dependence the business has on accessing technology resources. A key IT job is to be aware of this dependence and shape the environment so that access and availability are not in question. When management is able to deliver to this need IT's value to the business becomes clear. The benefits of implementing a well-designed IT Service Continuity Management program support this goal. Following are four additional benefits such a program can provide.

Stronger statutory and regulatory compliance

A sound IT Service Continuity Management program will provide an organization with the techniques for remaining in compliance with statutory and regulatory mandates. Today such mandates surround many aspects of information technology. Falling out of compliance can lead to financial penalties, negative publicity, and even criminal charges. And if an actual catastrophe occurs – a natural disaster, a man-made one – the fallout can be magnified exponentially. Of course, no continuity management program can completely remove all such risk, but a well-designed program can greatly reduce this risk, at the least keep it in line with expected practices. More importantly, such a program, when coupled with an IT service continuity initiative, can ensure that any ensuing damage is mitigated. ITIL's practices of security planning, implementation, and evaluation deliver a level of defensive positioning that supports the legal requirements associated with business information in the marketplace.

Better preparedness

This might be thought of as a psychological benefit, a 'soft' advantage that may seem to have little value in an IT environment. But when it comes to preparedness this value is quite tangible. Having at hand a proven service continuity program is a powerful way to deliver peace of mind, not only for IT management but – and perhaps more importantly – for the customer. In today's world threats and disasters can emerge from a myriad of sources. Knowing that its systems, data, and business processes are protected and in every event recoverable goes a long way to freeing an organization to focus on its primary goal of market success. And if a *force majeure* event occurs, the strategic, documented, and tested nature of an ITIL-based continuity program provides for targeted actions specifically designed for effective response. The proactive measures and techniques employed by the program provide a protective shield that serves to deflate the approach of major events, or at least minimize the depth of their impact. When an organization is able to place itself in this type of position it is much freer to pursue the common goals of its business and IT missions.

Reliable disaster recovery

Better preparedness and reduced operational risk might best be seen as substantial byproducts of an effective IT Service Continuity Management program. The most significant benefit however is a direct product of the program, its major product as it were, and that is reliable disaster recovery. This is the bottom-line goal of any continuity process. Even the most resilient of environments will experience, sooner or later, some form of catastrophe, big or small, natural or otherwise. Fire, typhoon, equipment failure, and malicious attacks – something sometime is going to go awry. With an ITIL-based IT Service Continuity Management program, mission and technical essentials are identified and protected; response plans are developed and tested; material is set into place to guarantee an ongoing state of readiness. Knowing that this level of assurance is in place provides a strong panacea for both the technology and business sides of an enterprise.

Reduced operational risk

Service continuity problems have the potential to affect so many aspects of IT operations that a well designed IT Service Continuity Management program can go a long way toward helping an IT organization meet its availability, capacity, security, and reliability targets. The result: an operating environment in which risk and exposure are reduced. That can readily translate into performance in line with SLA targets. A continuity program can positively affect incident rates, problem rates, and service levels. It can also bolster environmental security. Increased integrity of systems, data, and business flows follows. From this comes a higher level of quality relevant to service delivery and performance. Business processes face reduced risk. Service processes face reduced risk. Operational effectiveness and efficiencies rise.

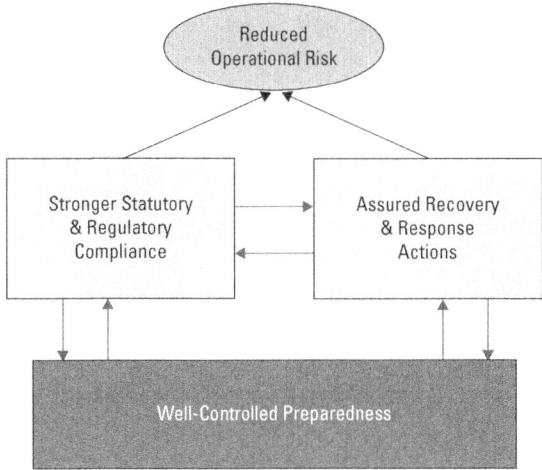

Figure 7.5 Benefits of effective IT Service Continuity Management

7.9. Implementation challenges and considerations

There are several aspects of IT Service Continuity Management that have the potential to affect how an organization might implement such a program. The first is the program's reach. Continuity management is rarely a local responsibility. More often than not it reaches across the enterprise, touching many components, systems, processes, and services. Next is the profound impact of *force majeure* events. Because they are hard to predict they are difficult to mimic. What's more, there is always the chance they may never show up in the first place, which sometimes strains the rationale to prepare for them. And then there is the issue of validating preparedness. In many environments, especially complex ones, testing continuity performance can be tricky. In line with these aspects, here are four challenges managers may wish to consider when implementing an IT Service Continuity Management program.

Maintaining a vigilant state of readiness

Vigilance as a posture may sound dramatic but it is a position that IT organizations should be willing to adopt as part of service continuity management. Maintaining a vigilant state of readiness, however, can be difficult to sustain. Especially in complex IT organizations it can be a challenge. Major disruptive events are not common occurrences. At the same time they are the kinds of events that require uncommon responses. The challenge comes from the fact that maintaining a constant state of readiness requires resources, and expending a quantity of those resources to maintain such a state (given that a disruption may not even materialize) may put pressure on corporate missions. As with other ITIL design processes, the key is to balance need with capability, capability with cost. In this case the organization should assess its environment against its continuity requirements, and from that determine the state of readiness that is most appropriate to its priority services and its position in the marketplace.

Acquiring and preparing contingency resources

When continuity events occur organizational teams typically have to shift into many different support roles and take on supplementary activities. This will usually require the use of staff personnel, special equipment, and certain facilities. It can be a challenge to acquire these contingency resources; capital investments may be required; teams will need to be trained and supplied; all of this can tax organizational resources. Part of an effective IT Service Continuity Management program will be planning in this area; the organization will need to determine what manner of contingency resources it can put into place and then direct them at the most crucial operating areas.

Thorough event and recovery testing

Thorough event and recovery testing can be a challenge because major events are such unpredictable and shape-shifting things. They are often difficult to mimic. Additionally, IT infrastructures today are almost by rule complex, sophisticated environments. Testing the full thread of an event's impact can be tough to design, strenuous to confirm. With this challenge it is helpful if the organization will reference its CMDB as a source for CIs related to services, CI dependencies, service map layouts, and technical streams of business services. The data can be used as a basis for test planning and test results validation. It is also helpful to recognize the time it takes to run through thorough test cycles. The organization should be sure to block out an adequate amount of time for test activity while accommodating minimal disruption to business activities.

Identifying and protecting essential functionality

Businesses operate through the delivery of many services, some however are more important to business missions than others. In the business impact analyses activity described for continuity management on page 143 the organization works to understand where its major service values lie and in what priority they might be considered. Such prioritization is important. Even the best of continuity programs cannot wrap a protective blanket around everything. For that reason it is important in continuity planning for IT management and business management to come together to identify core business processes that must receive first focus when major events occur. This can be a challenge in competitive environments where different groups naturally tend to view the work they do as paramount to corporate success.

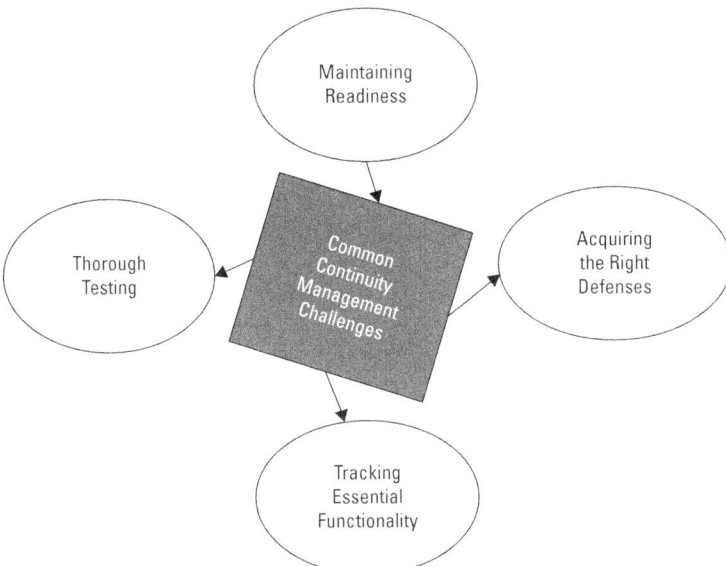

Figure 7.6 Implementation challenges and considerations for IT Service Continuity Management

7.10. Typical assets and artifacts of an IT Service Continuity Management program

An IT Service Continuity Management program requires a set of assets and artifacts that can be used to frame how program activities are managed. The assets provide the procedural guides and supporting materials for major activities. The artifacts shape the work products that the activities produce. Following is a list of some of the more common program materials that an organization is likely to employ when implementing an IT Service Continuity Management program. Your program may well require assets and artifacts not included here, but the set described below represents a typical baseline.

IT Service Continuity Management policy
This is an executive policy that stipulates the goals and objectives of the IT Service Continuity Management program. The policy, which ideally should be no longer than a few pages, documents at a high level the purpose of the program, the resources available to the program, the chief responsibilities of the program, quality targets, reporting hierarchies, and program measures. Endorsed by executive management, the policy is a demonstration of organizational commitment to the value and importance of IT Service Continuity Management across the enterprise.

IT Service Continuity Management Plan template
This template provides a structural guide for creating the organization's IT Service Continuity Management Plan. The template outlines the contents and sections that a properly documented plan should contain (see page 144). Such plans usually identify the following kinds of information: purpose and scope of IT Service Continuity Management, resources assigned to oversee IT Service Continuity Management activities, service continuity targets for each supported service, continuity measures and links to SLA targets, events that fall with IT Service Continuity Management domains, strategies for meeting service continuity targets, identification of IT Service Continuity Managers and key business stakeholders, types and frequency of IT Service Continuity Management reporting, report distribution channels, and a plan duration and review/revision schedule.

IT Service Continuity Management Plan
This is the organizational plan, based on the template above, that – once approved and adopted – stipulates how IT Service Continuity Management activities will be conducted over a set period of time.

IT Service Continuity Test Plan
This plan is a tactical extension of the IT Service Continuity Management Plan described above. This plan details how continuity strategies and capabilities will be periodically tested. Typically included are such details as: which services will be tested, what resources will be allocated for the testing, which user groups will be affected, what amount of downtime is expected, which data sets will be involved, how service interruptions or *force majeure* events will be mimicked, and what response and recovery outcomes are expected.

IT Service Continuity test results
These are the documented results from executing the IT Service Continuity Test Plan. It is distributed to Service Continuity Managers, senior IT managers, and key business stakeholders.

IT Service Continuity monitoring procedures
These are documented procedures that detail how business services, technical services, and service components will be monitored in the operational environment with regard to continuity. These procedures typically described the events to be associated with IT service continuity indicators, the thresholds of acceptable performance, identification of the tools that will monitor for prescribed events, and

descriptions of response activities to be invoked when thresholds are exceeded. These procedures are usually the basis for establishing OLAs between Service Continuity Managers and operations teams.

IT Service Continuity Management Measurement Plan Template
This template provides a structural guide for creating the organization's IT Service Continuity Management Measurement Plan. The template outlines the contents and sections that a properly documented plan should contain (see page 144). Such plans usually identify the following kinds of information: purpose and scope of measuring IT Service Continuity Management performance; resources assigned to establish metrics and performance reports; a description of each IT service continuity measure, how the data is to be collected, where the data is to be stored, and how data sets are to be analyzed. The plan also documents the type and format of measurement reports and also identifies stakeholders for receiving reports. Measures should be taken not only of IT service continuity performance in operational services but also of planning, design, and deployment activities. This plan is usually closely associated with continuity test plans.

IT Service Continuity Management Measurement Plan
This is the organizational plan, based on the template above, that – once approved and adopted – stipulates how IT service continuity measurement activities will be conducted over a set period of time.

IT Service Continuity Management reporting and distribution procedure
This is a documented procedure that describes how IT service continuity planning, design, and performance reports are created, how often they are generated, and to whom they are to be distributed. This procedure – and the ensuing reports – can be seen as a byproduct of the measurement plan described above. Together these artifacts provide for the generation of the kind of information IT management and customer groups need to understand the effectiveness of IT service continuity delivery and IT service continuity performance in order to identify opportunities for improvement.

Monitoring and control tools
The organization will need to acquire and configure a set of tools that can be used in operational services for monitoring IT service continuity performance and adjusting that performance as needed.

Organizational chart
This is a chart that shows the structural make-up of the IT Service Continuity Management operation. As with other organizational charts, the purpose is to identify teams, team relationships, and hierarchical flows, and so the chart's shape will depend on the organizational units and resources you are able to apply to the program. Most organizational charts of this sort are simple and basically linear. At the top, perhaps, there is a dotted box representing the key customer stakeholders. This extends down to a box for senior IT management, which then extends down to

the Service Continuity Manager. Below this might be three groups: service managers, service continuity analysts, and operation analysts. A dotted line from the Service Continuity Manager box might extend to a parallel support spot for the IT Service Continuity Management process owner (if this role is separate from the Service Continuity Manager). This chart may be service-specific or combine a set of service offerings.

Roles and responsibilities matrix

This matrix, an extension of the organizational chart, describes the various roles and responsibilities the organization has assigned to support IT Service Continuity Management activities. The roles typically include such positions as IT Service Continuity Management process owner, Service Continuity Manager, service continuity analysts (continuity designers and implementers), operations analysts, and (in consultative roles) senior IT management and service managers. Along with the job role definitions there should be descriptions of the responsibilities each role should account for, and references to how different roles interrelate and communicate. The matrix might take one of several forms: a spreadsheet, a series of database records, or a version-controlled text document. Ownership of this artifact is usually shared between IT management and Human Resource management.

8. Information Security Management

Information security troubles come in all shapes and sizes. In 2008, Heartland Payment Systems, a major credit card processing company in Princeton, New Jersey was alerted by both Visa and MasterCard about apparent suspicious activity surrounding its credit transactions. Heartland looked into it and found evidence that its systems had been hacked and malicious software had been compromising credit data that traversed its network. The size of the data breach affected an estimated 656 financial institutions and hundreds of millions of credit records. After reaching settlements with Visa, MasterCard, American Express, and Discover, Heartland's breach-related expenses topped $140 million.[1]

JE Systems Inc. is a fire alarm company in Fort Smith, Arkansas. In April 2010 the company got a call from its bank asking it to move more money into its payroll account, which was empty. Strange, because JE Systems had not yet made its mid-month payroll. What was discovered was that over the span of two days, someone had hacked into the account, stolen banking credentials, forged two payroll disbursements, and made off with $110,000. Because the confidential credentials used were legitimate, JE Systems and not the bank was on the hook for the loss.[2]

These kinds of electronic crimes, once unheard of, are now almost commonplace. The technological advances that provide for a truly global economy have also pushed businesses, governments, and other organizations into new transactional territories, often unfamiliar territories, and with that unfamiliarity comes a greater degree of risk. Today we are more and more aware of those risks and on guard against them. That is why information security has taken such a prominent position in IT organizations. Vulnerabilities, threats, social engineering, phishing, cookie mining, malicious code, spyware, viruses, distributed denials of service – these are just a few of the considerations an IT organization must face if it needs to operate on the assumption that its systems and data are protected and secure. And that is why Information Security Management represents a core ITIL process. ITIL defines the purpose of this process as:

"…To align IT and business security needs and requirements and ensure that information security is managed effectively in all services and Service Management activities."[3]

This is a two-fold responsibility. The first is to work to ensure that business security needs and IT security needs are aligned; that is, that they supplement and support

---
1 http://www.208breach.com
2 Dataloss DB
3 Foundations of ITIL. (2010). Van Haren Publishing

each other. This requires a consolidated, holistic approach. Next is to manage this approach, not just for the IT services being delivered but also for the management activities that support those services.

The objective ITIL provides for Information Security Management is:

"...To establish an environment where services, systems, and data are available when needed; that the integrity of those elements remains protected; that the confidentiality of those elements is assured; and that the authenticity of those elements is guaranteed."[4]

That objective shapes the content for this chapter. It describes the major considerations that should be addressed when security strategies and tactics are being set into place, either for a single service or a collection of services. These considerations include:
- Providing for confidentiality: ensuring that systems and data are governed in such a way that allows only for authorized access
- Providing for integrity: ensuring that systems and data are protected from intrusion, corruption, and theft

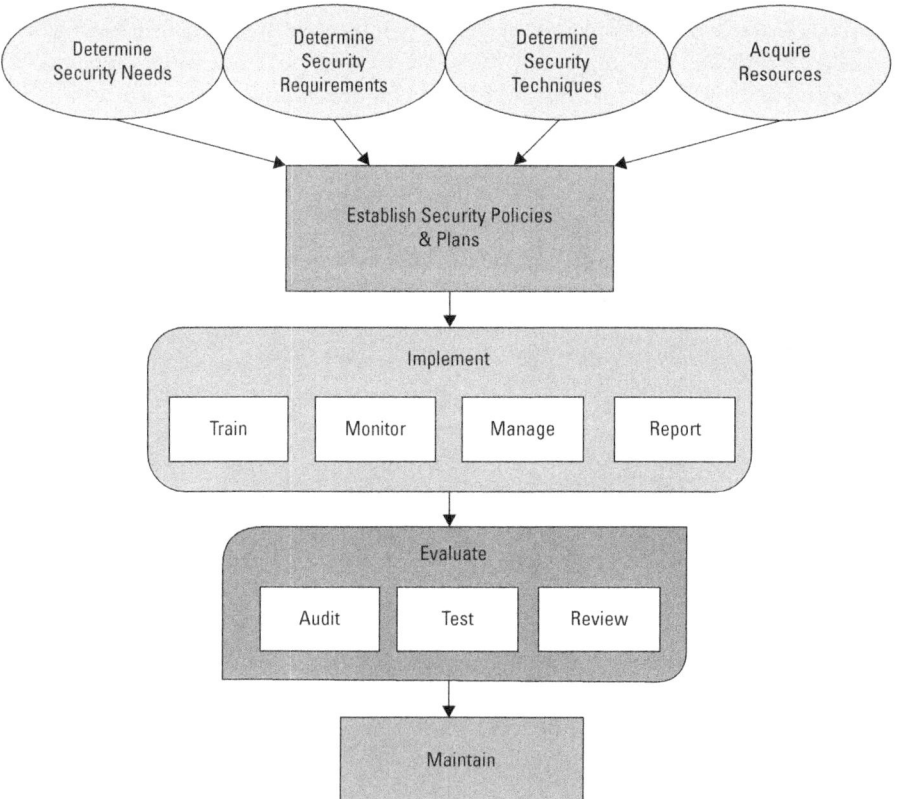

Figure 8.1 Typical Information Security Management process flow

---

4 Ibid.

- Providing for availability: ensuring that systems and data are presented in a controlled and protected manner for authorized use when needed by the business
- Providing for authenticity: ensuring that systems, data, and associated resources can be readily and reliably verified as authentic
- Providing for non-repudiation: ensuring that communications and authorizations can be reliably traced to originating sources
- Ensuring that the IT organization and the business comply with all applicable statutory and regulatory mandates

To delve into these considerations further let's begin with a look at the activities associated with the Information Security Management process.

8.1. Information Security Management activities

The four activities associated with Information Security Management closely follow, at a high level, the improvement method known as Plan-Do-Check-Act.[5] For this process the organization looks at its service mix and plans its approach to Information Security Management, based on configurations and needs. With approval in place the organization now executes the plan, setting its security methods and strategies to work. Next, the organization periodically evaluates the performance of the program, assessing its strengths and identifying ways to bolster any weaknesses. In the final step – rounding out a continuing cycle – the organization refines and adjusts the program over time so that it stays current with technology configurations, business needs, and market developments. ITIL terms these four activities:
- Planning
- Implementation
- Evaluation
- Maintenance

Here is a description of each.

1. Planning
Because Information Security Management is such a strategic point of focus, and because the impacts of low performance in this area can be significantly high, this first step of planning takes on special importance. Actually the term 'planning' may be a little misleading. What is really implied here is preparation: preparing the organization to establish a sound set of security policies, capabilities, and assessment mechanism. The work just naturally culminates in a plan. Planning involves five general sub-practices: identifying security needs, determining security requirements, identifying security techniques, and acquiring program resources then establishing a governing Information Security Management Plan.

---

5 For more on Plan-Do-Check-Act see Chapter 2.

Identify security needs. Every organization's service mix will have its own information security needs. The job of IT management at this stage is to identify those needs and prioritize them according to potential threats and vulnerabilities. Information security needs generally fall into a basic set of five considerations, as illustrated in the table below.

Table 8.1 Five considerations for determining security needs

Confidentiality	Which services and systems house sensitive data that needs special protection in order to remain confidential?
Integrity	How will the organization ensure that its services, systems, and data are protected from unauthorized access, corruption and theft?
Availability	How will the organization ensure that its services, systems, and data are available when needed by authorized users, while protected and controlled?
Authenticity	How will the organization verify that the services, systems, and data accessed by its users are genuine and authentic in nature?
Non-repudiation	How will the organization track and assess communications and authorizations in order to enforce non-repudiation?

It is important to note that, depending on the industries an IT organization operates in, security needs can also be strongly influenced by external regulatory and statutory mandates (e.g. HIPPA).[6]

Determine service security requirements. Once overall security needs have been identified, the organization can begin to look at individual services and determine their service level security requirements. Requirements in this domain cover three broad areas:
- Business service security requirements
- Technical service security requirements
- Service component security requirements

When eliciting in these areas the organization should seek to understand how the layers interact, how they depend upon on another, and possibly how they might make use of one another. Many such requirements will end up being common to the entire mix but each service will probably have its own particular requirements too. These need to be identified, agreed to, and documented. The work accomplished here will help establish security-related Service Level Requirements (for later use in SLAs). They are also valuable for establishing security-related OLAs for use by support teams and for establishing UCs with external providers.

Identify security techniques. Identifying security needs and service security requirements will point the way to appropriate security management techniques. Included here are incident monitoring and detection techniques, damage assessment

---

6 HIPPA: Healthcare Information Portability and Privacy Act (US government regulation)

and evaluation techniques, and prevention and response techniques. ITIL discusses five categories of such techniques as illustrated in the table below.

Table 8.2 Five common security management techniques

Preventive	These are measures taken to prevent vulnerabilities from maturing into threats. Examples include password protections and firewalls.
Reductive	These are measures taken to proactively minimize the potential damage from a security incident. Examples include daily data backups and off-site storage of records.
Detection	These are measures used to discover if a security incident has occurred. Examples include any variety of monitoring and control tools.
Repressive	These are measures taken to prevent a security incident from repeating itself or increasing. Examples include network rerouting and automatic device disabling.
Corrective	These are measures taken to correct damage caused by a security incident. Examples include data restores from backup and rollback plans as a response to system failures.

Acquire resources. The kinds of resources useful for implementing an Information Security Management capability will vary from organization to organization. But there is a base set and this includes people, design tools, industry standards, market guides, commercial off-the-shelf (COTS) products, production monitoring tools, and so on. Perhaps the most important resource to acquire, aside from skilled people, is some form of Information Security Management System (ISMS). This is an automated tool used by IT organizations to manage the assets of their information security programs. It is not a production tool *per se*; rather it is more of a strategic or positioning tool. With it the organization stores security designs, technical solutions, documentation, product information, production metrics, incident-problem resolution details, and other such aspects of functionality. Designers, architects, and security analysts must reference the ISMS when setting up new services or enhancing existing ones.

1. Establish information security plans and policies. Based on the information collected in the above sub-practices, the organization can now establish its baseline security polices and plans. Once drafted, policies and plans should be reviewed and approved by high level IT management and, when appropriate, by customer stakeholders. Once in place, the policies and plans should be carefully version-controlled. It is also important to remember to link security strategies and plans with service continuity strategies and plans. (For more on this, see Chapter 7).

2. Implementation. With implementation the organization deploys the program out into the IT environment. The program, with its policies, plans, practices, and resources, can now be put into operation. The stream of sub-practices associated with implementation include training on program use, monitoring real-time security performance, managing security breaches as they may occur, and issuing security activity reports.

Train relevant stakeholders. Training is an aspect of process implementation that is often overlooked, yet it is essential to program success. Training can include any combination of classroom instruction, one-on-one coaching, mentoring, and self-paced computer-based training (CBT). For the people who have to engage in Information Security Management activities, training will help them become familiar and comfortable with the policies and procedures that guide the process. Training material should be appropriately created to reflect the focal points of the program. Stakeholders should be identified based on the program's various operational domains. At this point instruction can be delivered and, once delivered, backed up with on-the-floor support.

Monitor program performance. There is a monitoring capability associated with each ITIL design process. This is the only practical way to confidently know how a service is operating in production. Monitoring can be done by tools or people. Whichever way or combination is selected, the key is to identify the essential security traits of a service, those that most need to be watched, and then track them. Data points should be collected, stored and analyzed according to plan (details of which are usually found in the organization's Information Security Management Plan). Monitoring is important for security breach management (it is an early-warning system) and provides input for security reporting. Monitoring should be applied to business services, technical services, and service components.

Manage security breaches. Security breaches may appear at any time, anywhere: malware, spyware, unauthorized access, denials o service. These are the kinds of events that monitoring activities are in place to detect. When an event does occur it is Information Security Management's job to manage it. How this is done will depend on the configuration of the environment, the type of breach, and its severity. The goal of security support is to get to the situation early, have adequate diagnostic and response tools available, then work to minimize impacts. With any incident, problem, or event, details concerning the breach should be thoroughly documented – including symptoms, causes, and corrective actions.

Report security activity. Monitoring security performance and managing security breaches lead naturally to security reporting. Periodically, Information Security Management should formulate and distribute reports that summarize the period's security activities. These reports, in whatever groups you may require, have three common target audiences. Operation teams can use them to gain insight into ongoing status and maintenance needs; they provide a picture of information security integrity in today's environment. Service managers can use them to gain insight into the status and stability of their particular business, technical, and component domains; they provide a picture of how well a service is operating inside existing security policies and practices. And senior IT management can use them as mission reports; they inform management as to how well the program is working with regard to enterprise level security goals and objectives.

3. Evaluation. Evaluation is a periodic, repeating activity for Information Security Management. Here management looks at the program's performance in order to determine its effectiveness. In some organizations and within some process frameworks (such as CMMI) this activity is grouped under Quality Assurance. And it does in fact have a process quality focus to it. The purpose of the evaluation step is three-fold: to perform assessments to verify that security policies and procedures are being followed, to test information security capabilities in order to validate that they are operating as intended, and to determine any adjusts or revisions that may be required to improve program performance.

Conduct security assessments. Assessments are spot checks on on-going information security preparedness. An assessment is an evaluation of performance; that is, a gauge of how well security teams are executing the organization's information security policies and practices. Assessments usually involve the review of process activities, inspection of work products, and interviews with team members. The results are then recorded and presented to the teams as well as to IT management. Based on the results, corrective actions – to the program or to the people – may be recommended.

Test security capabilities. Just as assessments reveal procedural preparedness, security tests demonstrate functional preparedness. The purpose of testing is to mimic in a harmless way intrusions and threats that may potentially affect the enterprise. Tests should be complete (moving through a full service chain) and reflect real-world variety and sophistication. Test cycles should be competently planned and scripted, with their executions carefully monitored. Results should be distributed to relevant stakeholders and used as the basis for identifying possible procedural or environmental improvements.

Review and revise. Based on the results of performance assessments and security testing, the organization may elect to review security requirements and strategies in light of industry practices and mandates and perhaps revise the requirements and strategies as needed.

4. Maintenance. This fourth step is in place to ensure that the Information Security Management program is maintained over time with a view to keeping it current with evolving market, business, and technical needs. The preceding steps provide input and direction for maintenance activities. The primary emphases here include periodic executive reviews of program performance; reviews of resource levels (staffing, tools, budgets, etc.); reviews of plans and policies; and reviews of emerging industry and market trends. The results of this set of reviews should reveal opportunities for program adjustments and improvements. That will lead to a fresh cycle of information security planning.

Relationship to ISO/IEC 27000 series

Information Security Management has close relationships with the ISO/IEC 27000-series (ISO/IEC 27001, 27002, 27002, 27003, 27004, 27005, 27011) which includes:

- Risk Assessment and Treatment
- Security Policy
- Organization of Information Security
- Asset Management Security
- Human Resources Security
- Physical Security
- Communications and Ops Management
- Access Control
- Information Systems Acquisition, Development, Maintenance
- Information Security Incident management
- Business Continuity
- Compliance

8.2. Process inputs and outputs

In a way that is similar to IT Service Continuity Management, Information Security Management is a process that takes two continual paths, planning and execution. *Planning* involves those activities necessary for setting the organization's security strategies and tactics into place. Because the factors that affect security performance are themselves dynamic (vulnerabilities, internal threats, external threats, etc.) the process of planning (or at least that of plan assessment) should be conducted on a scheduled basis. *Execution* mainly centers on the development and implementation of new information security requirements and measuring the performance of the resulting solutions. The entry state for the Information Security Management process is always predicated on one of three conditions: an IT service – new or enhanced – is being made ready for production, it is time to refresh security plans, or new security rules or regulations have been released. The triggers that set the process in motion may come from a variety of inputs: new requirements, security performance results, industry trends, emerging threats, etc. Triggers that indicate the process is complete are also fairly stable. They include new security strategies, new or refreshed design solutions, refreshed security plans, and lessons learned from PIRs. Below is a summary of common entry criteria and inputs, exit criteria, outputs of the Information Security Management process.

Entry criteria
The Information Security Management process is typically set into motion when one of three events occurs:
- A new or enhanced IT service is being readied for production (or)
- It is time to refresh existing security plans (or)
- New security regulations – internal or external – have been introduced.

Inputs
Inputs into the process can come from a variety of sources, individually or in combination. These inputs can include:

- Business strategies
- Existing Information Security Management policies and plans
- Existing security designs
- Statutory or regulatory requirements
- Security assessment results
- Security risk analyses
- Security performance reports from production that drive Requests for Change for any of the following areas:
  - Business security requirements
  - Service security requirements
  - Service security continuity requirements

Exit criteria

The process is typically recognized as having been completed when two general exit conditions are met:
- The new or enhanced service has been successfully transitioned into operation (or)
- The security environment has been realigned through new policies and plans.

Outputs

The Information Security Management process, once it has run its course, will produce a set of work products that support its procedural activities. At a minimum the set should includes the following artifacts:

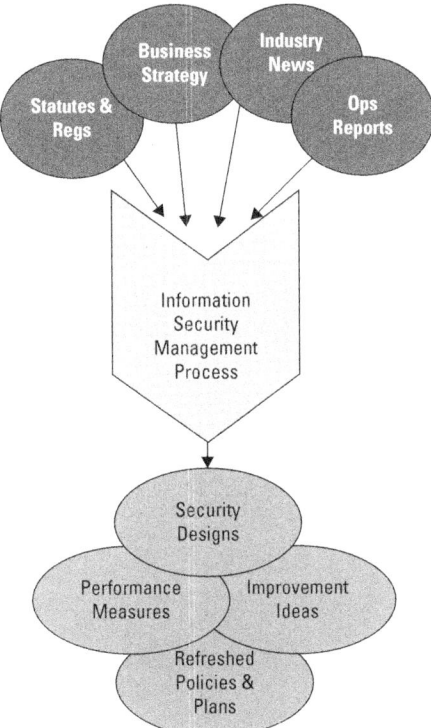

Figure 8.2 Inputs and outputs for Information Security Management

- New or refreshed Information Security designs
- Information Security performance metrics
- PIR notes
- Refreshed Information Security Management policies and plans

8.3. Processes related to Information Security Management

Information Security Management operates in a specialized domain and addresses very specific issues. It is through this process that Service Design factors such as confidentiality, integrity, availability, authenticity, and non-repudiation are considered. But it is important to note that these factors, while specialized, are not intended to function in isolation. Other aspects of Service Design and Service Management need to integrate into the methods and models established by Information Security Management activities. And so when implementing an Information Security Management program it is important to appreciate this need for integration, to recognize it, and provide links through which other ITIL processes can mesh successfully with security activities. In particular four of ITIL's core processes require at least some degree of integration with Information Security Management. They are:
- Availability Management
- IT Service Continuity Management
- Service Level Management
- Service Improvement

Availability Management
Availability Management and Information Security Management are closely allied. Security requirements shape in many ways how availability configurations might be designed. Likewise, business availability needs affect how security methods and models might be implemented. From an operational perspective, security intrusions or breaches may have significant impacts on availability levels, and so security performance needs to monitored with availability in mind, and vice versa. From the vantage point of improvement, security effectiveness should be evaluated in light of availability performance, identifying opportunities where adjustments to configurations in one area might lead to enhanced performance in the other. (For more on this topic, see Chapter 5.)

In summary:
- Availability designs have the potential to affect security performance.
- Security methods and models should account for business availability needs.
- Operational incidents or problems related to security have the potential to adversely affect availability levels, and vice versa.
- Improvement assessments relevant to security management should include assessments of availability configurations.

IT Service Continuity Management

Information Security Management is linked to IT Service Continuity Management in much the same way that it is allied with Availability Management. After all, IT Service Continuity Management is, in many ways, an extension of Availability Management, so similar considerations apply. Continuity tactics that deal with prevention and recovery need to support information security requirements and configurations. Disaster plans and continuity tests need to include Information Security Management as part of their scope. And when security methods and models are adjusted or improved, Information Security Management must be sure to communicate these changes to IT Service Continuity Management so new configurations may be absorbed into their plans and methods. (For more on this topic, see Chapter 11.)

In summary:
- The protection and response strategies inherent in IT Service Continuity Management need to support security requirements and configurations.
- Existing threats and vulnerabilities need to be accounted for in continuity plans and tests.
- Operational incidents or problems related to security have the potential to bring disaster recovery and other continuity methods into action.
- Changes and improvements made to security methods and models need to be communicated to IT Service Continuity Management stakeholders.

Service Level Management

Because of its high profile position as a necessary IT activity, Information Security Management is almost always included as an activity to be measured under SLAs. SLAs always include some targets for security capabilities, vulnerabilities, and threats. It is important for security managers to work closely with service level managers to negotiate appropriate security performance targets. Once SLAs have been agreed upon, security teams should work with service level managers to track ongoing production performance. Poor performance in such a visible area as information security can be detrimental not just to other technical targets but to customer satisfaction levels as well. For these reasons, a Service Level Management program should work to integrate and support the function and shape of an Information Security Management program. (For more on this topic, see Chapter 4.)

In summary:
- Information security performance – owing to its sensitivity – has direct bearing on service quality, and thus on the customer's perception of IT's overall value to the business.
- SLAs should realistically define and document Information Security Management performance expectations.
- Effective Information Security service levels can provide solid support for IT's effort to create strong and cooperative relationship with business management.

Service Improvement

Service Improvement is an umbrella activity for all aspects of an IT Service Management program and it is used with particular emphasis on ITIL design processes. With Information Security Management, improvement work falls into two broad categories. The first is technical: security analysts and operation teams investigate ways in which security policies, plans, designs, and tactics can be enhanced. The second category falls under procedural support. Security management teams (along with the Information Security Management Process Owner) work to identify improvement opportunities that can be applied to the program's processes, procedures, monitoring tools, and measurements.

In summary:
- A key responsibility of security analysts is to continually investigate and identify ways in which security designs and operating performance can be improved.
- Security improvements are not confined just to the technical arena; teams should seek improvements in management processes, monitoring tools, and measurements.

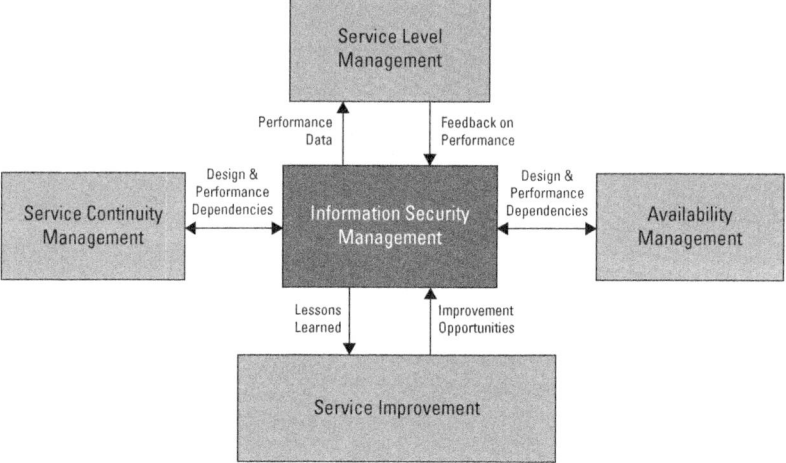

Figure 8.3 Processes related to Information Security Management

8.4. Tools and techniques

As much as with any of the other ITIL core processes, Information Security Management benefits from the use of supplementary tools and techniques. The main activities of this process require the organization to set protective security measures in place, monitor the integrity of the enterprise, and respond effectively when security incidents occur. Establishing a layer of protection suitable to the enterprise requires standards and guidelines, and some form of system to manage program data. Monitoring performance requires specialized tools. And response responsibly calls for a set of proven and reliable tactics. Below are five common tools and techniques often employed for Information Security Management:

Table 8.3 Tools and techniques for Information Security Management

Information security assignment and update guidelines	Many organizations implement security guidelines that control how often security profiles are reviewed and updated. This practice safeguards against profiles becoming outdated or inappropriate to current business roles; in many cases profiles expire at a fixed time pending review. These guidelines apply to business services, technical services, and user profiles.
Incident management tactics	These tactics include the following types of security management techniques: • Preventive • Reductive • Detection • Repressive • Corrective These are used to address vulnerabilities and threats such as malicious code, unauthorized access, social engineering, cookie data lifting, identity theft, spyware, viruses, distributed denial of service, etc.
Encryption and data-locking masks	Many organizations that deal with sensitive or proprietary data encrypt their information so that if the data is compromised the party attacking the data will need a special key to access the contents.
Production monitoring and control tools	It is essential for protection and performance assessment that information security performance is monitored and controlled in live operation as far as possible. Monitoring tools provide recorded feedback of security activity and access over time; this contributes to the creation of security trend baselines and models.
Information Security Management System	The ISMS is a tool – typically automated – that is used to configure security profiles, enforce access and then track and manage profiles over time.

8.5. Key Performance Indicators

KPIs for an Information Security Management program can be used to measure progress toward the program's critical success factors (see following section). The kinds of KPIs typically included in a baseline program fall into two broad categories: configuration and response. The configuration KPIS deal with the number of types of security profiles associated with business services, technical services, and user groups. This data shows the scope and complexity of the security landscape. The response KPIs cover the range of security actions typically invoked to respond to a security threat or breach event. These actions include preventive, reductive, detective, repressive, and corrective actions. Descriptions of these KPIs follow.

Number and types of business security profiles in place

This is a breakdown of the number and types of different business security profiles in place across the organization. The shape of these counts will naturally vary from organization to organization, but it is common to see profiles set up along lines of business (e.g. accounting, marketing), by functional area (e.g. Amsterdam office), or by business service (e.g. email, ledger posting). These profiles address the particular needs of specific business groups and help establish the scope of security concerns and responsibilities from a high-level business perspective. It also gives management an appreciation for the levels of effort associated with maintaining this volume of profiles on an ongoing basis.

Number and types of technical service security profiles in place
This is a breakdown of the number and types of different technical service security profiles in place across the organization. Just as with business profiles, the shape of these counts will vary. It is common to see profiles set up along system and system component bases. Contrary to business profiles, the security profiles are configured at a deeper layer and are often brand-specific. Applications, servers, routers, queue managers, and other similar components may require their own profiles and these profiles may be of a proprietary or exclusive nature. These profiles address the particular needs of technical services and help establish the scope of security concerns and responsibilities at the operational level. These counts can give management an appreciation of the types and numbers of resources needed to maintain the portfolio of profiles on an ongoing basis.

Number and types of user security profiles in place
This is a breakdown of the number and types of user security profiles in place across the organization. This is, in effect, a count of everyone who has an individual profile and a breakdown of what type that profile is. It is common to see profiles set up by job role, as a pointer to business and technical services. These profiles are usually configured as an extension to a business profile and are often contained as 'child' records to more general business profiles. A shipping clerk, a software manager, a marketing VP will each require distinct and different security profiles. An analysis of these profiles can help establish the scope of security concerns and responsibilities at the individual job role level. These counts can give management an appreciation of the types and numbers of resources needed to maintain this portfolio on an ongoing basis.

Number and types of security breaches
This is a basic count of the number and types of security breaches experienced for a set period of time. These counts may be further broken down by business service, technical service, or user group. This data gives an indicator of the general stability and functional integrity of the security environment – and provides insight into the effectiveness of the organization's strategic security plan. This is a macro view of the operability of the Information Security Management program.

Number and types of preventive measures taken
Preventive measures are proactive measures taken to secure the environment from threats. It is a primary job of Information Security Management and requires that security staff remain up-to-date on emerging threats and evolving preventive techniques. This metric is a basic count of the number and types of preventive security steps exercised in the environment for a given period of time.

Number and types of reductive measures taken

Reductive measures are proactive measures taken to secure the environment from threats by protecting the integrity of systems and data – by reducing the likelihood that a breach could cause actual harm. Examples of reductive techniques include performing backups and implementing operational redundancies. This metric is a basic count of the number and types of reductive security steps taken in the environment over a given period of time.

Number and types of detection measures taken

Detective measures are proactive measures taken to regularly monitor the environment in order to anticipate threats or identify breaches. The objective is to detect intrusions before the intruders have the opportunity to engage in any surreptitious or destructive behavior. This metric is a basic count of the number and types of detection security steps taken in the environment over a given period of time.

Number and types of repressive measures taken

Repressive measures can be either proactive or reactive. They are steps taken to suppress the environment so that a threat's potential for harm is disabled or significantly curtailed. The steps may be set into place in response to a specific breach or in anticipation of unknown breaches. Examples of repressive measures include the use of firewalls and signal blocking. This metric is a basic count of the number and types of repressive preventive security steps taken in the environment for a given period of time.

Number and types of corrective measures taken

Corrective measures are reactive in nature. They are taken to repair the effect of a security breach or to mitigate the breach's impact. Corrective actions may be self-contained or may include the implementation of preventive, reductive, repressive, or detection techniques. This metric is a basic count of the number and types of corrective security steps taken in the environment over a given period of time.

8.6. Critical Success Factors

A successful Information Security Management program is one that effectively positions the organization for operational security and data integrity. It is also one that succeeds in working to continually reduce threats, vulnerabilities, and breaches. The effectiveness and efficiency of such a program can be gauged by regularly measuring and assessing breach activity across the enterprise. Presented below are four such analytical measures, which you may find applicable as CSFs for your Information Security Management program. These are only common examples and are by no means exhaustive, but they are useful for demonstrating the value of the security program overall.

Number of security breaches over time
This metric provides a high level, global view of security performance over time by highlighting the volume of breaches. This may be the best single indicator of the tightness of an organization's security management practices. These measures are useful for establishing a breach-level baseline and then, as data accumulates over time, projection models that may help predict future security performance. The information shows the number of security breaches over a fixed period of time with the goal being to see a trend line of diminishing volumes, reflective of the Information Security Management program evolving and maturing with time.

Number of business security profiles versus security breaches over time
This metric provides the organization with a high-level look at security effectiveness and activity. These measures capture the number of security breaches, organized by type and by business line, for a given period of time. The data shows management the volume of security breaches compared to the number of business security profiles in place. This data can be used to help identify vulnerable or exposed lines of business. The desired goal is to see a trend indicating that the business units-to-breaches ratio remains favorable, or at least stable, even if business profiles change or expand.

Number of technical service security profiles versus security breaches over time
This metric provides the organization with a mid-level, technical look at security effectiveness and activity. These measures capture the number of security breaches for a given period of time organized by type, by technical service, and by service component. The data shows management the volume of security breaches compared to the number of technical service profiles in place, and may help identify poorly configured equipment or weakly supported systems. The desired goal is to see a trend indicating that the business units-to-breaches ratio remains favorable, or at least stable, even if business profiles change or expand.

Number of user profiles versus security breaches over time
This metric provides the organization with a detailed, line level look at security effectiveness and activity. These measures capture the number of security breaches, organized by type and by business line, for individual users for a given period of time. The data shows management the volume of individual security breaches compared to the total number of user-based security profiles, and may help identify problematic staff members or business domains within an organization. The desired goal is to see a trend indicating that the ratio of ratio of individual breaches-to-staff size remains favorable, or at least stable, even if staff levels fluctuate.

8.7. Information Security Management roles

The following job roles are typically seen in mature Information Security Management programs. Depending on the size and focus of an organization these roles may be full-time or part-time, combined, or shared by multiple individuals.

Information Security Management Process Owner

The Information Security Management Process Owner is the person (or persons) in the organization responsible for the development, deployment, and ongoing use of the Information Security Management program. It is common in many IT organizations that this process owner is the same person as the Service Security Manager, but this is not essential. The process owner champions the purpose and goals of Information Security Management, ensures that the program remains in a state of operational effectiveness, and interfaces with senior IT management and business representatives to facilitate program adjustments and improvements. To summarize, the Information Security Management Process Owner is responsible for:

- Developing and documenting the Information Security Management program
- Implementing the program across relevant teams
- Coordinating program training and mentoring
- Monitoring ongoing program use
- Measuring program performance over time
- Reporting on program effectiveness over time
- Soliciting and coordinating program improvements

Service Security Manager

Every IT service supported by the organization should have assigned to it someone responsible for managing the activities associated with security: security configurations, access profiles, security monitoring, and incident response actions. This position is typically known as the Service (or IT) Security Manager. This is a technical role because understanding, implementing, and controlling service security requirements are complex activities. Service Security Managers manage a technical staff of analysts, prepare and coordinate security plans, oversee design, monitoring, and test activities, and report on security performance to senior IT managers, service level managers, and the customer. To summarize, the Service Security Manager is responsible for:

- Establishing, maintaining, and monitoring strategic Information Security Management plans
- Coordinating the definition, management, and control of service security requirements
- Responsible for interfacing with user groups and IT management on security policies and issues
- Responsible for keeping up to date on statutory and regulatory security requirements
- Monitoring industry trends and developments

- Planning and coordinating security evaluation and test activities
- Collaborating with Availability Management, Capacity Management, Continuity Management, and Service Level Management teams
- Participating in Change Management activities as necessary
- Gathering program measurements and releasing program performance reports
- Facilitating security-related PIRs
- Identifying security improvement opportunities

Security Analyst

Security Analysts may be members of a specific service team but in most organizations they work at the enterprise level and account for multiple services or sets of services. They work under the direction of senior IT management and senior security managers (with tie-ins to service managers), their main responsibilities being to design, implement, and test security solutions. These solutions cover protective measures to reduce the likelihood of service interruptions (firewalls, access profiles, etc.) and recovery measures to mitigate the impact of security incidents should they occur. They are responsible for eliciting and validating security requirements, structuring solution designs, assisting in security related implementations, providing Tier 2 or Tier 3 support for security-related production issues, periodically testing protective and mitigation strategies, and providing assessments and advice to change control stakeholders. To summarize, Security Analysts are responsible for:

- Providing input into security strategies and plans
- Eliciting, documenting, and managing Information Security requirements
- Responsible for maintaining the Information Security Management System (ISMS)
- Responsible for configuring and tracking security profiles for services, systems, and users
- Establishing and maintaining security designs
- Monitoring service security performance over time
- Executing periodic service security evaluations
- Providing Tier 2 and Tier 3 security technical support
- Reporting on security effectiveness
- Providing security assessments and advice relevant to change control activities
- Participating in security-related PIRs

Human Resource considerations

The following are some typical traits that Human Resource staff may want to take into consideration when they are providing personnel, tools, and other resources for an Information Security Management program.

Experience and background. Security Managers should have experience that includes technical awareness of security vulnerabilities and risk-reduction techniques; sound understanding of security-related statutory and regulatory requirements (e.g. HIPPA); sound knowledge of threat prevention and protection techniques; good coordination and collaboration skills, sound planning skills, and the ability to interface effectively across functional teams and user groups.

Security Analysts should have the right level of technical experience in the areas of configuring and monitoring user access to services, systems, and data. They should also have experience monitoring the network for security threats, risks, and breaches.

Comfort working in a process-centric environment. IT Service Continuity management and staff should be comfortable working in a process-centric environment, and should be open to learning about the organization's program and contributing to its ordered growth

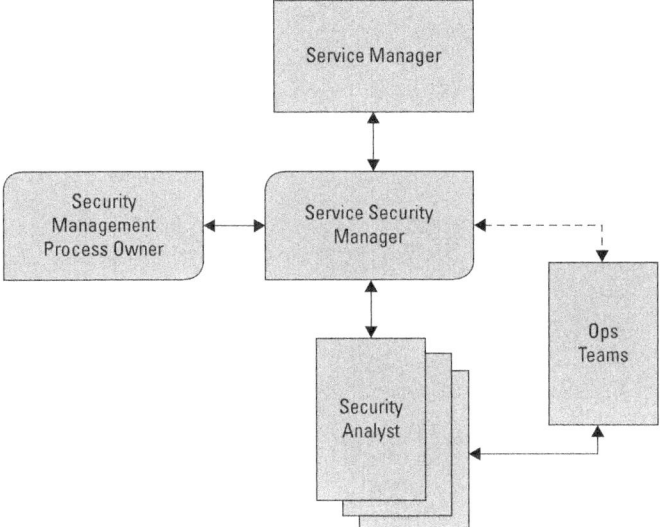

Figure 8.4 Information Security Management roles

8.8. Benefits of effective Information Security Management

Information security is so central a topic in today's IT environment that the benefits of implementing an effective Information Security Management process are compelling. The overriding benefit, of course, rests in the domain of fiduciary obligations: it is a *prime responsibility* of IT management to protect its customers' data, systems, and assets from the threat of loss or compromise. Out of all other IT responsibilities, this one comes closest to being legally binding, and in certain professions and industries there are indeed laws that set this as a fixed legal obligation (note HIPPA regulations as one example). IT organizations are expected to provide a secure environment, one that can be confidently managed and monitored. When an organization sets such a capability in place it can be seen as meeting its obligation for this domain. That single benefit can establish significant goodwill with the customer. Below are three other important benefits an Information Security Management program can deliver.

Stronger statutory and regulatory compliance

A sound Information Security Management program will provide an organization with the techniques for remaining in compliance with statutory and regulatory mandates. Today such mandates surround many aspects of IT management. Falling out of compliance can lead to financial penalties, negative publicity, and even criminal charges. And if an actual catastrophe occurs – an intrusion, a theft – the fallout can be magnified exponentially. Of course, no security management program can completely remove all such risk, but a well-designed program can greatly reduce this risk, and at the least keep it in line with expected practices. More importantly, such a program, when coupled with an IT service continuity initiative, can ensure that any ensuing damage is mitigated. ITIL's practices of security planning, implementation, and evaluation deliver a level of defensive positioning that supports the legal requirements associated with business information in the marketplace.

Reduced operational risk

Security management is a fixed requirement for any technology organization today. The risks to operations are so high, and the ramifications so profound, that the absence of such management is tantamount to a violation of fiduciary responsibility. Implementing a formal Information Security Management program is the recognized way to address these operational risks. But it will do more. It will also reduce business exposure to risk and therefore bolster the effectiveness of business processes. The recommendations in ITIL provide a pathway for realizing a program that accounts for business mission integrity, potential service vulnerabilities, defensive positioning, and appropriate breach responses. This scope of preparedness covers the spectrum necessary to secure data, services, and system components.

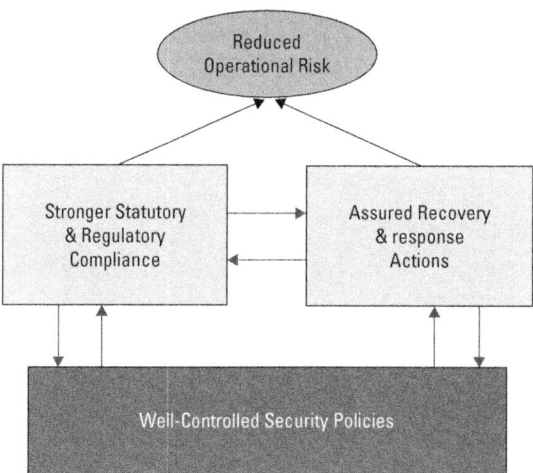

Figure 8.5 Benefits of effective Capacity Management

More assured response and recovery actions

The most tangible benefit of an effective Information Security Management program is that it provides the organization with proven response and recovery actions. If a security incident occurs business and technology stakeholders can know that prompt actions will be taken, impacts will be mitigated, and through event analyses defenses will be strengthened. A coordinated, managed program delivers these capabilities. It positions the business so that upfront its processes, assets, and data operate in an arena of reduced risk. It also buffers the business in such a way that, when events do occur, the potential for significant harm has been minimized.

8.9. Implementation challenges and considerations

The challenges and considerations of implementing ITIL's Information Security Management process have more to do with the nature of security management as a general IT concern than they do with the process itself. For an Information Security Management program to be effective, the organization must be in such a position that the program's practices can be applied to what might best be called a 'receptive' environment. This is one in which security staff have the experience and knowledge necessary to configure a secure environment; access profiles remain continually aligned with expanding or shrinking user needs; redundancies and defense mechanisms are appropriate to the environment; and the configurations of sensitive and essential data are well understood. Achieving this level of receptivity, however, is not always as straightforward as might be hoped for. Following are descriptions of four common challenges that many organizations face when they move to implement an Information Security Management program.

Keeping current with evolving security threats

The field of security management as a branch of IT discipline has become more and more organized and sophisticated over the years. Today it is strongly supported by the IT industry and the mix of security-related product offerings continues to grow and diversify. Nevertheless there can still remain challenges associated with implementing security processes. One of the biggest challenges is the perpetual need to keep security staff up to date on evolving threat technologies and techniques. It seems that as IT environments become more and more sophisticated, threats become more creative and ingenious. And as technology grows more and more endemic to business environments, so too will security risks take on new shapes and forms. This requires staff to be regularly exposed to new security methods and options. This can be accomplished through off-site training, in-house training, industry workshops, industry associations, and other knowledge avenues. Because this is a field that will probably never be free of risk, the organization's commitment to continual training and knowledge acquisition must be recognized as long term.

Keeping user security status appropriate

Keeping user profiles current with evolving job status can be a challenge for both large and small companies. People's roles naturally change over time. Job responsibilities change, people come and go. With these changes there is almost always the need to adjust security profiles. Security staff need to be aware of these changes so that the appropriate adjustments can be made. If this awareness is lacking in an organization or if there is significant delay between when a change occurs and when the adjustments are made, the risks of breaches or unauthorized access rise. Many security incidents can be traced to the simple fact that people have retained access and security rights that no longer hold relevance to their position in the company. To address this, IT management should work to promote some degree of integration between Human Resource management and security management. For example, the personnel policies and procedures executed by HR could be supplemented to contain triggers that invoke communications to security teams when certain employee profile conditions are met. This is very similar to how those same policies and procedures routinely trigger communications to payroll teams. The goal that IT management wants to achieve in this arena is a near-instantaneous ability to recognize a change, understand the nature of that change, and then reset security profiles to adequately reflect the requirements of that change.

Acquiring adequate redundancies and defense mechanisms

The legitimate desire to provide a robust security environment introduces the challenge of finding a balance between need and cost. Security incidents carry with them the potential for two distinct impacts: assets are stolen, or assets are corrupted. For the first point, an important aspect of any security environment is providing the right level of redundancy so that copies of data, systems, and infrastructure components can be made quickly available in the event that primary assets are compromised. For the second point, security management should provide a proper layer of defense mechanisms (e.g. firewalls) so that the potential for breaches is reduced. Of course, protecting thoroughly against theft and corruption can be expensive: too much rigor might not make economic sense; too little might leave the organization open to unnecessary risk. Management will need to look at this issue carefully: acquire an understanding of current security integrity, identify sensitive and high-value data (see the following challenge), identify known and potential risks, and develop a strategy for addressing those risks. Then the organization will be in a position to determine the right cost-benefit blend in a manner that makes sense for the business.

Identifying and tracking sensitive data

Identifying and tracking sensitive data may seem to be an obvious operational responsibility but many IT organizations find this to be a significant challenge. In today's widely distributed environments data can be spread across multiple centers, many systems, and maintained by many teams. It is also common to see it shared and processed into different information forms. A portion of this data might certainly be considered benign; that is, of no critical importance. But another portion – and it may even be the bulk – may be considered sensitive. It may reveal competitive positions, it may be proprietary, and it may be controlled by legal statutes. In short, the data contents and data integrity need to be protected, and it is a major responsibility of IT to provide this protection. In order to have as risk-proof an environment as possible IT management should undertake the job of identifying these essential and sensitive data sets and then tracking them so they can be adequately protected. This involves mapping the data sources, the data types, the repositories, the distribution channels, and all processing and delivery avenues. This can admittedly be a big job, but the fallout and consequences of not following through with it might exponentially outweigh the effort.

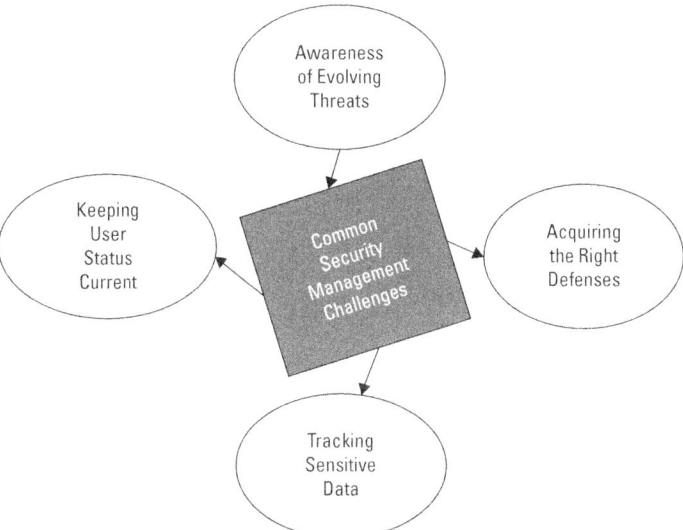

Figure 8.6 Implementation challenges and consideration for Information Security Management

8.10. Typical assets and artifacts of an Information Security Management program

Your Information Security Management program will require a set of assets and artifacts that can be used to frame how program activities are managed. The assets provide the procedural guides and supporting materials that govern the activities. The artifacts shape the work products that the Information Security Management activities produce. Following is a list of some of the more common materials that an organization is likely to employ when implementing ITIL's Information Security Management process. Your program may require assets and artifacts not included here, but the set described below represents a typical baseline.

Information Security Management policy
This is an executive policy that stipulates the goals and objectives of the Information Security Management program. The policy, which ideally should be no longer than a few pages, documents at a high level the purpose of the program, the resources available to the program, the chief responsibilities of the program, quality targets,

reporting hierarchies, and program measures. Endorsed by executive management, the policy is a demonstration of organizational commitment to the value and importance of the Information Security Management program across the enterprise.

Information Security Management Plan template
This template provides a structural guide for creating the organization's Information Security Management Plan. The template outlines the contents and sections that a properly documented plan should contain (see page 169). Such plans usually identify the following kinds of information: purpose and scope of Information Security Management, resources assigned to implement Information Security policies and monitor security activity, security performance targets for each supported service, response actions when security events occur, security measures and links to SLA targets, security monitoring techniques, strategies for meeting security performance targets, identification of information security managers and key business stakeholders, types and frequency of information security reporting, report distribution channels, and a plan duration and review/revision schedule. Also included, by service, are topics such as security configurations, prevention techniques, detection techniques, correction techniques, and evaluation techniques.

Information Security Management Plan
This is the organizational plan, based on the template above, that – once approved and adopted – specifies how Information Security Management activities will be conducted over a set period of time.

Information security design guidelines
These are guidelines that detail the technical, operational, and support factors that should be considered when designing security needs for specific services.

Information Security Management Information System (ISMIS)
This is some form of automated system (selected based on the needs of the organization) that can be configured as a prime repository for storing and managing information about security designs, security deployment factors, and security monitoring measures.

Information security monitoring and response procedures
These are documented procedures that detail how business services, technical services, and service components will be monitored in the production environment. They also address how security breaches, glitches, and other anomalies will be treated. These procedures typically describe the events to be associated with information security indicators, the thresholds of acceptable performance, identification of the tools that will monitor each event, and descriptions of response activities to be invoked when thresholds are exceeded or threats are realized. These procedures are usually the basis for establishing OLAs between security managers and operations teams.

Information Security Management Measurement Plan template
This template provides a structural guide for creating the organization's Information Security Management Measurement Plan. The template outlines the contents and sections that a properly documented plan should contain (see page XX). Such plans usually identify the following kinds of information: purpose and scope of measuring information security management performance; resources assigned to establish metrics and performance reports; a description of each information security measure, how the data is to be collected, where the data is to be stored, and how data sets are to be analyzed. The plan also documents the type and format of measurement reports and also identifies stakeholders for receiving reports. Measures should be taken of information security performance in operation and also of planning, design, and deployment activities.

Information Security Management Measurement Plan
This is the organizational plan, based on the template above, that – once approved and adopted – specifies how information security measurement activities will be conducted over a set period of time.

Information Security Management reporting and distribution procedure
This is a documented procedure that describes how information security planning, design, and performance reports are created, how often they are generated, and to whom they are to be distributed. This procedure – and the ensuing reports – can be seen as a by-product of the measurement plan described above. Together these artifacts provide for the generation of the kind of information IT management and customer groups need to understand the effectiveness of information security delivery and information security performance in order to identify opportunities for improvement.

Service Level Agreement
Security performance is a service trait so often linked with Service Level Management, the organization should ensure that there is a documented agreement between IT management, service managers, information security managers, and the customer that specifies the levels of performance that will be delivered concerning information security by service.

Monitoring and control tools
The organization will need to acquire and configure a set of tools that can be used in live service operation for monitoring security performance and informing relevant parties when performance indicates the need for intervention.

Organizational chart
This is a chart that shows the structural make-up of the Information Security Management operation. As with other organizational charts, the purpose is to identify teams, team relationships, and hierarchical flows, and so the chart's shape will depend on the organizational units and resources you are able to apply to the

program. Most organizational charts of this sort are simple and basically linear. At the top, perhaps, there is a dotted box representing the Service Managers. This extends down to a box for the Information Security Manager. Below this might be two groups: Information security analysts and operation analysts. A dotted line from the Information Security Manager box might extend to a parallel support spot for the Information Security Management Process Owner (if this role is separate from the Information Security Manager). This chart may be service-specific or combine a set of service offerings.

Roles and responsibilities matrix

This matrix, an extension of the organizational chart, describes the various roles and responsibilities the organization has assigned to support Information Security management activities. The roles typically include such positions as Information Security Management Process Owner, Information Security Manager, information security analysts (designers and developers), and (in tangential roles) operations analysts and senior IT management. Along with the job role definitions there should be descriptions of the responsibilities each role should account for, and references to how different roles interrelate and communicate. The matrix might take one of several forms: a spreadsheet, a series of database records, or a version-controlled text document. Ownership of this artifact is usually shared between IT management and Human Resource management.

9. Change Management

Change is a permanent characteristic of any IT environment. Business climates shift, service needs evolve, new technologies emerge. IT as a discipline may strive for stability, but as a function it is dynamic, and will remain dynamic. The philosophy of IT Service Management recognizes technology's continual evolution, so ITIL has made the ability to respond to change an important part of its framework. If you look at the structure of ITIL – with its five lifecycle phases – you will see that the assumption of change is embedded into each. Strategy, design, transition, operation, and improvement offer a clear cycle of change and provide a framework for ensuring that IT operations continually remain aligned with the needs of the business. An appreciation for change can be said to be an important trait of any IT Service Management program. It is the impetus by which services ultimately are controlled. That, of course, begs the question: How then is change managed?

ITIL provides an answer to this with its Change Management process. To begin this discussion let us begin with what ITIL means by the term 'change.' The ITIL definition of change is:

"...the addition, modification, or removal of authorized, planned, or supported services or service components and their associated documentation."

Here lies a point of interpretation. ITIL recognizes that Change Management may be invoked even when a work product is not moving into production. For example, if a capacity design that was delivered to developers has to be revised to fit some new-found technical need it is possible to manage this by creating a formal change request and invoking change control procedures. This is a valid approach, but it is not the most common one. In these kinds of pre-production cases, IT organizations tend to use the technique of Peer Reviews as a way to review and approve in-progress work products. They tend to engage formal change control only when work products are ready for production. Either approach can work well; look at the needs of your IT organization to determine the path for your program. For the sake of this chapter, however, we'll discuss Change Management in its chief domain, as a quality gate between design/development teams and the live production environment.

This definition logically places Change Management in the set of processes that make up ITIL's Transition phase. This phase is concerned with the orderly transition of new or enhanced services from design and development into live operation.[1] Change Management has been positioned in this phase as a sort of central fulcrum for transition activities. Everything must flow through Change Management before it can be released for operation. Its purpose in this role is that of gatekeeper. In the specification, ITIL offers a more formal purpose. To paraphrase:

The purpose of Change Management is "to provide an approach for the considered and controlled deployment of approved changes into the production environment with as little disruption to the business as possible."[2]

This purpose exists for an important reason: change is risky. If change is not well considered – that is, if it is not thoroughly assessed, intelligently designed, and properly implemented – the integrity of the environment may be placed in jeopardy. The same thing can happen if change is not controlled: if it is not documented, planned, tracked, and monitored. That purpose leads us to the objective of Change Management, which the specification cites as follows:

"The objective of Change Management is to ensure that requests for change are recorded, assessed, authorized, prioritized, planned, tested, implemented, documented, and reviewed in a controlled manner [by an appropriate set of stakeholders.]"[3]

Those elements make up Change Management's consider-and-control components. Another element to consider is the requirement embedded in the objective above, that change is made *"with as little disruption to the business as possible."* Even though change is unavoidable, business operations must take precedence. And when implementation time is available for change, business operations (systems, data, etc.) must be protected.

It is these three components – consideration, control, and continuity – that form the foundation of Change Management. The activities of documenting, assessing, reviewing, controlling, and ensuring all spring from this foundation. And they are realized through the use of an institutional change control workflow. In this chapter we will look at how this workflow operates and what you might wish to establish in order to support the program that operates around it.

It should be noted here, however, that the steps in the change control workflow are not just in place for the sake of Change Management. They support other key Transition processes as well, particularly Service Asset and Configuration Management and Release and Deployment Management. Change Management and Service Asset and Configuration Management (Configuration Management, for short) share a strong reciprocal relationship. The record details contained in the Configuration Management Database System (CMBD) inform change assessments as to the scope, impacts, and design requirements of a request. Conversely, change control activities often trigger subsequent updates to configuration records.

---

2 Foundations of ITIL V3, (2007). Van Haren Publishing.
3 Ibid.

For Release and Deployment Management (Release Management, for short) Change Management provides a set of primary inputs. Release scopes, plans, schedules, and dependencies are all derived from the approved changes that emerge from Change Management decision-making. The success of Release Management deployments can be used as one indicator of Change Management's effectiveness.

In this chapter we will approach Change Management from two perspectives. First we will look at the activities ITIL recommends for the change control workflow. Second, we will look at how an organization might take these recommendations and implement them into a formal program. Let's begin this approach with a look at the activities of the Change Management process.

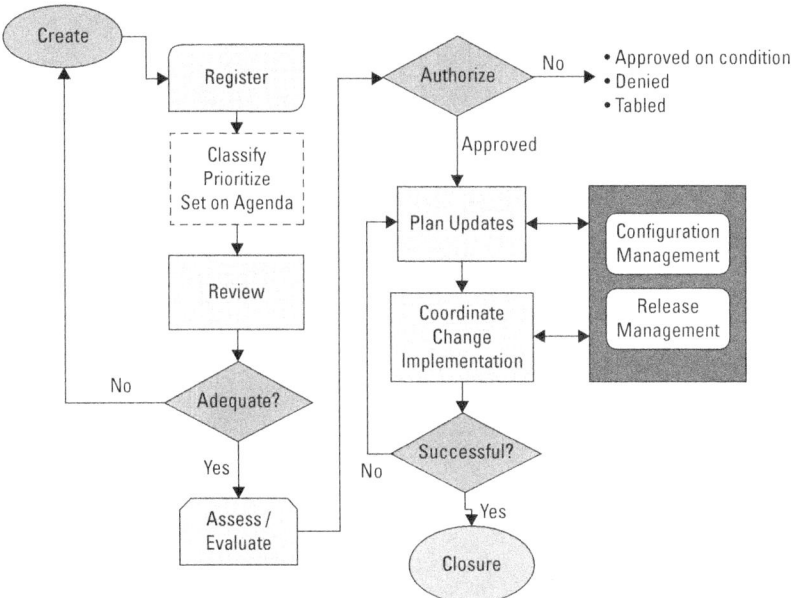

Figure 9.1 Typical Change Management process flow

9.1. Change Management activities

The activities ITIL describes for Change Management are in place to ensure that the objectives for this process area are met. As shown in Figure 9.1 above, the change control workflow is a fairly linear, stepped sequence with each Request for Change (RFC) moving through a series of decision points. With successful passage through each point, the RFC moves closer and closer to production. But before we examine these decision points, let's review some management concepts that are somewhat unique to the domain of Change Management.

The Change Board
Every Change Management program needs some form of Change Board. The Change Board is the body of members that governs the Change Management program. The

Change Board is comprised of organizational stakeholders, ideally both business and technical stakeholders. These members, with additional assistance as needed, are responsible for making decisions about RFCs. They work to ensure that changes are properly understood, that their value is legitimate, and that change decisions meet the needs of the business.

It is advisable that the size of the board should be kept manageable while at the same time accounting for all active services. Members should have the appropriate technical knowledge and authority to decision changes appropriately. The Change Manager chairs the board, sets its agenda, and facilitates RFC reviews. The Change Manager may also (though this is not essential) have special voting or veto powers. In terms of labels, the board can go by any number of names – Change Authorization Board, Change Control Board, Change Advisory Board.

You should charter the Change Board so that it is a formally recognized entity within the organization; reference formal meeting management guides (such as Robert's Rules of Order) as a basis for facilitating change control meetings.

Some organizations charter a Technical Review Board (or Engineering Review Board) in support of the regular Change Board. Technical Review Boards provide engineering insights for changes that are of an especially technical nature.

Types of changes

It is useful in a Change Management program to recognize three broad types of change. Each can be treated by the organization in its own way. The three types (with their common labels) are:

- **Normal change** – this is a change that is not subject to the change control process. In other words it is a request that needs only local approval to be implemented. An example of this is a service request to install a calendar application on a new desktop. Because requests like this fall into the bounds of normal, daily upkeep they are made exempt from Change Management activities.
- **Regular change** – this is a change that is subject to the full change control process. Depending on its size, a request of this type might be subject to one degree of rigor or another. Size is commonly categorized into three levels: Standard, Significant, and Major (see next section).
- **Emergency change** – this is a change that requires expedited attention. It is subject to change control but relies on the use of an Emergency Change Control process, a streamlined version of the regular process.

Size of change

Regular change is the kind that Change Boards deal with most often. Regular changes are requests that are subject to the formal change control process. But even here a further breakdown can be helpful. Not all regular changes are of the same size, and so not all may need to move through the same levels of rigor. Recognizing this, many organizations establish three size categories for regular changes. Here they are with their common labels:

- **Standard change** – changes of this size require only minimal review and assessment. Their approval is rarely in doubt. To accommodate standard changes, the change control process is often streamlined so that the Change Manager alone, or the Change Manager with a few key stakeholders, can deal with the RFC.
- **Significant change** – these are changes that require the normal, full attention of the Change Board and the process. Requests in this category are subject to all baseline review, assessment, approval, planning, and implementation activities.
- **Major change** – changes of this size require focused Change Management attention. Such changes tend to have one or more traits: they require large levels of effort, or they carry with them high risk, or they affect a large segment of the infrastructure. With these changes extra attention is paid to review, assessment, planning, and verification activities.

Managing change emergencies

From time to time the organization will have to deal with emergency changes. Any number of situations may prompt such action - equipment failures, system crashes, data corruption, even the needs of a VIP stakeholder. When such situations arise it is important to have an Emergency Change Control process that can be invoked to manage the emergency. Several assumptions operate in the domain of emergencies; s solution must be immediately implemented; implementation risks will be accepted: and approval need only come from a select management group. An Emergency Change Control (ECC) process is an essential part of any Change Management program. (The role of the ECC is illuminated throughout this chapter.) Some basic tips:

- Define precisely what constitutes a change emergency and communicate this to the organization.
- Establish a formal charter for an Emergency Change Board (ECB).
- Base emergency change control procedures on a streamlined version of the regular process.
- Establish emergency change communication channels.

With these management concepts introduced we can now take a look at the seven activities ITIL defines for the change control process.

1. Create and register the Request

The activities in this first step are in place to establish a request and then submit it to the organization for consideration. There are several implied sub-actions within these steps that may impact how you build your program. The first is that the organization should provide its users with some type of change request form, a template or guide that cues requestors to the types of information and detail that an acceptable request requires. Without such a template, requests will roll in, in no doubt, a variety of styles and degrees of acceptability. A request template can be deployed in a variety of formats, the most basic being a simple paper (or word processing) form. But what most organizations employ is some manner of automated change management tool. And that calls for another organization action – establishing a RFC Management System.

An RFC Management System (RFCMS) is a near-indispensible Change Management tool. Depending on the volume of change in your IT organization it may be the only practical way to track and manage change. In support of the 'create and register' step, a typical RFCMS provides two features. The first is a self-service entry form. This is an online form that users can readily access. With it they can create formal change request records. Designing the content of this record is an important job in establishing a Change Management program. The record should reflect the data elements that your Change Management resources will require to properly assess and make decisions on changes. The following table is provided for your reference. It is not exhaustive, but it is typical of the kinds of elements most IT organizations capture.

Table 9.1 Typical elements in a Request for Change database record

Change ID	A unique ID for the RFC record (usually assigned by the Change Tracking System)
Change Title	A summary description of the change

Description (Reason for Change)	A detailed description of the business and/or technical reasons for the request. (Often, external business justification documents or change proposals may be referenced or attached). Should include:
	    Business need and impacts
	    Technical need and impacts

Status	An activity code for the current working state of the change record
Category	A category code for the request
Priority	A priority code for the request. Typically a derivative based on urgency and impact
Risk	A description of the specific risks associated with the implementation of this change Note: Risks of not implementing the change are covered in the description field above
CIs Impacted	An identification of the Configuration Items that will probably be affected (added, modified, removed) if this request is approved
Level of Effort / Cost	An indicator of the level of effort that may be required to design, develop, test, and implement the change
Return on Investment	An estimate (and explanation) of the ROI that may be expected once the change is operating in production
Submitter	The ID of the person making the request. (May also employ an On-behalf-of field, also)
Submitter Contact	Contact information (e.g. department phone email) of the submitter
Date/Time	A time-stamp for when the change was registered
Service(s)	The ID(s) of the service(s) affected by this RFC
Technical Service Owner(s)	The ID(s) of the technical service owners whose services are affected by this RFC
Business Service Owner(s)	The ID(s) of the business service owners whose services are affected by this RFC
Assignee	The ID of the change analyst or stakeholders who have been assigned responsibility for this managing this RFC
Release	An indicator of the release this change has been approved for

Once the request has been created it can then be submitted. With a tool this is a simple process, usually the click of a button. The request is then channeled through the system and routed into a pending RFC queue visible to Change Managers.

Your organization may elect to allow users to submit RFCs in other ways too. Some common, non-technical means are:
- Phone calls to the Service Desk (service analysts initiate record creation and submission)
- Faxes to the Service Desk (initial level of detail provided; analyst creates and submits record)
- Emails to management (initial level of detail provided; management creates and submits record)

2. Review the Request

The first official job of the Change Manager and the Change Board members with regard to change control is to review new and pending RFCs. The intention at this step is not to decide on the merits of the request *per se*. That comes later. This step has more to do with quality screening. Change Managers review requests to make sure they are adequately documented, appear technically complete, and make sense from technical and business perspectives - in other words, to make sure they warrant further attention.

A good guide to employ for RFC reviews is a technique known as the "*7 Rs of Change.*" The 7Rs is a series of questions, each of which needs to be well understood before a request can be considered worthy of further consideration. These are the seven:
- Who **Raised** the change? What business or technical domains is the request coming from? Is the requestor a regular user or a VIP? What level in the organization is the request coming from?
- What is the **Reason** for the change? Is this a business or a technical driver? Does the reason appear to be well stated? Is the reason weak or strong? Significant or minor? What are the organizational impacts of the reason? What are the impacts on IT?
- What **Return** is expected from the change? Does it appear that the ROI is realistically formulated? Is the ROI proportionate to the apparent effort? Is there a time-length to the ROI? Might the ROI be exploited in other areas?
- What **Risks** are associated with the change? How risky is the change? What services or service components might be affected? What critical business processes might be affected? If the change fails, how can it be reversed? What damage might failure cause? What processes might need to be interrupted for implementation?
- What **Resources** are required? How much will this change cost? How much time will it take? How many people will be needed for development and other activities? Are special facilities or equipment required? Are these resources available?
- Who is **Responsible** for build, test, and implementation activities? If this change is approved, who will own the work? Can these people take on the job now or will we have to wait? Are the responsible parties technically capable of managing the work? Do the parties have the right tools and facilities needed for the work?

- Which **Relationships** exist between this and other pending or approved changes? Are there other pending or approved requests that might bear on how this one if worked? Is there a risk of redundancy with this RFC? Is there a risk of conflict? Could we process this RFC with other related ones?

One advantage of the 7Rs (or any standardized review technique) is that, being a shared format, it gives Change Managers a tool for achieving common consensus as to the purpose, scope, and general value of a change request. Reviews of this type are typically done separately by individual Change Board members, and then discussed during change control meetings. If a request seems clear and complete the record can be marked accordingly and the RFC can be placed in a queue for later assessment and evaluation. If the Change Managers feel that a certain request is lacking information or not clear enough they can always send it back to the author for additions or revisions.

3. Assess and evaluate the Request

The chief job of the Change Board is to assess and evaluate change requests. Three general sub-activities are helpful here. They are:
- Assign business and technical specialists for impact assessments
- Produce impact assessments
- Evaluate the assessed RFCs

Some RFCs may come to the Change Board fully formed; that is, fully studied and documented. More often than not, though, they arrive in a somewhat reduced form. Requestors simply do not always have the scope of knowledge needed to fully present all aspects of a change. The purpose of an impact assessment is to produce a technical and business study of the change, one intended to make the full benefits and ramifications of a request known. Because impact assessments require people with particular specialties, one task of the Change Manager is to work with the Change Board and with service managers to identify qualified change analysts who can produce the assessments.

Your change program can employ any kind of assessment approach appropriate for your organization. A typical assessment, however, will work to illuminate the following areas:
- Driver/reason for the change
- Scope of the change
- Alternative solutions
- Feasibility of the solutions
- Availability of required resources
- Risks of each alternative
- Dependencies
- Level of effort and estimated costs
- Potential return on investment

Once an assessment is complete, it and the full change request record can be presented to Change Managers for evaluation. Following are some tips on how each facet of a typical assessment might be considered.

Driver / reason – no matter what its size or scope, there should be a clear and compelling reason for any change, and this reason should be clearly stated. If the reason is 'soft' or vague the request may be of questionable value, or it may need to be returned to the author for further refinement.

Scope – the scope of the request needs to be well documented. Focused scope reveals potential impacts and highlights risks. It also ties directly into dependencies and costs. Change Boards should be reluctant to act on RFCs whose scopes appear to be fuzzy or overly broad. And RFCs with scopes that are necessarily large may be deemed to require special, focused attention.

Alternative solutions – there are changes whose solutions are direct and readily identifiable. But for many changes alternative approaches are possible. Alternatives carry with them different risks, costs, benefits, etc. That is why it is important to identify what options may be available for solving a particular problem or implementing a certain change. Change Board members should question RFCs that do not offer any such options, and then consider if the lack of options is warranted, and if the proposed solution is valid.

Feasibility – each solution proposed for a change should be evaluated for feasibility - how practical it is in light of the current environment. Solutions that may promise high efficiency may be prohibitively expensive. Others that might prove to be cost-effective may be overly risky. Judgment on the part of the Change Board is needed here; technical input from the outside might also be welcome. The goal is to avoid impractical solutions and promote effective ones.

Availability – solutions require resources, and in most IT organizations resources are usually limited. It is important to identify what resources will be needed in order to develop and implement the requested change. More important is to identify if these resources will be available when schedules require. If it looks like resources are probably not going to be available, the Change Board may wish to table the change.

Risks – identifying and understanding the risks associated with a change or with the solutions proposed for the change are essential for effective Change Management. When change decisions result in less than brilliant outcomes it is usually because some hitherto unseen risk materialized. Evaluating a change request is largely about evaluating risk. The goal is not to select only risk-free changes. Those kinds of changes are few. The goal instead is to identify and understand risk. If risk can be understood it can be anticipated. If it can be anticipated it can be mitigated. Roll-back plans help to mitigate risk – if things go wrong, a roll-back plan returns the organization to where it was before the change.

Dependencies – a large part of a change request's impact has to do with dependencies and interoperability. IT services often weave in and out of one another. A change to one service may require a change to another. The same is true with individual Configuration Items. The successful operation of one process might preclude adjusting another. Decisions about RFCs cannot be well made until such dependencies are made known and hierarchies of precedence are established.

Level of effort / cost – it is helpful for a change request to carry with it some estimate as to the level of effort and costs that are likely to be required to implement the change. Estimates cannot be taken for fact, but they do serve a useful purpose as indicators of the kind of commitment the change will require. A valuable asset for a Change Management program is standardized estimating algorithm that can be used by assessors when they perform impact analyses.

ROI – the point of all change is to somehow improve the environment. This improvement is the ROI, the return realized from the organization's committing to it. An ROI can be expressed in any number of ways. It can be a cash amount, an estimate of revenues earned or expenses saved. It can be functional benefit, perhaps improved business efficiency. It can even be something as simple as fulfilling a VIP's preference. Whatever form it takes, it does however need to be concrete. If the ROI appears sketchy or is overtly weak, the Change Board might well question its validity.

Based on an evaluation like this, Change Board members can come to a conclusion about the merits of the request and make a decision about the proposed change.

4. Authorize the Change

Once the request has been evaluated and its scope and impacts understood, the Change Board can now issue a decision about it. Depending on the size of the change (and the protocols of your change control procedures) this may involve the Change Manager alone, select members of the Change Board, or all members of the Change Board. Decisions can run the range across five options:
- Request approved as-is, and scheduled for release
- Request approved contingent upon other activity
- Request rejected in current form and returned for further work
- Request denied
- Request tabled for later consideration

Approved RFCs, because they are now headed for development, require some additional administrative steps. The Change Manager (or appointed designate) should update the change record to reflect a status of 'approved.' The fact that this request has been approved should be communicated to relevant stakeholders. The change itself should be tentatively assigned to a release. And a Forward Schedule of Change should be updated to include the new change. The final step in the change control stream is to assign the change to an ownership team, the team that will begin the work to develop the change into a releasable work product.

5. Plan updates

Here and in Step 6 the change control process begins to merge with Release Management. In this step, Change Management works with Release Managers to begin the process of organizing approved changes into sets that can be grouped into release packages. This topic – and the activities involved in the packaging and scheduling of releases – is addressed in depth in our discussion of Release Management. For more on this see Chapter 11.

6. Coordinate change implementation

In this step the change is transferred to new ownership. The new owner is the team that will now take responsibility for designing, developing, and delivering the solution. In some organizations this may be the particular service manager that this change chiefly affects. It may be the organization's Release Manager. It may be a member of the project management team. The shape of your organization will determine who this party should be. The point is that the Change Manager identifies who the new owner should be, works with the party to communicate knowledge about the change, and then officially transfers responsibility for the change to the new team.

7. Review and close the change

Some time may lag between when a change is approved and when the change is formally closed. Closure comes when production personnel are able to verify that implementation has been successful. For some changes this may be a matter of days; for others, months. In either case the record needs to be tracked and then the Change Manager oversees four final activities:
- Mark the change record as closed (upon confirmation)
- Capture and evaluate metrics
- Release performance reports
- Conduct a Post Implementation Review (PIR)

Marking the change as 'closed' is a way to remove the record from active work queues. It can also be used as a signal to transfer details of work associated with the change into the domains of Release Management or project management. This is now the appropriate time to collect performance measures surrounding activities for this change. Later on this chapter we will look at a series of key performance indicators (KPIs) and critical success factors (CSFs). These are examples of the kinds of measures you may wish to capture for change activity. Measures such as how long a change took to process, what the projected cost is, what size it was, what type it was, etc., provide the kind of information needed to help the organization evaluate program effectiveness. Once the measures have been collected, the data can be analyzed, and the resulting information made ready for performance reports. The reports can then be distributed to those associated with the change, and to those associated with overseeing Change Management in general.

The final step is to conduct a PIR. If you wish, you can do this with every processed change, or you can wait and conduct the PIR after a group of changes have been processed. The PIR is in actuality a performance review. Those associated with the

change (Change Manager, Change Board members, technical contributors, business stakeholders, etc.) meet to discuss how effective management of this change turned out. Four general questions are usually asked in a PIR:
- How effective was our overall handling of this change?
- What went well?
- What went poorly?
- How can we improve on this process the next time around?

Reference material for the PIR includes the change record, any attached material (e.g. impact assessments, estimates), and performance measures.

9.2. Process inputs and outputs

As we discussed at the start of this chapter, the change control process consists of a series of sequentially ordered activities. RFCs are submitted, they are reviewed, they are assessed and then evaluated; finally a decision is made as to their disposition. As with all processes, there are drivers that feed activity initiation and drivers that fuel activity closure. Below are descriptions of the inputs, entry criteria, outputs, and exit criteria usually associated with a Change Management process.

Entry criteria
The Change Management process is typically started by the occurrence of a single key event:
- A member of the organization submits an RFC requesting a change to the environment or to material that supports the environment.

Inputs
There are typically two modes of input that are derived from the entry criteria and inform the Change Management process. They are:
- Request for Change record
- Additional business justification as required

NOTE: In addition to the above inputs there are some triggers that can start the change control process. These triggers include:
- Problem reports
- Statutory or regulatory mandates
- Strategic changes
- Improvement recommendations
- New customer requirements

Exit criteria
Completion of the Change Management process will be signaled by the occurrence of two events:
- The RFC has been duly processed
- The RFC has been denied, or tabled

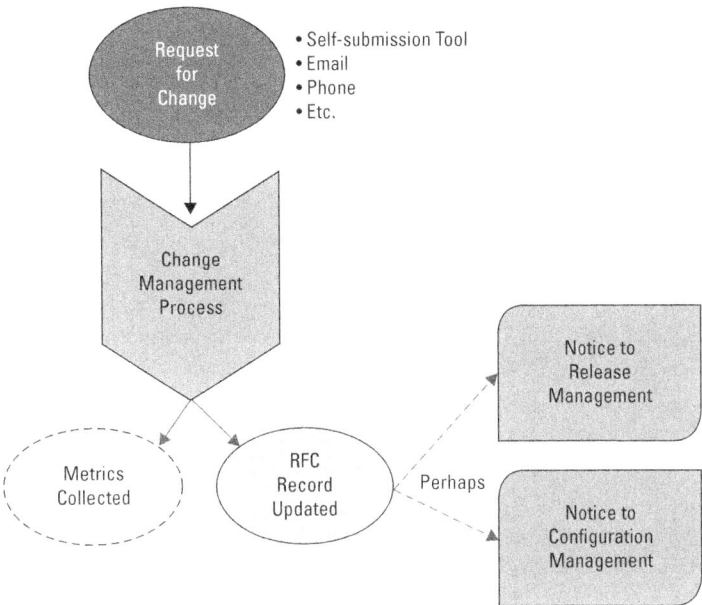

Figure 9.2 Inputs and outputs for Change Management

Outputs

Completion of the exit events above will result in a single discrete output:
- A duly-processed RFC (Approved/Denied/Tabled) record

NOTE: In addition to the completed RFC, the process may also result in some related outputs. These might include:
- Updated Forward-Schedule-of-Change
- Update notifications to Configuration Management
- Updates to problem records
- Purchase orders for new assets

9.3. Processes related to Change Management

Due to its focus and nature, Change Management has the potential to affect just about every facet of a Service Management program, from capacity designs to knowledge-base content, to process improvements. If it is an item that needs to be controlled it falls within the scope of Change Management. There are three ITIL processes, however, that share direct and active relationships with Change Management. Two of these – Configuration Management and Release Management – facilitate the record-keeping and deployment actions that are driven from Change Management decisions. The third – Service Level Management – reflects the performance outcomes expected to be realized once approved changes have been placed into production. The scope and needs of all three of these should be taken into consideration when building a Change Management program. Below is a brief description of each.

Service Asset and Configuration Management

Service Asset and Configuration Management (Configuration Management in short) is in many ways a record of, among other things, change activity. So much so that some service models (like CMMI) combine it with Change Management into a single process. Just as Change Management has the potential to alter any configuration item, Configuration Management is required to keep a history of those changes. Outputs from the Change Management process (approved changes) are inputs into Configuration Management (new assets acquired; existing assets changed). This flow works the other way, too. Outputs from the Configuration Management process (updated CI records) are inputs into change request assessment activities. Analysts use the CMDB as a source to determine how a change might affect current configurations.

In defining a Change Management program, IT managers should appreciate the close relationship between these processes. To make Change Management as effective as it might be, management should work to shape change and configuration procedures to work in harmony, and align change and configuration stakeholders to operate in a collaborative manner. (For more on this topic, see Chapter 10.)

In summary:
- Change analysts rely on the CMDB as a primary reference for RFC assessments.
- Configuration analysts rely on RFC assessments to inform them about any upcoming updates to the CMDB due to upcoming change implementations.
- Configuration managers are likely candidates to participate as Change Board members, or to attend change control meetings as relevant stakeholders.

Release and Deployment Management

There is a very thin line between where Change Management ends and Release and Deployment Management (Release Management in short) begins. Change Management provides the primary inputs into all Release Management activities. Release packages are, at their most basic, collections of approved changes, whether those are new functionality, enhancements, or fixes. Release Management takes these collections, packages them according to business needs, plans their implementation, deploys according to plan, and then verifies success. Often the very stakeholders who were instrumental in defining a change are the ones responsible for setting it into production. This symbiotic dependency requires a coordinated relationship between these two process areas. Change Management can foster this relationship by anticipating release needs in terms of categorizing pending changes, understanding current release schedules, and working with a view toward meeting business expectations. This will help ensure that these teams move synchronously in refining the environment. (For more on this topic, see Chapter 12.)

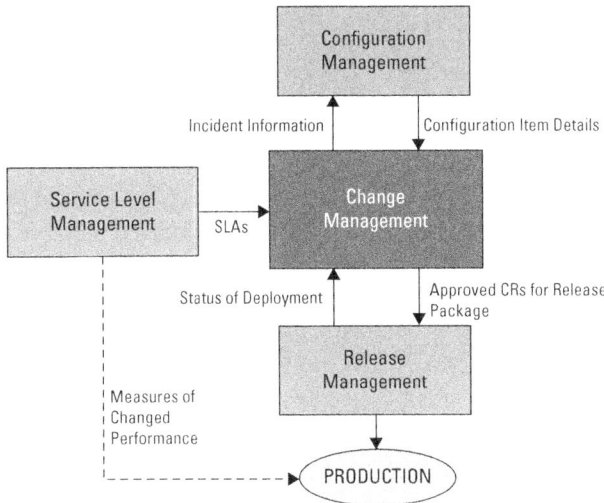

Figure 9.3 Processes and functions related to Change Management

In summary:
- Change Management should work to help time the release of related or dependent changes so they fall into common release packages.
- Change Management should work to help ensure that change approval timing meets business needs in terms of release schedules.
- To assist in release planning, Change Management should provide Forward Schedules of Changes to release managers.
- Release Managers are likely candidates to participate as Change Board members, or to attend change control meetings as relevant stakeholders.

Service Level Management

Change Management and Service Level Management are closely related but, unlike Configuration Management and Release Management, the relation – while distinct and important – is a little more indirect. The job of Service Level Management is to set performance targets for the organization, targets that govern service delivery and service quality. Change Management activities carry the potential to affect these targets and therefore need to support them. Production changes that do not contribute to SLA goals might legitimately be questioned, no matter what ROI they promise. In order to keep change control decision-making in line with SLAs, Change Managers should reference baseline SLAs as a primary source for assessing RFCs. RFCs that show relevance for contributing to SLA targets should take precedence over those that do not.

There is another indirect link, too - not an input or an output but a verification. Once changes have been implemented in the environment, management should measure the performance of reconfigured services. The intention is to verify that the changes have indeed delivered the ROIs associated with them. This provides feedback to

Change Managers as to how effectively change control procedures and decisions are working. (For more on this topic, see Chapter 4.)

In summary:
- Change management should use existing SLAs as a primary reference source when assessing RFCs.
- Measures of adjusted service performance compared to SLA targets can be used to inform service level managers as to the effectiveness of change control activities.
- Service level managers are likely candidates for participation as Change Board members, or to attend change control meetings as relevant stakeholders.

9.4. Tools and techniques

Change Management is not a complex process, nor is it a technical process. It is, if anything, a facilitation process. The Change Manager, together with the Change Board, facilitates a shared and common understanding of change across the organization. This is one area within ITIL that does not really take advantage of established tools or techniques. There are five, however, worth mentioning here. They are noted in the table below and are also discussed elsewhere in this chapter.

Table 9.2 Tools and techniques for Change Management

Request for Change (RFC) Categories	It is often helpful to provide categories or classifications for RFCs; e.g. standard, significant, and major. A 'Standard' RFC may represent a low-impact request and may be able to approved without full Change Board consent. A 'Significant' RFC may represent a change of a certain magnitude and may require careful assessment and full Change Board involvement. A 'Major' RFC may need the fullest of assessments, full Change Board involvement, and perhaps even extended stakeholder involvement.
Regular and emergency change control procedures	Regular change control procedures provide guidelines for conducting planned change control activities (meetings, assessments, approvals, etc.). Emergency change control procedures guide how a streamlined version of the process can be invoked when emergency or priority requests need to be addressed.
RFC tracking and communication system	This is an automated tool used to register, track, analyze, and manage Requests for Change. Most Change Management programs employ some kind of request tracking tool.
Impact assessment guidelines	These are guidelines that change analysts can use to produce impact assessments on change requests in a consistent and repeatable manner.
Forward schedule of change	This is a calendar that keeps track of upcoming releases and the changes associated with each release. It is a management tool to help in both Change Management and release planning.

9.5. Critical Success Factors

The KPIs noted in the following section describe a set of measures that can give management insight into the quality of various change control activities. They provide micro-views of performance. But how might management gain insight into how well a Change Management program is performing at the macro-level? This is where macro-measures can be employed: critical success factors (CSFs). These measures can be used to judge program effectiveness by looking at high-level organizational impacts. Strong CSF measures point to a strong program; weak measures to a program that might need improvement. Below are three sample CSFs that, taken together, can be used to demonstrate how well your Change Management program is operating for your IT organization.

Improved SLA performance

As explained in Chapter 4, an SLA is a contract of performance between the business and IT. SLAs set targets for how services and service support ought to perform. The obligation of the business is to help set realistic targets; IT is then obliged to meet those targets. Quite often it is the case that when targets are not being met change is required. It can be argued that changes should be considered valid for production only when they align with SLAs. What other measure of quality is there? In this light, a good Change Management program should result in SLA measures, more and more, falling within set performance ranges. Because of this the organization should use SLA measures and reports as a way to gauge Change Management effectiveness. If SLA performance is not what it should be, perhaps it is because needed changes are not being introduced, or perhaps it is because ineffective changes are being allowed through. With either case change control activities are involved. IT management is charged with regularly tracking SLA metrics, but it is important to remember to track them with reference to the Change Management program.

Stabilized (or diminishing) operational cost ratios

The effectiveness of a Change Management program can also be glimpsed by periodically monitoring operational cost ratios. Effective Change Management should contribute to enhanced operational effectiveness and efficiencies – an improved environment being one whose costs are proportionately in line with the mix of services being tendered. Senior management should evaluate operating costs over time with a view toward assessing the effectiveness of changes. If a Change Management program is working as intended, operating costs relevant to service support, should show a trend of stabilizing or (ideally) diminishing. If the ratios are pointing the other way, if efficiencies are declining, then the cause might well be found in the direction of change in the environment. Of course there are factors other than change that might affect these ratios, but change activity is certainly a significant influence in itself, and thus one that management should regularly account for.

Improved customer satisfaction

Measuring customer satisfaction levels regularly provides an IT organization with this third critical success factor. A well-run Change Management program will be shaped to address changes to the environment that are most important to meeting the customer's service delivery and service quality expectations. The result from this should be improved service operation. Falling or low customer satisfaction levels can be an indicator that Change Management is not working well; that customers perceive IT performance as being below the required standard, that the environment is not evolving in the right direction. Rising and high customer satisfaction levels point the opposite way. The improved SLA performance and stabilized operational traits noted above are evidence that IT Service Management is operating at cost-effective levels, and this means that change control is probably working well. With smooth, efficient IT operations, customers' views of IT's value to the business tend to rise, and with that, customer satisfaction levels tend to rise also.

9.6. Key Performance Indicators

Measuring the performance of a Change Management program is important for two main reasons. First, the change control process acts as a gatekeeper for new or enhanced operational functionality. It is through change control that the infrastructure is refined, improved, and extended. Second, this gatekeeper function is closely associated with cost. Functionality and cost are factors that drive IT management, and so in order for an IT Service Management program to be effectively controlled it needs to be measured. Defining and then using a set of KPIs is a good way to start down that road. Following are five KPIs commonly found in many typical Change Management programs.

Number of RFCs by category and type for a given period

This measure gives a picture of the volume of changes the organization must deal with for a given period. The count is of the total number of change requests received over a given period. These counts can include RFCs that were approved, denied, or tabled for later consideration. The data can be further broken down by category, type, and even submission route. This data gives management an insight into operational stability. If RFC volumes are disproportionately high, chances are there are issues with service delivery and service quality. If the volumes are comfortably stable or low, this is probably an indicator that user communities are generally content with service performance.

Number of RFCs pending implementation

This measure is a count of the total number of RFCs that have been approved but have not yet been deployed into the production environment; it is a look at upcoming workloads. One of the key jobs of Change Management is to align itself closely with Release Management to schedule timely releases of new or enhanced functionality. This typically stems from the organization's project work. Change Management then should keep a close eye on the pending RFC volumes. If they rise too high or too quickly, resources might not be available to focus on deploying project work in a balanced manner; that is, in a way that groups related changes into common, focused releases.

Cost of implementing approved RFCs for a given period

Change Management is an important gatekeeper not just for new operational functionality but for cost as well. This measure is a look at the costs associated with implementing approved changes over a set period (e.g., a fiscal quarter). Tangible costs are associated with any approved change. Contributions from people, equipment, and facilities may all be required. It is important that these costs are captured and tracked. Properly allocating costs to high value RFCs is key for effective IT Service Management. Change Management, being the fulcrum of RFC information and approval, is the appropriate function to track and manage these costs. This data will also help form the basis of assessing the realization of potential ROIs associated with RFCs (see the following KPI).

Anticipated RFC ROIs versus actual RFC ROIs

As we have noted earlier in this chapter, one attribute that should be attached to every RFC is an estimate of potential ROI – return on investment. In its purest sense, an RFC is a request to improve the environment, in a way that will improve the business. The better the organization is at capturing ROI the better will it be at Change Management. With this measure, the change control process captures estimated ROI early on and then, when the RFC is deployed, Service Operation personnel measure the changed performance to capture actual returns. This data can then be channeled back to Change Management, analyzed, assessed, and reported on. This data can be used to help assess the true effectiveness of changes, and to gauge the effectiveness of Change Management activities.

SLA performance measures for changed services

In the ROI-related KPI above the organization is looking at the value that an RFC or set of RFCs can deliver to the business once implemented. This measure is similar in spirit. It is a comparison of service level performance over time, with the view being to see if SLA targets after RFC deployment have improved, regressed, or remained the same. This metric can be seen as a sub-analysis of broader SLA measures. The expected trend line, of course, would be to see a direct correlation between RFC implementation and SLA performance. If improvements materialize, change activities are probably properly focused. If they do not, management may wish to investigate RFC creation, review, and decision-making protocols.

9.7. Change Management roles

In terms of industry depth, Change Management is one of IT industry's more mature and prominent processes. Most IT organizations, whether they are following standards or not, practice it in some way, so the roles associated with Change Management have been somewhat standardized over time. The following four roles are usually accounted for in some way in a Change Management program. As with other ITL processes, and depending on the size and focus of the organization, these roles may be full-time or part-time; combined or shared by multiple individuals. View the job titles and responsibilities described below as starting points for devising your own job descriptions.

Change Management Process Owner

The Change Management Process Owner is the person responsible for the use and performance of the activities associated with the Change Management program. Most commonly this person is the same as the Change Manager, but this is not essential. The Change Management Process Owner champions the purpose and goals of Change Management within the organization and ensures that the program remains in a state of operational effectiveness, one that will contribute to the overall IT and business missions of the company. To summarize, the Change Management Process Owner is responsible for:

- Developing and documenting the program
- Implementing the program across relevant teams
- Coordinating program training and mentoring
- Monitoring ongoing program use
- Measuring program performance over time
- Soliciting and coordinating program improvements

Change Manager

The Change Manager is responsible for coordinating the use of the change control program for a service or a set of services. There may be multiple Change Managers in any one IT organization or a single one; the key is to ensure that no service is left unaccounted for. The main job of the Change Manager is to unite technical stakeholders and business stakeholders in the orderly and considered evaluation of change requests. The Change Manager uses the change control process to ensure this happens on a scheduled and consistent basis. The Change Manager also works to ensure that proper communications surrounding RFC status is maintained, and also works closely with Release Management and Configuration Management with regard to the ongoing integrity of the environment. To summarize, the Change Manager is responsible for:

- Planning and organizing change control activities
- Planning and coordinating change control meetings
- Tracking status of active RFCs
- Ensuring the proper assessment of current RFCs
- Communicating change control meeting agendas and outcomes
- Ensuring the integrity of the Request for Change Management System
- Communicating approved RFCs to Release Management
- Communicating approved RFCs, as necessary, to Configuration Management

Meeting facilitator / scribe

Sometimes an organization will appoint meeting facilitators and scribes to work with the Change Manager as change control meetings are conducted and followed up. The facilitator's job is to host the meeting and keep its focus on track. The scribe's job is to take meeting minute notes and maintain a history of these notes over time. To summarize, the facilitator/scribe is responsible for:

- Facilitating change control meetings
- Taking change control meeting minutes
- Distributing meeting minutes to stakeholders
- Maintaining a history of meeting minute logs

Change Board members

As mentioned earlier in this chapter, the Change Board should be made up of a mix of IT and business stakeholders. (Just what that mix is you will need to decide for your own organization.) The members of the Change Board have three main jobs: review RFCs in light of potential organizational value; make decisions about RFCs (i.e., Approved, Denied, Tabled); and prepare their service teams for the eventual roll-out of approved requests. Those jobs place the Change Board members at the heart of the change control process. The Change Manager may govern the process, but it is the work of the Change Board membership that makes it effective. To summarize, Change Board members are responsible for:

- Representing customer interests with regard to RFCs
- Representing technical interests with regard to RFCs
- Active participation in change control meetings
- Providing input at to RFC ROIs, risks, impacts, etc.
- Appropriate follow-up to RFCs that affect Change Board member domains

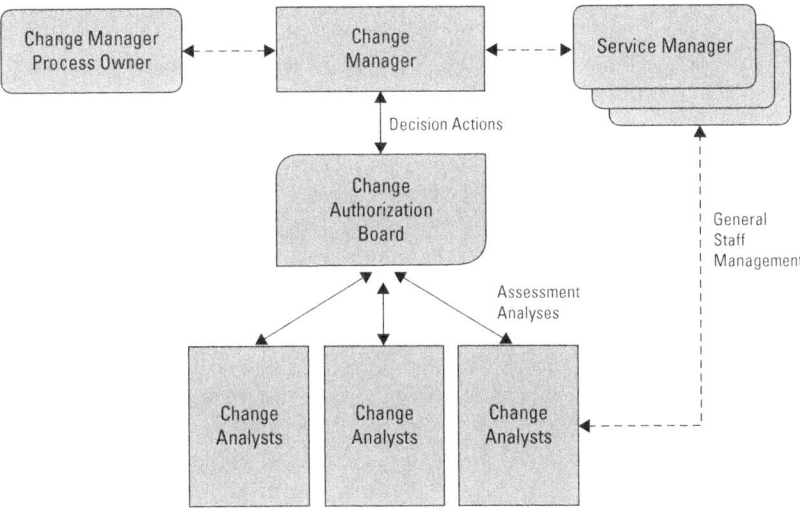

Figure 9.4 Change Management role relationships

Human Resource considerations

The following are some typical traits that Human Resource staff may want to take into consideration when they are providing personnel, tools, and other resources for a Change Management program.

Managerial experience and background: Change Managers should have an adequate technical background in order to facilitate and comment on the viability of change requests. They should have experience of organizing and mobilizing RFC review, assessment, and tracking activities. Change Managers should also have experience in team management as well as meeting organization and facilitation.

Comfort working in a process-centric environment: Change Management staff and Change Board members should be comfortable working in a process-centric environment, and should be open to learning about the organization's program and contributing to its ordered growth.

9.8. Benefits of effective Change Management

An ITIL-based Change Management program has the potential to benefit the organization in tangible ways. But the chief way – the way the others lead up to – is by protecting the integrity of the infrastructure. When change occurs willy-nilly, when it is not well planned or not well designed, the production environment can be negatively affected. Events, incidents, and problems can all become magnified. Though there are few statistics available, many IT professionals would probably identify disorganized change as one of the chief sources of IT service problems. With a Change Management program, however, disorganization moves to organization. Quality gates are set into place. Assessment and agreement become the norm. And the benefits begin to appear. Following are three such benefits that a Change Management program can deliver.

Managed (and responsible) control of the infrastructure

The infrastructure itself is the single most important asset of any IT Service Management program. And the top job of IT service managers is to see that this infrastructure remains operational and stable for the business. At the same time, IT infrastructures can be (and most usually are) highly complex environments, environments that are required to change over time. This complexity and dynamism can make a service manager's job challenging. Change Management is one way to ensure that the operation and evolution of the IT environment is attended to in a planned, orderly, and responsible way. Change control activities are intended to guard the integrity of the infrastructure. A well-designed Change Management program will make sure that no production changes are introduced without previous awareness and approval by both business and technical stakeholders. A Change Management program can serve in a very real way as a conduit for establishing contracts of agreement between IT and the business, and that is a highly responsible way for overseeing any enterprise.

Better planning and forecasting

Change Management, by its very nature, is a proactive process. Because of this, organizational planning is directly enhanced with the implementation of a Change Management program. Well-followed change control practices (in close conjunction with Configuration Management and Release Management practices) will over time provide the organization with an accurate and complete picture of the infrastructure. At the same time these practices will provide a thoroughly assessed and documented pipeline of what's to come – a forward calendar of change. Because Change Management fosters cross-organizational stakeholder participation and ongoing communications, common expectations can be established, and cost, resource, schedule and other needs can be shared and understood well in advance of action. Forecasting is also enhanced because the organization now has an agreed-upon repository of what it wants to roll out into production, with the characteristics of the items in this repository having already been thoroughly identified and assessed.

Improved IT and business performance

In the end, the overall results of effective Change Management should be evident in improved IT performance, reliability, and stability. Well-considered changes backed by well-controlled change, strengthens the IT environment. Defects and weaknesses are removed. Operational effectiveness is increased. New functionality is added. As IT service performance rises it follows that business efficiencies increase, too. Out of this should emerge stronger business results. That lasting business impact represents the major goal of any IT Service Management program: to further the missions of the business. IT plays its part in this goal by ensuring that it delivers high quality technical services and business services, and does so in a dependable and reliable manner. Change Management, acting as a quality gate into production, is a key player in this service delivery strategy.

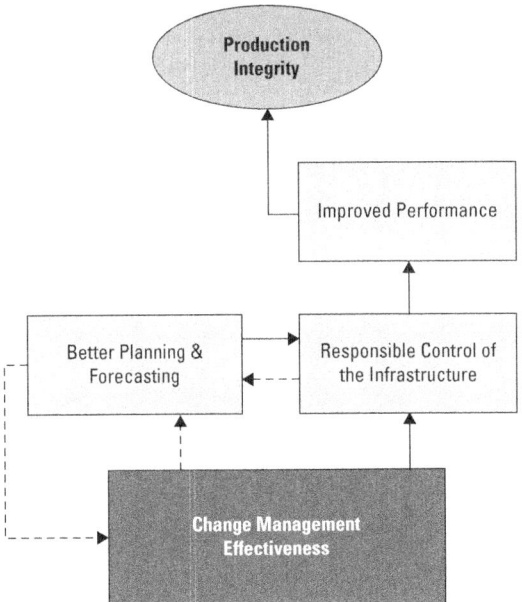

Figure 9.5 Change Management benefits

9.9. Implementation challenges and considerations

The activities that ITIL recommends for Change Management are not particularly complex or complicated. To the contrary, they are fairly straightforward. And yet Change Management as a program can be quite challenging to cement into the organizational culture. There are many reasons for this. For one, people who are used to having a basically free rein when it comes to adjusting the production environment may view change control as an impediment, as a gate that slows their responsiveness and ability to act. If these same people are required to participate in the process – as Change Board members, say – they may see such an assignment as a further drain on their time, one that takes them away from their chief duties. Both of these interpretations, and others that may surround them, are misguided of course. Change control is a gate, but it is a quality gate. And participation should indeed be seen as one of the main duties for service managers. But perceptions can be strong, and when they come from well-intentioned motives they can persist. Part of the effort with implementing a Change Management program will need to be devoted to dealing with such challenges. Toward that end, here is a set of four common challenges that you may find yourself facing when you move to implement your own Change Management program:

Realizing full participation in the process

For any Change Management program to be successful it must have full and active participation from its stakeholders. Passive representation will do little for the program and may easily lead to poor decision-making. But realizing full participation can be a real challenge for many IT organizations. Busy staff and managers may find it difficult to set aside what they might consider to be immediate concerns in order to participate in a more routine activity. If this perception is left unaddressed any Change Management program will weaken over time. It helps if senior IT management can engage with relevant stakeholders from both technical and customer teams and actively promote their participation in Change Management activities. It helps also if senior business management and senior IT management communicate the importance of this participation to the whole organization. Especially early on in program adoption, the level of participation should be closely monitored.

Sealing the back door

In organizations with minimal Change Management procedures, it is very common to see changes introduced by circuitous routes - routes that tend to skirt whatever process is in place. This is known in the industry as a 'back door' change. One of the biggest challenges when implementing a Change Management program is making sure that this back door is closed, locked, and sealed. Back door routing is unfortunately a common occurrence even in mature organizations. Associates who work well together work to support each other; they want to help each other out, do each other favors. It's a mark of *esprit de corpse*. Often one manager will come to another and ask that a change is allowed to detour the process, to slip around it for expediency's sake. Many reasons are given. This is a special, one-time need. It's a particular emergency.

It's just a 'little' change. And often the other manager gives in. This however is a risky business. And over time its practice will weaken a Change Management program. The best approach to deal with this may seem simplistic but it does work: executive communications. Senior IT management need to stress the importance of change control activities across its various teams, and it needs to support the Change Managers and the Change Board even when it might *appear* that important work is being delayed or that too much attention is being paid to procedural issues.

Properly assessing RFCs

The goal with any RFC is that its implementation will, in some way, make the environment a better place: faster, safer, handling more capacity, etc. This is the RFC's ROI, its potential for improved operational efficiency. In order to quantify this potential, RFCs need to be assessed. The job of coordinating this assessment typically falls to Change Management, and specifically to the members of the Change Board. The challenge is that it is not always easy to determine ROI. In complex or highly integrated environments this can be an especially tricky thing do. At the same time however, it is an essential thing to do. Off-the-mark evaluations can lead to production changes that bring no real value to the company; or worse, set the company back. So the challenge comes with establishing some approach for factoring a reliable ROI. In light of this the best path to take is for the organization to provide stakeholders in the Change Management process with documented guidelines on how to assess RFCs against aspects such as size, criticality, level of effort, impact, risk, cost – and ROI. This will at least provide a way for consistently assessing RFCs. And though it may not be perfect out of the gate, being formularized, it can be refined over time.

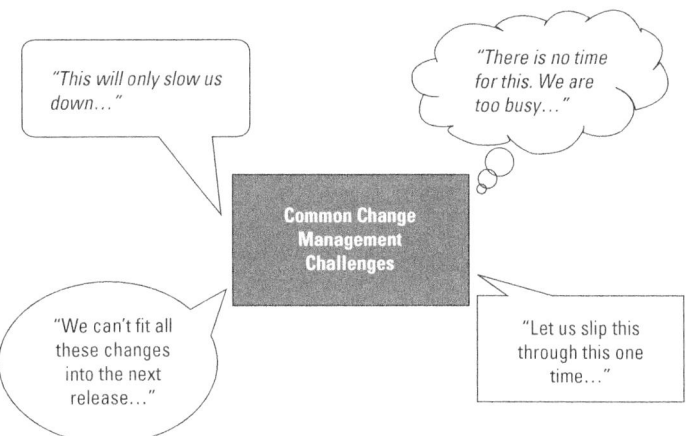

Figure 9.6 Change Management challenges and considerations

Balancing approved changes with release schedules

The close relationship required between Change Management and Release Management is important. But it can be a difficult one to achieve. The challenge comes with balancing the flow of changes between both of these organizational activities. And there can be a conflict here, too. Change Management's objective may be to drive major or high priority changes into the release in one 'basket'. Release Management typically prefers grouping related or complementary changes into a single deployment effort. Trying to fit a full set of these into a single design, test, and deployment cycle may be difficult for a Change Management program. While this challenge may not ever fully vanish, organizations should work to look at their volume of changes, the dynamism of the environment, and their available resources, and then synchronize their Change Management and Release Management programs so that they accommodate one another as well as possible.

Challenges and considerations face anyone implementing a Change Management program. Stakeholders may feel they do not have time to participate in the process. Others may think that the process will slow down work progress. There may be perceptions of an imbalance between approved changes and release bandwidth. And some may continuously try to circumvent the process.

9.10. Typical assets and artifacts of a Change Management program

A set of documented assets and artifacts will need to be created in support of your Change Management program. Assets are the program materials that bound the way the program is governed and run. Artifacts are those work products that emerge when operation teams engage in program activities. Following is a list of some common assets and artifacts that you would find in a typical Change Management program. While your program may require some of these, you will probably wish to create some things not described here; but this list, while not exhaustive, is typical.

Change Management policy
This is an executive policy that stipulates the goals and objectives of the Change Management program. The policy, which ideally should be no longer than a few pages, documents at a high level the purpose of the program, the resources available to the program, the chief responsibilities of the program, quality targets, reporting hierarchies, and program measures. Endorsed by executive management, the policy is a demonstration of organizational commitment to the value and importance of the Change Management program.

Change Advisory Board (CAB) charter
This charter is an official document that defines the purpose and role of the Change Advisory Board (Change Board or equivalent title) as an arm of Change Management. A charter of this kind typically includes details of CAB membership, who is eligible for appointment, how long they should serve on the board, what authority each member has, CAB meeting frequency, quorum rules, decision-making rules, communication channels, reporting requirements, and so on.

Change control process
This is a process that details the workflows inherent in the Change Management program. Establishing this process in an effective way is important. It will serve as the heart of the Change Management program. The process defines how all change control activities work. Such a process would usually define separate flows for degrees of change: standard changes, significant changes, and major changes. The process would also describe entry criteria, exit criteria, inputs, and outputs. And the process would identify the people needed to execute each defined activity. The process might also be supported by lower level procedures or work instructions.

Request for Change submission and tracking system
This asset is a system that technical and business users can use to submit RFCs for consideration to the Change Board. This system can also be used to update, status, and track RFCs over time. Systems of this kind are typically automated and play a central role in how change control is managed. The Change Manager will rely on the tool as a means for managing RFC status and Change Board meeting agendas. Change Board members will use the tool to update and review RFCs. And IT management will rely on the system to gain views into workloads, Change Management performance, and to collect change control measures.

RFC assessment guidelines
Guidelines for assessing newly submitted requests help Change Management stakeholders assess RFCs in a consistent manner. All requests need to be assessed for a variety of characteristics: size, criticality, complexity, risk, cost, ROI, and so on. If the assessments are done in a subjective or loose manner, the results may be off target; and change control, when performed by the book, may not be wholly effective. Because assessments are important to managing change properly, assessment guidelines give the Change Manager and the Change Board a tool that bounds RFC considerations, can be shared amongst members, and can be refined over time to further prove its value to the organization.

Forward schedule of change
This is a calendar that keeps track of upcoming releases and the changes associated with each release. It is a management tool to help in both Change Management and release planning.

Change Management Measurement Plan
Periodic performance measures are needed if a Change Management program is to be effectively controlled. The Change Management Measurement Plan is a tool for doing that. It identifies and defines the metrics to capture in order to assess the performance of change control activities. A typical plan will describe the set of measures, define how to collect them, stipulate where the collected data is to be stored, and provide formulae for analyzing the data. The measures you select for this plan will depend naturally on the needs of your IT organization, but the critical success factors (CSFs) and the key performance indicators (KPIs) described in this chapter may be

helpful examples of the kinds of measures you may wish to set up for your Change Management program.

Change Management reporting and distribution procedure
This is a documented procedure that describes how change control reports are created, how often they are generated, and to whom they are to be distributed. This procedure can be seen as an extension of the Change Management Measurement Plan described above. Together these artifacts provide the kind of information needed by IT management and customer groups to understand the effectiveness of change control activities and identify opportunities for improvement.

Organizational chart
This is a chart that shows the structural make-up of the Change Management operation. As with other organizational charts, its purpose is to identify teams, team relationships, and hierarchical flows. The shape of this chart will naturally depend on the general shape of your organization, and your Change Management program. Most organizational charts of this sort tend to be fairly simple. The box for the Change Manager is at the top. A dotted line extends to a parallel spot for the Change Management Process Owner (if this role is separate from the Change Manager). Below the Change Manager are two groups: the Change Board members (technical and business) and, supporting these, the facilitator/scribe roles. Sometimes it is also helpful to have a dotted line extending from the Change Manager at the top to Service Managers off in another parallel spot – but usually Service Management is covered by the Change Board membership.

Roles and responsibilities matrix
This matrix is an extension of the organizational chart. It is a matrix that describes the various roles and responsibilities the organization has assigned to support the Change Management program. The roles typically include such positions as Change Manager Process Owner, Change Manager, meeting facilitator, meeting scribe, and Change Board members. Along with the job role definitions there should be descriptions of the responsibilities each role should account for, and references to how roles interrelate and communicate. The matrix might take one of several forms: a spreadsheet, a series of database records, or a version-controlled text document. Ownership of this artifact is usually shared between IT management and Human Resource management.

10. Service Asset and Configuration Management

One could convincingly argue that no IT Service Management program can be effective without a robust Service Asset and Configuration Management program. The reasoning is pretty straightforward. Services cannot be intelligently managed if service configurations are not understood and available. When thinking about operation processes such as Incident Management and Problem Management there is a heavy reliance on configuration information. ITIL's set of design processes are the same way. Service Level Management, at the core of a Service Management program, does little more than provide performance targets against current configurations. In fact, an organization's IT infrastructure is nothing more than a collection of service components – technology assets –configured in a particular way. Managing technology assets, and how those assets are configured, provides the foundation for this ITIL process.

ITIL defines Service Asset and Configuration Management as:

"...a method to provide a logical model of the IT infrastructure. In this model IT services are related to the different IT components needed to supply business and technical services. The model is detailed down to the service component level."[1]

The purpose of Service Asset and Configuration Management is described as follows:

"To identify, control and audit the information required to manage IT services by defining and maintaining a database of controlled items, their status, lifecycles and relationships and any information needed to manage the quality of IT services cost effectively."[2]

Service Asset and Configuration Management is really about two closely related but separate tasks. In many organizations you will find that this process is built as two independent but welded programs.

Service Asset Management deals with equipment that is typically not 'live'; that is, in inventory, not having been released yet into production. Asset Management controls how this inventory is acquired, tagged, tracked, released, and then (eventually) recovered. Because Asset Management can be so capital-intensive it is not uncommon for this part of the program to be largely controlled by an organization's purchasing or accounting departments; it is closely linked to financial requirements. In many

---
1 Foundations of ITIL. (2007). Van Haren Publishing
2 Ibid.

organizations, especially large or mature ones, Asset Management is an already well-defined discipline.

Configuration Management deals with equipment that is typically 'live'; that is, assets in live operation and configured to support the delivery of IT services. Configuration Management deals with how baseline descriptions of equipment configurations are controlled and maintained as Configuration Items (CIs). It is through Configuration Management that a logical view of the infrastructure is established. It is also through Configuration Management that this logical view is periodically reconciled with the physical environment.

Service Asset and Configuration Management has strong ties to Change Management and Release and Deployment Management. All three of these ITIL processes are presented as part of the Service Transition lifecycle phase. They work together to help ensure the smooth transition of new or enhanced services from design and development teams into live operation. Let's begin the discussion of ITIL area by looking at the activities associated with the process.

NOTE: For the sake of brevity, throughout the rest of this chapter we will refer to Service Asset and Configuration Management simply as Configuration Management.

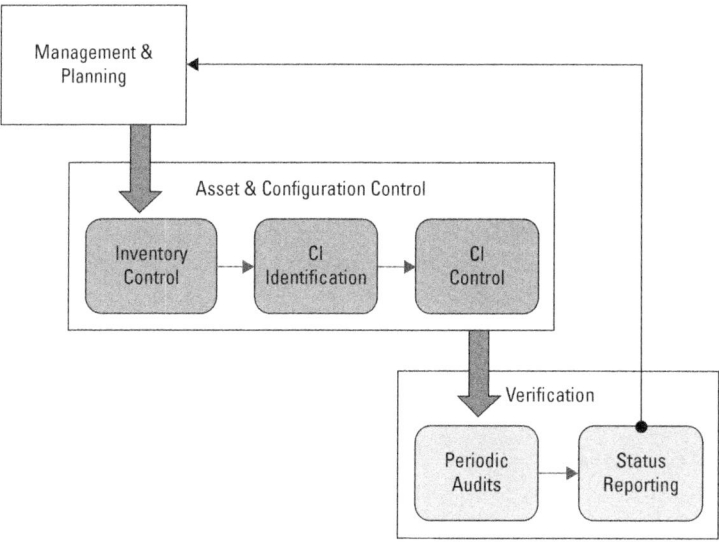

Figure 10.1 Typical Configuration Management process flow

10.1. Configuration Management activities

Configuration Management is a continual activity within an IT organization. If IT environments were static, stable places the task of Configuration Management would be clear and relatively easy. But IT environments are not such places. They are dynamic; they are constantly evolving. And so the task of Configuration Management

takes on significant importance. In order to manage change and shape workplace evolution intelligently, IT management must have a firm grip on the current shape of the infrastructure. That is what Configuration Management provides. As a workflow it consists of five general steps, which sub-activities indicated for each step. The five steps are:
- Management and planning
- Configuration identification
- Configuration control
- Status accounting and reporting
- Verification audit

Here is a brief description of each.

1. Management and planning
Establish a Configuration Management Plan. Because Configuration Management is a controlled activity it needs to be planned. Configuration management can be done on several levels. It can be performed at the organizational level. It can be performed at the service level. It can even be performed at the component level if that is practical for your IT organization. Whatever level you select, the shape of the shape of the plan will be generally consistent. At its base level a Configuration Management plan should contain the following:
- A statement defining the mission of the Configuration Management program within the organization.
- Identification of the services and CIs that will be managed under the plan.
- A description of the ways in which Configuration Management activities will interrelate and collaborate with Change Management activities.
- A description of the inputs that will be required for the various Configuration Management process activities.
- A description of the outputs that will be required for the various Configuration Management activities.
- A procedure or rule that defines how service managers will determine when configuration updates are needed.
- A procedure or rule that defines how service managers will inform configuration managers as to the need for configuration updates.
- A schedule stipulating when configuration audits will be conducted.
- A table or list identifying the staff and roles that will support Configuration Management activities.
- Identification of the CMDB repository with a description of access policies.
- A table or list identifying the stakeholders (internal and external) that will be involved in Configuration Management activities.
- A plan approval page.

Implement a Configuration Management Database (CMDB). A CMDB is typically the central tool in use by a Configuration Management program. The CMDB is the repository that holds Configuration Records throughout their lifecycle – note that there may be more than one CMDB in use in an organization. The Configuration

Management System maintains one or more CMDBs, and each CMDB stores attributes of CIs, and relationships with other CIs. The CMDB also commonly holds the service maps, diagrams that show how business services, technical services, and service components are linked. The CMDB often has an inventory module, too, through which inventory levels and disbursements are tracked. It is not essential that the CMDB is an automated tool, but for most IT organizations such a tool is indispensible.

Establish policies and procedures. As with all other ITIL processes it is important to provide the documented policies and procedures that people can use to operate safely and effectively within the program's boundaries. This is especially true of Configuration Management. Proper policies and procedures are essential because Configuration Management has direct impacts on service delivery and operational efficiencies. The costs, complexities, and business dependencies associated with the infrastructure are of such a nature that firm and explicit controls are necessary to ensure service integrity. IT management should take ample time to develop these policies and procedures in line with the overall shape of its Configuration Management strategy, plan, and program.

2. Configuration identification

The major task when implementing a new Configuration Management program is identifying and labeling all of the existing CIs in place across the infrastructure. This can be a major effort. And it is a task that remains in place as a key activity even once the program is up and running. Configuration identification is the job of recoding an assets online configuration in the CMDB. It takes a Configuration Management program to its most detailed level. It is these CI records that will comprise together how technical services are composed, and later how business services are composed. Creating the CI records and maintaining them over time is the central responsibility of any Configuration Management program.

NOTE: A Configuration Item (CI) is simply this: a technology asset whose configuration you wish to control. There may be, of course, many, many service components across an IT infrastructure, but you may not need to control every one of them. Hence not every service component needs to be classified as a CI. Part of the strategic task of Configuration Management is to look at your environment and determine what you need to manage and what you don't.

Identify Configuration Items (CIs). Certain CIs (e.g. servers, printers, telephony lines, software, etc.) will prove to be crucial to the delivery of IT services. IT management will want to identify these items and record their descriptions in the CMDB. Typical information attributes include:
- CI ID
- CI Description
- CI Type
- Model Number
- Serial Number

- Version Number
- Manufacturer
- Vendor Contact Information
- Date of Acquisition
- Expiration Date
- Last Date of Servicing
- Location (Building / Floor / Room / Rack)
- Associated Service(s)
- Dependent CIs
- Service Owner
- Service Owner Contact

Create service maps. IT services usually exist in three logical domains: service components, technical services, and business services. Service components combine together to make up technical services. Technical services combine to produce business services. A service map is a diagram showing how services are structured. They are useful because they illustrate the linked nature of IT environments. Service components can be shared across technical services; technical services can be shared across business services; one component may be dependent on another; one service may rely on another. Service maps help make these interrelationships and interdependencies clear. They are an invaluable aid to service design, service development, and troubleshooting service operations, so they need to be maintained with the same level of rigor and attention to detail as CI records.

Provide inventory control. Depending on your organization's current structure for managing capital equipment and handling purchasing activities, this aspect of configuration management may or may not be in IT management's domain. But the basic idea is worth noting. In addition to maintaining records of equipment in active use (the CIs in the database) it is important also to maintain track of equipment that is not in active use; that is, assets that have yet to be placed in operation or have been retired from operation and are awaiting some further disposition action.

3. Configuration control

The key maintenance activity for a Configuration Management program is configuration control. With this step the organization protects the integrity of configuration descriptions by restricting access to the CMDB and authorizing updates only with official approval from Change Management.

Place CIs and service maps under formal Change Control. Configuration item descriptions should only be changed under two conditions: with the approval of a service-related Request for Change (RFC); or when an audit reveals a configuration discrepancy. With both of these situations, Change Management should be involved. Configuration management as an organizational responsibility should always operate under the direct guidance of Change Management (see the following section).

Coordinate with Change Management and Release Management. Configuration Management teams should work with Change Management teams and Release Management teams to ensure that communication about operational deployment flows freely and in a timely manner among these three groups.

4. Status accounting and reporting

Through the activities of Change Management and Release Management, descriptions of any group of CIs are likely to change over time. It is the responsibility of the configuration manager to ensure that change and release actions are accounted for in the CMDB and that any CMDB updates are properly communicated to relevant stakeholders. Two tasks are involved: establishing baselines of configuration information, and reporting on baseline status as it evolves.

Establish and release baselines. Part of the value of a CMDB is that most can be configured to hold a complete history of a CI's past configurations. A user can look to any point in the past and see how an item was set. Such a snapshot is called a baseline and part of the job of the configuration manager is to ensure that baselines are available for access by authorized users of the CMDB. The team should establish business service baselines, technical service baselines, and CI specific baselines.

NOTE: A baseline is an item's current configuration along with any approved changes that have yet to be applied to that configuration. To maintain integrity between the logical and physical environments, baselines should always recognized as the definitive source of configuration information.

Track baseline status. Periodically, and in line with levels of activity around the CMDB, the configuration manager should coordinate the release of status reports noting current CMDB update and management activity. These reports should also announce and identify the release of new baselines. The audiences for these communications are typically service managers, support managers, and operation managers.

5. Verification audit

Periodically it is important for the organization to verify that its logical view of the infrastructure (the CMDB) is aligned with the physical environment. This is what this fifth step accounts for. A verification audit compares the logical model with the physical model and then records the results. If there is a mismatch between the two then either the logical model or the physical environment should be adjusted.

Audit CMDB contents. Auditing the CMDB requires that a team of analysts coordinates the activity across the organization, as inspecting operational equipment may present some degree of service interruption (although that does not always have to be the case). There are three common ways to conduct the audit:
- A select set of records in the CMDB – for a specific service, a specific customer group, etc. –is pulled and then verified in the field.

- A random sample set of records in the CMDB is pulled and then verified in the field.
- The entire CMDB is audited against configurations in the field.

Report audit results. The results of the audit should be sent to relevant IT and business stakeholders. Based on the results, these stakeholders may conclude that the logical and physical environments are aligned, that adjustments need to made to CIs in the environment, or that updates to the CMDB are required.

Providing information for the Configuration Management System (CMS)

The CMDB (or CMDBs) is an important part of the overarching CMS, which is a set of tools and databases that are used to manage the IT service provider's configuration data. The CMS also includes information about Incidents, Problems, Known Errors, Changes and Releases. Depending on its required scope, the CMS may also contain data about employees, suppliers, locations, business units, customers and end-users. The CMS includes tools for collecting, storing, managing, updating, and presenting data about all Configuration Items and their relationships. The CMS is maintained by Configuration Management and is used by all IT Service Management processes.

10.2. Process inputs and outputs

Configuration Management is a process of planning, identification, control, reporting, and auditing – activities that are in place to manage the various components that make up a technology infrastructure. The process is initiated whenever it is necessary to adjust the configuration of the environment or when it is time (as planned) to verify the configuration of the environment. Various inputs may be used to feed this initiation, but when the process runs its course the same work products emerge – configuration records synchronized to the environment, and updated management plans.

Entry criteria

One of three criteria needs to be in place in order to initiate the Configuration Management process. The three (and they may occur individually or in combination) are:
- The Configuration Management Plan indicates that it is time to initiate the Configuration Management process; (or)
- Updates to the infrastructure are being made [equipment installed, reconfigured, or retired]; (or)
- An audit of serviced assets has been requested.

Inputs
A variable set of inputs can be used to support each of the three entry criteria above. Following are the four most common ones:
- Scheduled audit via the Configuration Management Plan
- Purchase / Requisition Order
- Approved RFC (with accompanying technical detail)
- Ad hoc request for an audit

Exit criteria
At the end of the Configuration Management process, the organization has performed some degree of status accounting across the enterprise, sometimes in a limited way, sometimes in an expanded way. Proper closure of the process requires the organization to verify that certain exit criteria have been met. The four common conditions that signal the end of the process are listed below:
- The audit has been completed and results reports distributed
- CI records and service maps in the CMDB have been duly updated
- Equipment has been acquired and checked into inventory or deployed
- The Configuration Management Plan has been duly updated

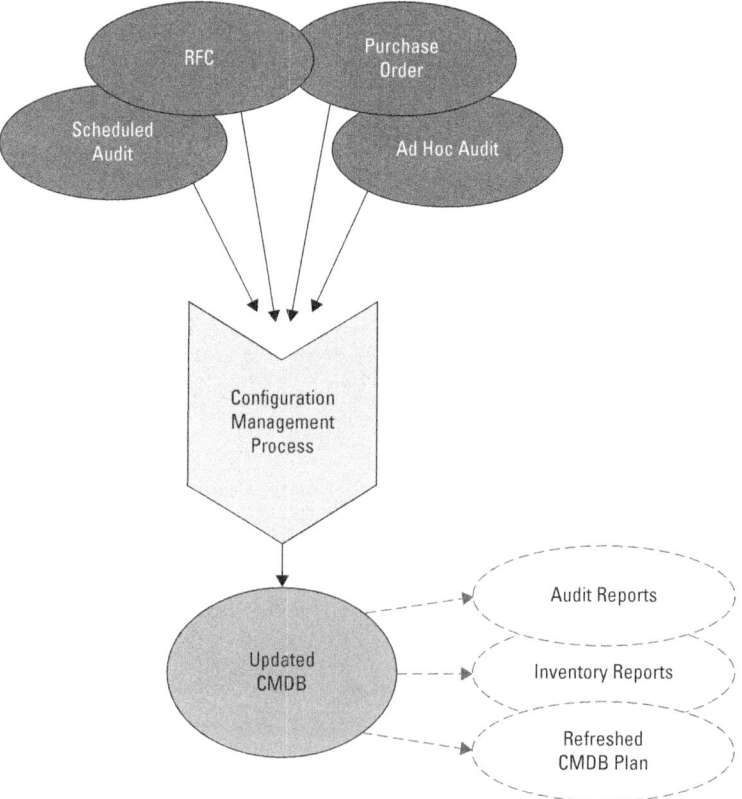

Figure 10.2 Typical Configuration Management inputs and outputs

Outputs
Outputs of the Configuration Management process reflect the work that goes into each aspect of the exit criteria. The common outputs are:
- Updated CMDB records
- Updated inventory management reports
- Verified audit results reports
- Refreshed Configuration Management Plan

10.3. Processes related to Configuration Management

Configuration Management is intricately linked to two other processes, Change Management and Release and Deployment Management (Release Management in short). In a very real way, these processes together are responsible for how the entire infrastructure is shaped over time. Uncouple any one from the other two and the organization's level of control suffers. If you were to trace the process activities in each of these areas you could easily see a single thread that moves through change control into Configuration Management and into Release Management. Such commonality can be used to view these three as blended components of one large process; call it Service Management Control, if you will. It is these three components together that provide for the smooth transition of services from design and development teams into production.

Change Management
Configuration Management goes hand in hand with Change Management. There is a reciprocity of reference at the crux of this relationship. When newly proposed changes need to be assessed, change analysts will turn to the CMDB to review technical information and current configuration details. It is this reference step that informs change managers and design teams how changes may affect environments and how solutions might be best engineered. Then, as changes are placed into production, a second reference occurs. CIs in the CMDB are updated to reflect new production configurations. This updating includes adjustments to individual CI records and to the integrated service maps as well. Through this relationship, change decisions can be made based on complete and accurate information, and approved production reconfigurations can be readily incorporated into organizational records. (For more on this topic, see Chapter 9.)

In summary:
- Change Management references CMDB information in order to inform change-related decision-making.
- Configuration Management relies on Change Management decision detail as input for updating CMDB CI records and service maps.

Release Management
Release Management picks up an assignment once the Change Board has approved a change. From this point on the job of Release Management is to realize an efficient

technical solution relevant to the change. In line with this, Release Management relies on the service details contained in the CMDB in order to plan, design, develop, test, and deploy such solutions. If the information in the CMDB is incomplete or inaccurate, solutions may be less than capable. Configuration Management provides an important verification role in support of Release Management. In return, Release Management provides a reciprocal verification service. Through deployment activities in the field, release teams are able to provide feedback to configuration analysts about current configuration profiles of installed equipment. This helps promote the synchronous refinement of the environment across teams. (For more on this topic, see Chapter 12.)

In summary:
- Release Management relies on Configuration Management to provide complete and accurate service configuration information.
- Service designs, development efforts, testing, and deployments are largely based on CMDB record sets.
- Configuration Management relies on release and deployment activities to provide the synchronicity that exists between CMDB data sets and field configurations.

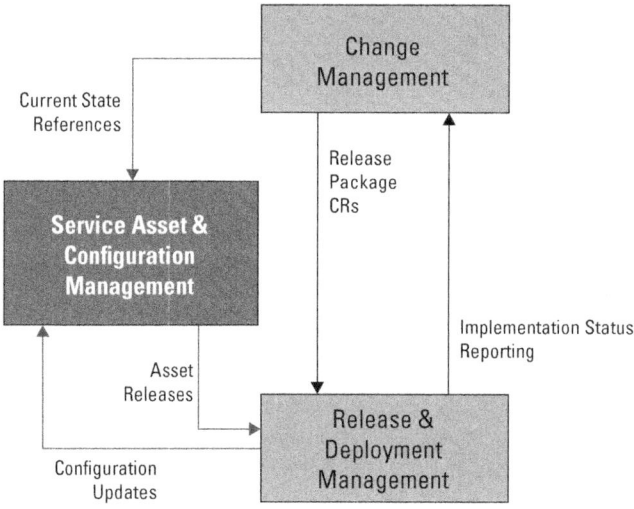

Figure 10.3 Processes related to Configuration Management

10.4. Tools and techniques

Configuration Management is usually founded, in a physical sense, on some form of database management system. This database is used to store and maintain CI records, service maps, and inventory information. It is these three management areas – CIs, service maps, and inventory – that require the program's most typical tools and techniques. Their most common types are described below.

Table 10.1 Tools and techniques for Configuration Management

Configuration Management System (CMS)	The CMS is a set of tools and databases that are used to manage configuration data. The CMS also includes information about Incidents, Problems, Known Errors, Changes and Releases. Depending on its scope, the CMS may also contain data about employees, suppliers, locations, business units, customers and end-users. The CMS includes tools for collecting, storing, managing, updating, and presenting data about all Configuration Items and their relationships. The CMS is maintained by Configuration Management and is used by all IT Service Management processes.
Configuration Management Database (CMDB)	The CMDB is the central repository for storing and managing CI information. This tool is most often realized as some form of database management system, but can be any tool that is right for the organization. The contents of the CMBD are carefully maintained over time and protected through adequate change control procedures. The use and maintenance of the CMDB is the responsibility of the Configuration Manager.
Service maps	Service maps are diagrammatic schematics that detail how business services are derived from technical services, and how technical services are derived from linked service components. Service maps are useful for understanding the current configuration of the infrastructure. They are also valuable for understanding service interoperability and interdependencies.
Inventory tracking system	Most operation-based organizations need to maintain some level of inventory, whether this is new equipment, replacement parts, or retired assets. To manage these assets effectively, organizations employ various forms of an inventory management system. Often this is an extension of the CMDB.

10.5. Key Performance Indicators

Measures of Configuration Management activities are usually set in place to provide insight into three operational areas: the current mix of configuration service and items that the organization is required to support, how closely the CMDB has remained aligned with configuration units in the field, and the level of asset activity for a given period of time. In this section we present a series of nine key performance indicators that can be used to present an operational picture for each of those areas. These nine are not exclusive but they are commonly used. You might find that these are beneficial for your Configuration Management program.

Number of business services by type
This is a count of the total number of business services offered by the organization. These counts may be broken down by business category or business type or any other subset that helps you get a good picture of the scope and spread of services across the enterprise. The counts may also be segmented by status: active services, services in design (forthcoming), and retired (inactive) services. This high level view forms the basis of a general Service Catalogue, the business services portion of the catalogue. This KPI is useful here because the configuration details of business services will need to be regularly maintained in order for the CMDB to realize its value for the organization.

Number of technical services by type
Like the business metric above, this measure is a count of the total number of technical services offered by the organization. You might find it helpful to break the counts down by technical category or technology type or – as with the business services – any other subset map the services across the enterprise. The counts may also be segmented by status: active technical services, technical services in design (forthcoming), and retired (inactive) technical services. Technical services operate individually or in combination to make up business services. It is important then that technical service configurations are maintained so that business service configurations remain accurate. Maintenance of this data can also provide for the technical services portion of a Service Catalogue.

Number of service components by type
This count is the most detailed of these first three services KPIs. It is a look at the total number of service components installed in the environment. As with the two measures above, these counts might readily be broken down by category, technology type, etc. Service components, when integrated, provide for the delivery of technical services, and it is here with service components that configuration detail becomes the most specific. A KPI of this type can help configuration managers track components and maintain the detail so that technical service configurations and business service configurations remain aligned and complete.

Number of configuration changes over period
This is a count over a set period of time of the number of updates made to CIs in the CMDB. This data can be used to help assess the volatility of the environment and to track the nature and direction of the infrastructure's evolution. This data is also helpful from another perspective. It can be used as a quality check against both change control and Configuration Management activities. For example, if for a given period the measures indicated a very low count of CMDB updates while for the same period the Change Board approved frequent and significant changes, then there might be a valid reason to conduct an audit of the CMDB against the environment. This is to verify that, indeed, appropriate updates have been made.

Number of RFCs without corresponding CI updates
This KPI is related to the one above, and supports analysis of CMDB update activities. The metric is a count of the number of changes to the infrastructure that were made without corresponding updates being made to CI records. It is not always the case that an approved change naturally leads to a CI update, but the data provides a good indicator of what sort of update ratio you night expect to see, given your organization's trend of change activity. This measure can be used to help assess organizational use of the CMDB and its compliance with current Configuration Management policies and procedures.

Number of unauthorized configurations over period
This is an analysis of the number of changes made to CIs in the field or in the CMDB that were not authorized or properly approved. As with the KPI above, this is a

useful performance measure. These counts help assess adherence to Configuration Management policies and procedures. Unauthorized changes have deep potential to introduce risk into the environment. High counts might indicate any number of things: that change control is missing some needed practices, that Configuration Management access is not secure, or that operations staff need additional training.

Number of failed deployments due to inaccurate CMDB data

This is a count of failed or troubled deployments due to inaccurate information in the CMDB. When approved changes are engineered for release, design teams and release managers look to the CMDB to collect technical information for deployment. If this information is complete and accurate changes should deploy successfully. If configuration data is missing, outdated, or incomplete the risk of deployment problems rises. This data can be used to help assess the current integrity of the CMDB and evaluate how well environmental changes and database updates are being coordinated. The data can also be used to articulate the level of risk that uncoordinated change poses to the organization.

Number of incidents and problems due to inaccurate CMDB data

This KPI is related to the metric above. It is a look at the numbers of incidents and problems that arose (for a particular period) due to inaccurate information in the CMDB. Mis-configurations in the field are a common source of incidents and problems. In fact, occurrences of incidents and problems are a primary source for discovering that something somewhere has become misaligned. Investigations by support staff can uncover these issues and documented resolutions can provide the evidence that serves as the basis for collecting these counts.

Number of assets released and recovered by type

This is an analysis of Asset Management activity. It looks at two facets. First is a count of the total number of assets that were released into the environment for a given period. This might be broken down by categories such as type, business unit, location, charge account, etc. Next is a count of the number and types of assets that were recovered; that is, that were removed from the environment and returned to inventory or retired. These counts provide a general picture of asset rotation requirements and general equipment stability.

10.6. Critical Success Factors

A successful Configuration Management program will be one in which assets are well controlled and the configuration information about those assets is regularly maintained. If you choose to implement the KPIs described in the previous section you will be well on your way to understanding these levels of control and maintenance. However, you can get a higher level picture of program success by looking at two somewhat removed CSFs. These CSFs exist because of the very close relationship Configuration Management has with two other ITIL processes, Release Management and Change Management. Both of these processes rely heavily on effective Configuration Management; when one (or both) of these processes works well Configuration Management can be seen as working well. Consider using the following two sample success factors as indicators of the effectiveness of your Configuration Management program.

Effective Release Management activities

When Configuration Management is conducted well, an organization is able to readily identify the system components that need to be updated in order for new or enhanced services to be designed, developed, and deployed. The CMDB, a central part of a Configuration Management program, provides the baseline information that implementation teams require to understand what needs to change, how it needs to change, and where those changes should occur. When the data sets available to these teams are accurate and complete, Release Management activities should execute smoothly. When data sets are weak or questionable, problems are likely to occur. It is helpful for IT management to identify the success of its Configuration Management program by looking at the performance of its Release Management program. A strong Release Management program is not solely contingent on sound Configuration Management practices, but it certainly points in large part to effective use of such practices.

Effective Change Management activities

The contribution that Configuration Management makes to effective Change Management is significant. Change Management will operate largely in the dark in the absence of configuration information. Change Management's practices of review, assessment, approval, and assignment all rely almost exclusively on CI descriptions. Descriptions that are missing or off-base may set the stage for misdirected decision-making. When this happens one can expect to see problematic designs, deployments, and performance levels. In order to understand the impact, value, and cost of proposed changes, it is essential that the organization has an accurate baseline of the infrastructure's shape, links, and configurations. A sound Configuration Management program will provide such a baseline, accurate and complete logical and physical views of the environment. A resource of this type will lead naturally to better change control (not perfect change control, but certainly better), so it is helpful for IT management to look to Change Management just as it can look to Release Management as an indicator of Configuration Management effectiveness. Typically, you will find that effective Change Management programs are being actively supported by successful Configuration Management programs.

10.7. Configuration Management roles

In terms of industry depth, Configuration Management is one of ITIL's more mature and prominent processes. Most IT organizations, whether they are following standards or not, practice it in some way, so the roles associated with Configuration Management have been somewhat standardized over time. The following four roles are usually accounted for in some way in a Configuration Management program. As with other ITL processes, and depending on the size and focus of the organization, these roles may be full-time or part-time, combined or shared by multiple individuals. View the job titles and responsibilities described below as starting points for your own job descriptions.

Configuration Management Process Owner

The Configuration Management Process Owner is ultimately responsible for the use and performance of all the activities aligned with the Configuration Management program. Often the process owner is also the Configuration Manager (see below), but this does not have to be the case. The Configuration Management Process Owner champions the purpose and goals of Configuration Management across the organization and ensures that the program remains in state of operational effectiveness, one that will contribute to the overall IT and business missions of the company. To summarize, the Configuration Management Process Owner is responsible for:
- Developing and documenting the Configuration Management program
- Implementing the program across relevant teams
- Coordinating program training and mentoring
- Monitoring ongoing program use
- Measuring program performance over time
- Soliciting and coordinating program improvements

Configuration Manager

The Configuration Manager is responsible for the maintenance and integrity of the contents of the organization's CMDB, and for overseeing authorized access into this repository. The scope of this data in the repository includes configuration item records, technical service maps, and business service maps. In addition to overseeing this body of core information the Configuration Manager is responsible for coordinating CI-related activities with Change Management and Release Management, communicating status to service and business stakeholders, conducting periodic audits between field configurations and CMDB configurations, and capturing and reporting on Configuration Management performance measures. To summarize, Configuration Managers are responsible for:
- Establishing, maintaining, and monitoring the Configuration Management Plan
- Managing Configuration Management resources (including the CMDB)
- Planning and coordinating CI updates
- Coordinating configuration audits
- Communicating configuration updates and audit results
- Verifying approved changes with Change Management, Release Management, and service managers
- Collecting performance measures and distributing performance reports
- Coordinating inventory control activities with asset managers

Asset Manager

Asset Managers work with Configuration Managers to control the physical inventories of the IT equipment that make up the infrastructure. The job responsibilities are three-fold: to ensure that inventory levels are maintained, tracked, and protected; to govern the release of equipment into the environment in a controlled and documented manner; and to recover equipment from the environment, when required, in a controlled and documented manner. Often the Asset Manager and the Configuration Manager are one individual in the same role; many times in larger organizations they are divided into two distinct roles. If there is a distinction to be made it is that Asset Managers usually deal with equipment that is not active and thus separate from production. Configuration Managers deal with equipment that is 'live' in production. To summarize, Asset Managers are responsible for:

- Maintaining the integrity of physical inventories
- Maintaining inventory records
- Controlling the release of assets into the environment
- Coordinating the recovery of assets from the environment
- Participating in CMDB audits
- Communicating asset-related activities to Change Management, Release Management, and service managers
- Collecting performance measures and distributing performance reports
- Coordinating inventory control activities with Configuration Managers

Configuration Analyst

The role of the Configuration Analyst is two-fold. The first is to populate and maintain the organizational CMDB with up-to-date CI records and service maps. The service maps should cover active business services and technical services. (The analyst should also facilitate access to this information by other teams in the organization.) Second, the analyst provides input and insight to Change Management about working RFCs, and to Release Management about information necessary for planning releases and conducting deployments. To summarize, Configuration Analysts are responsible for:

- Operating and maintaining the CMDB
- Updating CI information as required
- Issuing required CMDB reports
- Participating in CMDB and field audits
- Providing input into Change Management and Release Management activities

Human Resource considerations

The following are some typical traits that Human Resource staff may want to take into consideration when they are providing personnel, tools, and other resources for a Configuration Management program.

Technical experience and background: Configuration Management resources should have an adequate technical background in order to design, operate, and maintain the CMDB so that baselines accurately reflect the equipment in place across the infrastructure. Staff should have experience of planning, executing, and monitoring configuration update, review, auditing, and verification activities. Configuration Managers should have experience in team management and in cross-functional support techniques.

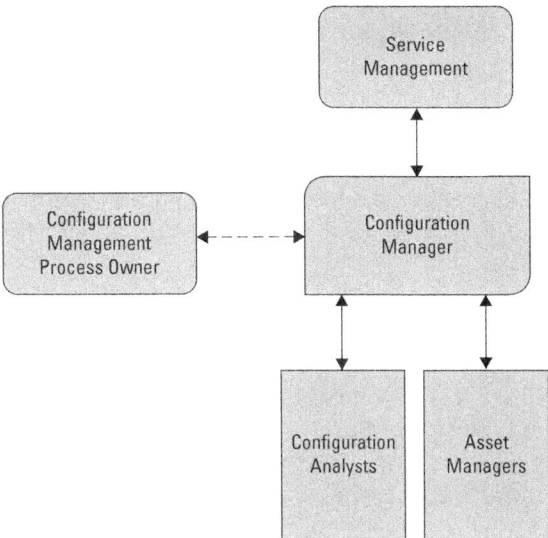

Figure 10.4 Roles for Configuration Management

Comfort working in a process-centric environment: Asset and Configuration Management staff should be comfortable working in a process-centric environment, and should be open to learning about the organization's program and contributing to its ordered growth.

10.8. Benefits of effective Configuration Management

Any IT infrastructure, large or small, is a complex enterprise. Rare are the environments that contain only a simple set of components. IT infrastructures are also highly dynamic. As business and technical needs change, they are continually being refined, enhanced, and extended. When these kinds of environments are not managed, or are poorly managed, the scope and function of IT services can become quickly jumbled. As a result, Service Management becomes problematic. This is a common occurrence in more than a few IT organizations. But when the environment is well documented and then controlled in a planned manner, service delivery and quality become much more manageable. This increase in manageability is the goal of an ITIL-based Configuration Management program. The rewards of such a program cover a wide range of benefits. Here are four of the main ones.

More effective IT Service Management
The base benefit of a Configuration Management program is simply more effective IT Service Management. When the CMDB is complete and accurate, managers and technicians will have up-to-date information on the details of how any mix of IT services operates. With this information at hand, services can be handled with reduced risk. Problems and incidents can be quickly diagnosed. Enhancement and extension alternatives can be intelligently assessed. Delivery and quality targets can

be more readily tracked. These operational benefits are complemented by a set of strategic benefits. Configuration histories can be analyzed to identify productive growth paths and avoid problematic ones. Service mix efficiencies can be studied to inform capacity, availability, and security designs. Environmental reconfigurations can be presented as a way to weigh cost, demand, and performance alternatives. All of these targeted benefits, across operational and strategic domains, add up to service management that can be more responsive, proactive, efficient, and forward thinking.

Accountable cost control

The asset management portion of a Configuration Management program provides controls for one of the biggest areas of potential corporate spending, technology equipment. Controlling costs in this domain, in an accountable way, is not only an integral facet of Configuration Management, it is an essential component of business success. The manner in which assets are requisitioned, acquired, inventoried, released, and recovered sets a foundation for how efficiently services are managed. Asset management sets this foundation in place. Many times, due to fiscal necessity, asset management crosses functional boundaries and becomes in large part a responsibility of financial management (corporate planning groups, accounting units, etc.). But the link into IT can never be fully displaced. The trace to activity on the ground level, where the disposition of assets takes place, must remain a line clearly drawn. However it is organized, asset management combines with Configuration Management to provide for accountable cost controls for this major area of corporate investment.

Better planning and forecasting

Because of the fullness of data that will reside in a mature CMDB, IT and business management will have a sound reference for understanding how the environment is structured and how services perform technically. With this understanding, planning for service enhancements and service extensions can become more accurate, mainly because the logical picture contained in the CMDB will mirror the physical environment precisely, down to the service components level. Forecasting is also enhanced because the organization now has a solid as-is picture of the environment; this greatly facilitates strategic decision-making (the projection of to-be states) when it comes to assessing potential environmental enhancements or extensions. The value here is quickly realized when one appreciates that changing the infrastructure always carries with it some degree of risk. That risk can be significantly reduced when plans are built on reliable information and when forecasts are able to take into account past performance and earlier configurations.

Improved IT and business performance

The result of effective Configuration Management should be demonstrated in improved IT performance, reliability, and stability. This is true to the extent that the importance of this process's relationship to service quality cannot be overemphasized. The logical view of the infrastructure that a program of this type provides gives the organization a safe 'proving ground' for environmental decision-making. It is not far off the mark to say that Change Management, Release Management, Incident Management, and Problem Management would all operate much less efficiently in the absence of a Configuration Management program. This depth of impact extends out from the domain of IT and into business domains. When Service Management proceeds in a smooth manner, when IT equipment costs can be controlled and accounted for, and when plans and forecasts become more accurate business missions can only be advanced.

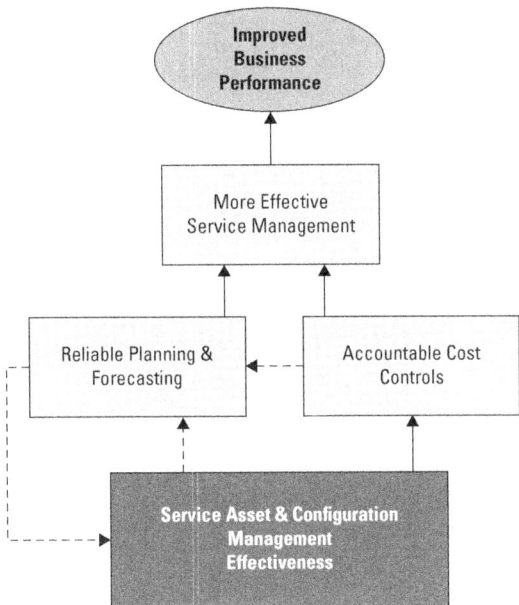

Figure 10.5 Potential benefits of a typical Configuration Management program

10.9. Implementation challenges and considerations

Managing service assets and maintaining up-to-date configuration records are two activities absolutely essential for effective IT Service Management. In their absence, an organization's ability to truly understand (and thus manage) its environment can be seriously handicapped. Most IT managers appreciate the value here. And yet implementing a rigorous Configuration Management program carries with it a set of challenges and considerations that have been know to give even mature IT organizations pause. The reason is not that the practices of Configuration Management are intrinsically difficult. It is rather because the practices require that the organization acquires – and then controls – an accurate and complete picture of the infrastructure. Because IT infrastructure tends to be both large and complex and because such environments tend to evolve in unexpected ways over time, such acquisition and control can be daunting. There are three aspects to this that program implementers should be aware of when designing and deploying a Configuration Management program. They are described below.

Establishing the CMBD
A CMDB will typically be at the physical heart of any Configuration Management program. If the organization does not have one already, the job of installing and designing a CMDB can be a major task. To move from initiation to utilization, the organization will need to evaluate potential products, make an acquisition, invest in installation, work through a carefully considered design, and then commit the right resources to its ongoing use and maintenance. And while the CMDB that the organization elects to employ does not have to be elaborate or complex, it will need to be well matched to the needs of the IT organization. Challenges can come from people's reaction to such an effort. Without an appreciation for the value a well-managed CMDB can bring to the environment, staff might question why such a tool is needed when, perhaps, operation teams have been able to do without one. The expenses involved and resources required may be seen as better applied elsewhere, perhaps in areas where shorter-term rewards might be realized. And then there is the fact that centering a program on a CMDB may require the organization to adopt new skill sets and operational policies, things that are often uncomfortable for many. There are no quick resolutions to any of these potential objections. Management's best path is to itself understand the value inherent in the CMDB, be able to articulate it to others, and then develop a solid plan for realizing such a tool in the IT organization.

Inventorying the environment
This may be the toughest job (and thus the biggest stumbling block) when it comes to establishing a Configuration Management program. In order for its value to be realized the CMDB will need to contain complete and accurate information about every CI important to the organization, those CIs essential for delivering services. To reach this state of completeness and accuracy, the organization will need to conduct in some form or fashion a physical inventory of the infrastructure, recording what equipment is currently in place and what current configuration states are. There are some automation tools that can be used to remotely scan networks and discover what is out there; but even so, it is almost inescapable that teams will need to be sent across the workspace and conduct physical inspection and verification activities. The effort called for here will likely be a large one, and that fact alone tends to derail many Configuration Management programs. The apparent size of the effort simply overwhelms people. And, in fact, the effort can be overwhelming. This perceived burden can be minimized through a selective design: by staggering the effort to focus first on certain areas, and then later on others. But the bottom line, no matter how it is approached, will not be easily changed: design, transition, and operation processes require complete and accurate configuration information in order for service delivery and service quality to be controllable.

Creating service maps
Establishing service maps is an effort that flows from the inventory activity described above. And it is often just as big a challenge as establishing the baseline inventory itself. Service maps are diagrammatic flowcharts or schematics that present a picture of how IT components are linked to form technical services and, one step up, business services. The maps show interrelationships among technical components and services,

and highlight interoperability and interdependency intersections. They are a valuable part of any complete Configuration Management system mainly because they give analysts and support personnel a holistic view of service designs. Such maps are a central aid when it comes to service strategy, design and support considerations. However, there is the need to create the maps in the first place: business service maps that present a macro view of service configurations, and technical service maps, which give more of a component-level micro view. Two things are required to set these maps down; each has particular challenges associated with it. The first thing required is people's time. Some group of resources is going to have to take the time to draft the maps, review them with stakeholders, finalize them, and then maintain them over time. Who those resources will be, given that IT organizations are already stretched thin, may be hard to identify. The second thing is knowledge. The people who will be ultimately needed to contribute to service map creation may cover a broad expanse of the organization. Where will they find the availability and 'thinking time' to make these contributions? These two factors push the commitment about service maps to one of significant proportion. But realizing this, the organization should ask a complementary question: In the absence of access to service maps, how truly effective and reliable will our service-related decision-making be?

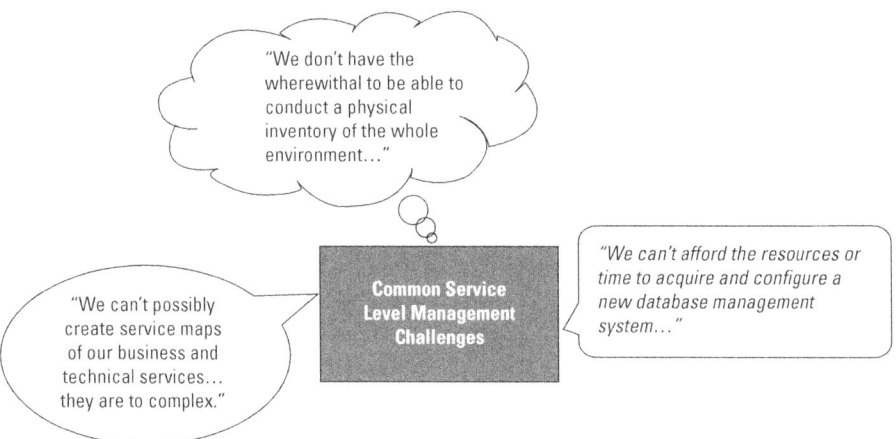

Figure 10.6 Implementation challenges and considerations for a Configuration Management program

10.10. Typical assets and artifacts for a Configuration Management program

A Configuration Management program will require a set of program materials to cover both asset management and configuration management. These materials provide the boundaries for asset and configuration management activities to operate in, and frame the form and function of the work products produced by these activities. Following is a list of some common program materials you are likely to encounter in a typical Configuration Management program. While your program may call for some of these, you will likely wish to create some things not described here; but this list, while not exhaustive, is typical and might be useful as a starting point for your program.

Service Asset and Configuration Management policy
This is an executive policy that stipulates the goals and objectives of the Service Asset and Configuration Management program. The policy, which ideally should be no longer than a few pages, documents at a high level the purpose of the program, the resources available to the program, the chief responsibilities of the program, quality targets, reporting hierarchies, and program measures. Endorsed by executive management, the policy is a demonstration of organizational commitment to the value and importance of the Service Asset and Configuration Management program.

Configuration Management process
This is a process that details the workflows inherent in the execution of Configuration Management activities. The process defines how all such activities work and usually accounts for configuration item identification, CMDB referencing, communications with Change Management and Release Management, CMDB updates, configuration audits, and performance reporting. The process would also describe entry criteria, exit criteria, inputs, and outputs for major activities, and identify the actors needed to execute each. The process might also be supported by lower level procedures or work instructions.

Asset Release and Recovery process
This is a process that details the workflows inherent in the execution of asset management activities. The process defines how all such activities work and usually accounts for asset acquisition, inventory control, asset release, asset tracking, asset recovery, asset disposition, interfaces with Configuration Management, and performance reporting. The process would also describe entry criteria, exit criteria, inputs, and outputs for major activities, and identify the roles needed to execute each. The process might also be supported by lower level procedures or work instructions.

Configuration Management Plan template
This template provides a structural guide for creating the organization's Configuration Management Plan. The template outlines the contents and sections that a properly documented plan should contain. Such plans usually identify the following kinds of information: Purpose and scope of Configuration Management, resources assigned to the team, management and key stakeholders, location of the CMDB, security rules for CMDB access, required contributions to Change Management, required contributions to Release Management, triggers for CMDB updates, update verification rules, audit schedules, and audit report distribution channels.

Configuration Management Plan
This is the organizational plan, based on the template above, that – once approved and adopted – stipulates how Configuration Management activities will be conducted over a set period of time.

Configuration Management Database system (CMDB)
The CMDB is typically the central tool used in a Configuration Management program, within a CMS. The system is a repository that authorized technical and business users can access to record details about individual CIs, create and manage service maps, and (sometimes optionally) maintain equipment inventories. IT managers and technicians rely on the CMDB as the authoritative reference for information about how business services, technical services, and service components are configured, linked, and operated.

Configuration Management audit procedure
This is a process that details how periodic audits of the CMDB and CIs on the floor will be conducted. Procedures of this type usually cover how audits will be scheduled, what items will be inspected, what conditions the auditors expect to find, what organizational stakeholders will be involved, how issues will be identified, and how disagreements about the findings will be managed. The procedure should also identify the audit results reports that will be produced, to whom they will be distributed, and where composite audit results data will be stored.

Organizational chart
This is a chart that shows the structural make-up of the Configuration Management operation. As with other organizational charts, its purpose is to identify teams, team relationships, and hierarchical flows. The chart's shape will depend on the organizational units and resources you are able to assign to the program. Most organizational charts for this process have two branches. At the top is a box for the Configuration Manager. A dotted line extends to a parallel support spot for the Asset/Configuration Management Process Owner (if this role is separate from the Configuration Manager). Below the Configuration Manager are two groups: the Asset Manager and Configuration Analysts. Under Asset Manager there may be a box for Inventory and under Configuration Analysts perhaps a box for the CMDB. Sometimes it's also helpful to have a dotted line extending from the Configuration Manager at the top to Service Managers off to another parallel spot, an indicator of their general involvement and input into the process.

Roles and responsibilities matrix
This matrix, an extension of the organizational chart, describes the various roles and responsibilities the organization has assigned to support asset management and configuration management activities. The roles typically include such positions as Asset and Configuration Management Process Owner, Asset Manager, Configuration Manager, and configuration analyst. Along with the job role definitions you should have descriptions of the responsibilities each role should account for, and references to how roles interrelate and communicate. The matrix might take one of several forms:

a spreadsheet, a series of database records, or a version-controlled text document. Ownership of this artifact is usually shared between IT management and Human Resource management.

11. Release and Deployment Management

In the line of ITIL core processes Release and Deployment Management occupies the bridge between service development and live operational service. This is a process whose scope includes a wide range of activities, perhaps wider than any other ITIL process. The ITIL definition for this process reveals this breadth:

"Release and Deployment Management aims to build, test and deliver the capability to provide the services specified by service design that will accomplish stakeholder requirements and deliver the intended objectives.[1]"

This is supplemented by the purpose of Release and Deployment Management, which is:

"To ensure that new releases are thoroughly planned and controlled so that deployments are successful, there is appropriate knowledge transfer to production, and there is minimum disruption to the business.[2]"

The 'and' in the title of this process signifies a conjunction of related activities. Under **release management** are the activities associated with strategic planning, project oversight, service development, and testing. Under **deployment management** are the activities associated with validation, implementation, and verification. Under both of these areas are three overriding responsibilities.
- Ensure that services, as built, meet customer expectations
- Confirm that service integrity is adequate for production
- Manage deployments so that business disruptions are minimized

This being the mission of Release and Deployment Management, it is easy to understand why this process reaches by necessity into multiple functional areas of the enterprise. Release and Deployment Management interacts with project management, Application Management, and Requirements Management teams. It must be closely allied with ITIL's core design processes. It must interface continually with change control teams. It relies heavily on Configuration Management records. It provides a level of oversight and coordination for test activities. Its planning responsibilities require it to interact with business stakeholders and its verification responsibilities require it to interact with service managers and service level managers.

---

1 Foundations of ITIL. (2007). Van Haren Publishing.
2 Ibid.

This family of interactions and objective shapes the content for this chapter. It also alludes to the major considerations that should be addressed when release strategies and deployment tactics are being set into place, either for a single service or a collection of services. These considerations include:
- Providing a manageable and responsive organizational release strategy.
- Planning releases and coordinating release package contents.
- Validating technical solutions and providing build resources.
- Providing testing and, as needed, piloting services.
- Providing for the removal and retirement of obsolete assets.
- Ensuring adequate documentation and knowledge transfers.
- Verifying implementation success.
- Providing support for newly deployed systems.

To delve into these considerations further let's begin with a look at the activities associated with the Release and Deployment Management process.

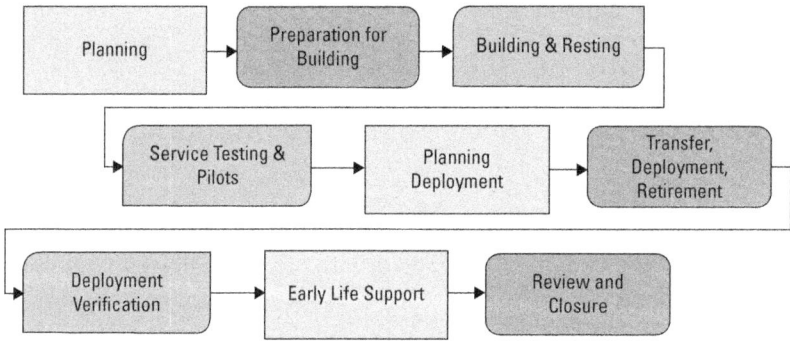

Figure 11.1 Typical Release and Deployment Management process flow

11.1. Release and Deployment Management activities

The Release and Deployment Management process consists of a series of nine general activities. These are used to cover the full scope of release management and deployment responsibilities, which are broader than in any of the other ITIL core components. For most of the general activities there are a series of sub-practices. Taken as a whole, the process leads the organization through the steps needed to establish a release management strategy, introduce a service development capability, provide test and other verification resources, establish a deployment strategy, and provide early production support for newly deployed services. The nine general steps in the process are:
- Planning
- Preparation for building
- Building and testing
- Service testing and pilots
- Planning deployment
- Transfer, deployment, and retirement

- Deployment verification
- Early life support
- Review and closure

In the following sections we'll take a brief look at each.

1. Planning

The term 'planning' might be better interpreted as 'preparation', for in this step the organization sets its release management and deployment management capabilities into place. Four steps are defined for this activity: establish a release strategy, define deployment requirements, establish development resources, and establish test and pilot facilities. It is important to note that these broad recommendations may require deep work by the organization. In any event they will be likely to require some reshape of existing operating units.

Establish a Release Management strategy. The Release Management strategy represents the organization's approach to evolving its service mix and shaping its infrastructure. The strategy usually sets definitions for a minor release, a major release, and an emergency release. It also specifies how often or under what conditions each release can be initiated. For example it is common for many organizations to allow minor releases every month, major releases every quarter, and emergency releases under conditions aligned with the policies of emergency change control (see Chapter 9). Additionally the strategy should specify interfaces with Change Management and Configuration Management. And it should identify roles, responsibilities, and assignments necessary for process management. These roles include Release Manager, Deployment Managers, and Implementation Analysts, each of which may or may not be service specific. Once this information has been determined it should be collected into a Release Management plan, reviewed, approved, and then managed under version control.

Establish deployment requirements. Deployment requirements are those factors that need to be accounted for when deployments are being prepared. The requirements serve as a foundation for establishing a Deployment Plan template. Typical requirements in this domain include:
- Describe the scope, purpose, and objectives of the deployment.
- Define the success criteria expected at the close of the deployment.
- Document back-out strategies and methods.
- Identify the members of the deployment team along with their roles.
- Identify relevant service and business stakeholders.
- Describe the implementation approach.
- Describe verification methods.
- Establish the deployment schedule with major milestones.
- Establish the deployment budget (as required).
- Describe communication avenues and status reporting methods.

Establish development resources. The goal is to introduce those design and build resources necessary to support service development activities. This includes technical staff, development equipment, development tools, workspaces, and all the other provisions found in a traditional technology development department.

Establish test and pilot facilities. These facilities include technology equipment that mimics the capabilities of production, workspaces and equipment housings, office provisions, etc.

2. Preparation for building

This activity is designed to prepare the organization to engage in building activities. These steps prepare the organization to shape services to the needs and objectives of the business environment and to do so in a consistent and predictable manner. This includes establishing design criteria, implementing a technical solution capability, and linking build work to Configuration Management assets.

Establish design criteria. Design criteria provide the organization with a way to standardize design efforts so that they take into consideration those operational factors that are important to business and technology performance. Design criteria help technology teams work in a consistent and predictable manner. (For more on this see the chapters on Availability, Continuity, Security, and Capacity Management.)

Establish a technical development capability. A technical development capability is established by instituting policies and standards that restrict the range of technologies the organization can employ when designing service solutions. They define a set of authorized tools (programming languages, operating systems, server brands, etc.) that support the operational and business needs of the organization.

Link to Service Asset and Configuration Management. Building activities should be linked to configuration management so that development teams have access to the Configuration Management Database (CMDB). This is for two reasons: to be able to check configuration item (CI) records for current configuration information; and to be able to determine how configurations will need to change in order to support new solution deployments.

3. Building and testing

Building and testing includes the technical activities involved with creating service designs to meet service requirements, implementing the designs to realize technical solutions, conducting unit and integration testing of service components, and developing the documentation necessary for service support. The beginning point for this step is to provide for requirements traceability.

Establish requirements traceability. Requirements traceability is a thread that runs through every part of the service development lifecycle. Traceability is a way to take individual requirements and account for them as they move across definition, design, development, test, and implementation activities. Traceability serves two main purposes.

On the front end it aids in planning activities, helping to establish the scope for major project phases. On the back end it provides a way to demonstrate to the customer that the requirements have indeed been embedded into the solution at each major milestone. Traceability can be realized in something as simple as a spreadsheet or by way of a sophisticated tool; the key to its effectiveness, however, arises not from form but from function: the matrix needs to be carefully managed and updated across the lifecycle.

Create and implement service designs. This step has strong connections to ITIL's Availability, Capacity, Continuity, and Security Management processes. Here technical teams use design criteria to design solutions to meet service requirements. In technology IT organizations this usually includes establishing architectures, mapping designs, programming software, configuring and integrating components, performing unit testing, and performing some degree of integration testing. This step represents the heart of service development.

Document service solutions. With service development comes the need for service documentation. In this step technical teams create the kinds of documentation needed to maintain solutions over time. Typically this documentation falls into three categories: technical documentation as a reference for further development activities (designs, commented source code, architecture schematics, component integration maps etc.); operation documentation referenced for the production use and maintenance of the service (concept-of-operations manuals, maintenance manuals, etc.); and user documentation, functional and training documents for those users who work with the service or interface with it on a regular basis.

4. Service testing and pilots

Service testing represents a more robust form of testing than is found in the Build and Test activity above. It is designed to accommodate full-scope testing in the way that system and regression testing do. Pilots are an extended form of testing. They are typically conducted in isolated environments that are monitored for a set span of time. The steps in this activity include establishing test plans, developing test scripts and cases, executing tests, evaluating the results, establishing pilot plans, executing pilots, and evaluating pilot results.

Establish test plans. Test planning is used to manage testing efforts. They establish the scope of the effort and document the resources and configurations that need to be in place in order for testing to proceed. Depending on the scope and shape of the release there may be a series of individual test plans or a single master integrated plan. Before execution, test plans should be reviewed and approved by stakeholders affected by the outcome of the tests. Test plans usually contain the following kinds of information:
- Objectives of the test effort
- Business scope of tests (processes and service features)
- Technical scope of tests (infrastructure components)
- Key business and technical stakeholders
- Test team members

- Required test environment configuration
- Required test data
- Success criteria (Go/No Go)
- Schedule
- Assumptions / Risks / Constraints
- Budget (as needed)
- Communication and reporting channels

Establish test scripts and cases. Test scripts and test cases should meet three criteria. They should uphold the integrity of traceability, tying directly to requirements. They should mimic actual business and technical processes to as complete an extent as possible. And they should push the functionality – availability, capacity, security, etc. – to the extent that real-world operation might push them.

Execute test plans and evaluate results. According to plan, testing should be executed with test cases and scripts run and the results monitored and recorded. As they accumulate the results should be reviewed with relevant stakeholders and compared against success criteria. If the results warrant it the service package can be readied for pilot – if one is in order – or moved on for operational deployment. If the results indicate otherwise, that the service package needs to be reworked, it can be returned to the development team with an action to adjust the deployment plan.

Establish pilot plans. Pilot plans are very similar to test plans and contain basically the same types of information. A few notes:
- Pilot plan schedules are typically much longer than test schedules, often several months in duration.
- Pilot teams usually include members of the customer community who are subject matter experts in relevant business domains.
- Pilots usually demand exclusive (or at least significant) use of select infrastructure assets.
- Pilots almost always require the use of targeted monitoring and control techniques.

Execute pilots and evaluate results. As with testing, the pilot should be run with the results of business processes and technical performance monitored and recorded. As results accumulate over time they should be reviewed with relevant stakeholders and compared against success criteria. If the results warrant it the service package can then be made ready for production deployment. If the results indicate that the service package needs to be reworked it can then be returned to the development team with an action to adjust the deployment plan.

5. Planning deployment

Deployment plans are release-specific and provide documentation on how a service package will be implemented in the environment. Deployment plans contain the kinds of information common to all management plans. These include objectives, success criteria, deployment milestones, schedules (with deployment dates selected to minimize business disruptions), budgets (as required), personnel and roles, stakeholders, and communication avenues. The development of deployment plans uses as its foundation the deployment requirements identified in the planning activity described in Step 1 above. One essential aspect of a deployment plan is a rollback (or back-out) strategy. This is a contingency for returning the environment to its previous configuration if for any reason the implementation fails.

6. Transfer, deployment, and retirement

With this step the deployment plan is executed and the actual implementation activities begin. Three steps are involved. The first is termed 'transfer'. Transfer involves the movement of assets and resources from a planned or pending status into production. This may include any number of things needed for the release to operate and can cover financial resources, capital equipment, people, and support materials. With that completed actual deployment can begin. This is where physical installation takes place. The key recommendation ITIL makes about deployment is that it should be scheduled at a time most convenient to the business; in other words, on a schedule that will require the least disruption to business processes. Deployment should be a carefully monitored activity, one whose status is regularly communicated to relevant stakeholders. Once implementation activity is complete and the infrastructure has been changed, the final step is to remove any superfluous equipment and retire it according to asset management policy.

7. Deployment verification

With completion of Step 6, the release or release package has been installed and configured. Major deployment activities have been finalized. It is at this point that the new release can be 'turned on'. The job for the deployment team now is to verify that the components of the release work as they should, that the full streams of affected services are functionally intact. This is typically accomplished by running a selected series of live transactions and monitoring system performance. If performance problems are noted, corrective actions can be implemented. If the corrective actions are not effective, the team can implement its rollback strategy. If performance appears to hold its integrity the deployment *pro forma* can be considered complete. Reports on the results of deployment verification should be sent to relevant service managers, senior IT management, and business managers.

8. Early life support

Early life support (ELS) is an activity in which design and development staff provide on-call support for elements of a release newly implemented in operation. The aim is to closely monitor the solution for a fixed period of time in order to evaluate its operational proficiency. If there are problems the ELS team can respond accordingly with corrective action. The ELS team is also available to mentor production staff in first-line monitoring and maintenance techniques. During ELS, operational issues should be documented and periodically reviewed by senior IT management. At the end of the period, ELS results should be reviewed with a view toward full transition to operations teams. Periods for ELS can vary in length depending on the scope and complexity of a release. In some cases a couple of weeks might be adequate; other instances may require three months or more.

9. Review and closure

The final step in the Release and Deployment Management process is a review of all activities associated with the release. This is typically conducted as a Post Implementation Review (PIR). A PIR is a meeting in which major stakeholders convene to assess project performance. The participants evaluate want went well, what went poorly, and what might improved for the next release. Notes from these discussions are captured, distributed later to stakeholders, and then incorporated as inputs into continual service improvement activities (see Chapter 15). Once the PIR has been conducted the release can be considered finalized and the project can be officially closed.

11.2. Process inputs and outputs

Release and Deployment Management is an ongoing activity for any IT organization. Through the activities of change control and the acquisition of new capabilities infrastructure configurations are regularly being adjusted. It is through these activities that release and deployment procedures are initiated. As noted in the section above, the process itself is not so much cyclical as it is linear: it moves from a point of coordination to a final validation on implementation. Below is a summary of common entry criteria, inputs, exit criteria, outputs of the Release and Deployment Management process.

Entry criteria

The Release and Deployment Management process is typically set into motion when one of three events occurs:
- A new service has been developed or acquired and scheduled for a particular release.
- A Request for Change (RFC) has been approved and timetabled for a particular release.
- A combination of 1 and 2 above occurs.

Inputs

Inputs into the process can come from a variety of sources, individually or in combination. These inputs usually include:
- New services (e.g. custom systems, commercial off-the-shelf (COTS) products, etc.)
- Change control impact assessment reports
- Approved RFCs
- Service package requirements
- Forward schedule of change
- CI records
- Active release plans
- Known Errors

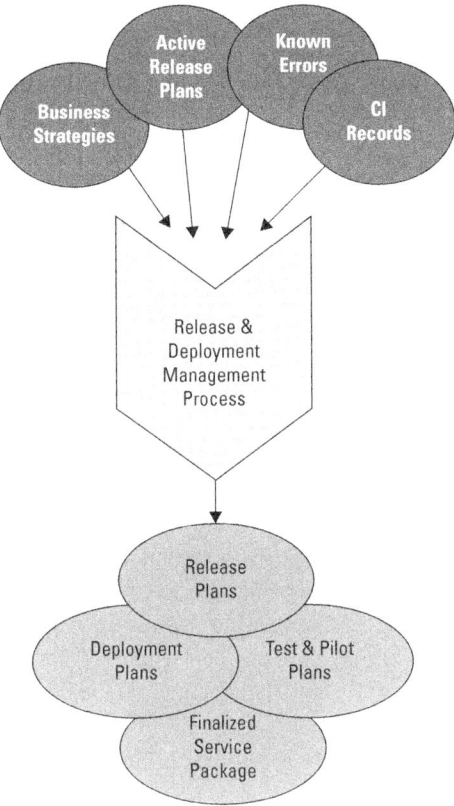

Figure 11.2 Inputs and outputs for Release Management

Exit criteria
The process is typically recognized as having been completed when three general exit conditions are met:
- The service package has been successfully deployed into production.
- Service performance has been validated.
- The service is being monitored and controlled by operations staff.

Outputs
The Release and Deployment Management process, once it has run its course, will produce a set of work products that support its procedural activities. At a minimum the set should include the following artifacts:
- The deployed service package
- Technical support, maintenance, and operation documentation
- PIR assessment notes
- Release and deployment activity metrics
- Also created during the process and archived as support material:
  - Release plans
  - Deployment plans

- Design schematics
- Test plans
- Test cases and scripts
- Test results

11.3. Processes related to Release and Deployment Management

As noted in the introduction to this chapter, Release and Deployment Management touches a variety of ITIL's core processes. The design processes Capacity, Availability, Continuity, and Security Management provide inputs on the front end into service development activity. Service Level Management establishes the reference for traceability, verification, and test activities. And the investigative and diagnostic work associated with Incident and Problem Management uses the documentation and other knowledge transfer artifacts provided by Release and Deployment Management. There are two other core processes that have an even stronger relation with this process. They are Change Management and Service Asset and Configuration Management.

Change Management

In many ways Release and Deployment Management can be seen as an extension of Change Management. Change Management controls the gate into Release Management. It is the grouped collection of approved changes (new services and enhanced services) that make up the contents of release packages and drives release schedules. Change Management also determines the scope of Release Management work. From that process come the requirements Release Management must oversee in terms of development, testing, and implementation. There is also the factor of collaboration. Change Management and Release and Deployment Management need to work closely together to ensure that approved changes can be accommodated in existing schedules and that schedules meet the business needs of the organization.

In summary:
- Approved changes shape the agenda for Release Management.
- Change Management supplies the requirements that must be realized under Release Management oversight.
- Change Management must coordinate the timing of approved changes with Release Management.
- Release schedules need to accommodate priority changes in accordance with business drivers.

Service Asset and Configuration Management

Service Asset and Configuration Management supplies Release and Deployment Management with the fundamental configuration information upon which implementation strategies and deployment plans can be based. Without Configuration Management, deployment management would be a hit or miss affair. Referencing accurate CMDB information is a prerequisite for effective production changes. Release and Deployment Management also provides valuable input back into Configuration Management. Once deployments are complete and their success has been verified, deployment management is the proper avenue for communicating CMDB updates. The CMDB is also the proper repository for storing and managing the technical documentation needed to support a service once in production, documentation delivered by deployment teams.

In summary:
- For accuracy and completeness, deployment needs to reference CI information in the CMDB.
- Deployment activities may trigger changes to configuration records.
- The CMDB is the appropriate repository to manage service documentation provided by deployment teams.

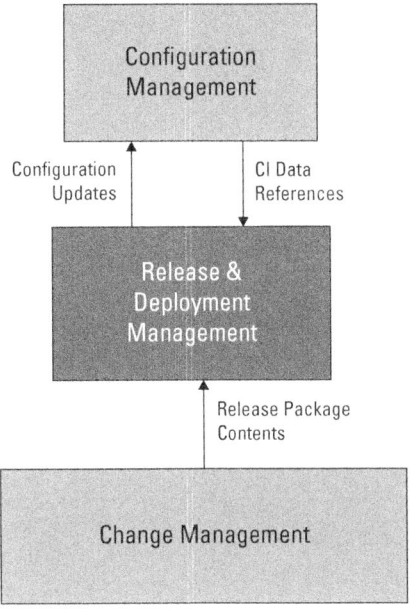

Figure 11.3 Processes related to Release and Deployment Management

11.4. Tools and techniques

In the same way that Change Management might not be considered a 'technical' process, Release and Deployment Management is not usually considered one either. Being part of ITIL's Service Transition phase it is mainly focused on logistics, how teams can be managed so production changes occur smoothly. There are, however, some tools and techniques that are useful when working toward these ends. Below are four common tools and techniques often employed for Release and Deployment Management programs:

Table 11.1 Tools and techniques for Release and Deployment Management

Project management practices	Release and Deployment Management can be seen as a domain that includes the need for project management practices. Project management provides a way to steer a service project through the development lifecycle. This lifecycle includes planning, requirements, design, development, testing, training, and implementation. Frameworks such as PMBOK's PMI, PRINCE2, and CMMI Maturity Level 2 all contain proven project management components that may be of value to a Release Management program.
Reflective test environments	One key to effective Release and Deployment Management is comprehensive testing. Testing is used to verify two conditions: • The technical solution works and is sound (i.e. free of defects) • The solution meets the customer's original specification In order to test accurately and completely, the organization needs a test environment that as closely as possible mirrors the production environment. Aspects such as interoperability, data sets, services, processes, and component configurations should all be considered when establishing the test environment. The goal is to gain assurance before deployment into live operation that the solution will operate as intended.
Requirements traceability	Requirements traceability is a technique for accounting for individual customer requirements across the service lifecycle, from design to build to test to implementation, etc. Requirements traceability allows for forward planning and backward verification. But the chief use of requirements traceability is to provide an output that can be shared with customers in order to demonstrate that the technical solution accommodates the full set of original specifications.
Configuration Management Database system (CMDB)	The CMDB is the central repository for storing and managing CI information, including service designs and builds, thus it is a valuable Release Management tool. The definitive software library (DSL) stores running versions of service builds (i.e. Service Packs). The definitive hardware library (DHL) stores running versions of service component specifications and service maps. Both the DSL and the DHL are typically included as part of the overall CMDB.

11.5. Key Performance Indicators

Measuring the performance of a Release and Deployment Management program is important for two main reasons. First, Release Management is the vehicle by which approved changes to the production environment are funneled. Under this domain service features are developed, tested, validated, and deployed. Second, due to the broad range of activities under its scope, Release and Deployment Management is likely to deal with projects of significant size and cost. In a very real way it is the project management arm of an IT Service Management program. Therefore it is important that this process's components are effectively controlled, and to do that they needs to be measured. Defining and then employing a set of KPIs is a good way to start down that road. Following for your reference are seven KPIs commonly found in many typical Release and Deployment Management programs.

Number and types of deployments by service for given period
This is a basic count of the total number of deployments broken down by business and technical service for a given period. This measure helps release managers understand where their work is coming from and paints a picture of the 'shape' of the Release and Deployment Management program. Analyses of this information can help managers plan for needed resources, skill levels, equipment, and training needs.

Number of deployment rollbacks by cause
This is a count of the number of deployments that necessitated a rollback. This measure can be segmented by release with a 'cause' code(s) attached. High rollback rates are red flags that indicate problems somewhere with validation activities. This means that the release package is not being appropriately assessed for production worthiness. This may be due to improperly configured test environments, inadequate test runs, weak implementation plans, or ill equipped staff. In addition to capturing the rollback data and categorizing them it is also helpful to record the outcome of the rollback, if it was successful or not.

Number and types of deployment errors
This measure is a count of the total number of deployment errors that were noted during deployment and Early Life Support. Two types of errors are typically tracked: configuration errors and operating errors. Configuration errors are implementation mis-steps, usually due to invalid configuration information or mistakes made by implementation teams. Operating errors are bugs, usually due to design or development errors. Analyses of this information are important for understanding the stability and integrity of the entire release lifecycle. Consistent configuration errors may indicate the need to improve deployment or CMDB practices. Consistent operating errors may indicate the need to review design, development, and test practices.

Number of build cycles per release
This is a count of the total number of build cycles that the release went through before being delivered for implementation. These numbers may give an indication of the integrity of design and build processes. If low numbers of build cycles correlate to troublesome deployments this may indicate the need for development practices to be examined. If unusually high numbers of build cycles are appearing this may indicate the need to examine design, development, and test practices.

Number of test cycles per release
This count is similar to the one above. It is a measure of the total number of test cycles that the release went through before being delivered for implementation. These counts may give an indication of the integrity of design, build, and test processes. Few test cycles associated with troublesome deployments may indicate a need for more thorough testing. Unusually high numbers of test cycles – spinning through multiple design, development, and test activities –may indicate that design and development work is not being produced in an effective manner.

Number of pilots versus deployments
This measure is a count of the number of pilots that were conducted during the release period versus the number of deployments. This analysis is helpful for determining the value that piloting might bring to your IT organization, as an extended quality control tool, If your deployments have a tendency to be troublesome or result in the need for above average early-production support, you may want to invest in a broader use of pilots. On the other hand, if deployments are typically smooth the time and expense of piloting may need to be relegated only to special projects.

Number and types of RFCs in each release
This measure provides an analysis of the number of approved RFCs that were contained in each release package. This data is used to help assess the average size and scope of both planned and emergency releases. With efficient programs, release packages are shaped to address families of prioritized RFCs and related RFCs in such a way that deployment efforts can be harmonized and business impacts maximized. With less efficient programs you tend to see releases that address few or scattered RFCs, as if they had been shaped in an ad hoc manner.

11.6. Critical Success Factors

Release and Deployment Management, as an ITIL process, can be constructed in part by borrowing from the discipline of project management, so the CSFs relevant to release and deployment activities are very much like those you would expect to find in a project management program. In that domain success is traditionally determined along three broad lines: did the project finish on time, did the project finish within budget, and were the customer's expectations met? While the KPIs described in the section above will help you understand the nuances of release and deployment performance the following three factors will help you understand the program's overall level of success.

Number and types of deployments for given period
The metric breaks down release activity to give you a picture of program performance shape for a given period. The first way to break down this data is to organize releases by type; this typically includes linking releases to the services they affected. For each of these types further breakdowns can be made, such as the number of planned releases versus emergency releases, the number of major releases versus minor releases, and the number of successful deployments versus failed deployments. Analyzing this information will give you a lead in determining how well balanced your program is. Data that points to a large number of emergency releases, high volumes of minor releases, or multiple failed deployments may indicate a need to make adjustments to release management or deployment procedures.

Planned release duration versus actual release duration
This is a basic and familiar project management measure. The goal is for the actual duration of a release (project length) to approximate what had been planned for it.

Protracted schedules may indicate program components that are either ineffective or inefficient. Schedule problems of this kind can extend beyond the domain of the release. They can cause the entire release mix to fall off balance. And, as is well known, extended schedules almost always result in escalating costs.

Planned release cost versus actual release cost

This is another traditional project management measure and is companion to the schedule metric above. Here the goal is to find that actual project costs approximate to what had been budgeted for the release. Cost controls are an important facet of a Release and Deployment Management program because developing, testing, and deploying a release package can be a large and significant undertaking. The umbrella that is Release Management covers a lot of ground. Across all of IT Service Management this is the area where most major expenditures are commonly realized.

11.7. Release and Deployment Management roles

The following job roles are typically seen in mature Release Management programs. Depending on the size and focus of an organization these roles may be full-time or part-time, combined, or shared by multiple individuals.

Release and Deployment Management Process Owner

The Release and Deployment Management Process Owner is the person (or persons) in the organization responsible for the development, deployment, and ongoing use of the Release and Deployment Management program. It is common in many IT organizations that this process owner is the same person as the Services Release Manager, but this is not essential. The process owner champions the purpose and goals of release and deployment management, ensures that the program remains in a state of operational effectiveness, and interfaces with senior IT management and business representatives to facilitate program adjustments and improvements. To summarize, the Release and Deployment Management Process Owner is responsible for:

- Developing and documenting the Release and Deployment Management program
- Implementing the program across relevant teams
- Coordinating program training and mentoring
- Monitoring ongoing program use
- Measuring program performance over time
- Reporting on program effectiveness over time
- Soliciting and coordinating program improvements

Release Manager

The Release Manager coordinates the assimilation of new functionality and approved change requests into service packages. The service packages then move through development, test, verification, and implementation activities. It is the Release Manager's job to ensure that all of these activities are planned, coordinated, monitored, and successfully completed. A Release Manager may focus on a single

service or be responsible for a set of services. Because Release Management serves as a gateway into production, Release Managers should work closely with service design stakeholders, service operation stakeholders, Change Management, and Configuration Management. To summarize, the Release Manager is responsible for:
- Establishing, maintaining, and monitoring the strategic Release Management plan
- Planning and coordinating release and deployment staff and activities
- Coordinating deployment efforts
- Interfacing with Change Management and Configuration Management personnel
- Gathering program measurements and releasing program performance reports
- Facilitating Post Implementation Reviews (PIRs)

Deployment Manager

The Deployment Manager typically oversees a subset of duties under Release Management. The main duties involve coordinating smooth implementation of new service packages, in a way that ensure the least disruption to ongoing business processes. The Deployment Manager creates plans for implementations, coordinates installation and validation activities with technical and operations staff, monitors deployment activities, and oversees handoff of service responsibilities to production personnel. Deployment Managers may specialize in a particular service or manage deployments for a range of services. They may also oversee multiple deployments and deployment teams across a variety of environmental domains. To summarize, the Deployment Manager is responsible for:
- Establishing and monitoring deployment plans
- Coordinating production implementations (reviews, testing, installations, etc.)
- Ensuring service package readiness
- Communicating deployment progress and status
- Producing and distributing deployment status reports
- Participating in PIRs
- Providing input into Change Management and Configuration Management activities

Implementation Analyst

Implementation Analysts are typically members of a deployment team, with members having different areas of technical specialty required for the successful deployment of the service package in question. These specialists perform most of the hands-on implementation work, including installation, component configuration, system integration, performance validation, and operational training. The analysts work closely with production personnel to ensure smooth transition of responsibilities. They may also provide a period of production support during the early phases of service operation. To summarize, the Implementation Analyst is responsible for:
- Implementing new or enhanced services into operation
- Collaborating with operations staff
- Providing status and progress reports to Deployment Management
- Ensuring that all support materials (e.g. documentation) are available to support production changes
- Participating in PIRs

Human Resource considerations

The following are some typical traits that Human Resource staff may want to take into consideration when they are providing personnel, tools, and other resources for a Release and Deployment Management program.

Experience and background: Release Managers should have managerial experience that includes technical awareness of the infrastructure, good coordination and collaboration skills, sound planning skills, and the ability to interface effectively across functional teams. Deployment Managers should have sound project management skills, good inter-team facilitation skills, and a solid familiarity with the technical aspects of the environment. Implementation analysts should have the right level of technical experience in the areas of testing, documenting, installing, and supporting solutions into specific environments.

Comfort working in a process-centric environment: Release Management and Deployment Management staff should be comfortable working in a process-centric environment, and should be open to learning about the organization's program and contributing to its ordered growth.

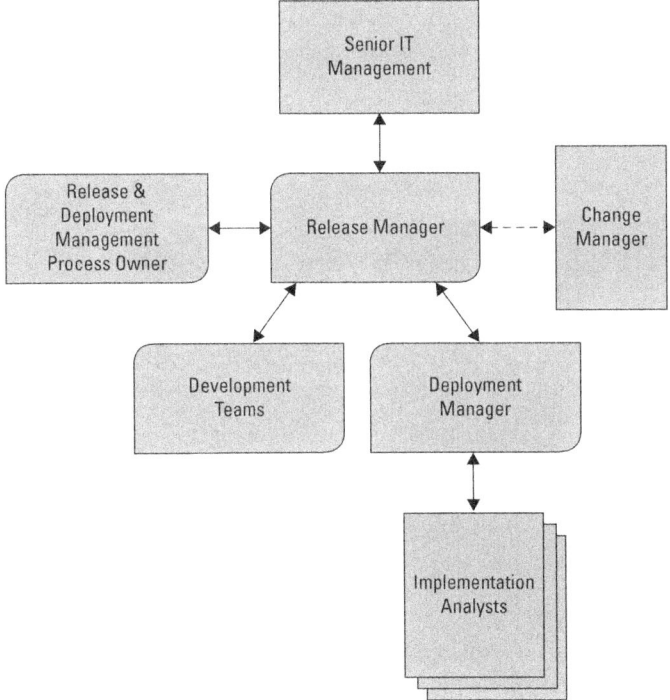

Figure 11.4 Release and Deployment Management roles

11.8. Benefits of effective Release and Deployment Management

Out of ITIL's core components, Release and Deployment Management is the process that is positioned at the entrance to production. All of its activities are in place to ensure that what moves through it does so in a way that will enhance operational efficiencies (improved service) while minimizing service interruptions (smooth implementations). Neglect any of the process activities and production problems may ensue. There are therefore numerous benefits to be derived from sound release management and deployment practices. These include better control of service delivery and service quality, fewer operational incidents and problems, and better management of SLAs. Below is a brief description of each of these three.

Better control of service delivery and quality
The main push behind Release and Deployment Management is, of course, to deploy improvements into the environment. When you are working with an effective Release and Deployment Management program the organization is able to roll these improvements out in a planned, controlled and cost-effective manner, one that coordinates with a wide spectrum of stakeholders. The result should be a Service Management program that is improving and becoming more efficient over time. This should result in better service delivery, quality, and management overall.

Fewer operational incidents and problems
A well-designed and executed Release and Deployment Management program will work to ensure the reduction of service events and infrastructure deficiencies. This will result in fewer incidents and problems, which will happen two ways. First, the development work at the heart of this process will be 'scrubbed clean' through the various Release Management lifecycle steps. This should prevent the introduction of unforeseen or hidden issues into the environment. Secondly, through Release Management's close integration with Change Management and Service Asset and Configuration Management, the content of new service packages can be designed to remove known errors from the environment. This range of service responsibilities (with the addition of requirements management, design activities, build activities, and test activities) focuses on embedding quality and functionality – and when this is done in a managed way, one that is verified and validated, the result should be the delivery of robust services.

Better management of Service Level Agreements
The result of effective Release and Deployment Management should be demonstrated in improved IT performance, with heightened reliability and stability; and out of this should emerge stronger business results. The stream of work that runs through this ITIL process can be channeled to achieve all of the above because Release and Deployment Management is an actualizing agent within ITIL. It starts with new service features or approved changes and steers these through the development lifecycle, integrating with Service Design activities then moving through production,

verification, deployment, and validation. Each of these steps can be shaped as a quality gate at which requirements and performance capabilities can be assessed and evaluated. When the full stream is followed, by the time early-life-support has begun release and deployment teams should have a solid understanding for how well the services in question will meet operational expectations.

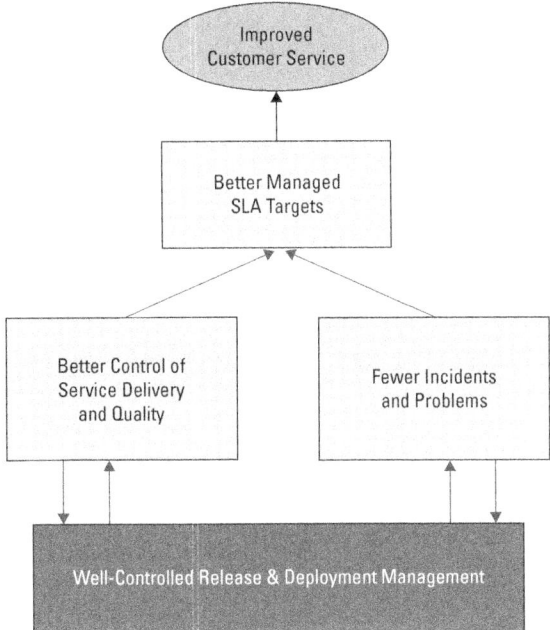

Figure 11.5 Benefits of effective Release and Deployment Management

11.9. Implementation challenges and considerations

Because Release and Deployment Management covers a lot of ground there can be many implementation challenges and considerations associated with it. The very fact that this is a large process – one with the broadest of scopes – makes it so. This can be complicated by the fact that Release Management activities and deployment activities span everything from project management and development to testing and installation. Following are four particularly common implementation challenges that you may wish to consider as you plan to design and build out this ITIL process.

Limiting release cycles

IT organizations are often pressured to run a large number of release cycles. Customers want new features as fast as they can get them. Technical teams see pressing opportunities for improvement. But living in a frequent release cycle world can put an organization at risk. Planning, reviews, and quality checks must necessarily be compressed. Hectic activity can lead to less-than-polished results. It is to the organization's advantage to set release cycles at a manageable level, giving each adequate time for proper planning, design, development, and verification work. The cycle frequency you determine to be right will naturally depend on the needs of your IT organization but a recognizable frequency might be along the limited lines of major releases made quarterly; some even use a half-yearly system. It can be a challenge in busy or dynamic IT organizations to limit this number of releases, especially when stakeholders feel compelled to push as much functionality or value out to production as they hope the IT organization can support. Unfortunately in those cases, the effectiveness of Release and Deployment Management programs suffers.

Coordinating logical sets of RFCs

The more related a set of approved changes is, the more likely the release they are embedded in will be successful. However, in many environments the amounts of change flowing through the Change Management process are not only significant, they are scattered, touching multiple areas across the infrastructure. This presents a challenge to change managers, release managers, and service managers alike. Typically releases can be better managed and more efficiently realized when the changes they contain are ordered and grouped into logical sets. Coordinating such grouping takes foresight, advanced planning, and inter-team cooperation, but this can be difficult to accomplish when there are many stakeholders involved, perhaps with competing goals and business objectives. It will aid a Release and Deployment Management program if the organization can work to establish some guides and practices that will help prioritize the implementation of approved RFCs so as to harmonize the scope and focus of individual releases. This will require give-and-take on the part of stakeholders but the result should be more effective management, better scope control, and smoother implementations.

Tracing requirements through releases

Successful releases need to demonstrate that the customer's requirements have been fully accounted for in the implemented solution. Not only that, design, build, test, and deployment activities must also be able to account for each requirement. In order to do this it is important for release teams to establish mechanisms for requirements traceability. Many IT organizations struggle with traceability; it can admittedly be difficult to achieve, especially with large or complex releases or projects of extended duration. But traceability has a payoff that is worth its ongoing maintenance. It provides the customer with a level of assurance about the viability of the deployed solution and it is a definition of quality. If IT management can clearly trace the requirements across every stage of the Release Management process, customers have an obligation to (at least temporarily) agree to the results. Likewise, customers and IT managers both can reference traceability matrices as a tool to spot misses or glitches before they move deep into the production process.

Testing deployments fully

The challenge that comes with the issue of robust testing may well be one of the thorniest in the domain of technology development. This can be a challenge in many IT organizations and for several reasons. Tight project timeframes often force management to spend less time on test activities than has been planned. It can often be impractical to equip and configure test environments so they adequately mimic the production environment. Test teams may not have the experience or exposure to test the intricacies of specialized business processes. And so on. Perhaps no area of deployment planning raises as much risk as the integrity of testing. The fact is, there might be little some IT organization scan do about this. In the absence of strict management insistence or capital investment the only practical approach might be to recognize the deficit and track it as an active, ongoing risk.

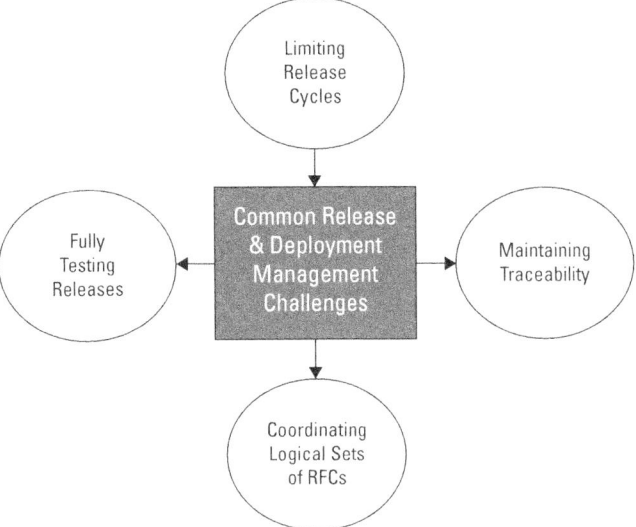

Figure 11.6 Implementation challenges and considerations for Release and Deployment Management

11.10. Typical assets and artifacts of a Release and Deployment Management program

The Release and Deployment Management program your organization develops will need to be founded on a set of documented assets and artifacts. Assets are the program materials that bound how the program is governed and run. Artifacts are those work products that emerge when your teams exercise the assets. Following is a list of some common assets and artifacts that are found in typical Release and Deployment Management programs. Your program may call for some of these; you may wish to create some things not described here; but this list, while not exhaustive, is typical.

Release Management policy
This is an executive policy that stipulates the goals and objectives of the Release and Deployment Management program. The policy, which ideally should be no longer than a few pages, documents at a high level the purpose of the program, the resources available to the program, the chief responsibilities of the program, quality targets, reporting hierarchies, and program measures. Endorsed by executive management, the policy is a demonstration of organizational commitment to the value and importance of the Release and Deployment Management program across the enterprise.

Release Management process
This is the process used to guide the organization's approach to Release Management. This approach typically includes procedures to cover scoping, planning, scheduling, communications, verification, validation, review, and reporting activities. The Release Management activities described throughout this chapter can be used as a foundation for setting this process in place.

Emergency Release process
This is a streamlined version of the Release Management process used for developing and moving service packages into production due to particularly urgent conditions.

Deployment process
This is the process used to guide a project approach to Deployment Management. This approach typically includes procedures to cover packaging, scheduling, communications, verification, implementation, review, and reporting activities. The Deployment Management activities described throughout this chapter can be used as a foundation for setting this process in place.

Release Management Plan template
This template provides a structural guide for creating the organization's Release Management Plan. The template outlines the contents and sections that a properly documented plan should contain. Such plans usually identify the following kinds of information: purpose and scope of Release Management, resources assigned to Release Management activities, the organization's planned release schedule, supported business and technical services, interfaces with Change Management and Configuration Management, activity reports to be created, reporting distribution avenues, interfaces with Deployment Management, Release Management metrics, and PIR criteria. (This plan template is often integrated with the measurement plan described below.)

Release Management Plan
This is the organizational plan, based on the template above, that – once approved and adopted – stipulates how specific Release Management activities will be conducted over a set period of time.

Deployment Plan template
This template provides a structural guide for creating the project-specific deployment plans in support of Release Management activities. The template outlines the contents and sections that a properly documented plan should contain. Such plans usually identify the following kinds of information: purpose and scope of Deployment Management, resources assigned to a particular deployment effort, the planned deployment schedule, supported business and technical services, interfaces with Release Management and Configuration Management, activity reports to be created, reporting distribution avenues, interfaces with service stakeholders, deployment

management metrics, and PIR criteria. (This plan template is often integrated with the measurement plan described below and with the Release Management Plan template described above.)

Deployment Plan(s)
This is the set of plans, based on the template above, that – once approved and adopted – stipulates how deployment activities will be conducted for service packages over a set period of time.

Release and Deployment Management Measurement Plan
In order for a Release and Deployment Management program to be effectively controlled, it needs to be measured. The measurement plan is a tool for doing just that. It identifies and defines metrics to be captured in order to assess the performance of release management and deployment activities. A typical plan will describe the measures, define how to collect them, stipulate where the pulled data are to be stored, and provide formulae for analyzing this data. The measures you select will depend naturally on the needs of your IT organization, but the CSFs and the KPIs described in this chapter are examples of the kinds of measures you may wish to set up for your measurement program.

Release and Deployment Management reporting and distribution procedure
This is a documented procedure that describes how release and deployment activity reports are created, how often they are generated, and to whom they are to be disseminated. This procedure can be seen as an extension of the Release and Deployment Management Measurement Plan described above. Together these artifacts provide the kind of information needed by management and the customer to understand the effectiveness of release and deployment practices and identify opportunities for improvement.

Organizational chart
This is a chart that shows the structural make-up of the Release and Deployment Management program. As with other organizational charts, the purpose is to identify teams, team relationships, and hierarchical flows, and so the chart's shape will depend on the organizational units and resources you are able to apply to the program. Most organizational charts of this sort are a simple tiered hierarchy. At the top, there is a box representing the Service Managers and senior IT management. This extends down to a box for the Service Release Manager. Below this might be Deployment Managers and under them, teams of Implementation Analysts. A dotted line from the Service Release Manager box might extend to a parallel support spot for the Release and Deployment Management Process Owner (if the role is separate from the Service Release Manager). This chart may be service-specific or combine a set of service offerings.

Roles and responsibilities matrix

This matrix, an extension of the organizational chart, describes the various roles and responsibilities the organization has assigned to support Release and Deployment Management activities. The roles typically include such positions as Release and Deployment Management Process Owner, Service Release Manager, Deployment Manager, and implementation analyst. Along with the job role definitions there should be descriptions of the responsibilities each role should account for, and references to how different roles interrelate and communicate. The matrix might take one of several forms: a spreadsheet, a series of database records, or a version-controlled text document. Ownership of this artifact is usually shared between IT management and Human Resource management.

12. Incident Management

Incident Management may be the most visible of all ITIL processes, and it is certainly one of the most important in terms of core processes. Incident Management has acquired this reputation for several reasons. First is the fact that it is so strongly customer facing. Incident Management is the route by which most customers interact with IT personnel, and it is through this route that customers most often form their opinions of IT service delivery in general. Second, Incident Management serves as a mirror of IT service quality. Environments where incident volumes are abnormally high or where resolution activities are inconsistent or unreliable typically reach that state due to weak or unfocused Service Management strategies. Finally, Incident Management is prominent because it is by nature an extension of a fairly mature business domain: customer service and call center support. There is a broad base of best practices in this domain, practices that most users are familiar with and have come to expect when dealing with their own Service Desk personnel.

The importance of Incident Management places it at the center of an effective Service Management program.

ITIL V3 places Incident Management in the Service Operation lifecycle phase together with the processes Problem Management, Request Fulfillment, Access Management, and Event Management; and the functions Service Desk, Monitoring and Control, and IT Operations. ISO/IEC 20000 includes Incident manager under the section Resolution Processes, where it is defined together with Problem Management.

It is a key activity of the Service Desk, and it contributes significantly to the operations of Problem Management, Service Level Management, Change Management, and Configuration Management. Implementing a successful Incident Management program is a strong indicator that the organization is positioned for a successful Service Management program. In this chapter we will look at the various aspects of Incident Management, with a view to the options and considerations necessary for effective design and deployment. A good place to begin is with a definition of what, exactly, an incident is.

ITIL V3 offers a very specific definition:

An incident is "any unplanned interruption to an IT service, or a reduction in quality of delivery of an IT service."[1]

There are a few points to appreciate here. An incident is unplanned in that it is not anticipated. A scheduled system backup may cause a service interruption but because it is a planned activity the interruption is not considered an incident. Also: incidents

---

[1] Foundations of ITIL V3, (2007) Van Haren Publishing

do not have to be rote interruptions; service degradations may qualify. Slow response times from otherwise speedy services may well meet the definition of an incident. And then there is the relationship between incidents and problems. Many incidents (but not necessarily all) can be thought of as the surface symptom of a problem; the problem as the underlying root cause of the incident. It is important to understand that an incident may be validly resolved while the underlying cause remains in place. This leads to the purpose of Incident Management.

ITIL V3 states the purpose of Incident Management as:

"To address incidents in such a manner that the normal IT state of affairs is resumed as quickly as possible."[2]

In other words, take action so that users may return to their business activities. This may be accomplished through a permanent fix (e.g. replacing a hard drive) or through some manner of temporary fix (e.g. re-routing network traffic). But, whether it is permanent or temporary, one characteristic remains: it should be quick. Incidents almost always demand prompt attention. Problems, on the other hand, can be (and should be) dealt with in a more considered manner. The Incident Management process supported by ITIL is structured to promote this streamlined approach to incident

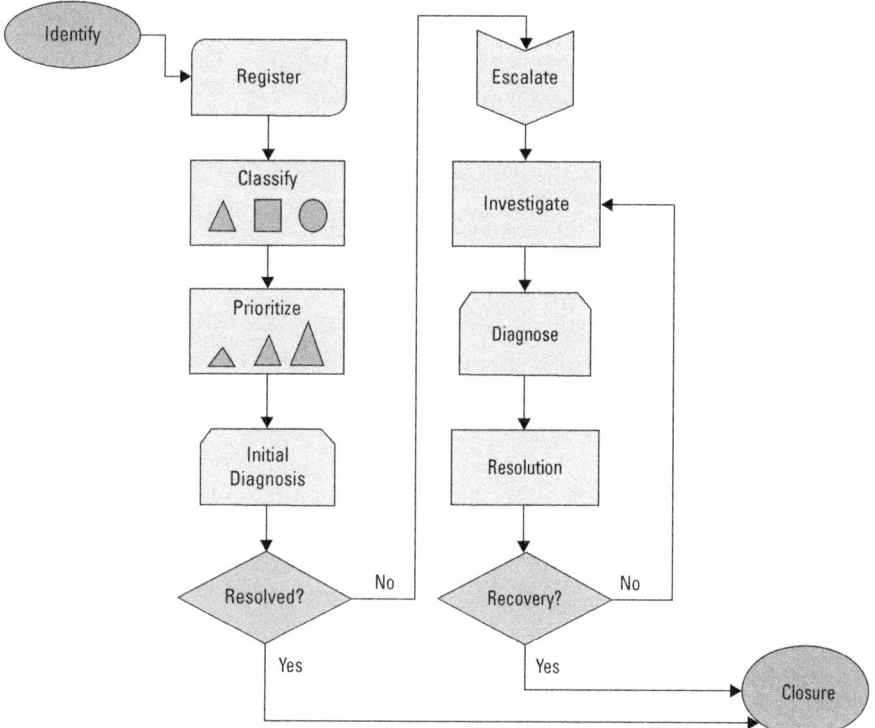

Figure 12.1 Typical Incident Management process flow

---

2 Ibid.

handling. Its workflow is basically linear in form. Incidents are identified; they are registered; they are addressed, and then tracked to closure.

The following section contains a review of the basic activities that make up the Incident Management process.

12.1. Incident Management activities

The Incident Management process is described in ITIL V3 as a workflow represented by nine activities. These are archetypical incident handling steps, long recognized in customer service domains. Here is a description of each in the order they typically occur.

1. Identification

The first activity described for the Incident Management process is that of identification: becoming aware that an incident has occurred (or perhaps is about to occur). There are three common ways the Service Desk might become so aware. The first is that a monitoring tool detects an over-threshold condition and sends out a notice or triggers an alarm. The second is that a member of the technical staff becomes aware of a condition that may imminently interrupt service and contacts the Service Desk. The third way – and perhaps the most common – is that a user experiences some manner of interruption (in their mind, a 'problem') and contacts the Service Desk or submits a trouble ticket. With this identification, the procedural steps that cover registration-diagnosis-resolution are engaged.

2. Registration

Registration is the action of taking an incident report and turning into a manageable incident ticket. This is done most commonly through the use of an Incident Management Tracking System (IMTS), but registration actually tends to cover a series of sub-steps. The Service Desk analysts confirms caller identification, takes detail on the issue, and then makes some attempt to verify the interruption. At the heart of registration is creation of the incident ticket. When registering an incident it is helpful to record such detail as shown in the table below.

Table 12.1 Incident ticket registration items

Incident ID	A unique ID for the incident (usually assigned by the Incident Management Tracking System)
Incident Title	A summary description of the incident
Description	A detailed description of the incident (including observed cause and resulting impacts)
Category	A classification code, or set of codes, for the incident
Urgency / Impact / Priority	A set of related codes that set the criticality level for the incident
Submitter	The ID of the person or tool reporting the incident
Status	An activity code for the current working state of the incident

Submitter Contact	Contact information (e.g. department phone email) of the person reporting the incident
Date/Time	A time-stamp on when the incident was registered
Owner	The ID of the person or team to whom the incident has been assigned
Initial Follow-on	A brief description of the follow-on action prompted by the incident report

These elements are added as work on the ticket proceeds (Table 12.2).

Table 12.2 Additional items on incident ticket

Diagnosis	A text entry describing the probable cause of the incident, the configuration item (CI) affected and any other relevant technical or functional information
Initial Resolution	A text entry that describes the initial solution approach proposed for the incident. This is a first take on how to deal with the incident and is useful for technicians as a starting point for working toward a final action.
Verified Resolution	This is a text description of the final verified steps taken to resolve the incident.

Once the incident has been registered, the Service Desk begins to track it toward resolution. This involves the additional steps as described below.

3. Classification

In order that incidents are well managed it is helpful to classify them. Classification is a way to tag a ticket so that it may be directed through the proper work channel. In this way, classification is useful as a kind of pointer; if the ticket can be resolved on First-Call the tag serves as an historical pointer; if the ticket needs to be escalated, it serves as a directional pointer. In most IT organizations there are teams that work in specialized domains (e.g. network teams, application teams, telecom teams, etc). Escalated incidents affecting certain domains should be sent to those particular teams. A classification scheme can help you set those tags. With ITIL you are free to design any scheme you deem best, but when implementing an Incident Management program try to choose one that reflects the approach your organization takes for customer management and technical specialties.

There are many options available for how an organization might structure a classification schema. Following are a few common examples:
- Classify by service (e.g. email, networking, printer support, etc.)
- Classify by service component (e.g. file server, exchange server, router, smartphone, etc.)
- Classify by incident type (e.g. access, security, reporting, desktop application, etc.)
- Classify by platform (e.g. PeopleSoft, DB2, Oracle, Outlook, etc.)
- Classify by customer group (e.g. accounting, marketing, shipping, etc.)

The implementation advice is to shape the classification scheme in line with what brings most value to your teams.

Distinguishing incidents – major and minor: In your Incident Management program, consider how your teams might distinguish between major and minor incidents. Such a distinction is common in most mature IT organizations. Some service interruptions are by nature more critical than others; some are severe. These kinds of major incidents may require a special set of incident handling procedures, a sort of emergency protocol that can be invoked when needed. Minor incidents – the day-to-day routine ones – need a less rigorous protocol, the 'regular' Incident Management process. As your organization begins to build this program, keep this in mind. Classification code schemes, prioritization levels, ownership assignments, and escalation paths can all be shaped with this two-path approach in mind – a full-scale approach for major incidents, a lighter one for minor incidents.

4. Prioritization

Once an incident has been classified, the Service Desk will have a better idea as to how it should be handled. At this point it becomes important to consider prioritization. Prioritization is a way to recognize that IT resources are limited. It simply is not possible to immediately resolve every incident that flows to the Service Desk or other support teams, so it is helpful in Incident Management to establish some ordering guidelines. By using priority criteria and associated priority codes, the Service Desk can assess the key characteristics of an incident and assign it a code that will shape its visibility in work queues. This way, incidents of higher criticality can receive higher priority codes and receive quicker attention. In the ITIL specification, a calculation to derive priority is offered:

impact + urgency = priority

Through this formula the impact of an incident is assigned a value (the organization sets the value range): a high value for high impact, a low value for low impact. The same approach is followed with urgency. Very urgent incidents get higher urgency values. Here is an example: A server's power supply burns out. Because that failure shuts down the server completely, the Service Desk might assign this incident an impact code of 5 (high on a scale of 1 to 5). But because the Service Desk analysts know that that particular server is just one of four redundant backup servers, they might give it an urgency code of only 2 – thus a final priority value of 7 would be assigned.

When this priority code (together with the classification code) brings the incident to the attention of the right technical team, the team can begin the process of diagnosis.

5. Diagnosis

Incident resolution and subsequent recovery are dependent on an accurate diagnosis of what precisely caused the service interruption to occur. Working with the user and collecting as much information as is available, Service Desk analysts assess symptomatic detail and make an attempt to set the situation right. The ready availability of business and technical references is helpful for getting quickly to a sound diagnosis and an effective response. This includes material such as documented procedures for handling common incidents, up-to-date technical specifications that accurately describe the infrastructure, and a Known Error Database of existing functional and operational issues. Using these references the Service Desk can:

- Resolve the incident, update the record, and communicate status to the customer; or
- Determine that it does not have the expertise or resources to address the incident and thus move to escalate the ticket to the next tier of support.

6. Escalation

The primary goal of the Service Desk is to resolve each support call that comes its way, right then in real time. This is known as First Call Resolution. But there will always be incidents that Tier 1 support teams cannot adequately address. They may lack the technical expertise, or may not have necessary access to services or equipment. In these situations, escalation is required. The Service Desk assigns the tickets to parties at Tier 2 or Tier 3 and there the ticket will be worked again.

A quick note on terms: Throughout this book the term Tier 1 is used to represent the first line of technical support, the Service Desk. Tier 2 is used to designate desk-side support or other internal but specialized technical support teams. Tier 3 designates those technical analysts whose primary jobs may be in service design or development but who contribute to incident handling when they are needed. Tier 2 and Tier 3 support can point to any teams that the organization wishes to label those ways. For an Incident Management program it is not important to use the terms Tier 1, Tier 2, and Tier 3. Label your tiers with any terms you wish, and implement as many or as few levels as your organization needs.

In thinking about escalation and developing escalation guidelines, the organization will want to trace identified Tier 2 staff to the customer groups and services systems they support, and the Tier 3 staff to the services and service components they support. From this the organization should then define the criteria for when moves from Tier 1 to Tier 2 to Tier 3 should be made and how communications between levels will be initiated, continued, and managed.

Two types of escalation: functional versus hierarchical. Escalation is a method used to move ticket assignment from one support level to another. ITIL provides for two types of escalation. Functional escalation is the more common of the two and usually applies to more routine incidents. Using predefined escalation channels, support teams move the incident from Tier 1 to Tier 2, etc. as it becomes necessary. Hierarchical escalation usually applies to more serious incidents (e.g. major incidents or Priority 1 incidents). In these cases, support teams involve IT management. Management evaluates the situation and, based on impact and urgency, moves the incident directly to the party that ought to address it, skipping tiers as required.

7. Investigation and diagnosis
Investigation and diagnosis here is different from Step 5 above. At this point the incident has been escalated. Now Tier 2 or Tier 3 teams (or others as your IT organization requires) are assigned the task of resolving the incident. Using the foundation data established by Tier 1 and recorded on the incident ticket, these teams conduct their own investigation and then, based on these results, make a diagnosis. The teams should work closely with Tier 1 support during this stage as they document their findings; it may be important to explain a solution's rationale in order to get buy-in from IT management and the customer. Once the solution has been agreed to, plans can be made for the fix.

8. Resolution and recovery
With this step we reach the main objective of Incident Management: resolving the incident and recovering the normal state of IT affairs. Here the fix or workaround that was determined in the investigation and diagnosis phase is delivered.

9. Closure
Throughout the activities above, the incident record will have been regularly updated as work toward its resolution progressed. Once resolution is complete the record can be marked as closed. This should remove it from any active work queues so that resources may be free to work on other pending incidents. This act of closing is also a cue to communicate this final status to the customer and any other relevant stakeholders who may have been connected with the incident.

NOTE: In addition to marking the incident as closed, the Incident Manager should check other conditions before having teams move on to other work. This includes making sure that relevant documentation and CIs have been properly updated, and confirming that appropriate entries have been made into the Known Error Database (KEDB) and the Service Knowledge Management System (SKMS).

The *Known Error Database* is a repository where the organization stores records of all known errors in the infrastructure. You can think of a known error as an existing defect. In other words, something recognizable is wrong with the environment, but the organization – for one reason or another – can't deal with it right now. Most of the time what organizations do with known errors is to create workarounds. A workaround is a temporary patch that alleviates the symptoms without addressing the real cause. In the ideal world, workarounds are temporary measures set in place until a real fix can be made. But that's not always the case. Sometimes workarounds stick around for a long time. Because of this you want to know about them so that you can minimize how they affect the efficiency of the infrastructure. The KEDB (that's ITIL shorthand) helps you keep track of the known errors while they exist.

The *Service Knowledge Management System* is a repository where the organization stores configuration and technical information about each of its services. Because it is a knowledge center for the entire portfolio, the SKMS (more shorthand) serves as a key reference tool for the Service Desk in the mission of incident management. In fact, the SKMS is most often used not just for Incident Management but for all of ITIL's operating programs. Into this central repository the organization places technical documentation, policies and procedures – in short any material that helps the shop manage the environment and deliver its services.

12.2. Process inputs and outputs

The Incident Management process can be seen as a fairly linear chain of events. What might be seen as somewhat unique about Incident Management, though, is that the process itself is never invoked *automatically*. It is a *people-driven* process and its inputs and outputs are people-driven, too.

Entry criteria
The Incident Management process is typically started by the occurrence of one of three events:
- A user experiences a service interruption and notifies the Service Desk.
- A support analyst monitoring the environment notices an emerging or potential service anomaly.
- A monitoring tool issues an alert or notification to a support analyst.

Inputs
There are typically two modes of input that are derived from the entry criteria to inform the Incident Management process. They are:
- Information obtained from the customer during incident notification (phone call, email, fax, etc.), or
- A technical notification or report issued by a support analyst to the Service Desk

Exit criteria
Completion of the Incident Management process will be signaled by the occurrence of three events:
- Service has been restored to the normal state of affairs.
- The customer has confirmed service restoration.
- The incident ticket has been appropriately updated and closed.

Outputs
Completion of the exit events above will result in two discrete outputs:
- The incident ticket has been marked as 'closed'.
- The user has been notified that the incident has been closed.

NOTE: An automated output may be the programmed collection of record-related metrics.

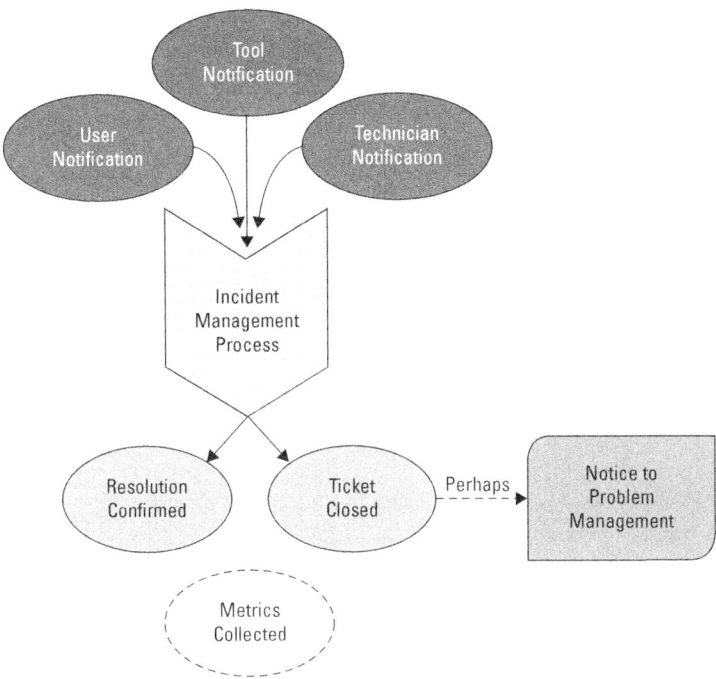

Figure 12.2 Inputs and outputs for Incident Management

12.3. Processes related to Incident Management

As a process, Incident Management has a distinct point of entry and a definitive end. But Incident Management does not directly rely on other ITIL processes to initiate its beginning or end. In that sense Incident Management can be thought of as a standalone process. That understanding, however, has only a very limited use. Incident Management might not be chained to other program elements but it is certainly highly integrated with the reach and purpose of these other elements. For example, an incident's resolution might trigger a Configuration Management action. It might inspire the creation of a change request. It might lead to a renegotiation of a service level requirement. Incident Management should be seen as a process with the potential to inform many of the other processes and functions in a Service Management program. In this section we will look at three core ITIL areas that are most strongly affected by an Incident Management program. These areas are the Service Desk, Problem Management, and Service Level Management.

Service Desk

Service Desk is described in ITIL V3 not as a process but as a function. A function is an operational unit within an organization that uses processes, so it is easy to see why the Service Desk is so directly affected by Incident Management. That process is one of the major (if not *the* major) responsibilities that a Service Desk operates from. That strong link prompts most organizations to develop their Incident Management processes and Service Desk functions together, as if they were two facets of the same program. And often the Service Desk manager and the service incident manager are the same person.

Service Desk activities are by necessity embedded between the lines of the Incident Management process. The inputs and entry criteria that start Incident Management arrive from the user community via the Service Desk. The registration and tracking of subsequent incident tickets are managed by the tools and facilities of the Service Desk. And the resolution and closure of incidents is controlled by Service Desk analysts. Both of these areas should support and complement one another in design and execution. (For more on this topic, see Chapter 14.)

In summary:
- The Service Desk is the unit that typically takes charge of incident handling activities.
- The Service Desk executes most Incident Management processes and procedures.
- The Service Desk is typically seen as the 'face' of Incident Management.
- The success of incident handling activities will depend largely on compatibility between Incident Management operations and Service Desk functions.

Problem Management

Incidents and problems are closely related. As noted at the beginning of this chapter, incidents are defined by ITL as service interruptions (or potentialities); problems are the underlying cause of repeated interruptions. Problem Management can be seen as a logical extension of Incident Management. Problem Management seeks to remove the possibility of certain kinds of incidents from reappearing. For this reason it is important to shape a Service Management program whereby these two processes are provided with a set point of convergence, in which incident analysts and problem analysts are encouraged to work closely together. This relationship between Problem Management and Incident Management is so close that many organizations shape the teams so that they even use the same tools: a common tracking system, shared diagnostic information, a common Known Error Database, a common Knowledge Management System, and so on. (For more on this topic, see Chapter 13.)

In summary:
- Repeated or recurring incidents inform Problem Management about areas of investigation and focus
- Incident resolution techniques can provide Problem Management with established and proven long-term corrective actions
- Problem Management personnel are very often the same analysts and technicians who contribute to Tier 2 and Tier 3 incident support
- Over time, Problem Management success will enhance Incident Management success

Service Level Management

Incident Management and Service Level Management exist in a shared closed-loop system of targets-performance-feedback. One informs the other. Service Level Agreements (SLAs) establish the priorities and areas of focus that Incident Management most typically operates under, and they set the performance levels that Incident Management activities are expected to attain. More so than perhaps other processes in a Service Management program, the visibility of Incident Management should prompt IT managers to closely align service level expectations with the capabilities and performance potential of its Incident Management teams. It is also important to understand how Incident Management performance may affect business relationships and to work with customer stakeholders to reach practical and achievable Incident Management performance goals. (For more on this topic, see Chapter 4.)

In summary:
- Service Level Management provides the prioritization by which Incident Management may focus its resources.
- Service Level Management establishes the performance yardstick against which Incident Management is measured.
- Incident Management performance over time provides a close-loop feedback system by which SLAs may be, in part, refined or renegotiated.
- Customer satisfaction levels, which are key to successful SLAs, are significantly influenced by Incident Management performance.

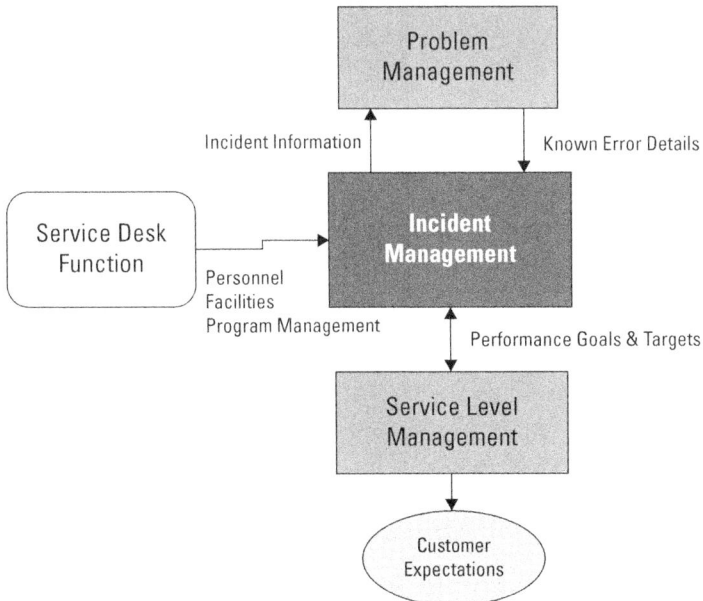

Figure 12.3 Processes and functions related to Incident Management

12.4. Tools and techniques

When implementing Incident Management programs, organizations usually account for more than just the activities that ITIL describes for this process. The relative maturity of Incident Management, especially in the customer service industry, has taught IT businesses the value of supplementing their process activities with a series of tools and techniques that complement and deepen those activities. The following table presents some of these most common tools and techniques.

Table 12.3 Tools and techniques for Incident Management

Incident Management Tracking System (IMTS)	This is essential in just about any Incident Management program. The IMTS is an automated tool used to register, track, update, and manage service tickets. Popular IMTS tools include FrontRange's IMTS, BMC's Remedy, HP's ServiceNow; and there are many others. The use of some kind of tool is probably the best way to ensure that individual tickets get the attention they deserve when volumes are coming in to the Service Desk.
Escalation guidelines	These are descriptions of the conditions and steps to employ when tickets need to be escalated from Tier 1 to Tier 2, Tier 2 to Tier 3, etc. The guidelines should include details that govern such factors as response timeframes and communication requirements. Guidelines like these are helpful because they bring consistency and repeatability to how tickets are handled, and they help ensure that the right tier of attention is being delivered by the right party.
Service Knowledge Management System (SKMS)	In the domain of ITIL an SKMS is a master repository of information on each service that the organization supports. This information can be technical or operational. Its purpose is to provide the details necessary for the regular use and maintenance of the service. Information in an SKMS can be accessed by support analysts in an Incident Management program as a tool for resolving common or previously encountered incidents, or for providing general information to a customer or technician.
Known Error Database	The *Known Error Database* is a repository where the organization stores records of all known errors in the infrastructure. You can think of a known error as an existing defect. In other words, something recognizable is wrong with the environment, but the organization – for one reason or another – cannot deal with it right now. Most of the time organizations address known errors by creating workarounds. A workaround is a temporary patch that alleviates the symptoms without addressing the real cause. In the ideal world, workarounds are temporary measures set in place until a real fix can be made. But that is not always the case. Sometimes workarounds remain in place for a long time. Because of this you want to know about them so that you can minimize how they affect the efficiency of the infrastructure. The KEDB helps keep track of the known errors while they exist.
Scripts and workflows	These are pre-configured support aids for use by the Service Desk and other support teams. Scripts can be set up to guide analysts through a series of diagnostic steps when working with customers to solve issues. Workflows lead analysts through a chain of support activity, a chain that has typically been shown to be effective for solving common or previously encountered issues.
Soft skills and problem-solving training	This kind of training is intended to enable Incident Management personnel to be effective when working with business customers. Soft skills training provides a basis for effective customer interactions, communications, and collaborative problem solving. Problem solving training provides analysts with the ability to more effectively diagnose, investigate, and solve customer issues.

12.5. Key Performance Indicators

KPIs are especially important for an Incident Management program because Incident Management is such a customer-facing activity. Most customers' dominant impression of overall IT performance is shaped by their interactions with the Service Desk, so it is important for management to be able to capture and analyze quantified snapshots of this performance. Following are some traditional KPIs that typical IT organizations tend to adopt. You may find these useful for your program.

Number of incidents

This is a simple base count of the total number of incidents that have occurred over a given period of time. It is useful as a macro-level performance indicator. It gives management an appreciation for the volume of work their operations teams have to deal with in support of the user community. This base measure can also be used to plot, over time, a high level trend lines to show how incident volumes are changing (descending, ascending, stabilizing) in relation to incident handling activities.

Incidents by type and/or category

Most organizations will classify incidents by type and/or category. This is a way to both order incidents and channel them to appropriate teams to be worked. As an example, an incident might be labeled a desktop failure, or an application failure, or perhaps a server failure. These type/category classifications reflect the shape of the infrastructure. Measures of incident volumes broken down by type and category can help management and operation teams understand better where to apply support resources. These measures can reveal where systemic weaknesses exist in the infrastructure, and thus reveal opportunities for refinement and improvement.

Incidents by severity

This measure is similar to the Type/Category one above. Here the number of incidents is broken down by severity level. Again, most organizations find that incidents can be better managed when they are prioritized according to severity. High severity levels take precedence over lower levels. A metric of this sort is useful because it quantifies the relative stability of the environment. Low or declining rates of high-severity incidents (major incident versus minor incidents) probably indicate that both the environment and support activities are well controlled.

Number of repeated incidents

This is another type of measure that can be used to reveal a picture of operational stability. Incidents that tend to repeat themselves usually indicate one of two things: there is a defect in the environment or users are following improper workflows. In either case a problem is indicated, so this KPI helps identify problems that are embedded either in the environment or in people's use of the environment. With this data as a starting point the problem can be identified, diagnosed, and resolved.

Number of incidents by customer group
These counts can be used to help management understand how effectively its customers are interfacing with the IT infrastructure. If the data points to a high number of incidents coming from a particular group, management may wish to investigate that group's IT components or the customer's use of those components. What may be indicated here is that the components need to be reconfigured or the customers themselves may need to receive some additional training.

Number of incidents by IT domain (Service)
This KPI is very similar to the one above; it can be seen (and used) as a complementary companion to that measure. Here the data is broken down into incident volumes by service. These number help management understand how effectively its business and technical services are operating. Just as with the KPI above, a trend pointing to a high number of incidents coming from a particular domain may warrant the investigation and reconfiguration of that domain's components. Or it may call for adjusting the customer's methods of interacting with those components

Number of incident escalations
These counts break down incidents by their movement from Tier 1 to Tier 2 to Tier 3 (etc.) support. This information can be used to highlight the percentage of incidents that are able to be solved by the first point of contact, the Service Desk crew, and the percentage that needed to be moved up to more specialized teams. The information here reveals two aspects of the environment: how well equipped the Service Desk is for dealing with incidents, and the nature of incident volumes in terms of complexity.

Number of internally resolved incidents versus externally resolved
This count shows the number of incidents that teams internal to the organization were able to resolve, compared with those that needed the attention of external support parties. This information is helpful to management because internal resolution usually means faster response times and lower costs. When an incident is of such a nature that it needs to be escalated to an external third party, time, effort, and costs go up. This information is also helpful because it serves as an indicator of how well equipped internal teams are for the day-to-day care of its environment.

Average time to resolve
This count can be either a global or a categorized look at the average time it takes to move an incident ticket from being in an 'initial' state to reaching a 'closed' state. The configuration of the organization's Incident Management tracking system will help capture this information as records are updated in the course of being managed. The time metric gives the organization an idea of support team responsiveness – how quickly the teams are able to move on and resolve incidents.

Average cost to resolve
This KPI is related to the time measure above. It is a calculation of the average cost invested to move an incident from its 'initial' state to a 'closed' state. Typically this cost is based on a combination of time-value plus any capital equipment/replacement

outlays. (Each organization will need to formulate this calculation based on its own business parameters.) This cost metric gives management an idea of the level of investment the operations teams are required to expend in order to resolve their mix of incidents.

Average number of resources to resolve

This count combines with the time and cost measures above to give a rounded picture of Incident Management business drivers. This is a look at the average number of staff needed to intervene in order to move the incident from the 'initial' state to the 'closed' state. A well-configured Incident Management Tracking System will update a ticket each time it is escalated or assigned to another party. This establishes a history of how many hands the ticket had to move through to reach resolution. In most IT organizations, the more hands that touch a ticket the longer resolution takes and the more expensive the resolution is.

12.6. Critical Success Factors

The KPIs noted in the section above can be used to establish targeted Incident Management performance. In this section we will address an additional set of metrics: measures that can be used to help determine the overall success of your program. These critical success factors (CSFs) can be seen as operational objectives, quality goals that, when reached, result in an Incident Management program that is fulfilling its organizational mission. Following is a series of typical CSFs you may wish to consider for your program.

NOTE: Once you define the CSFs that are right for your Incident Management program you may find it helpful to establish them as performance baselines in your service level agreements (SLAs). For more information on SLA development and use, see Chapter 4.

Service Desk availability

A successful Service Desk is going to be available when its customers need it. So this first CSF is a measure of how available Service Desk support is to the customer base. The target you select will need to be one that you work out with your customer; it needs to be mutually agreed-upon. Some Service Desks will need to be available 24 x 7. Others may simply need to be available during normal business hours in a common time zone. The availability factor you come up with will depend on your industry, your available resources, and the needs of your customer. In terms of the target, many organizations set an expected availability rate of 99.98% and many organizations set a minimum availability rate of 99.96%.

First call resolution rate

This is a measure of the number of incidents resolved on the initial call to the Service Desk. First call resolution rates (FCRs) are important because they indicate responsive, quality support delivery. The more FCRs an IT organization can deliver the higher customer satisfaction rates typically are. This is another target you will need to work with your customers to select. Because this is a high profile measure it is important to select a *practical* FCR target, and that requires that you have a good understanding of the nature of your environment and of the types of incidents your Service Desk typically receives. Many typical IT organizations set an expected first-call-resolution rate of 65%, and a minimum FCR rate of 60%.

Average speed to answer
This is a measure of how fast Service Desk analysts are able to pick up on a customer's call. When speed-to-answer is slow, customer frustration can rise, and call abandon rates (see next CSF) also rise. A successful Service Desk is one staffed and configured so that calls are answered quickly. So, as you shape your Incident Management program, work with your customers to select a target speed for how quickly Service Desk personnel should answer calls. Many organizations set an expected speed-to-answer rate at less than 15 seconds and a minimum at no more than 20 seconds.

Call abandon rate
This is a measure that shows how many calls to the Service Desk were abandoned by callers. Abandonment is usually (but not always) due to slow answers, no answers, or unusually long hold times. Low call abandon rates indicate a responsive and properly staffed Service Desk. Many organizations set expected call-abandon rates at less than 5% of total calls, with maximum call-abandon rates being set at 6% total calls.

Average resolution time for Priority 1 incidents
This is a measure of how fast Service Desk analysts are able to resolve Priority 1 incidents. In typical IT organizations incidents are classified as 'Priority 1' when they have both high impact and high urgency associated with them. These are the kinds of incidents that are highly visible either in terms of service interruption or user importance (e.g. a VIP executive). Target resolution times for Priority 1 incidents should be established between IT management and the customer so that adequate resources can be applied when Priority 1s arise. Many organizations set this expected target resolution time at 1 hour with a maximum resolution time of 1.5 hours.

Priority 2 through 5 incidents
These measures are identical to the one above. They break down resolution times for other incident priority levels. Note that it is not necessary for your program to use this 5-level priority schema, but you will probably want to employ some classification method in order to separate high-priority incident handling from low-priority handling.

12.7. Incident Management roles

The following job roles are typically seen in mature Incident Management programs. Each plays a part in ensuring that the program's activities are carried out as designed. Depending on the size and focus of the organization these roles may be full-time or part-time; combined or shared by multiple individuals. View the job titles and responsibilities described below as starting points for your own job descriptions. You will probably want to refine each of these to the particular needs of your IT organization.

Incident Management Process Owner

It is customary in ITIL-based Service Management programs to assign someone the duty of managing specific portions of the program. In this sense, the Incident Management program should have a process owner. The main roles of the process owner are to make sure that the program is developed in line with organizational needs, that it is appropriately documented and implemented, and that it is used in a compliant way by the right teams. In short, the process owner oversees use of the program for IT management. To summarize, the Incident Management Process Owner is responsible for:
- Developing and documenting the program
- Implementing the program across relevant teams
- Monitoring ongoing program use
- Measuring program performance over time
- Coordinating program improvements
- Coordinating program communications, training, and performance assessment

Service Incident Manager

The domain of IT Service Management introduces the concept of technology delivery in terms of services. An IT organization identifies which services it will offer its customer base (e.g. email, application hosting, etc.) and then sets up a management infrastructure to deliver those services. Typically each service is assigned a service owner, someone (usually on the technical staff) who is responsible for the delivery and quality of the service. It is also common to assign someone to be responsible for managing incidents that occur across that service's delivery spectrum. This is the service incident manager. The main job of the service incident manager is to make sure that incidents occurring for that service are being addressed in a timely and thorough manner. This manager is usually responsible for:
- Managing incidents related to a specific service or set of services
- Coordinating a service's Incident Management resources (Tier 1, 2, 3)
- Ensuring that critical performance levels as related to SLAs in the domain of Incident Management are consistently met
- Working with the Incident Management Process Owner to refine and develop the program in an effective manner over time
- Analyzing Service Desk performance data

- Analyzing customer satisfaction data
- Interfacing with Change Management and Problem Management

Tier 1 support

Tier 1 support (a common term, but not one you need to necessarily adopt) is usually interpreted as being the staff of the Service Desk. This team serves as the initial and primary point of contact for the user community when seeking technical support. This team initiates incident tickets and serves as the ultimate ticket owner across the resolution lifecycle. Typical responsibilities for this team include:

- Providing customers with a single point of contact for technical and business service support
- Providing telephone, self-submission, email, and fax intake
- Providing first-line incident investigation, diagnosis, and resolution
- Working in close collaboration with Tier 2 and Tier 3 staff
- Escalating ticket assignments when necessary
- Collecting Service Desk performance data
- Collecting customer satisfaction data

Tier 2 support

Tier 2 support personnel are typically internal analysts with a degree of specialty about technical support services. Very often they are called 'desk-side support' because they will actually visit customer work sites when needed to resolve an incident or service request. In any regard they provide the second line of support when Tier 1 teams are not able to resolve an issue. Typical responsibilities for this team include:

- Supporting Tier 1 Service Desk personnel in incident investigation, diagnosis, and resolution
- Providing desk-side support as needed
- Dealing with user equipment failures or reconfigurations
- Working in close collaboration with Tier 1 staff
- Escalating to Tier 3 staff when necessary

Tier 3 support

Tier 3 support teams are usually analysts with service specialties and major responsibilities apart from technical support. For example, an application architect might be made available from time to time to provide Tier 3 support. Tickets are usually escalated to Tier 3 when Tiers 1 and 2 need help with incident investigation, diagnosis, and resolution. Typical responsibilities for these teams include:

- Providing major component infrastructure support
- Dealing with infrastructure or enterprise failures or reconfigurations
- Working in close collaboration with Tier 2 staff
- Involving the input of external third party providers when necessary

Human Resource considerations

Following are some typical traits that Human Resource staff may want to take into consideration when they are providing personnel, staff aids, tools, and other resources for an Incident Management program.

Matching technology background: IT infrastructures are diverse environments. In order to properly support this diversity it is important that technical staff have familiarity and experience with the kinds of equipments and systems that make up the environment. This is certainly true when it comes to Service Desk personnel and Tier 2/Tier 3 analysts. Incident Management staff should be able to demonstrate that they have the background and experience that closely mirrors the infrastructure they are required to support. This experience may come from on-the-job work or training; but regardless the organization should view this state of competency as an obligation of ongoing continuing education.

Communication skills: Because Incident Management as a function deals closely with communications, support staff should be able to demonstrate strong verbal and written communication skills. These skills should fall into two areas. The first is the area of customer service: the ability to communicate work with non-technical business users in a professional and patient manner as solutions to issues are worked out. The second is the technical arena. Support staff should be able to communicate effectively with technical personnel while issues are being investigated, diagnosed, and resolved.

Comfort working in a process-centric environment: Incident Management staff should be comfortable working in a process-centric environment, one structured across culture-based practices and organizational assets, and one that promotes teamwork over individual 'heroics'. They should be open to learning about the organization's Incident Management program and contributing to its ordered growth.

Affinity for collaboration and teamwork: Incident Management staff must deal with a wide range of stakeholders – both business and technical. Thus it is helpful that they are adept at working in a collaborative manner within and across teams. This appreciation for teamwork is important to the success of the program as a whole. Incident registration, tracking, and resolution are seldom isolated activities. They involve coordination and cooperation across multiple units of the enterprise.

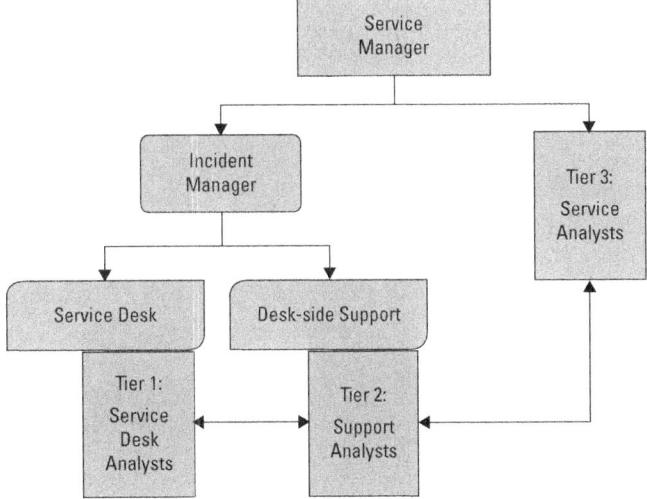

Figure 12.4 Incident Management role relationships

12.8. Benefits of effective Incident Management

The primary benefit to implementing a well-considered Incident Management program is clear: business missions can be realized in a more efficient manner. In fact, this can be taken as the primary benefit of an IT Service Management program as a whole. If this is to be considered a macro benefit, there are still other, micro benefits that an organization may enjoy when implementing Incident Management. Following are four of these benefits that arise naturally from the recommendations ITIL V3 makes for this particular process.

Establishes mechanisms for protecting the infrastructure's integrity

The key to high quality IT service delivery is a reliable infrastructure, one that can be shaped to the evolving needs of the business. Incident Management plays an important role in this shaping of the infrastructure. Incident Management serves as a foundation-level window, one that gives the organization a view into the workings of the environment. It is here, through this view, that issues and problems are often first made known, and it is here that resolutions, refinements, and long-term improvements may first come to light. An Incident Management program is one way to establish mechanisms to protect the integrity of the infrastructure. Through accrued assessments of Incident Management activities and trends over time, the organization will be able to identify ways to improve service performance, raise service quality, and ensure service integrity.

Develops a progressive capability for managing the infrastructure

As with any improvement initiative, an ITIL-based Service Management program is meant to be grown over time. Its eventual strength and return-on-investment (ROI) comes from this gradual maturation. This holds true for the Incident Management portion of the program. When an organization implements thoughtfully designed incident handling activities it is setting into place routines not just for addressing immediate concerns but for looking at long-term possibilities as well. The program is not just a tactical resolution activity but a strategic learning activity: what works well, what could be improved. Over time, an Incident Management program – as described by ITIL – can provide for the build-up of best-practice operational knowledge so that service performance traits can be progressively improved and refined as knowledge and experience advances.

Provides a means for demonstrating performance and responsiveness

The purpose of any IT Service Management initiative is for the program to demonstrate its value to the business; to show that the program advances the cause of the business. Incident Management, because it is so strongly customer-facing, is an ideal way to demonstrate IT's performance and responsiveness for the business. The measures an organization collects from its incident handling activities (see the CSF and KPI section earlier in this chapter) can be used by management as indicators of its commitment to both technical and business success. Resolving customer issues, investigating potential defects, providing ready advice and information, identifying opportunities for improvement: all of these further the ability of the business to meet its mission and market objectives, and indicate IT's contribution to these business goals.

Links business and IT missions

It is with Incident Management, through the Service Desk, that business users interact with IT the most. And it is here that users may most readily come to appreciate IT's contribution to their various business tasks. Helping restore normal business routines may seem at first to be an on-again/off-again activity, but over time the impression that Incident Management makes on the user community is one of reliable partnership. The immediacy of Incident Management combines with its dependable availability to make it a prime source for linking business missions with the mission of IT Service Management. When technology teams consistently reinforce their customers' job roles this partnership becomes a real part of the business, an integral part of the business. And from this there comes a blending, the merging that is anticipated in IT Service Management, where business and technology missions are no longer separated but become one and the same.

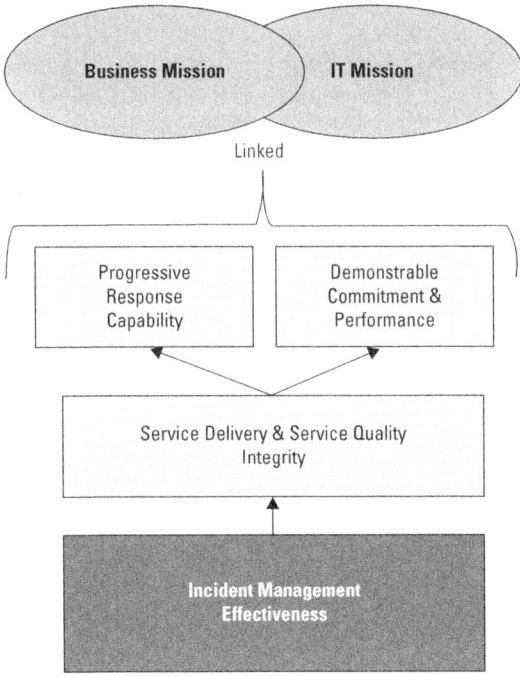

Figure 12.5 Incident Management benefits

12.9. Implementation challenges and considerations

Because the activities of Incident Management are so thoroughly customer-facing, an organization developing an Incident Management program should do so with a well-rounded view of what it will take to make that program successful. Perhaps more so than any other ITIL process, implementation of Incident Management carries with it a set of (practically) pre-established requisites, factors proven over time and experience as being central to Incident Management success. These factors are not complex so much as sophisticated. They require solid executive commitment and the application of resources over time; and so accounting for these factors can be challenging even for mature organizations. But when you consider the function of the Service Desk (as discussed in Chapter 14) and the goals of Incident Management it is hard to relegate any of these – there are six – to the sideline. Consider these as you begin to build your program and make plans to implement it.

Developing well-trained, experienced support staff

Perhaps the single greatest challenge for effective Incident Management is developing and retaining a well-trained, experienced technical support staff. It is easy to appreciate the value of such a staff when you consider the mix of skills they are required to move seamlessly between. For instance, they should have polished and patient interpersonal skills. They should also possess acute investigative and problem solving abilities. They should have a solid technical knowledge of what is likely to be a complex and diverse IT environment. And they should be dependable record-keepers. Developing such a staff requires smart hiring practices, continuing education, the provision of up-to-date support materials, and a focused employee retention program. The organization that works to mold such a qualified staff however will find that its Incident Management program is equipped to meet even the toughest of performance expectations

Establishing effective incident reporting and notification avenues

Incident Management is at heart a people activity, not a tool activity. And so it is important to any Incident Management program that there are very clear and easy-access channels for reporting incidents and communicating their assignment and status across the incident lifecycle. Without such channels tickets may get waylaid, or set aside due to lack of ownership. To facilitate such channels, the organization should provide effective processes and procedures for managing incidents across different support tiers, accounting for staff assignments, resolutions activities, and status updating at set milestones. The organization should also provide effective communication and status routes, routes that can be used to inform customer stakeholders as well as IT management about resolution activities.

Configuring sound ticket tracking and management tools

Incident Management may be a people activity but it is an activity that relies in large part on the effective management of incident tickets. That is why virtually all Incident Management programs are physically based around some form of ticket tracking and management system. The reason is clear: an incident is ultimately a record, a record of an anomaly. Being a record it is documented, transferred to parties, updated, and tracked. That requires a tool. In large, dynamic, or sensitive environments such a tool is indispensible. When implementing its Incident Management program, the organization should provide incident tracking tools appropriately configured to the needs of the program. Key activities to account for should include: registration, ownership assignment, classification, prioritization, journal entries, status updates, and resolution descriptions.

Providing accessible service documentation
This factor is simple, but it is a challenge for most organizations. Its importance, however, cannot be overestimated. In order for support staff to address incidents effectively, those people need easy and ready access to current and complete service documentation – business service and technical service documentation. And yet all too often that documentation is lacking. Many IT organizations, for whatever reasons, are not well versed at establishing good service documentation and maintaining that documentation over time. When it is missing, incomplete, or out of date, even the most talented support teams may struggle to investigate incidents and resolve them in a timely manner. Although it is such a challenge, every organization implementing an Incident Management program should ensure that technical support teams have access to complete and accurate service documentation. The organization should make an ongoing investment in the creation of this documentation and in its regular maintenance and upkeep.

Establishing balanced Service Level Agreements
This implementation challenge rests more with IT management than it does with the Incident Management program. Yet it needs to be considered, because the shape and requirements of the SLA will go a long way to interpreting the success of an Incident Management program. The challenge is to establish *balanced* SLAs. As noted in Chapter 4, SLAs should reflect realistic performance targets for Service Management activities, and that includes Incident Management. In order to do that, IT management and the customer together must agree what 'realistic' really means. That will require input from incident managers and participation in the SLA negotiation process. In addition to establishing SLAs with documented Incident Management goals and objectives, the organization should regularly report on Incident Management performance levels.

Promoting stakeholder communications
This implementation challenge, not being a tool or document or tangible skill set, might be considered 'soft' in nature. But it lies at the heart of why many Incident Management programs fail to achieve the high level of customer appreciation IT managers feel they deserve. Customer communications – proactively and regularly informing the customer about the progress and status of incidents – is essential for any Incident Management program that wants to be *perceived* as being effective. That perception is important. Customers who report issues to the Service Desk do not want to be left in the dark about what is happening with their issues. Yet many Service Desk operations tend to focus solely on solving the issue rather than communicating with the customer. And yet when customer communication is shown to be high, customer satisfaction levels tend to rise – despite the resolution outcomes. It follows that IT organizations should promote open and on-going customer communications as a core ingredient of its Incident Management program.

12.10. Typical assets and artifacts of an Incident Management program

The Incident Management program your organization develops will need to be founded on a set of documented assets and artifacts. Assets are the program materials that bound how the program is governed and run. Artifacts are those work products that emerge when your teams exercise the assets. Following is a list of some common assets and artifacts that are found in typical Incident Management programs. Your program may call for some of these; you may wish to create some things not described here; but this list, while not exhaustive, is typical.

Incident Management policy
This is an executive policy that stipulates the goals and objectives of the Incident Management program. The policy, which ideally should be no longer than a few pages, documents at a high level the purpose of the program, the resources available to the program, the chief responsibilities of the program, quality targets, reporting hierarchies, and program measures. Endorsed by executive management, the policy is a demonstration of organizational commitment to the value and importance of the program.

Incident tracking system
Virtually every IT organization will implement some form of Incident Management Tracking System to support its Incident Management program. This system is employed as the key tool for recording, tracking, and managing incident tickets. It is central to how incident handling activities are conducted. Service Desk personnel are the main users of the system, but are by no means the only users. Tier 2 and Tier 3 teams will rely on the system for managing escalations, and IT management will rely on the system, for views into workloads, performance, and measures.

Ticket resolution guidelines
Because an IT community is, at least at the macro level, a fairly stable environment, most organizations will find that they tend to encounter common types of incidents. In order to address these in the most efficient way possible it is handy to create a set of ticket resolution guidelines. These guidelines detail the steps required to move an incident ticket from an open state to a resolved state. For commonly occurring incidents the guidelines can also provide discrete resolution steps that have proved to be effective in addressing the incident on past occasions. These guidelines might take the form of a paper or online document; they might even be configured as workflows invoked by the Incident Management system you are using.

Ticket escalation guidelines
In order to manage incident tickets in a consistent and controllable manner, the different technical support teams will need to know how and when tickets should be escalated. Documented ticket escalation gguidelines can provide that knowledge.

They detail the rules surrounding how and when to escalate ticket ownership from one support tier to another. They set down the conditions, modes of transfer, methods of tracking, and communication rules for each tier of support you have instantiated. (Note: an Operational Level Agreement - OLA - should be established to help cement these guidelines across teams.)

Incident Management measurement plan

In order for an Incident Management program to be effectively controlled, it needs to be measured. The Incident Management Measurement plan is a means for doing just that. It identifies and defines metrics to capture in order to assess the performance of the incident handling activities. A typical plan will describe the measures, define how to collect them, specify where the pulled data are to be stored, and provide formulae for analyzing this data. The measures you select will depend naturally on the needs of your IT organization, but the CSFs and the KPIs described in this chapter are examples of the kinds of measures you may wish to set up for your Incident Management program.

Incident Management reporting and distribution procedure

This is a documented procedure that describes how Incident Management reports are created, how often they are generated, and to whom they are to be disseminated. This procedure can be seen as an extension of the Incident Management Measurement Plan described above. Together these artifacts provide the kind of information needed by management and the customer to understand the effectiveness of incident handling activities and identify opportunities for improvement.

Service Level Agreement

An SLA in this case is a documented agreement between Incident Management personnel (via IT management) and the customer. The agreement defines performance expectations about how incidents are handled (e.g. response times, priorities, communications, etc.). The items that are usually covered are: incident identification, tracking, resolution, and reporting. An Incident Management SLA is important because it establishes common performance expectations between parties and sets a quality target for the Incident Management program to aim for. (For more on the shape and structure of SLAs, see Chapter 4.)

Organizational chart

This is a chart that shows the structural make-up of the Service Desk and other Incident Management teams. Its purpose is to identify teams, team relationships, and hierarchical flows. The shape of this chart will naturally depend on the general shape of your organization. But if you were to visualize a textbook shaped Incident Management Program you might see a chart with three trunks. The main trunk would flow down from Incident Manager to Help Desk (with perhaps a dotted line connecting Incident Manager to Incident Management Process Owner). The Service Desk would be linked horizontally to the second trunk, Tier 2 Support (perhaps Desk-side Support); and Tier 2 to Tier 3 Support (e.g. Technical Service Analyst). The Tier

2 and Tier 3 units might have a vertical line reaching up to their own management units but also have a dotted line connecting them, at least lightly, to Incident Manager.

Roles and responsibilities matrix

This artifact is an extension of the organizational chart above. It is a matrix that describes the various roles and responsibilities the organization has assigned to support its Incident Management program. The roles typically include such positions as Incident Manager Process Owner, Global Incident Manager, Service Incident Manager, Service Desk Analyst, Desk-side Support Analyst (Tier 2 Support), Technical Service Analyst (Tier 3 Support), and so on. Along with the job role definitions come descriptions of the responsibilities each role should account for, and references to how roles interrelate and communicate. The matrix might take one of several forms: a spreadsheet, a series of database records, or a version-controlled text document. Ownership of this artifact is usually shared between IT management and Human Resource management.

13. Problem Management

In the previous chapter we looked at Incident Management. In this chapter we address Problem Management. Incident Management and Problem Management are in fact very similar. Both processes deal with essentially the same activities: identifying operational issues, diagnosing them, and then setting resolutions into place to neutralize the impacts. The main differences with these two are timing and the angle of focus. As we have seen, Incident Management is almost always a 'right now' activity. Since its goal is to restore the normal state of IT affairs as quickly as possible incidents tend to be addressed in real time. On top of that, the resolutions reached by support analysts are not always technically robust or complete. These are only required to be good enough to get the user up and running again. Things are slightly different with Problem Management. To appreciate that, let's start with a definition. ITIL V3 defines a problem as:

"...the underlying cause of a set of related incidents or an incident that affects multiple users."

Through this definition Problem Management can be seen as a logical extension of Incident Management. The purpose of Problem Management supports this extension. ITIL V3 states that the purpose of Problem Management is...

"To identify and remove the root cause of incidents either through correction or the implementation of a workaround."

At the base of this purpose statement are two key points:
- Problems are the underlying causes of many (but not all) incidents; incidents are often (though not always) the symptoms of problems.
- Problem Management seeks to remove these underlying causes so that the incidents and problems do not reappear.

This sets the stage to note the angle of focus Problem Management is concerned with. While incidents demand prompt attention, problems usually required more considered attention. As incidents are typically addressed in an immediate (real time) manner, problems are typically addressed in a 'slower time' (planned and scheduled) manner. The core activity of Problem Management is root cause analysis (RCA), which takes time and requires specialized resources. The complexity and sophistication of most IT infrastructures make these prerequisites a necessity. On top of that, multiple solutions may be available with which to address a problem; these alternatives need to be evaluated and compared. Finally, problem resolutions may require the reconfiguration of IT components, and this may require that the resolutions move through a formal approval process, such as change control. The considerations that Problem Management addresses can be summarized as follows:

- How to detect and identify problems as they emerge
- How root causes are investigated and evaluated
- How potential corrections and workarounds are determined and assessed
- How known errors are tracked and managed
- How corrections and workarounds are planned and implemented

In this chapter we will look at the activities that ITIL recommends for Problem Management and then investigate how such a process might be effectively configured for an IT organization. To begin, let's look at a typical Problem Management process flow:

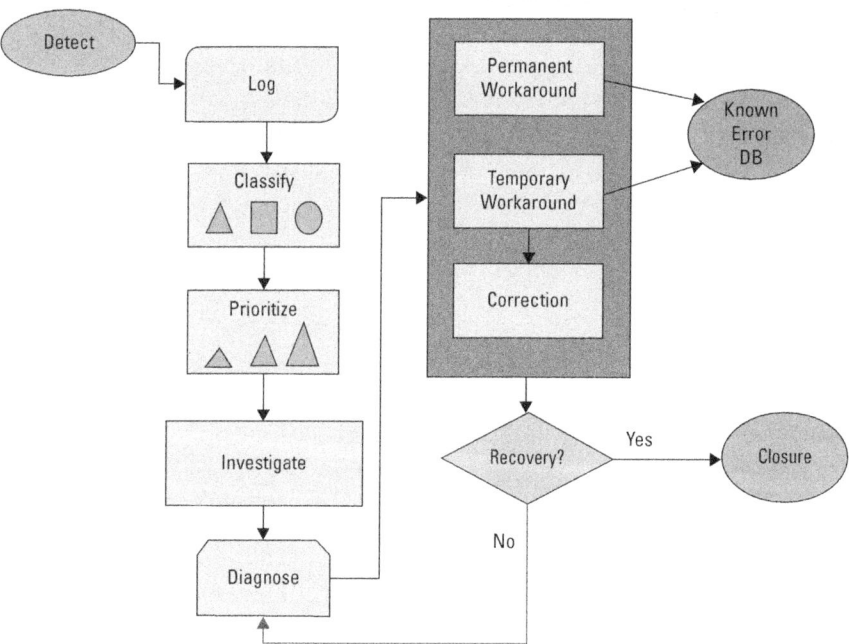

Figure 13.1 Typical Problem Management process flow

13.1. Problem Management activities

The Problem Management process is intended to work operational issues toward a successful resolution, one with technical integrity and lasting effect. ITIL V3 recommends nine steps in the Problem Management workflow. Here is a description of each in the order they typically occur.

1. Detection

The first activity described for Problem Management – the entry state, so to speak – is that of detection, becoming aware that a problem exists. Detection usually takes one of three forms. The first form appears at the Service Desk; it comes from incident analysis. If Service Desk analysts notice a series of seemingly related incidents or a string of repeated incidents they will usually conduct a focused investigation, one that may even involve escalated (Tier 2 or Tier 3) support. This investigation may result in a problem being discovered: a single cause driving the incident sets. The second appears with monitoring and control activities by IT operation teams. These analysts, in monitoring the environment, may detect a problem when a control device signals an alert or when a severe technical event (such as a power outage) occurs. The operations team may then issue an internal problem notification. The third form takes shape as an external notification. This occurs when a vendor or some other third party sends a notice to the organization informing of a defect in a service component or system and offering advice on corrective action.

2. Logging

Once a problem is detected it should be logged. Many Problem Management programs make use of a Problem Tracking System, a database for creating, updating, and managing problem records. Logging is the first step in Problem Management. Logging includes establishing a baseline description of the problem and then ensuring that this baseline is updated as work on the problem proceeds over time. The following elements are typical of the kinds of attributes you might wish to record for each active problem.

Table 13.1 Typical elements of a problem record

Problem ID	A unique ID for the problem (usually assigned by the Problem Tracking System)
Problem Title	A summary description of the problem
Description	A detailed description of the problem (including observed cause and resulting impacts); may be updated over time
Submitter	The ID of the person or tool reporting the problem
Status	An activity code for the current working state of the problem
Submitter Contact	Contact information (e.g. department phone email) of the person reporting the problem
Date/Time	A time-stamp on when the problem was logged
Owner	The ID of the person or team to whom the problem has been assigned
Initial Follow-on	A brief description of the follow-on action prompted by problem registration

And then these elements are added as work on the ticket proceeds (Table 13.2).

Table 13.2 Additional elements of a problem record

Root Cause	A narrative text entry describing the investigation results and documenting the problem's root cause. This description may be updated over time, and often features a link to an external, fuller RCA document.
RFC ID	The ID of any request for change that may be associated with this problem
Resolution Alternatives	A narrative text entry that describes the potential alternative solutions that should be considered in response to the RCA results. Each alternative should contain a technical approach, an impact analysis (cost and benefits), and a risk analysis.

Workaround	If the selected solution to the problem includes a temporary or long-term workaround, then the elements of that workaround should be described in detail here. The description should touch on the configuration of the workaround, its required maintenance, and any performance tradeoffs that might ensure from implementation. A reference to a record in the Known Error database might also be included here.
Verified Resolution	This is a text description of the final verified steps taken to resolve the problem.

3. Categorization

In order that problems can be worked on by appropriate teams it is helpful to assign them to some form of operational category. Categorization is a way to tag a problem record so that it may be directed down the proper channel. Categorization serves as a kind of pointer. As problems are, by definition, specialized events they require the attention of specialized teams. In most IT organizations teams work in particular domains (e.g. network teams, application teams, telecom teams, etc). Particular problems should be owned by their particular teams. A categorization scheme can help you set that ownership.

There are many options available for how an organization might structure a Problem Management categorization schema. The following are a few common examples (you will notice that they are closely allied to the kinds of classification schemes that support Incident Management):

- Categorize by service (e.g. email, networking, printer support, etc.)
- Categorize by service component (e.g. file server, exchange server, router, personal digital assistant, etc.)
- Categorize by problem type (e.g. access, security, printing, desktop application, etc.)
- Categorize by platform (e.g. PeopleSoft, DB2, Oracle, Outlook, etc.)
- Categorize by customer group (e.g. accounting, marketing, shipping, etc.)

The implementation advice is to shape the categorization scheme in line with what brings most value to your teams.

4. Prioritization

Once a problem has been categorized, the problem manager will have a better idea about how to handle it. At this point it becomes important to consider prioritization. Prioritization is a way to line up Problem Management work so resources focus on the most critical issues first. It is helpful for a Problem Management program to establish some ordering guidelines. By using priority criteria and associated priority codes, problem managers can assess the essence of a problem and assign it a code that will shape its visibility in work queues. Problems of higher criticality can receive higher priority codes and thus receive quicker attention. As with Incident Management, ITIL offers a calculation to drive Problem Management prioritization:

impact + urgency = priority

Through this formula the impact of a problem is assigned a value (the organization sets the value range): a high value for high impact, a low value for low impact. The same approach is taken with urgency. Very urgent problems get higher urgency values. Here is an example: A lightning strike incapacitates a data center's cooling system. Because that outage threatens the performance of a significant portion of the infrastructure, Problem Management might assign this issue an impact code of 5 (high on a scale of 1 to 5). And since certain essential business operations are timed to run imminently, Problem Management might give the situation an urgency code of 5 also. Thus a final priority value of 10 would be the result.

When this priority code (together with categorization) brings the problem to the attention of the right technical team, the team can begin the process of investigation and diagnosis.

5. Investigation and diagnosis
Investigation and diagnosis in the domain of Problem Management takes the form of root cause analysis (RCA). RCA is a formal discipline in which a problem is analyzed for the purpose of determining its originating source. Address the source appropriately and the problem should go away. Miss it and symptoms will be likely to persist. RCA is a cornerstone activity in Problem Management; and it should be a focal point of any Problem Management program. Once RCA has revealed the problem's true nature, problem teams may then apply their technical expertise to come up with possible resolutions. Alternatives should be identified and then compared in terms of reliability, impact, time to deliver, cost, etc. As we see in Step 6 below, alternatives may include workarounds as well as permanent corrections.

6. Establishment of workaround
A workaround is an operational detour. If a permanent fix for a problem is not currently possible or feasible, the best solution may be to work around it, to set in place a patch that will alleviate the impact of the problem without perhaps directly removing the underlying source. Sometimes workarounds are used while permanent solutions are being designed. Sometimes they are employed because a permanent solution proves too expensive or too resource-intensive. When an organization elects to deploy a workaround in place of a technical correction it is important to ensure that the workaround is thoroughly documented – see Step 7.

7. Creation of Known Error Record
A known error is a defect in the environment that has been addressed through a workaround. A common tool in many Problem Management programs is a Known Error Database (KEDB). The KEDB stores a record of every known error in the environment. It is a repository for all information on the errors (most typically infrastructure defects and vulnerabilities) and includes detailed descriptions of the design and configuration of their associated workarounds. Every time a workaround is accepted as part of a problem's resolution a new known error record should be created.

8. Resolution

Problem resolution can take form in one of three states. First, the organization might simply implement a permanent fix in response to the problem. A basic example of this might be replacing a computer's power supply. Second, the organization might set a temporary workaround in place while a permanent fix is being prepared. Once the fix is available the workaround is removed. This is usually done when the fix requires significant design consideration or construction work. Third, the organization might elect to implement a workaround and treat it as the permanent solution. This is often the case when a corrective fix would be prohibitively expensive or not technically practical. In all of these cases, however, the end result is that the problem has been addressed and the operability of the environment is once more under control. That is the main goal of resolution.

NOTE: Often, the correction or workaround is of such a nature that before it can be selected and worked it will need to first move through the formal change control process (for more on this, see Chapter 7).

9. Closure

With Problem Management, closure comes when a permanent correction or an acceptable workaround has been set into place and the problem's negative potential is no longer a threat to operational productivity. Once the user community has confirmed that the resolution is indeed complete the problem record can be marked as closed. This will remove it from any active work queues and free up resources to work other pending problems. This act of closing is also a cue to communicate this final status to the customer and any other relevant stakeholders who may have been connected with the problem resolution activities.

13.2. Process inputs and outputs

Compared to the Incident Management process, the Problem Management process can be seen as a process that is not in real time; that is, it is conducted not so much with a sense of urgency as with a sense of thoroughness. It is a *planned* activity. Additionally, the inputs and outputs that drive this process are almost always clear and unambiguous (as they might not be with Incident Management). Here is a look at the typical entry criteria/inputs and exit criteria/outputs that bound traditional Problem Management activities.

Entry criteria

The Problem Management process can be started when a single, simple entry condition is met:
- The organization becomes aware of a problem through either an encounter (an event) or a notification.

Inputs

The entry criteria are usually met when the organization receives one or more of the following:

- A review of related or repeated incident tickets reveals the existence of a likely problem, or
- An internal operational assessment reveals the existence of a likely problem, and a problem notification is released; or
- An external notification is sent to the organization describing the presence of a likely problem, or
- A *force majeure* event occurs.

Exit criteria

Completion of the Problem Management process is typically signaled by the occurrence of three conditions:

- A solution has been implemented such that defects have been mitigated and IT service has been restored to the normal state of affairs and
- The customer has verified service restoration, and
- The problem record has been updated with resolution detail (and perhaps an entry in the Known Error Database has been made).

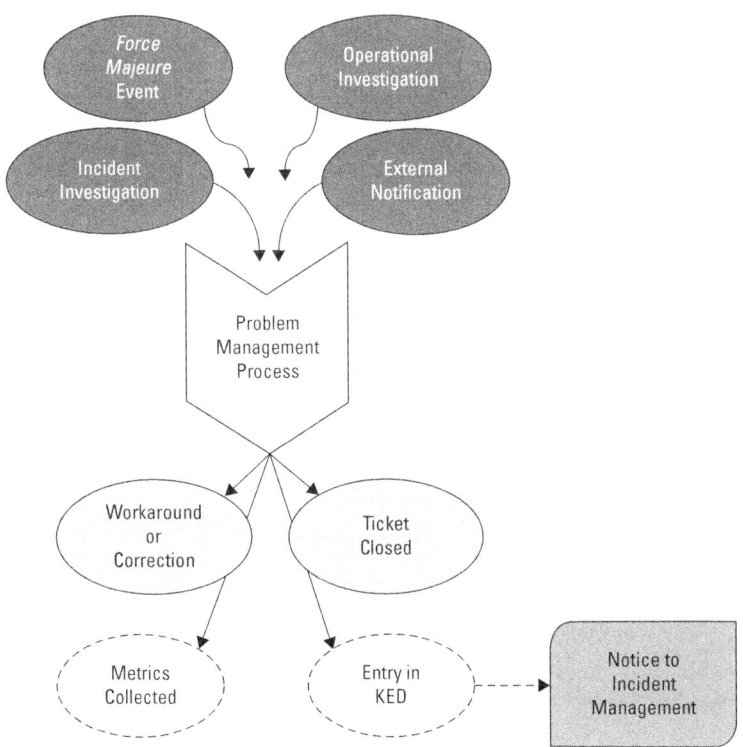

Figure 13.2 Inputs and outputs for Problem Management

Outputs

Completion of the above exit events will result in two discrete outputs:
- The problem record has been marked as 'closed'.
- Notification that the problem has been resolved and closed has been sent to relevant stakeholders.

NOTE: An automated output may be the programmed collection of activity-related metrics. (See the Key Performance Indicator section later in this chapter.)

13.3. Processes related to Problem Management

Problem Management can be seen as a continual improvement activity. Operations are monitored, weaknesses are spotted, opportunities are assessed, improvements are implemented, monitoring begins again. This is why Problem Management is such an important core ITIL process. Its impacts radiate not just across Service Operation domains, but across Service Strategy, Service Design, and Service Transition domains as well. As you begin to design your IT Service Management program, consider the global role that Problem Management can play. At the same time, look at the micro level. There are three other processes in the core set that work hand-in-hand with Problem Management, each directly supporting the other. In building your program you will want to keep these relationships in mind. In this section we will take a brief look at these three. They are Incident Management, Service Asset and Configuration Management, and Change Management.

Incident Management

Problem Management and Incident Management are so closely related that even their process steps track together. As was mentioned at the start of Chapter 12, Incident Management is a resolution activity that takes place in near real-time. Problem Management is a resolution activity that takes place in slower time. Incident Management is reactive; Problem Management is planned. But they are both aimed at identifying, investigating, and resolving issues. At the same time, Incident Management as a process is an important source of input for Problem Management. It is usually through Incident Management that problem trends are first identified. Service Desk analysts are key players, noticing related or repeated incidents and tracing them to apparent common causes. In fact, Incident Management investigations across all tiers – not just the Service Desk – often result in the identification of hitherto unknown problems. Finally, Incident Management activities provide a verification step to gauge the effectiveness of problem resolutions once they have been implemented.

In summary:
- Incident notifications to the Service Desk are usually the first indication that a problem has developed.
- Incident handling activities provide first-line investigation data to problem analysts.
- Incident Management observations provide insight into problem resolution effectiveness.

Service Asset and Configuration Management

Because problem resolutions may require the acquisition of new service assets or require configuration changes to existing assets, it is important to link Problem Management considerations with Service Asset and Configuration Management activities. When this link is not made, information in the Configuration Management Database (CMDB) can quickly become out of date, inaccurate. Then not only is the integrity of reference material lost, but coming full circle, subsequent problem investigations may suffer as well. An effective IT Service Management program will promote an ongoing alignment between Problem Management and Configuration Management. (For more on the subject of Service Asset and Configuration Management, see Chapter 9.)

In summary:
- Problem resolutions may require the acquisition of new service assets.
- Root cause analysis activities will need to account for current service component configurations.
- Problem resolution assessments will need to reference configuration data in order to weigh such factors as impact, risk, and scope.
- Problem resolutions may require that service components be reconfigured and thus configuration item (CI) records updated.

Change Management

Many routine problem solutions will be of such a minor nature that they may be implemented with but a minimum of oversight, much in the same way that incidents are. There will be, however, problems whose resolutions are significant enough that their implementations need to be more tightly controlled. For these situations problem resolution activities should be moved through the Change Management process. This is especially true when a resolution carries a high degree of risk, has wide ranging impacts, requires significant resources, or is capital-intensive. Change control protects the production environment by establishing a series of quality gates and communication channels, ensuring that proposed solutions are reviewed, assessed, and then decided on by key stakeholders across the organization. Many organizations, in developing their Problem Management programs, establish criteria (risk, impact, resource levels, etc.) which can be used to weight proposed problem solutions, distinguishing those that need to move through change control from those that do not. (For more on the topic of Change Management, see Chapter 8.)

In summary:
- Problem resolutions may be significant enough that they need to move through the formal change request and review process.
- Proposed problem resolutions may need to be assessed against pending or approved requests for change (RFCs) in order to understand any potential conflicts or overlaps.
- Certain resolutions may need to be packaged in scheduled releases that are set by Change Management.

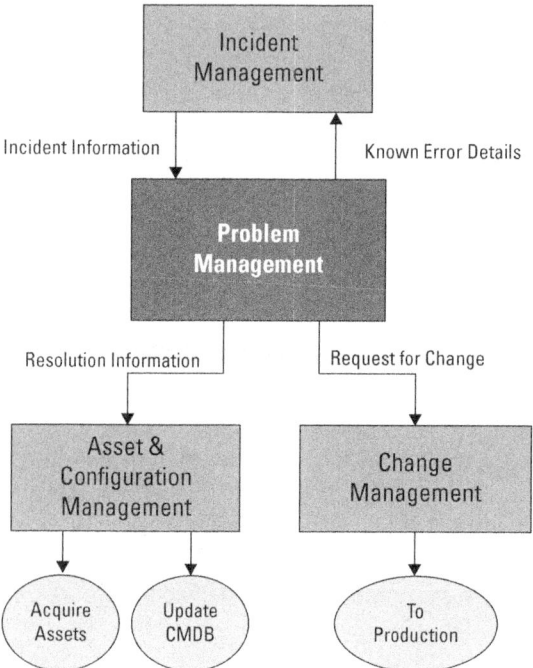

Figure 13.3 Processes related to Problem Management

13.4. Tools and techniques

Problem Management programs are usually supported by a set of problem solving techniques and the use of some Problem Management tools. The tools and techniques your organization elects to employ will depend largely on the shape of your program and the needs of your environment. However, over time the industry has come to recognize that many Problem Management programs adopt a common set of what might be called 'base' tools and techniques. The following table presents a listing of these.

Table 13.3 Tools and techniques for Problem Management

Problem Tracking System	A *Problem Tracking System* (PTS) is an automated tool used to help manage the documentation associated with work on problems. The system houses a record for each problem. The record initially contains identifying information for the problem (e.g. ID, description, priority, status, etc.). As work on the problem proceeds, the record will be updated to reflect such data as root cause and solution alternatives. When the problem is finally resolved, the record will be updated to reflect implemented solution. The PTS can also be used to establish work aids such as prioritized work queues, and status reports.

Root Cause Analysis guidelines	One of the main jobs for Problem Management teams is to perform *root cause analyses* (RCAs), to determine the underlying source of environmental defects. There are various approaches one can take with RCAs. Failure Mode Analysis, fishbone diagramming, and brainstorming are three common techniques. Whichever approach the organization takes, it is helpful to establish guidelines so that problem teams may approach RCA in a consistent and predictable way. These guidelines will typically cover things such as investigation techniques, evidence gathering, data analysis, root cause documentation, root cause testing, solution analysis, and solution proposal documentation.
Service Knowledge Management System	The *Service Knowledge Management System* (SKMS) is a master repository of information on each service that the organization supports. This information typically blends technical specifications with operational data. Its purpose is to provide the details necessary for the regular use and maintenance of each service. Information in the SKMS is important to problem analysts because it provides reference that can be used when investigating how services should be configured, how they are expected to operate, and what service components support each.
Known Error Database	The *Known Error Database* is a repository where the organization stores records of all known errors in the environment. Often the KEDB is a module within the SKMS. Problem analysts might use the KEDB one of two ways. First, they will reference the KEDB as part of initial problem investigations, in order to determine if the source of the current problem might have been previously identified and documented. Second, if the solution to a current problem is to implement a workaround into the environment (temporary or long-term) then the problem analysts will document this workaround and make a new entry into the KEDB.

13.5. Key Performance Indicators

The desired situation for any Problem Management program is that activity levels are low. In other words, there are very few problems. Such an ideal may, however, be hard to achieve. With infrastructures that are relatively immature, that embrace new technologies, that are in difficult environments, or operate in dynamic industries, problems are a real and unavoidable part of the picture. KPIs in this area can help IT management better understand just what part of the picture operational problems are occupying. Following are some common KPIs that typical IT organizations adopt. Some of these may have a useful place in your program.

Number of problems

This is a simple base count of the total number of problems that have occurred over a given period of time. It is useful as a macro-level performance indicator. It gives management an appreciation for the volume of problem-related work, and a view into the overall stability of the environment. This base measure can also be used to plot, over time, high-level trend lines to show how problem volumes are changing (descending, ascending, stabilizing) in relation to Problem Management activities.

Number of change requests related to problem activity
This measure is a count of the number of problems that led to the creation of formal change requests. An analysis of this metric can reveal two things. First, it can show management the level of problems significant enough to be placed under Change Management, thus the severity of problems being dealt with. Also it can help management evaluate how problem activities are affecting the core business of the organization. In other words, it can show to what degree attention to problems is distracting the IT organization from its more forward-thinking work.

Incidents-to-problem relationships
These counts establish the relationship between incidents and problems. In a typical many-to-one relationship, the measure links related or repeated incidents to the problem that proved to be the underlying cause. This data is helpful for understanding the stability of the infrastructure, showing what sets of incidents flow from which sets of problems.

Problems by severity
With this KPI, the number of problems is broken down by severity level. Most organizations find that problems are better managed when they are prioritized according to severity. High severity levels take precedence over lower levels. A metric of this sort is useful because it quantifies the relative stability of the environment. Low or declining rates of high-severity problems probably indicate that both the environment and support activities are well controlled.

Number of problems by customer group
These counts can be used to help management understand how effectively its customers are interfacing with the IT infrastructure, and how well that infrastructure is serving the customer base. If the data points to a high number of problems coming from a particular user group, management may wish to investigate that group's IT components or the customer's use of those components. What may be indicated here is that the components need to be assessed for their configurations or the customers themselves may need to receive some additional training and support.

Number of problems by service component
The numbers here help management understand how stably the IT infrastructure is operating and how reliable certain components are. A trend pointing to a high number of problems coming from a particular domain, a specific brand of equipment, or a certain type of asset may warrant investigating the equipment's service record and market dependability. This information can become very useful when infrastructure expansions are being planned or when new equipment purchases are being considered.

Number of problems by project type
These counts break down problems by the development efforts they are associated with. This metric is useful as a means of tracing the originating source of a problem. Many problems are *deus ex machina* events, out of the organization's control. But others are self-imposed. (Software bugs are a ready example.) This metric groups

problems by the development projects they appear to have sprung from. It is a way to trace the origination of problems to the teams who created the work. This analysis may reveal the need to support the teams with additional tools, resources, or training.

Number of problem-initiated development projects

This count shows the number of problems that needed to be addressed through the establishment of formal projects in order to be resolved. This is an important metric because IT resources are limited. An organization can undertake only a finite number of projects. If the numbers here show that a disproportionate number of projects are dedicated to retrofitting functionality, in effect, the indication is that the IT organization's limited resources are being diverted from forward-moving activities to basic everyday activities.

Number of externally resolved problems

This measure shows the number of problems that needed to be resolved by teams external to the organization. This metric is useful for two purposes. First, it gives management a view into the average complexity (severity) of problems. Those that require external intervention usually prove to be of a complex nature. Second, it links Problem Management effectiveness to cost. If internal teams need to rely more than usual on external help, resolution costs will probably be higher than planned and internal Problem Management effectiveness may be lower than desired.

Average time to resolve

This count can be used as either a global or a categorized look at the average time it takes to move a problem ticket from being in its 'detected' state to reaching a 'closed' state. The configuration of the organization's Problem Tracking System can help capture this information as records are updated in the course of being managed. This time metric gives the organization an idea of service team responsiveness – how quickly the teams are able to move problems through the Problem Management lifecycle.

Average cost to resolve

This KPI is related to the time measure above. It is a calculation of the average cost invested to move a problem from its 'detected' state to a 'closed' state. Typically this cost is based on a combination of time-value plus any capital equipment/replacement outlay. (Each organization will need to formulate this calculation based on its own business parameters.) This cost metric gives management an idea of the level of investment the service teams are required to expend in order to resolve their mix of problems.

Average number of resources to resolve

This count combines with the time and cost measures above to give a rounded picture of Problem Management business drivers. This is a look at the average number of staff needed to intervene in order to move the problem from its 'detected' state to a 'closed' state. A well-configured Problem Tracking System will update a problem ticket each time it is assigned to a specific party. This establishes a history of how many hands the ticket had to move through to reach resolution. In most IT organizations, the more hands that touch a ticket the longer resolution takes and the more expensive the resolution is.

13.6. Critical Success Factors

A successful Problem Management program is not one in which no problems occur. Here we discuss a series of potential CSFs that might be employed to track the ROI this process brings to the organization. These sample success factors can be seen as measures that demonstrate the effectiveness of the Problem Management program overall.

Problem trends by service
In order to be effective, a Problem Management program must have a view into the general performance of the organization's Service Catalogue. Measuring problem trends by service provides that view. These measures (which can include both active and resolved problems) can be aggregated to show performance trends over time. Management can use these trends to assess how effective service design, deployment, operation, and maintenance activities are. They can also use the measures to determine how well integration and interoperability work. The hope of course is to see trend lines that point to declining problem rates over time, or at least to a balance between problem volumes and increasing service functionality.

Age of active problems
This measure captures the age of problems that are being worked on in the organization. The data can be broken down by service, category, or type if that is helpful. Management can use this information to understand the effectiveness of problem resolution activities. If problems are ageing past certain limits this may indicate that proper resources are not being applied, that resolution activities are not proving effective, or that the IT organization's problems are of a complex or significant nature. In many IT organizations, senior management sets a time limit governing the span from when a problem is first identified to when it should be resolved and closed. When a portion of the problem workload slips past this time limit, management is cued to take intervening action. Effective Problem Management programs will be designed to guard against the severe ageing of active problem initiatives.

Age of active workarounds by service and type
This metric captures a picture of workarounds in the infrastructure: how many there are, how old each is, which services they affect, what types they are. Because workarounds tend to be less-than-ideal solutions, an infrastructure with lots of workarounds is one that can be considered at risk. Management can use the information in this measure as a way to understand the evolving shape and stability of the environment. If the data indicates a trend of more and more workarounds, management may want to take steps to strengthen the environment, or at least strengthen contingency preparedness. Management may also wish to set a time limit on how long a workaround is allowed

to be deployed in response to a problem – although it is important to appreciate that sometimes workarounds must be deemed permanent. One key to successful Problem Management program is to set into place practices that ensure temporary workarounds (which should be the majority of workarounds) are addressed with permanent (i.e. reliable) resolutions within a given timeframe.

Costs of problem resolutions

Tracking the costs associated with resolving problems is a key metric for determining a program's general success. There can be various contributing factors that make up these costs: analysts' time, equipment purchases, and so on. Capturing this information is important because the ultimate cost of a Problem Management program should end up being less than the deficits the collected problems cost the business. A too-high allocation here may indicate systemic environmental weaknesses, or perhaps misdirected resolution activities. An allocation that is within budget or is reasonably balanced with workloads shows a program that is working. Senior management should establish percentage targets for the proportion of the IT budget allocated to Problem Management and then monitor planned costs to actual costs over time.

13.7. Problem Management roles

The following job roles are typically seen in mature Problem Management programs. Each role plays a part in ensuring that the program's activities are carried out as designed. Depending on the size and focus of the organization these roles may be full-time or part-time; combined or shared by multiple individuals. View the job titles and responsibilities described below as starting points for your own job descriptions and assignments. You will probably want to refine each of these to fit with the particular needs of your IT organization.

Problem Management Process Owner

As with the governance of other ITIL processes, it is customary with Problem Management that the organization assigns someone the duty of managing the program's institutional use and evolution over time. In this sense, the Problem Management program should have a process owner. The main roles of the process owner are to make sure that the program is developed in line with organizational needs, that it is appropriately documented and implemented, and that it is used in a compliant way by appropriate teams. In short, the process owner oversees use of the program for IT management. The Problem Management Process Owner is usually responsible for:
- Developing and documenting the Problem Management program
- Implementing the program across relevant teams
- Monitoring ongoing program use
- Measuring program performance over time
- Coordinating program improvements
- Coordinating program communications, training, and performance assessment

Service Problem Manager

The mission of Problem Management is to protect ongoing service delivery and quality through the use of the Problem Management techniques. Most ITIL IT organizations appoint problem managers for their services. Depending on the size and complexity of the IT organization and its service mix, there may be one problem manager for each service or a single problem manager for a set of services. Either way, the main task of the service problem manager is to coordinate problem identification and resolution activities across teams when problem events occur. This manager is usually responsible for:

- Implementing Problem Management for a specific service or set of services
- Managing those Problem Management resources (technicians and analysts) responsible for a service or set of services
- Ensuring that critical performance levels as related to SLAs in the domain of Problem Management are consistently met
- Working with the Problem Management Process Owner to refine and develop the program in an effective manner over time
- Communicating problem resolutions to service managers, IT management, and customer stakeholders
- Contributing to Change Management assessments

Problem analyst

Problem analysts perform the technical work required for problem resolutions. These resources are usually specialists who have deep operational knowledge of the environment's IT services and can thus reliably investigate problem sources, propose valid solution alternatives, and configure selected solutions for implementation. These analysts are typically responsible for:

- Tracking problem tickets through to closure
- Working to investigate problem sources through RCA
- Identifying and documenting potential problem resolutions
- Configuring approved solutions for implementation
- Working in close collaboration with external third party providers
- Contributing to Change Management assessments

Human Resource considerations

The following are some typical traits that Human Resource staff may want to take into consideration when they are providing personnel, staff aids, tools, and other resources for a Problem Management program.

Technical experience and background: In order for Problem Management staff to be productive it is important that they possess a solid understanding of the services they are required to support. There are two aspects to this understanding:

- Since many services perform specific business operations, these teams should be able to account for some degree of knowledge in these business areas. As business services are founded on IT services, Problem Management personnel should have training and experience working with the kinds of service components that are present in your infrastructure. This training and experience should encompass

not only the service components themselves but also interoperability between components.
- Problem Management staff should have the breadth of knowledge that will enable them to identify appropriate methods and techniques to resolve problems embedded in the environment.

Sound problem solving skills: Technical experience and background can go a long way to enabling qualified Problem Management resources, but another trait is also highly desired: sound problem solving skills. For Problem Management staff to be effective they will need to possess a range of problem solving skills, including investigative techniques, RCA, solution option assessment and selection, technical documentation ability, and solution configuration.

Comfort working in a process-centric environment: Problem Management staff should be comfortable working in a process-centric environment, one structured across culture-based practices and organizational assets, and one that promotes teamwork over individual 'heroics'. They should be open to learning about the organization's Problem Management program and contributing to its ordered growth.

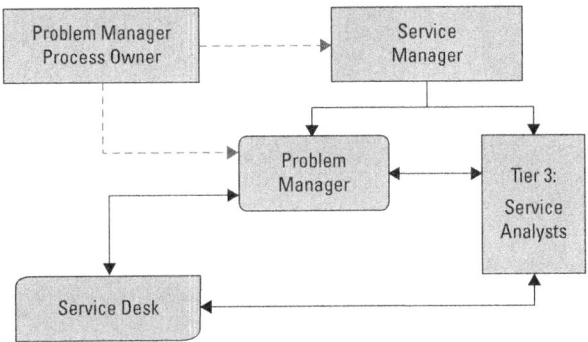

Figure 13.4 Role relationships with Problem Management

13.8. Benefits of effective Problem Management

A running theme through all of ITIL is a focus on customer satisfaction. High customer satisfaction levels are a sound indicator that the organization is delivering on expectations. But nothing can derail customer satisfaction as much as an environment with widespread problems. Frequent service interruptions – major or minor – will quickly frustrate users and may create perceptions of IT as being unresponsive. The value of a Problem Management program comes from the fact that the organization focuses resources on removing problems from the field, and provides the tools and techniques to make those activities effective. Over time, the major benefit of a well-run Problem Management program comes down to rising customer satisfaction levels. Supporting this are other operationally-oriented benefits as well. Four of the major ones are as follows.

Enhanced operational stability
Prompt and effective attention to problems results in a more stable and functionally productive environment. As defects are detected and removed, interruptions are reduced; infrastructure weaknesses are removed. This results in more reliable service delivery, higher service quality, and stronger service performance. This increasing stability allows the organization to focus more of its resources on forward-thinking activities and a lighter proportion on everyday maintenance. It also positions the organization to better meet its SLA targets and goals, and that can result in stronger business relationships.

Proactive incident reduction
An effective focus on Problem Management will result in a stronger environment and this will usually lead to a reduction over time in the number and types of service incidents. As mentioned at the beginning of this chapter, incidents are usually symptomatic of an underlying problem. The symptoms may take multiple forms and crop up in different areas. It is quite common for a single problem to present itself initially as sets of incidents. Once the problem is removed, however, the incidents disappear. As problems are methodically addressed over time, as their root causes are identified and removed, incident levels will follow the same course and also drop.

Responsive problem resolutions
A well designed Problem Management program will provide for the resources and techniques that make problem removal an effective and efficient organizational activity. This directly links to ITIL's focus on customer satisfaction. No environment will be free of problems, and most customers appreciate this. The job of the organization is to demonstrate to the customer its commitment to rapid and thorough problem resolutions. This is what a practiced Problem Management program can help the organization do. The program's performance results can be used to demonstrate the commitment IT has made to the business and the value IT is delivering to the business.

Identification of improvement opportunities
Perhaps one of the strongest yet least appreciated of Problem Management benefits is its ability to help the organization identify improvement opportunities. Problem analysis is in itself a continual improvement activity. The practice of identifying defects, assessing their cause and effects, and determining appropriate corrective action will result over time in a deeper understanding of the environment – one that can be used to further strengthen existing service components and, with expansions into new business areas, deliver better service solutions.

13.9. Implementation challenges and considerations

All organizations, whether they have a structured approach or not, practice Problem Management. It is a mandated activity. Avoid it and service levels will certainly fall. The key to effective Problem Management, however, is to adopt a structured approach. Problem investigation, solution designing, and solution implementation can best be controlled and refined when practiced in a consistent, repeatable, predictable way. ITIL's recommendations for its Problem Management process help you achieve those traits. Yet there are challenges and considerations you should be aware of as you design your program and set it into place. These challenges and consideration concern the framework within which a Problem Management program operates. Certain parts of this framework need to be in place in order for the program to reach its full potential. The challenges and considerations spring from these. Here are five that most organizations, to one degree or another, commonly face.

Establishing clear service ownership channels

Problems are most often specific to particular services; that is, they spring from a service's specific configuration. In order to address problems effectively, the organization should have effective control of the teams and other resources that are responsible for service operation. When problems are identified these resources can then be called into play. However, in some IT organizations these ownership channels are not clear. The idea of IT as a service may not be clear. Ownership may be recognized only at the traditional level, at the service component level where people are responsible for pieces of equipment. When this is the case, the documented mix of components that make up a service may not be well established, and so when problems occur the teams that need to be involved in resolution may not be easily identified. In order to implement an effective Problem Management program, IT managers should promote the service view of IT delivery, map service components to service definitions, and then clearly link personnel and resources to service ownership. That way, responsibility for service delivery, and the resolution of problems that impede delivery, will be clear.

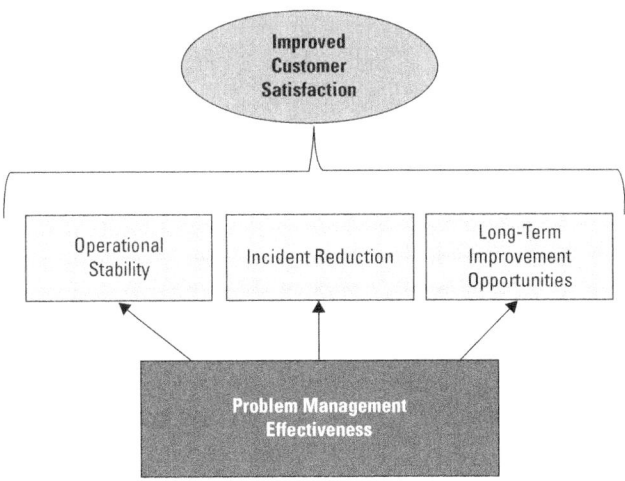

Figure 13.5 Benefits of Problem Management

Maintaining an up-to-date Configuration Management Library

Problem Management relies heavily on Configuration Management for its success. In order to understand problems and then identify, track, and manage problem resolutions it is important to have a good understanding of the CIs affected by the problem. It is particularly important to know how those CIs have been configured. Indeed, the first stop for many problem investigations is the CMDB. Problem analysts reference the data in the CMDB to establish a baseline that will make a problem's source and solution clear. But this does require that the organization has a CMDB in place that is complete and up-to-date, which can prove difficult for many IT organizations. Often, immature IT organizations or those new to IT Service Management have not had the time to develop a robust CMDB. Other IT organizations may not have the resources required for the ongoing task of keeping CMDB entries current. Still others simply lack a focus on managing this area. Yet it should be a prominent and upfront consideration for any organization wishing to implement a sound Problem Management program. Without ready access to accurate configuration reference information, problem analysts will struggle to get to a problem's true underlying cause, and then find that they are forced to experiment when developing potential solutions.

Maintaining the Known Error Database

For Problem Management, the Known Error Database (KEDB) is as important a reference tool as the CMDB. The KEDB can be used by problem analysts in two ways. When a problem is first detected analysts should check the KEDB to determine if the problem has been already identified. The KEDB will hold records of known defects across the infrastructure with details of the workarounds that have been set in place to mitigate their impacts. Referencing this information may reveal the trouble spot, or it may point the analysts to a similar situation that might be addressed in an already proven way. That is the front-end of Problem Management. The KEDB comes into use on the back-end, too. If problem analysts determine that the best solution for a current problem is to implement a workaround then those analysts will need to create a fresh entry in the KEDB, documenting all the details of the problem and workaround configuration. The challenge is similar to that of maintaining the CMDB above. The value of the KEDB comes from its completeness and currency. If it is out of date or incomplete, problem analysts may find it contributes little to their investigation and resolution efforts. Regular and ongoing maintenance of the KEDB is essential for Problem Management activities to be as effective and as efficient as possible.

Establishing sound change control procedures

Resolving problems often requires reconfiguring the environment, and this may necessitate moving a problem through the change control process, even if it is an emergency (i.e., streamlined) change control process. In the absence of sound Change Management processes, the smooth and orderly implementation of problem resolutions may be difficult to achieve. If Problem Management becomes a rushed or ad hoc activity, proper consideration may not be given to how resolutions are shaped. It is preferable for Problem Management to become a gated activity, and Change Management provides for those gates. With a change control process, a problem's proposed resolution can be assessed for effectiveness before being accepted into production. Redundancies can be identified, conflicts can be addressed, benefits can be evaluated, and implementation can be planned. Change control procedures provide for all of these requirements; they can help turn Problem Management from being a rushed activity into one that is more appropriately considered. The challenge for the organization is to resist the temptation to rush resolutions into place, to take the time necessary for Change Management's communications, analyses, and evaluations.

Providing good project management methods
Problem resolutions often result in the initiation of formal projects. This occurs when the scope of the solution is such that it is necessary to assign resources, elicit requirements, establish designs, build, test, deploy – in short, all those stages of work that typically accompany a development project. It is important for an organization to have some set of project management methodologies in place. Such methodologies are helpful for running small, medium, and large-sized projects; the challenge comes in terms of organizational reach. There are many options available, such as the PMI's PMBOK, the SEI's CMMI, PRINCE2, and others, which all offer good project management frameworks. But they require concentrated efforts to implement, easily equal to that required for setting up an IT Service Management program. An organization might simply not have the bandwidth to accommodate that. The risk is of course clear: in the absence of project management methods, projects may exceed budgets and timelines, functionality may suffer, business missions might get cloudy, and when deployed the organization might find that new problems have been introduced into the production environment.

13.10. Typical assets and artifacts of a Problem Management program

The activities and practices that make up a Problem Management program will need to be supported by a defined set of assets and artifacts. Assets set the framework for the activities and practices; artifacts are the work products that result from their execution. Following is a list of some common assets and artifacts found in what might be considered a typical Problem Management program. You may recognize the need for some of these in your program. This list is presented to help you begin down the path of identifying those elements your organization's program will require.

Problem Management policy
This is an executive policy that stipulates the goals and objectives of the Problem Management program. The policy, which like all policies should be concise (ideally no longer than a few pages), documents at a high level the purpose of the program, the resources available to the program, the chief responsibilities of the program, quality targets, reporting hierarchies, and program measures. Endorsed by executive management, the policy is a demonstration of organizational commitment to the value and importance of Problem Management activities.

Problem tracking system

Problem tickets need to be managed and tracked in the same way that incident tickets do. To accomplish this, most Problem Management programs employ some manner of Problem Tracking System. This system, most commonly an automated database management system, is used to register, document, track, and manage problem tickets. The tool may also serve as a central repository for housing root cause analyses (RCAs), resolution proposals, and other problem related information. Problem managers and problem analysts are the chief users of the Problem Tracking System.

Root cause analysis guidelines

RCA is a central activity of Problem Management. RCA is a technique for studying a problem in order to determine the underlying cause of its occurrence. There are many approaches that can be used for root causes analysis (brainstorming, fishbone diagrams, etc.). The choice of approach is, of course, dependent on the needs of the organization. The key is to ensure that RCA may be conducted across different teams in a consistent and familiar way. That is why RCA guidelines are important; they describe the steps that teams should consider when performing RCA on a problem; the can also include criteria for determining potential solutions, and recommendations for documenting solution proposals and outcomes.

Problem Resolution Review Guidelines

Problems that are significant may require solutions that are significant. Such solutions, when proposed, may need to be reviewed by appropriate stakeholders before their implementations are considered. (For example, an organization may wish for some types of problem resolutions be channeled through the formal change control process.) To assist with this process is helpful for the organization to provide its teams with Problem Resolution Review Guidelines. These guidelines set out the criteria that govern what types of resolutions need to be assessed by certain stakeholder groups in order to be accepted for implementation. These guidelines help ensure that production changes which may have significant operational impacts are not made in the absence of proper review and approval.

Problem Management Measurement Plan

Measuring an organization's Problem Management program provides a basis for improving it over time. The Problem Management Measurement plan, as described here, is a tool for doing that. The plan identifies the metrics that will be captured in order to assess the performance of the problem resolution activities. A typical plan will define the measures, document where to find them and how to collect them, specify where the data is to be stored, and provide formulae for analyzing different data sets. The measures selected will depend naturally on the needs of your IT organization, but the CSFs and the KPIs described in this chapter are examples of the kinds of measures you may wish to set up for your Problem Management program.

Problem Management reporting and distribution procedure

This is a documented procedure that describes how Problem Management reports are created, how often they are generated, and to whom they are to be disseminated. This procedure can be seen as an extension of the Problem Management Measurement Plan described above. Together, these artifacts provide the kind of information and analysis needed by IT managers and business customers to understand the effectiveness of problem resolution activities and identify opportunities for improvement.

Organization chart

This is a chart that shows the structural make-up of the various Problem Management working units. Its purpose is to identify teams, team relationships, and hierarchical flows. The shape of this chart will naturally depend on the general shape of your organization, but if you were to visualize a textbook shaped Problem Management Program you might see a chart with vertical layers. The top layer would be Service Management, those executives responsible for the delivery and quality of a service or set of services. The middle layer would be Service Problem Managers, the managers assigned to coordinate RCA and resolution activities when problems occur. The third layer would be problem analysts, those analysts with specialized service skills who are able to identify causes and propose valid resolutions. In some IT organizations the middle layer might have a dotted line out to the Problem Management Process Owner, and the third layer might have a dotted line out to the Service Desk or Incident Management teams.

Roles and responsibilities matrix

This artifact is an extension of the organizational chart described above. It is a matrix that describes the various roles and responsibilities the organization has assigned to support its Problem Management program. The roles typically include Problem Manager Process Owner, Service Problem Manager, and Service Technical Analyst. Along with the job role definitions you should have descriptions of the responsibilities each role should account for, with references to how the various roles interrelate and communicate. The matrix might take one of several forms: a spreadsheet, a series of database records, or a version-controlled text document. Ownership of this artifact is usually shared between Problem Management and Human Resource management.

14. Service Desk

Service Desk is, in itself, not an ITIL process. It is a function, an operational unit within an organization. As a function it employs one or more ITIL processes. For Service Desk the main process used out of all ITIL's core processes is Incident Management. But Service Desk also employs elements of Problem Management and Service Level Management as well. Service Desk is accounted for under the Service Operation lifecycle phase and when you look at the five ITIL processes that comprise this phase you will see that they all point more or less to the Service Desk. In fact, when most people think of service operations the image that comes to mind is the Service Desk. In well run IT organizations it is not uncommon for the IT experiences of customers to be largely limited to encounters with this function.

Two themes common to ITIL are that Service Management exists to support the business missions of an organization, and the chief objective for IT is to ensure that its customers are satisfied with the value IT brings to the business. Naturally a lot goes into realizing those two themes, and it would be shortsighted to state that it's solely through the Service Desk that they are achieved. But the importance of a well-run, well-integrated Service Desk cannot be overestimated. Strategic planning and positioning, management judgment, resource allocations, industry experience and a host of other characteristics ultimately determine the level at which an IT organization performs. But because the Service Desk represents, so to speak, the front line, it is the Service Desk that most often sets the *perception* of how well IT is run. And customers who are not aware of the complexities inherent in information technology will often treat perception as reality, and based on what might be micro level considerations they may make macro level decisions.

In this chapter we'll take a look at how ITIL structures the function of the Service Desk. We'll look at the specific responsibilities it assigns and we'll explore some potential key performance indicators that can be used to help measure how well what you set up is working in practice. But first let's look at what ITIL means when it uses the term Service Desk. Here's what ITIL defines as the mission of the Service Desk:

"…to serve as the single point of contact for IT users when it comes to dealing with all incidents and service requests."[1]

In order to realize this mission there are many considerations about the design of a Service Desk function. This design depends largely on the shape, size, and focus (business and technical) of the organization. The IT organization will need to decide if it wants a centralized Service Desk or perhaps multiple decentralized Service Desks. It will want to look at business bases and locations and ensure that the Service Desk can support the geographic, time zone, and language needs of its customers. And it

---

1 Foundations of ITIL. (2010). Van Haren Publishing

will want to look at various other operating factors to make sure that Service Desk help is available when the organization's customers are working. With that in mind, let's take a general look at what ITIL recommends for setting up and maintaining an effective and responsive Service Desk function. We will begin with the Service Desk's core responsibilities.

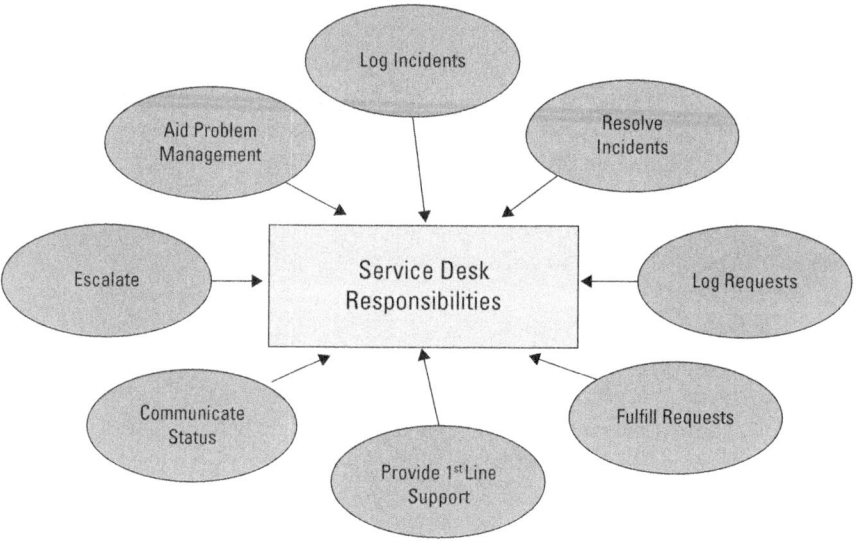

Figure 14.1 Responsibilities of the Service Desk function

14.1. Service Desk responsibilities

ITIL identifies eight responsibilities for the Service Desk. In most IT organizations these are the primary tasks the Service Desk performs and are readily recognizable to most. How to account for each of the eight is up to the individual organization and how it elects to design its Service Management programs. A Single Desk operation might handle them all; or you might elect to spread these responsibilities across separate teams. In any event here are the eight responsibilities.

1. Log incidents

'Log incidents' involves more than just registration. Logging begins the management chain that will lead ultimately to resolution. The act of logging the incident is the opportunity to record the incident and describe its attributes so that it can be properly worked. Two other activities flow contiguously from this first one. Managing the incident covers the set of activities needed to investigate, diagnose, and decide on an appropriate response. Here is where the incident owners apply their technical acumen. Then there is tracking incident status. The incident owners need to periodically check the status of active incidents to verify that they are indeed being worked in a responsive way; the owners can then use this information as an opportunity for contact with the customers, to keep them informed on progress toward a solution (see Item 7 below).

2. Resolve incidents

This is probably the most visible responsibility of the Service Desk. Resolving incidents, ideally on the first call, is what the Service Desk exists to achieve. When a customer reports an incident it is because something – big, small, or in-between – is interrupting their business duties. And since IT's chief job is to keep business operations running, the issue needs to be resolved quickly. Usually this is done in one of two ways. Either the support analyst recognizes the source of the issues and applies a permanent fix (like, say, a password reset) or the analyst, in place of a permanent solution, provides a workaround, a detour that enables the customer to get back to work. There are also times when the first-line analysts are not able to achieve a resolution. At this point they use their system knowledge and documented guidelines to escalate the situation to the proper technical team while still retaining ownership of the incident record (see Item 6 below).

3. Log service requests

Service requests are requests from an end-user for an addition or extension to an existing technology configuration. Service requests typically require no special approval. The responsibility to log service requests carries with it the activities associated with tracking and managing them. The main difference from logging incidents, indeed if there is one, is one of intensity. Incidents, in the minds of the customers, are usually 'problems' that need to be resolved immediately. Managing service requests should be a much more straightforward process for two reasons. First, because you'll have a finite set of request types; second, because the method to fulfill each type can be structured and documented in advance. The job of logging service requests also aligns with logging incidents in relation to customer service. Satisfaction levels tend to rise when you keep the customer informed about the progress of the request during the management process.

4. Fulfill service requests

Fulfilling requests in a responsive manner promotes the same rewards as resolving incidents. There is also an important learning and improvement opportunity that should be mentioned here. It applies both to resolving incidents and fulfilling service requests. As your Service Desk program becomes established and your people, over time, come to deal with common incidents and common requests they will acquire a familiarity with how the environment works from a practical standpoint (the environment's strengths and weaknesses), and from this can emerge new strategies and tactics for more efficient resolution and fulfillment activities.

5. Provide first line investigation and diagnosis

This responsibility works like a two-sided shield. By providing a first line of investigation and diagnosis you give your customer a convenient single point of contact for engaging with IT resources. At the same time, this protects your downstream technical specialists from dealing with a free-form stream of (potentially) minor or scattered issues that are not their top priority. It is this first line responsibility that prompts most Service Desk operations to adopt a 'generalist' position, employing generalists who can handle a broad range of different interaction types, applying to these types pre-prepared paths of diagnostic approaches (such as scripts and how-to steps). Only when the efforts of this first line have been exhausted will there be a need to go 'deeper' into the IT organization to request assistance from Tier 2 or Tier 3 resources.

6. Escalate

With a well-run Service Desk the desired end of each customer interaction is first-call resolution; i.e. resolving the issue right then, in real-time. Unfortunately not all issues are able to be resolved with the first call. Escalation can be *functional*: sometimes Tier 1 resources are not equipped to address the issue; they might lack the expertise, information, or access required. It is in these situations that the Service Desk staff will escalate a ticket to the next tier of support. The key to coordinated escalation is to equip your staff with the guidelines that enable them to do two things: channel the issue to the right technical team, and still maintain control of the ticket even while they are bringing in additional help.

Hierarchic escalation may also be necessary from time to time: if there is a serious incident (for example Priority 1 incidents) the appropriate IT managers must be notified, for informational purposes at least. Hierarchic escalation is also used if the 'Investigation and Diagnosis' and 'Resolution and Recovery' steps are taking too long or proving too difficult. Hierarchic escalation should continue up the management chain so that senior managers are aware and can be prepared and take any necessary action. Hierarchic escalation is also used when there is a dispute about allocation of the incident.

7. Communicate status to users

This may be the single most important responsibility of any Service Desk. Customers appreciate communications. When they need help they want to know they are getting help, the kind of help it is they're getting, and the status of the help being applied. In fact, communicating status to users may even be more important than providing solutions. The human element, and the soft skills associated with dealing with that element, is often overlooked when managing an infrastructure. But the Service Desk is the logical unit with the opportunity to take that factor into consideration. Customers respond to proactive interactions. Even when a customer's needs are not being met in a timely manner, for whatever the technical or business reason, if the support staff at the Service Desk are communicating this to the customer in a professional and open manner, the customer's patience tends to last longer than the problem at hand.

8. Contribute to problem identification

Incidents and service requests are most often handled in a real-time manner. That is, they are worked in line as they appear. And if there is not a sense of urgency about them then there is at least a window of time in which they are expected to be addressed. It is not the same with problems. Problems are usually worked on in slower time and are addressed with more management rigor and control. And they are typically worked on by Tier 2 or Tier 3 teams. The Service Desk teams, however, in their Tier 1 space, are uniquely positioned to realize, before most, when problems are beginning to emerge. Chains of related incidents are typically the first clue. Because of this, Service Desk personnel are often sought out by those who deal with Problem Management to consult on emerging problems or on potential causes and solutions for identified problems.

14.2. Processes related to Service Desk

The Service Desk operates by using the two key resolution processes established by the IT organization for Service Management: the customer-facing Incident Management process and the diagnostic Problem Management process. From the perspective of the ITIL core set and from the viewpoint of ISO/IEC 20000, the main charter of the Service Desk is to resolve service issues, whether they are issues with delivery or quality. Because the Service Desk function has frequent and direct contact with the customer base, SLAs also influence how the function operates. Service Desk performance targets are usually significantly represented in SLAs.

Incident Management

Incident Management and Service Desk operations are pretty much inseparable. The Incident Management process involves all those activities associated with addressing service interruptions: identification, registration, classification, resolution, etc. And it is the staff of the Service Desk who duty it is to carry out these activities. When most IT organizations create an Incident Management program they do so with the Service Desk in mind. The tools that are selected, the metrics that are defined, the kinds of performance reports that are developed, all of these are done by the Service Desk. More so perhaps than with any other relationships in ITIL, this function and process are intricately linked.

In summary:
- Incident Management governs how the Service Desk manages the intake, tracking, and resolution of service incidents.
- Incident Management influences the key performance indicators (KPIs) captured by the Service Desk.
- The tools and techniques included in a typical Incident Management program are employed by the Service Desk to manage day-to-day operations.
- Escalation guidelines included in an Incident Management program are used by the Service Desk to coordinate ticket assignments across support teams.

Problem Management

The main activities of Problem Management (see Chapter 13) are typically carried out by service specialists. Service Desk analysts, however, are often involved in the auxiliary activities that support this process. The Service Desk is frequently the first party to become aware that a problem may exist or that one is emerging. Evidence of incident patterns may point them to this conclusion. Service Desk analysts can also provide valuable input and insight during root cause investigations, helping service specialists diagnose source issues and derive potential corrective actions. The

Service Desk is also positioned to be able to confirm, once resolutions have been set in place, that they are effective and service operation is back to normal. Finally, the Service Desk is the proper source for communicating the status of ongoing Problem Management with the user community.

In summary:
- Service Desk analysts are positioned to identify and report problems through their work in diagnosing and investigating incidents.
- Tier 1 and Tier 2 support analysts, through their front-line work, can provide insight to problem analysts about potential problem root causes and likely solutions.
- Service Desk analysts are positioned to keep the user community informed about the impacts and workarounds of known errors and existing problems.

Service Level Management

As a process, Service Level Management should be shaped to account for Service Desk activities. As an organizational responsibility, it is invariably required to address Service Desk performance. Most traditional SLAs will contain a good number of performance targets that tie directly to the Service Desk. This creates a two-way dependency: service level negotiations should be conducted with Service Desk capabilities in mind in order to reach reasonable targets; and Service Desk configurations should be shaped to reflect SLA goals. Then there is the issue of customer satisfaction. This is a major focal point for Service Level Management. At the same Service Desk performance is a major contributor to satisfaction levels.

In summary:
- SLAs typically contain a significant degree of performance targets derived from Service Desk activities.
- Service Desk configurations (resources, tools, etc.) should be set to adequately account for SLA requirements.
- Service Desk performance has a significant impact on customer satisfaction levels.

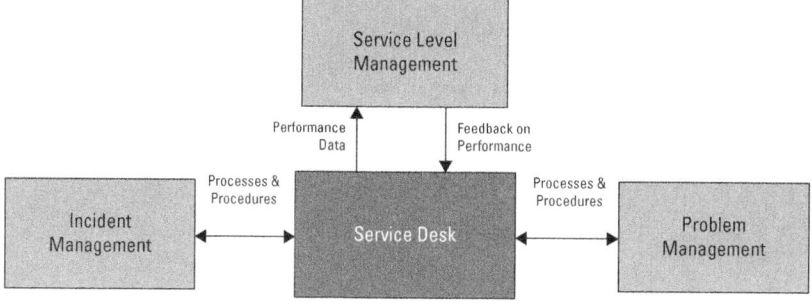

Figure 14.2 Processes related to the Service Desk

14.3. Tools and techniques

Most ITIL-based Service Desk functions are built around a series of tools and techniques. This is the same for any kind of call center. Look inside one and you will find sophisticated telephony systems, switches, pagers, personal digital assistants (PDAs), remote access aids, monitoring devices, dashboards, etc. These are just a few examples of what it takes for an organization to set up a Service Desk. And for any given organization the configuration will be unique. There is a common foundation, however, at the base of this function. On that foundation rests the need to engage with customers, manage work tasks, and collaborate across teams. Toward that end then here are five assets you will find present, at least in some form, in nearly all Service Desk programs.

Table 14.1 Tools and techniques for Service Desk

Service ticket tracking system	This is an automated tool used to register, track, update, and manage service tickets. Practically every Service Desk operation will employ some kind of tool like this. The main items processed through this tool are incident records and service requests. Through the system tickets can be categorized, prioritized, assigned ownership, escalated, notated with journal entries, time-tracked to ensure timely completion, placed in queues for special management; and reported on. Popular tools in this class include Service Desk Plus, H2Desk, Autotask, and Incident Management Tracking System (IMTS).
Escalation guidelines	These are guidelines that govern how service tickets are escalated from one support tier to the next. In order for a ticket to be managed effectively escalation activities need to be controlled. Tickets should be escalated at the right times within the right timeframes to the right parties with the right level of communication and with accountability chains still intact. Without such guidelines support analysts may be left to adopt willy-nilly ticket handling and hand-off practices. These guidelines provide for a measure of consistency, predictability and quality assurance related to ticket assignments.
OLAs and UCs	Operational Level Agreements (OLAs) and Underpinning Contracts (UCs) set up support agreements across internal teams and external providers. These are important for the Service Desk because of the need to occasionally escalate tickets. OLAs and UCs will help ensure that when escalation is needed the right level and type of support to be delivered will be understood by all relevant parties.
Service Knowledge Management System	Many Service Desk operations give their analysts access to a Service Knowledge Management System (SKMS). This is a repository of service information that can be referenced for information helpful in resolving common or previously encountered incidents service requests or for answering general tech questions. The SKMS is usually structured as a database management system containing content categories of knowledge articles. Categories can be in classifications such as How-To, How-do-I? or they can be service-related as in Email Order Entry etc. The knowledge articles themselves are usually brief and to the point, able to be scanned quickly by the analysts in order to get to the heart of the matter.
Scripts and workflows	These are pre-configured support aids for use by Service Desk and other support teams. They may be manual references or automated work paths configured within a Ticket Tracking System. Scripts guide analysts through a series of diagnostic steps when working with customers to solve issues. Workflows lead analysts through a chain of support activities, a chain that has typically been shown to be effective for solving common or previously encountered issues. Scripts and workflows can help a Service Desk operation provide consistent service across teams with differing levels of expertise and experience. They can also be used to capture and promote best practices.

Soft skills and problem-solving training	These two areas of training enable Service Desk personnel to be more effective when working with business customers. Soft skills training provides a basis for effective customer interactions, communications, and collaborative diagnostics. Problem-solving training provides staff with enhanced ability to creatively and more effectively diagnose, investigate, and resolve customer issues.

14.4. Key Performance Indicators

Measuring Service Desk performance is essential for the development of any responsible (i.e. responsive) Service Desk function. And if you look through Chapters 12 and 13 you will see already identified a variety of KPIs and critical success factors (CSFs) that can be used toward this purpose: measures of Incident Management and Problem Management activities, two major areas of focus for the Service Desk. These can go a long way toward providing you with the data you need to capture Service Desk performance, understand underlying trends, and improve overall effectiveness. Below are four additional measures that may be helpful to add to the mix. These four are defined to directly gauge Service Desk response time, that is, how efficiently a caller can move from dialing for help to getting it. Here is a brief description of each measure.

Average time to answer
This is the average time it takes for a customer's call to be answered. This initial answering might be by the support analyst who will work on the issue. It might be by a ticket agent who will direct the call to a qualified analyst. It might even be an automated routing system that will direct the call to the qualified analyst, through a series of prompts ("Press 1 for...") The goal is to provide a system in which the call is answered promptly; that it does not just ring and ring and ring until the customer is wondering if there is really anybody at the other end. You and the customer should set this limit to any length deemed reasonable. On average, across different companies, it is common that this time is set in the area of ≈ 15 seconds.

Average time on hold
If it weren't for elevators and hold buttons there would be no Muzak™ industry. In the world of customer service, the more time a customer spends on hold the more of a performance issue the Service Desk has (or at least appears to have). The hold is measured as the time between when a call if first answered – either by a Service Desk agent or a routing system – to when a qualified support analyst picks it up. For most customers, being placed on hold initiates an Einsteinian condition: time seems to slow down. Ten seconds seem like thirty. Two minutes like fifty. Long hold times usually indicate one of two situations. Either there are too few support resources for the given environment or there has been an anomaly in the environment that has caused an atypical spike in service calls. Measuring average hold times can help you track both of these situations and respond accordingly.

Call abandon rates

Here is a measure of frustration. You will find that it falls in proportion with the first two measures. When customers feel they have to wait 'forever' for someone to pick up the phone, they might simply give up and hang up. That is a cardinal sin for a Service Desk operation and one that management should keep a close eye on. If the mere *attempt* to get access to help is thwarted how much faith will the customer community be able to develop in what lies past that attempt? Having the right number of online resources and the right mix of call center equipment will help your customers establish a seamless connection to the Service Desk. Call abandon rates, which most SLAs set at around 4% or lower, will help you understand if you have got those numbers and that mix right.

First call resolution rates

This metric is a traditional Service Desk 'top measure'. It is one that IT management and customers are always interested in looking at. First time resolution simply measures the number of times in which an incident was resolved with the analyst and the customer on the initial call, in real time. IT management is interested in this metric because it reveals how prepared and effective their first line of support is in dealing with IT issues. Customers are interested in this metric because it tends to shape their impressions of the overall value the IT organization is delivering to the organization; i.e. through knowledgeable response and speedy help. As might be expected, this measure and measures of customer satisfaction have a compatriot relationship: as first time resolution rates rise, so do customer satisfaction measures.

14.5. Critical Success Factors

Throughout this book we have looked at CSFs for the various components of an ITIL-based Service Management program. Collectively all of them apply to the Service Desk. Whether talking about Incident Management, Problem Management, or Capacity Management, those CSFs will have direct impacts on how well a Service Desk performs. Two additional measures are also beneficial.

Service Desk performance aligned with SLA targets

This is an essential measure (or set of measures) for any Service Desk operation. When operational performance consistently falls in line with SLA targets, the Service Desk is, in all likelihood, performing to the expected levels of quality and professionalism. Because of the high visibility of Service Desk activities and their impact on customer quality perceptions, meeting these targets consistently is a priority for most IT organizations.

Customer satisfaction levels

This is an essential measure (or set of measures) for any Service Desk operation. It indicates how satisfied customers are with the help being provided to them. In a typical ITIL program the work of collecting this data falls under the process Service Level Management, but it is worth mentioning here. ITIL is such a customer-focused quality framework that no program, even a basic one, should be set without means to gauge satisfaction levels. Customer satisfaction is most commonly determined through the use of satisfaction surveys. The questions/comments on the survey cover the range of services that the Service Desk provides and is designed to solicit (without prejudice) a collective subjective impression of Service Desk performance. Together with the hard measures the organization collects (see the KPI sections in Chapters 3 through 12) you will be able to get a full picture of current performance and from this, identify actions toward service refinement and improvement. Consistently high satisfaction levels are strong indicators that Service Desk performance is acceptable to the customer.

In addition to the above measures there are four organizational traits that influence the success of a Service Desk operation. These traits are success factors in the sense that they need to be in place, to some degree at least, for Service Desk performance to reach its full potential. These traits help to support how a Service Desk is initially shaped. The four are:
- Committed organizational support
- Skilled service desk personnel
- Well designed SLAs
- Appropriate monitoring tools

Organizational support

When an IT organization sets up a Service Desk it is investing in more than just a telephone and a desk. What is usually happening is that it is setting up a call center. For that reason broad organizational support is key. The IT organization must invest in the right equipment: phones, computers, switches, routers, messaging centers, displays, monitoring tools, etc. Then there is the need for staff. This requires hiring, training, equipping, provisioning office space, and all the other Human Resource requirements that come with creating work teams. This level of commitment has to come from the highest executive level of the IT organization. When the IT organization is in-house, that commitment has to come also from the highest executive levels of the business.

Skilled Service Desk personnel

Every IT environment is different. Even environments that feature the same brands of hardware and software are different. So when staffing a Service Desk it is a misconception to assume that all support analysts are equal. Hiring skilled people means hiring the kinds of people with the right blend of soft and hard skill-sets, skills matched to the shape of your environment. The 'soft' skills (as they are called in the customer service business) are those that promote smooth customer interactions; such as a professional manner, strong communication abilities, analytical aptitude, and so on. And then there are the hard skills: direct experience with environments similar to yours. After all, the main things the Service Desk deals with are incidents, requests, and – tangentially – problems. Incidents, requests, and problems all spring from some condition in the environment. The more familiar your new hires are with that environment and its components, the more effective they will be.

Service Level Agreements

Well designed SLAs are essential to the successful operation of a Service Desk. Without them, how can IT and the customer agree to the quality of services? SLAs (and we might as well include OLAs and UCs) represent the cooperative agreement established between parties about performance. It is important to appreciate that the stipulations in an SLA should not just go one way, as in: "you achieve this." They should always go both ways, as in "you achieve this and we'll recognize it as successful." SLAs should be negotiated and defined to find that common ground where both parties can work comfortably. With the Service Desk and its focus on issue resolution and request fulfillment, SLAs become especially important. Here is the place where temperatures can run high, where pressures can mount, where urgencies and priorities are everyday considerations. The boundaries featured in an SLA, when they are collaborative and practical, help set realistic expectations that can dissipate heat and help ease pressures to more normal levels.

Monitoring tools

Tools used to monitor systems and performance serve the mission of the Service Desk in three ways. First, they can alert Service Desk staff when something in the environment is beginning to go wrong. With that, analysts can anticipate what might ensue and prepare to initiate corrective action or make ready in advance to handle the calls that might be coming in. Monitoring tools are also useful for resolving incidents and fulfilling requests. They can provide support staff with real-time views into the effectiveness of their own actions. The tools can inform staff about the effectiveness and status of these actions, and can verify that they are indeed achieving desired results. And then there is the issue of hindsight. Monitoring tools can be configured to capture performance data. Once the data has been collected it can be processed, analyzed, and turned into the kinds of information and reports useful for understanding Service Desk performance, strengths, and weaknesses over time.

These success factors, taken with the others we've discussed throughout this book, can provide an organization with what a service operations program requires to succeed. From this insight you can position the organization to shape a Service Desk function structured to contribute effectively to the success of your overall Service Management program.

14.6. Service Desk roles

The following job roles are typically seen in mature Service Desk operations. Depending on the size and focus of an organization these roles may be full-time or part-time, combined, or shared by multiple individuals.

Service Desk Manager

The Service Desk Manager is responsible for ensuring that the Service Desk function operates as planned. The management duties include scheduling and overseeing resources, collecting performance measures, issuing performance reports, maintaining compliance with policies and procedures, and interfacing with senior IT management and customer stakeholders to improve performance. Another key role of the Service Desk Manager is to guide Service Desk operations in such a way as to meet SLA performance targets. To summarize, the Service Desk Manager is responsible for:

- Ensuring Service Desk operations run according to established policies and procedures
- Scheduling and coordinating staff duties and availabilities
- Overseeing Incident Management and request fulfillment activities
- Coordinating involvement with Problem Management
- Measuring Service Desk performance
- Reporting on Service desk performance
- Working with Service Level Managers to gauge Service Desk effectiveness
- Working with senior IT management, Incident Management Process Owners, Problem Management Process Owners, service level managers, and customer stakeholders to improve Service Desk responsiveness and effectiveness

Service Desk analyst (Tier 1)

Service Desk analysts are those Tier 1 members who staff the phones and monitoring devices to provide a primary point of support for the user communities. These analysts take support calls, provide first-line investigation and diagnosis, and work to deliver first-call resolutions. They create, update, and manage service tickets. They assign tickets to Tier 2 and 3 teams when needed. They coordinate and collaborate on escalated issues and on Problem Management. They also provide status and update information to customers. To summarize, Service Desk analysts are responsible for:

- Providing customers with a primary point of contact for technical and business service support
- Providing first-line incident investigation, diagnosis, and resolution
- Fulfilling service requests
- Providing support for problem investigations, diagnoses, and resolutions
- Escalating service tickets when necessary
- Working in close collaboration with Tier 2 support staff
- Working with external third party providers as required

Tier 2 analyst

Tier 2 analysts usually provide desk-side support for customers experiencing technical issues, or they provide service-specific assistance along lines of specialty. They are typically the second line of defense when incidents arise and thus must work closely with their Tier 1 colleagues. They are also responsible for escalating tickets to Tier 3 support when that level of intervention is required. Tier 2 analysts are also directly involved in Problem Management, often taking the lead in root cause analyses and solution proposals. These teams usually work as Tier 2 support on a part-time or

as-needed basis, usually having prime technical responsibilities in dedicated service areas. To summarize, Tier 2 analysts are responsible for:
- Assisting Tier 1 teams with service support
- Providing desk-side and other forms of specialized technical support
- Supporting the fulfillment of service requests
- Providing support for problem investigations, diagnoses, and resolutions
- Escalating service tickets when necessary
- Working in close collaboration with Tier 1 support staff
- Working with external third party providers as required

Tier 3 analyst
Tier 3 analysts are usually highly specialized internal resources or external vendor representatives. With finely focused areas of expertise these analysts are engaged when Tier 1 and Tier 2 teams have exhausted their resolution efforts or the issue faced exceeds their knowledge domains. To summarize, Tier 3 analysts are responsible for:
- Assisting Tier 1 and 2 teams with specialized service support
- Providing service and service component specific technical support
- Providing support for problem investigations, diagnoses, and resolutions

Human Resource considerations
The following are some typical traits that Human Resource staff may want to take into consideration when they are providing personnel, tools, and other resources for a Service Desk operation.

Technical experience and background: Service Desk managers should have experience of managing support teams, assessing the design of call center configurations, understanding technical support roles and responsibilities, interfacing both with senior IT managers and customers, and using statistical analyses to chart and understand Service Desk performance.

Service Desk analysts should have an appropriate technical background that includes experience with the types of components in the current environment. They should also have a broad and general knowledge of environmental needs and configurations related to hardware and software. Good diagnostic, organizational, and interpersonal skills are also important, as is attention to detail.

Tier 2 and Tier 3 analysts should have specialized skills in specific services and/or service components in place in the environment. They should also possess strong diagnostic and resolution design skills.

Comfort working in a process-centric environment: Service Desk management and support staff should be comfortable working in a process-centric environment, and should be open to learning about the organization's program and contributing to its ordered growth.

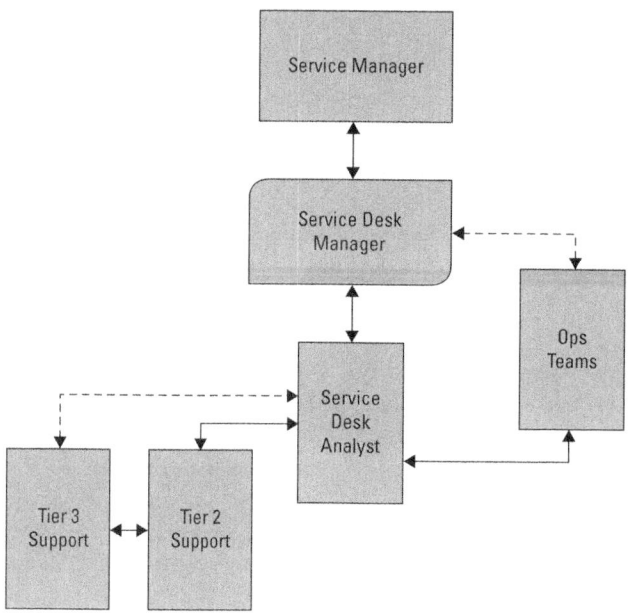

Figure 14.3 Role relationships with respect to the Service Desk

14.7. Benefits of a well-executed Service Desk function

The core focus of IT Service Management, as a discipline, is to meet customers' needs as they relate to using an IT infrastructure. The experience and value of IT service delivery is most often seen from the business end as a byproduct of Service Desk activities. That is why it is important to design the Service Desk well, staff it with skilled resources, manage it with the same customer emphasis you would a direct-sales program, and continually monitor its performance. Through these actions you will find that the central benefits any IT organization is after – customer satisfaction with your work – will materialize and increase with time. Toward that end here are three are major benefits a well-run Service Desk function can deliver.

Enhanced customer service
The reason customer satisfaction levels rise with a well-run Service Desk is due to the quality of customer service. When incidents are resolved efficiently and requests are fulfilled in a timely way the complexities of IT vanish for the customer and what remains is productivity. That level of service is what customers naturally expect from their IT resources. When such levels are consistently delivered the mission of IT is generally seen as having been achieved.

Improved operability
One reason why customer service is enhanced with a well-run Service Desk is because the operability of the environment improves. Things become smoother. This improvement stems from two factors. First, because Service Desk responsiveness

is now enhanced (controlled through proven practices) customers experience less downtime, service interruptions are less intrusive, and times to fulfill requests are streamlined. The second is due to the fact that environmental defects and weak configurations should begin to diminish. The activities that ITIL recommends for Service Desk management will, over time, lead to proactive refinements across the infrastructure, weeding out problems and improving services. What emerges will be improved service quality, more efficient service delivery. Not only will the environment be easier to manage and maintain; as a result of these refinements, customers will experience smoother service operations.

Controlled support expenses

In IT organizations where support activities are conducted in an ad hoc manner or in 'firefighting' mode, the tendency is for support costs to escalate in proportion to the size of the service mix and customer base. This is mainly because the function is left to rely on individuals to see the mission of the Service Desk through. But this tendency is reduced when the organization takes a more controlled approach. When it uses trained staff, proven practices, process methodologies, and integrated tools as the basis for running its Service Desk more work can get done without a proportional increase in expenses. That is because, when compared to a collection of varying individual capabilities, the controlled approach produces a uniform organizational capability, one that is not only economical but scalable and flexible as well.

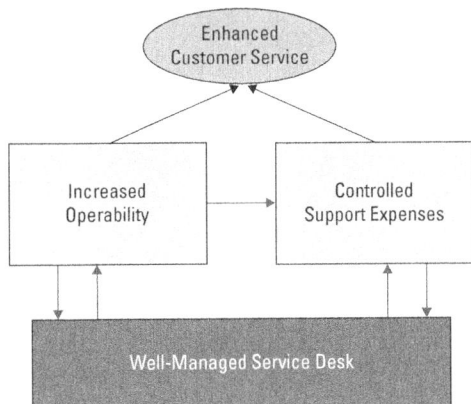

Figure 14.4 Benefits of a well-executed Service Desk function

14.8. Implementation challenges and considerations

Setting up a Service Desk is a major task for any organization. Even relatively small Service Desk operations require a host of resources: staff, communications equipment, computers, service ticket management systems, scheduling systems, monitoring tools, and so on. Both a solid commitment and significant investment are required. Nevertheless the Service Desk is an essential - even central - part of an IT Service Management program. As noted in the section above, a well-executed Service

Desk function can deliver distinct benefits to an IT organization. Behind these benefits, though, there is a series of implementation challenges and considerations that should be evaluated when you are setting this capability into place. Four of the most significant are as follows.

Developing well-trained support technical staff

Developing and retaining talented support staff is a challenge for many call centers. In order for technical support analysts to be effective they are required to possess a somewhat rare blend of talents. They should have deep familiarity with the technical environment they support. They should have thorough knowledge of the range of IT services and the spectrum of service components that span the infrastructure. They should also be proficient both at customer interactions and diagnosing technical issues. This rarity can be compounded by the fact that many employees view support staff roles as stepping stones in an IT organization, a temporary stint leading to better opportunities. While such views may well continue to be held in our industry, IT organizations should nevertheless work to find talented analysts, develop them in line with the shape of the infrastructure, and reward strong performance as it is delivered.

Access to accurate service documentation

In order to resolve incidents, fulfill service requests, and address problems efficiently, Service Desk and support teams need to have access to accurate and complete technical documentation. The logic of this need is self-apparent; however, in many organizations the presence of such materials is noticeably lacking. Documentation seems to be the one artifact that IT organizations skimp on time and again. Whatever the reason, the lack of documentation has negative impacts on the Service Desk's ability to meet customers' needs. Results are likely to be difficulties with clear resolutions, extended request fulfillment times, and difficult operational inconsistencies. The solution is clear enough. Early in the service lifecycle the IT organization should invest in the creation of appropriate design, operations, and maintenance documentation so that support teams may have access to this information when service issues arise.

Negotiating balanced Service Level Agreements

The subject of negotiating balanced (read: realistic) Service Level Agreements was covered in Chapter 4 but it is worth repeating because Service Desk performance targets are so often featured in SLAs. The challenge appears in the form of expectations. Business users' views of customer service levels may not always be in line with the Service Desk's capability to perform. Negotiating too rigid expectations may result in misleading interpretations of actual customer service. Conversely, if the IT organization fails to deliver an appropriately staffed and equipped Service Desk function even generous expectations are likely to fall victim to poor service. A proactive negotiating position is recommended for this situation. Business and IT stakeholders should work together to understand reasonable and recognizable customer service levels, quantify these, then set them into formal agreements.

Promoting customer communications

Though the Service Desk is often referred to as technical support it is probably more appropriate to view it as *customer* support. It is ultimately a people-service function. Compared with the other branches of IT Service Management it may indeed be one of the most people-oriented functions. For this reason, customer communications in this domain is so important. Interacting with customers to understand issues, working with them toward resolutions, and keeping them informed of progress all require communication. But this aspect of service delivery is often underemphasized in favor of technical duties. Many support functions fail to realize that regular, open communication has the potential to affect customer satisfaction levels to the same degree as implementing technical solutions. What is needed here is for the organization to recognize the value of customer communications, promote it to their support teams and then follow up with good communication tools and sound communication guidelines.

14.9. Typical assets and artifacts of a Service Desk function

A well designed Service Desk function requires a set of assets and artifacts that can be used to frame how the function's activities are run. The assets provide the procedural guides and supporting materials for associated activities. The artifacts shape the work products that the activities produce. Following is a list of some of the more common materials that an organization is likely to employ when implementing a Service Desk

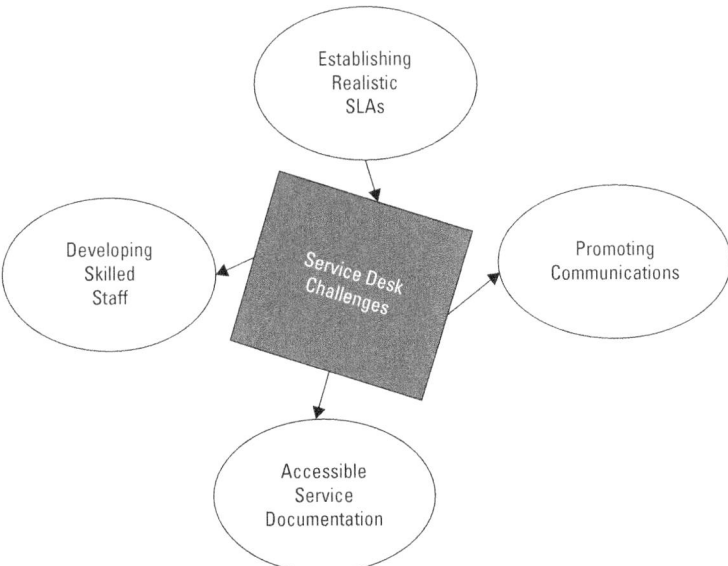

Figure 14.5 Implementation challenges and considerations for the Service Desk

function. Your program may require assets and artifacts not included here, but the set described below represents a typical baseline.

Service Desk policy
This is an executive policy that stipulates the goals and objectives of the Service Desk function. The policy, which ideally should be no longer than a few pages, documents at a high level the purpose of the function, the resources available to support it, the chief responsibilities of its teams, quality targets, reporting hierarchies, and program measures. Endorsed by executive management, the policy is a demonstration of organizational commitment to the value and importance of the Service Desk function.

Ticket tracking and management system
This is some form of automated system (selected based on the needs of the organization) that can be configured as the primary tool for creating, tracking, and managing incident, problem, and service request tickets.

Ticket resolution guidelines
These are documented guidelines used to establish standards for how support calls and service requests should be handled. The guidelines provide a degree of consistency, predictability, and control across support teams. When based on proven practices they also ensure a level of speed and quality when it comes to support and request resolutions.

Ticket escalation guidelines
These guidelines set the rules and boundaries for how support teams will assign ticket ownership to other teams. They help ensure that hand-offs are made under appropriate conditions and to appropriate parties. These guidelines often reference OLAs and UCs because escalation involves coordination and collaboration across support groups.

Service Level Agreement
Service Desk performance is so closely tied to service quality that it is invariably linked with Service Level Management. Performance measures, such as those associated with the CSFs and KPIs discussed earlier in this chapter, typically make up a significant portion of SLA performance targets. The organization should ensure that there is good understanding between Service Desk management, senior IT management, and the customer about expectations for Service Desk responsibilities, activities, responsiveness, and availability.

Service Desk performance measurement plan
This plan defines and describes the set of metrics that will be captured as a way to measure Service Desk performance and effectiveness. Earlier in this chapter we looked at the CSFs and KPIs many Service Desk functions adopt. These are the kinds of measures typically associated with a Service Desk function. Whatever measures you select for your program, ensure that the plan identifies where the data is to be found, how it is to be collected, where it is to be stored, and how it is to be analyzed.

Also, be sure to identify the parties responsible for each of these activities. It is also helpful to make sure that the measurement plan is closely allied with any existing SLAs focused on Service Desk performance.

Service Desk performance reporting and distribution procedure

This is a documented procedure that describes how Service Desk performance reports will be created, how often they will be generated, and to whom they are to be distributed. This procedure – and the associated ensuing reports – can be seen as a logical byproduct of the measurement plan described above. Together these artifacts provide for the generation of the kind of information IT management and customer groups need to have in order to understand the Service Desk effectiveness and performance in light of agreed-upon SLA targets.

Organizational chart

This is a chart that shows the structural make-up of the Service Desk function. As with other organizational charts, the purpose is to identify teams, team relationships, and hierarchical flows. The chart's shape will naturally depend on the organizational units and resources you apply to this function. Most organizational charts of this sort tend to be simple and basically linear. At the top perhaps there is a dotted box representing the Service Desk Manager(s). Extending down from this, there is a box for Tier 1 support (the Service Desk analysts). Below this might be two parallel groups: Tier 2 support teams (e.g. desk side support and/or service specific supports) and Tier 3 teams (e.g. offsite or vendor representatives). Dotted lines might also link the Service Manager to the organization's Incident Manager, Incident Management Process Owner, Problem Manager, Problem Management Process Owner, Service Level Manager, and the Service Level Management Process owner. This chart may be service-specific or combine a set of service offerings.

Roles and responsibilities matrix

This matrix, an extension of the organizational chart, describes the various roles and responsibilities the organization has assigned to staff and support the Service Desk. The roles typically include such positions as Service Incident Manager, Service Desk analysts (Tier 1 support), Tier 2 support analysts, and Tier 3 support analysts. Along with job role definitions for these positions you should have descriptions of the responsibilities each role should account for, and references to how different roles interrelate and communicate. The matrix could take one of several forms: a spreadsheet, a series of database records, or a version-controlled text document. Ownership of this artifact is usually shared between IT management and Human Resource management.

15. Service Management and Service Improvement

At the center of IT Service Management and the core ITIL processes associated with it is the concept of continual service improvement. This concept is essential to both of these disciplines for two reasons. First, business environments are forever changing and it is the mission of IT Service Management to ensure that IT objectives and business objectives continue to remain aligned. Second, a primary goal of ITIL is to bolster an IT organization's competitive position in the marketplace, and to do that its service offerings must be subjected to ongoing scrutiny. And so Continual Service Improvement enters the picture as the last of the service lifecycle phases. The word 'last' however implies a linear flow that is not accurate. Continual Service Improvement contains processes that apply equally at the beginning of a new service as they do to every step in that service's growth and evolution. It is a view that wraps around all other ITIL phases and processes. In this chapter we'll take a look at the key process under Continual Service Improvement, which is Service Improvement.

Here is how the ITIL specification defines Service Improvement:

"To provide an on-going approach for assessing evolving business needs, service performance, and potential service improvements."

This definition establishes the scope of Service Improvement. The key word in the definition is probably 'on-going.' Continual improvement should be seen as a regular, routine activity, one that is embedded into the culture of the organization. It is more than just an activity. It is a philosophical approach to IT management; it is a way of doing business. In its absence, IT Service Management cannot succeed as intended.

(Note the semantic difference between 'continual' and 'continuous.' Continual, as applied to process, is an activity that starts and stops at set intervals. Continuous, on the other hand, is an activity that, once started, does not stop. Literally applied, continuous process improvement can overwhelm and even subdue and organization. Continual process improvement is an approach more readily managed.)

Toward that end, here is how ITIL states the purpose of Service Improvement:

"To identify, assess, and implement service improvements that improve IT efficiencies and effectiveness while lending value to the achievement of business missions and objectives."

The role that Service Improvement plays in the operation of an IT Service Management program management is important to both the IT organization and the business, yet its scope is fortunately somewhat constrained. But that is not to say

that it is insignificant or secondary. There are multiple considerations that need to be addressed when improvement strategies and tactics are being set into place. These considerations include deciding on the best ways to:
- Identify and prioritize high-value services
- Identify and prioritize high-value processes
- Determine the organization's ability to measure service performance
- Determine the organization's ability to measure process performance
- Establish protocols for measuring service performance
- Establish protocols for measuring process performance
- Capture, collect, and analyze service and process measures
- Assess service and process metrics
- Share service and process performance information with IT and business stakeholders
- Identify opportunities for improvement

To investigate these considerations further let's begin with a look at the activities associated with the Service Improvement process.

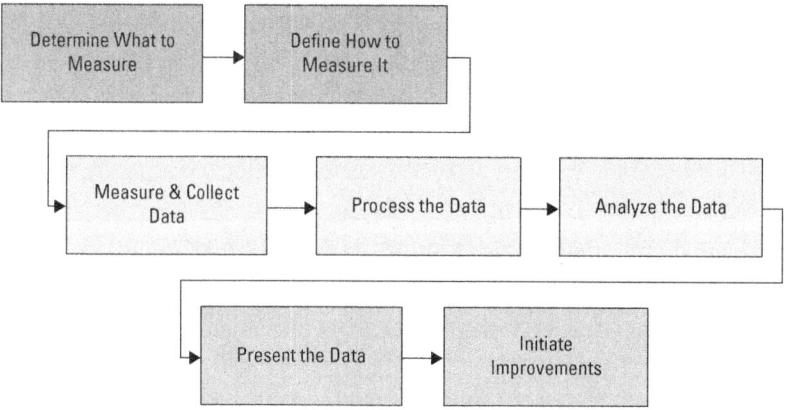

Figure 15.1 Typical Service Improvement process flow

15.1. Service Improvement activities

The approach behind Service Improvement is two-fold: quantitative analysis and qualitative assessment; in other words, measurement combined with judgment. Quantitative analysis need not reach the level of sophistication many of us associate with high-end statistics, but it is a numbers-based approach. The rationale is that we cannot make informed decisions about what to improve if we do not have a clear picture of how the environment performs. We get this picture by measuring selected infrastructure components, then comparing the results with what we expected (or hoped) to find. This gives us an objective and empirical base for decision-making. For most IT organizations most of the time, basic statistical techniques are sufficient. Means, modes, trend lines, and other similar data amalgamations can determine that empirical picture to the degree of confidence required. Qualitative assessment comes in once measurement data has been processed. Here is where IT managers and business stakeholders assess the metrics information and, using their experience, judgment, and expertise, identify opportunities for improvement from the information. ITIL accommodates this dual approach through a process comprised of seven activities. A description of each activity follows.

1. Determine what to measure

There are two parts to this first step: understand what you *can* measure and out of that, know what you *should* measure. A common temptation with improvement programs is to want to improve everything. A better strategy is to work to determine those aspects of your IT Service Management program that are that are priorities for improvement, those that will return the highest value to the organization. Look at the full range of IT services that the IT organization supports and do so in light of the business services and business missions the IT organization helps to support. Through this view, determine what aspects of business and IT services are primarily essential for delivery and quality. Identify what measures might be taken to track these aspects

NOTE: It is helpful to remember that Service Improvement is most effective when focused on two domains: service performance (the way IT services work) and process performance (the way the processes and procedures used to manage service delivery and operations) work.

2. Determine how to measure it

With an understanding of what ought to be measured the organization should establish a Service Improvement Measurement Plan. Often this plan is embedded in the general Service Improvement Plan. Sometimes it is a document in its own right, one that takes its lead from the service-specific measurement plans (see the Typical Assets and Artifacts section at the end of each process chapter). Whichever way you choose to go, the information set in place will need to be the same. The idea is to build a plan that will guide the organization in how to measure for service improvements. The structure of a measurement plan should contain, at a minimum, the following points of detail:

- Services to be measured
- Processes to be measured
- Specific measures for each
- Methods of data capture (tools, people, etc.)
- Data capture responsibility
- Data capture frequency (schedule)
- Data collection methods and frequencies
- Data storage and access methods
- Analysis techniques
- Reporting methods and frequencies
- Analysis and reporting responsibilities

Once the contents have been established the plan should follow the management cycle below:
- Draft the plan
- Review with relevant stakeholders
- Revise (as necessary) based on feedback
- Present for final review
- Approve the plan
- Control the plan
- Execute the plan

3. Measure and collect data
With this step the measurement plan is executed and over time measurement data is captured, collected, stored and made ready for analysis.

4. Process the data
Processing the data is the simple (i.e. direct) step of applying analytic techniques (formulae, quantitative analysis, qualitative assessments, etc.) to convert the raw data into useful information interpreted in the context of IT performance and business needs. Note that while the step may be simple the analytical techniques you apply may indeed be, in some cases, quite complex. But in most cases, typical of most IT organizations, basic analyses are able to provide useful, applicable results.

5. Analyze the data
Using business and technical perspectives the information is consolidated into fresh organizational knowledge. The processed data can then be analyzed to identify organizational strengths, weaknesses, and opportunities for improvement. Proper analysis of the data should also help determine potential return on investment (ROI) for each opportunity, which should in turn help you and your team to weight and prioritize the opportunities in light of organizational needs.

6. Present and assess the data
The process of Service Improvement places emphasis on the relationship between IT management and business stakeholders. For effective improvement both parties should participate in assessments of performance data. So at this point it is important that IT management shares acquired knowledge with key business and service stakeholders. Together they assess the knowledge in light of business and technical needs, strategies, and plans, and from this they determine improvement opportunities collaboratively.

7. Implement improvements
The phrase 'implement improvements' implies that you do two things: create a Service Improvement Plan, and then execute improvement activities according to the plan. 'Improvements' fall into two categories: incremental improvement, in which existing functionality is refined; and innovation, in which new functionality is introduced. Both may be represented in the Service Improvement Plan. It is also important to

remember that improvement can (and often should) be identified for management processes as well as for business and technical services. As Service Improvement is a cyclic activity, it is often necessary in this step to refine an existing Service Improvement Plan to reflect the refreshed direction of the organization.

REMEMBER: Service Improvement operates through a recurring cycle, so consider that the template for the Measurement Plan described in Step 2 above can be included as an integral part of the Service Improvement Plan.

15.2. Process inputs and outputs

Because the Service Improvement process is strategic in nature it can be initiated in two ways. It can begin on a planned basis, in accordance with the schedule in the organization's Service Improvement Plan. It can also be executed in an on-demand manner, if senior management decides that service performance needs an improvement effort. The process is closed in a similarly strategic manner - that is, when identified improvements have been implemented and when support materials (e.g. refreshed plans, service documentation) have been developed and published.

Entry criteria
The criteria used to trigger the beginning of the Service Improvement process signify the need to adjust service in either a planned or on-demand manner. These criteria include:
- At the pre-set time in accordance with the Service Improvement Plan, management initiates its service improvement process.
- Due to concrete service performance issues, IT management or the customer request an on-demand focused improvement initiative.

NOTE: Service Improvement Plan -based improvement efforts are typically done on an annual or semi-annual basis. Too frequent change tends to cause confusion; infrequent changes tend to miss opportunities

Inputs
The inputs that are typically used to start the Service Improvement process rolling are artifacts that include the following:
- Strategic IT and business plans
- Previous Service Improvement Plans
- SLA performance numbers
- Process performance reports
- Customer satisfaction levels
- Incident Management summary reports
- Problem Management summary reports
- Requests for Change (RFCs)

Exit criteria

The criteria used to signal that the Service Improvement process is complete indicate that the organization has reviewed performance, targeted opportunities for improvement, and acted on a select set of these opportunities. These criteria include:
- The organization has identified a set of service improvements.
- The organization has implemented service improvements.

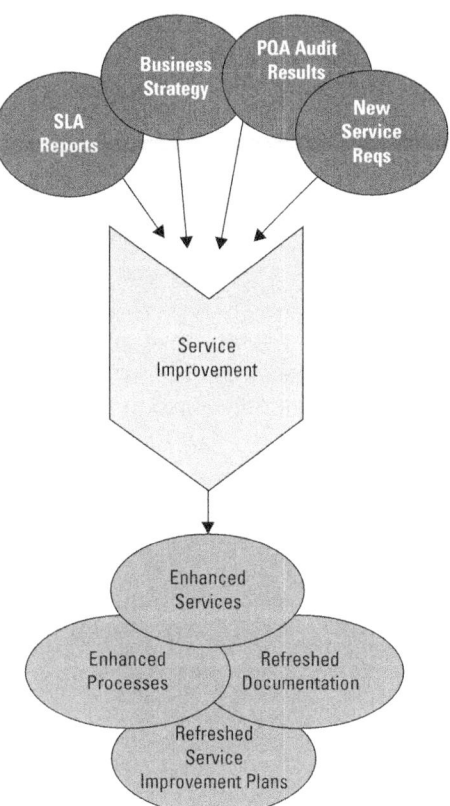

Figure 15.2 Inputs and outputs for Service Improvement

Outputs

Once the process has run its course the improvement activities carried out will have led to the production of artifacts that reflect this work. Three common outputs include:
- Refreshed Service Improvement Plan
- Modified service (or sets of services)
- Refreshed service documentation (operational or managerial)

15.3. Processes related to Service Improvement

Every ITIL process is related to Service Improvement. Look at the image used by itSMF to show ITIL's lifecycle phase structure and you will see how Continual Service Improvement circles all the other phases. It is an all-encompassing activity. Every aspect of an IT Service Management program is subject to improvement scrutiny, whether it is a functional characteristic of a service or a method by which the service is managed. One of these processes, though, does stand out because it has a unique relationship with Service Improvement. This process is Service Level Management.

Service Level Management

As we noted in Chapter 4, Service Level Management deals with managing service performance so that it falls in line with customer expectations. With Service Level Management, service delivery and service quality are monitored and measured, the measures are then reported to the customer and compared with the service targets defined in SLAs. The goal of course is for performance levels to meet or exceed agreed-upon levels. This is where Service Improvement comes in. Service Improvement is the process used to adjust characteristics of service delivery and service quality so that performance does indeed fall in line with expectations. The seven step process of deciding what to measure, determining how to measure it, then measuring, processing analyzing performance data, presenting it to management (and the customer), and then implementing improvements is the primary tool for enhancing the environment, within an IT Service Management program. And the guide for what direction these enhancements should be steered in should be that primary contract of agreement, the SLA. (For more on this topic, see Chapter 4.)

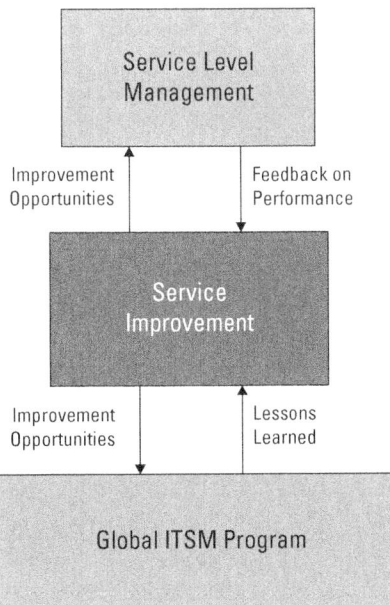

Figure 15.3 Processes related to Service Improvement

In summary:
- SLAs specify expectations for service delivery and service quality levels; in short, how a service should perform.
- SLAs provide primary input into how Service Improvement initiatives should be strategically positioned.
- Service Improvement results should be traceable back to SLAs, demonstrating that enhancements are indeed having a positive impact on delivery and quality levels.

15.4. Tools and techniques

Service Improvement is not a particularly complex process, nor is it a particularly technical process. It is, if anything, a strategic facilitation process. In this endeavor, monitoring tools may be employed but they do not belong to the specific domain of this process; this is one area within ITIL that does not really take advantage of established tool sets. There are, however, techniques that can be applied when executing a Service Improvement program. Three that are almost always present in a Service Improvement program are worth mentioning here. They are noted in the table below.

Table 15.1 Tools and techniques for Service Improvement

Strong customer relationship	Service Improvement requires firm agreement between the customer and IT management about specific areas of focus. IT management and business management should forge a close relationship in this respect so that IT objectives and business objectives can be aligned as closely as practical. When IT management and business management work in a committed partnership to refine and improve services over time, improvement efforts invariably produce results.
An effective Process Quality Assurance (PQA) Program	To obtain objective insight into IT Service Management process utilization and performance across the organization, management should implement an assessment mechanism (Process Quality Assurance) in which teams move out across the enterprise and periodically conduct assessments for process performance. This program should include activities such as QA planning, assessment, management of performance issues, and performance reporting. The results from such assessments provide a wealth of information and insight valuable for positioning improvement efforts. (For more on this, see chapter 16.)
Effective service delivery and service quality monitoring	To capture solid metrics of service delivery and service quality performance, the organization will need to have effective service monitoring tools in place. These tools will need to promote and facilitate the capturing, storing, analyzing, and presenting of performance data on a regular basis. This capability is closely tied to the mission of a Service Level Management program. (For more on this, see Chapter 4.)

15.5. Key Performance Indicators

Measures of Service Improvement activities are usually set in place to provide insight into three operational areas: how well the organization is meeting its SLA performance obligations, how well the organization is meeting its process performance goals, and how effective the organization is at achieving its customer satisfaction targets. In this section we present a series of six KPIs that can be used to present an operational picture for each of those areas. The six are not exhaustive but they are commonly used. You might find that these are beneficial for your Service Improvement program.

SLA performance measures
Service Improvement performance is closely linked to SLA performance and Service Level Management. The key performance indicators defined for Service Level Management are just as valid and useful for Service Improvement and should be applied here. (For more on this, see chapter 4.) The SLA performance measures noted above help to capture metrics of service delivery and service quality performance. The following KPIs help to capture metrics in the domain of IT Service Management process performance.

Number of Process Quality Assurance assessments
This is a count of the total number of Process Quality Assurance (PQA) assessments that were conducted over a set period if time (usually as reflected in the organization's Service Improvement Plan and in individual PQA plans). The purpose is to assess if the number of executed assessments aligns with the number of planned assessments. Since assessment is an essential component of the Service Improvement process, lack of assessment activity may be an indicator that the assessment mechanism may need to be improved or – as is more commonly the case – requires stronger enforcement. While the total number of assessments is an important piece of information this KPI can also be further broken down to segment assessments by service types or by particular technical teams.

Number and types of performance issues
This count shows the total number of performance events that were revealed during the assessment period. The total might be further broken down to show performance issues by type, service, or team. This information is important because it indicates areas within the organization where the process is (or appears to be) being neglected – either because it is not working or staff members are not familiar with how to use it properly. Performance issue rates are a key management indicator, and not just from the perspective of cultural discipline. They point the way toward service improvements; they provide insight as to where you might direct improvement strategies and resources.

Performance rates by service
As part of a Service Improvement Plan, organizations should set performance rates for the teams that attend to its mix of IT services. (See the process activities section earlier in this chapter.) This KPI is a reflection of that benchmark. It is a breakdown

by business service and IT service of overall process performance rates; that is, how well teams are adopting and using recognized policies, processes, and procedures. This data should emerge from the assessment activities that make up a part of the overall Service Improvement process. The information that comes from this data is helpful for assessing which areas in the organization are adhering to the established management approach and which ones may be in need of assistance (e.g. training, mentoring, etc.)

Performance trend rates by service over time

This KPI is a consolidation of the data in the above KPI. This an analysis that shows performance rates over time, usually first by business service and then by IT service. The organization would want to see that performance rates are rising over time. Fluctuating or falling rates are typical indicators of some form of operational issue.

Number and types of corrective actions

This count shows breakdowns of the number of corrective actions that resulted from management of performance issues over the assessment period. A breakdown of finalized (fulfilled) corrections is helpful when compared to the number of outstanding corrective actions. Managing performance issues through corrective actions is a key facet of Service Improvement. As mentioned in the introduction to this chapter, this is more of a micro-focused, reactive improvement tactic when compared to the improvement activities in the organization's strategic Service Improvement Plan. The trend this data can reveal shows how readily teams are adopting improvement concepts and incorporating refinements into routine workflows. A large volume of unfulfilled corrective actions may require some management intervention.

15.6. Critical Success Factors

The CSFs that benefit Service Improvement are the same factors that indicate you are operating a successful IT Service Management program. The three main CSFs in this domain are at the top of a layer made up of the other KPIs and CSFs so far discussed in this book. The three main ones are: SLA targets are being met, process performance targets are being met, and target customer satisfaction levels are being met. These success factors can be seen as reliable measures demonstrating the effectiveness of the Service Improvement program overall.

SLA targets are being met

A successful Service Improvement program must, over time, have positive impacts on operational efficiencies and effectiveness. That is the *raison d'etre* behind the process. The enhancements and innovations that emerge from the program should be demonstrated in delivery improvements and quality improvement, and thus lead to more efficient realization of SLA targets. Effective Service Improvement will ensure that the performance, capabilities and infrastructure are constantly being scrutinized and continually being aligned with customers' service needs and expectations.

Process performance targets are being met
In order for service delivery and service quality performance to move toward defined targets in a consistent and predictable manner, it is important for IT teams to follow the organization's established processes and procedures. These are the assets that make up the heart of any IT Service Management program. Perform process well and the IT organization can consciously manage its work methods. Ignore process and management progress becomes highly dependent on individual capabilities, not on the organization's institutional capabilities; that is a risky position to be in. The periodic program assessments associated with Service Improvement will provide insight into levels of performance across the organization. A well-managed Service Improvement program will always have associated with it solid and stable levels of performance within the process program.

Customer satisfaction targets are being met
Meeting customer satisfaction expectations is just as important as performance levels with regard to service delivery and service quality. As most IT professionals know, both are in fact strongly interrelated. A well-managed Service Improvement program will have the ability to respond to operational weaknesses and changing customer needs in such a way that the customer is aware of IT's work in this domain, participates in improvement activities, and is kept informed of progress toward shared goals. In this type of cooperative atmosphere, satisfaction levels tend to rise; even more so when the improvements begin to show fruit.

15.7. Service Improvement roles

The following job roles are typically seen in mature Service Improvement programs. Depending on the size and focus of an organization these roles may be full-time or part-time, combined, or shared by multiple individuals.

Service Improvement Process Owner
The Service Improvement Process Owner is the person (or persons) in the organization responsible for the development, deployment, and ongoing use of the Continual Service Improvement program. The process owner champions the purpose and goals of service and process improvement, ensures that the program remains in a state of operational effectiveness, and interfaces with senior IT management and business representatives to facilitate program adjustments and enhancements. To summarize, the Service Improvement Process Owner is responsible for:
- Developing and documenting the Service Improvement program
- Implementing the program across relevant teams
- Coordinating program training and mentoring
- Monitoring ongoing program use
- Measuring program performance over time
- Reporting on program effectiveness over time
- Soliciting and coordinating program improvements

Service Improvement Manager

The Service Improvement Manager occupies the same role as that of a Quality Assurance Manager in traditional organizations. Service Improvement Managers conduct quality planning, which is realized in an organizational Service Improvement Plan. They control the ongoing execution of this plan, coordinate periodic performance assessments, report results to executive management, identify opportunities for improvement, and oversee a team of process quality assurance analysts. To summarize, the Service Improvement Manager is responsible for:

- Facilitating Service Improvement meetings and reviews
- Planning and coordinating Service Improvement activities
- Ensuring the proper assessment of service delivery, performance, and quality
- Communicating improvement potentials and improvement activities with business stakeholders and IT management
- Managing development and execution of the Service Improvement Plan
- Coordinating reviews and revisions of the Service Improvement Plan

Process Quality Assurance Analyst

Process Quality Assurance Analysts (PQA Analysts) work with service managers to establish PQA plans, the quality assurance plans used to gauge a service's compliance with policies and standards. The plans include schedules of assessments and the PQA Analysts conduct these assessments. They record assessment results, manage any performance issues or corrective actions that emerge from the assessments, and communicate the results to service managers and senior IT management. PQA Analysts are also responsible, from the insight gained by organizational assessments, for identifying potential opportunities for improvement as well as operation strengths. These can be used as input into the Service Improvement Plan planning process. For more on this role, see Chapter 16. To summarize, the PQA Analyst is responsible for:

- Establishing service-focused PQA plans
- Conducting scheduled assessments
- Managing performance-related and corrective action issues
- Coaching and mentoring teams as needed
- Reporting assessment results to service managers and senior IT management
- Identifying opportunities for improvement
- Executing assigned portions of Service Improvement Plans

Human Resource considerations

The following are some typical traits that Human Resource staff may want to take into consideration when they are providing personnel, tools, and other resources for a Service Improvement program.

Experience and background: Improvement Managers and PQA Analysts should have an adequate technical background in order to facilitate and comment on the viability of potential improvements to existing or new services. They should have experience organizing and mobilizing teams for improvement review, assessment, and implementation activities. And they should have strong experience in team management as well as meeting organization and facilitation.

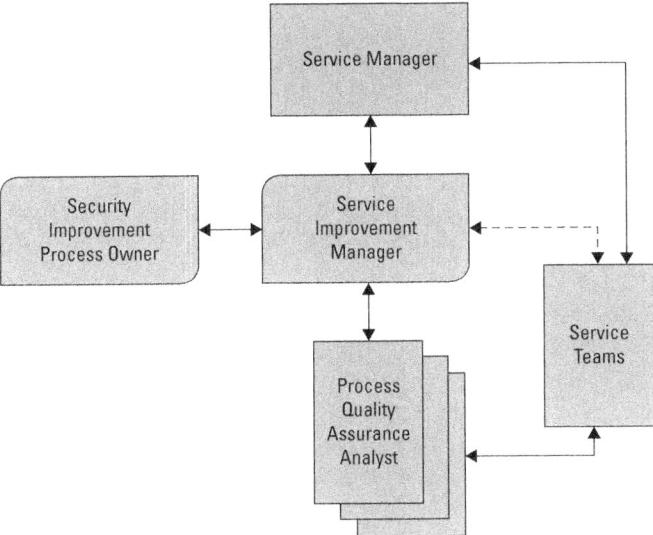

Figure 15.4 Service Improvement role relationships

Comfort working in a process-centric environment: Improvement Managers and PQA Analysts should be comfortable working in a process-centric environment, and should be open to learning about the organization's program and contributing to its ordered growth.

The Service Improvement process requires several interrelated roles. The Service Improvement Manager facilitates all organizational improvement and planning activities. The PQA Analysts plan and conduct service assessments, and report results to senior management. Service Managers are stakeholders in this process. And the Service Improvement Process Owner is responsible for the use and maintenance of the program across the organization.

15.8. Benefits of effective Service Improvement

When compared to processes like Information Security Management and Capacity Management, Service Improvement could be called an 'elective' process. That is, it is not a mandate from the viewpoint of service engineering. Rather, the organization chooses to conduct business under the philosophy of continual service improvement. And so, being an elective choice, the entire push of this process is to bring benefits to the organization. Conscientiously and collaboratively working to improve services – either through innovation or incremental growth – should enhance Service Management. IT service should become more reliable and more capable, leading to more effective business processes. Enhanced business processing should lead to realized business missions. All of this taken together should lead to increased customer satisfaction levels and the recognition that IT has delivered on its commitments. Three of the practical benefits you can expect from a sound Service Improvement program are described below.

Managed (and responsible) control of the infrastructure

IT infrastructures can be (and most usually are) highly complex environments. At the same time they are dynamic, required to change over time. Service Improvement is a way to ensure that the evolution and responsiveness of the enterprise with regard to infrastructure growth and development is addressed in a planned, orderly, and responsible way. The use of a management-approved Service Improvement Plan along with continual improvement methods channels strategic goals into coordinated, tactical action. It replaces a willy-nilly approach to meeting (perhaps ad hoc) technology needs with one designed to tie technology needs to the needs of the business. Carried out this way, Service Improvement ensures that potential changes are identified upfront, assessed for their practical returns on investment (ROIs), communicated to relevant stakeholders, and deployed with precision. This targeted approach can positively influence many operational characteristics of IT, including incident rates, problem rates, performance levels, etc.

Better planning and forecasting

Planning is enhanced with Service Improvement because the activity itself is a proactive management approach. Because it includes cross-organizational stakeholder participation, common communications and expectations are established for service evolution, and cost, resource, schedule and other needs can be shared and understood well in advance of action. Forecasting is also enhanced with Service Improvement because, through this process, the organization establishes an agreed-upon repository of what it wants to roll out into production by way of enhancement, and provides for the thorough assessment of items in the repository along with their operational characteristics.

Improved IT and business performance

In the end, the result of effective Service Improvement should be demonstrated in improved IT performance, reliability, and stability. This is the philosophy at the foundation of any process improvement program. And when such a program is harnessed from the start to the mission and needs of the business, stronger business results should naturally emerge out of the improvement efforts.

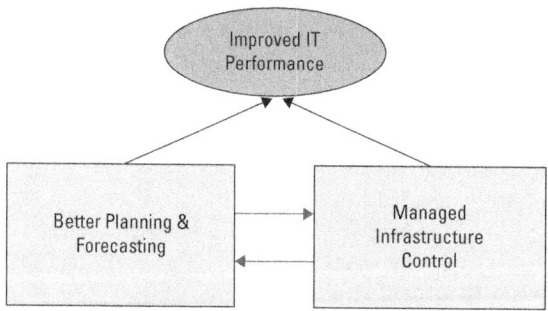

Figure 15.5 Service Improvement benefits

15.9. Implementation challenges and considerations

As noted in the section above, Service Improvement activities can deliver distinct benefits to an IT organization. Behind these benefits, though, there is a series of implementation challenges and considerations that should be evaluated when you put this process into place. Three of the most significant are as follows.

Realizing full participation in the process
In order for Service Improvement to be effective, stakeholders from across the enterprise must participate in the process. This is the only way likely to reveal opportunities for improvement with the potential to yield high ROIs. But getting this full degree of participation is often challenging to do, especially in complex, busy IT organizations. This is complicated by the realization that Service Improvement requires the active involvement of customers almost as much as that of IT teams. To make this easier, Service Improvement teams should work closely with IT management and business management to identify relevant stakeholders from both technical and customer teams and endorse their participation in improvement activities. Senior management can further promote this participation by communicating the importance of these efforts participation to the organization. Success in this arena requires an emphasis on partnership, collaboration, and the value that the IT Service Management program overall delivers to the business.

Capturing practical sets of high-value improvements
In any typical IT environment, improvement opportunities are not difficult to come by. Just the opposite, they probably proliferate. For a Service Improvement program to be effective however the trick is not to find the opportunities, it is to find the opportunities that deliver the strongest returns. When improvement managers forget to focus in this area the risk is two-fold: identifying unwieldy sets of improvement ideas, and identifying ideas that may require strong efforts without significant ROI. To minimize these risks improvement managers should take time to facilitate discussions and evaluations of improvement opportunities so that a valuable, finite, and manageable set can be selected. In the absence of this identify-assess-select approach, the organization may find itself burdened with a lot of work that may not have correspondingly high value.

Managing sets of in-progress improvements
Just as identifying high-return improvements can be challenging, so can managing the implementation of those improvements. Diligent improvement planning is required so that this step goes smoothly. The challenges can come from a variety of factors. If the improvement sets are large or unwieldy they may strain available resources. If they touch on a multitude of domains they may require an impractical depth of stakeholder involvement. And if the improvements are inadvertently under- or over-engineered they may actually reduce the program's overall effectiveness. A combination of capabilities is required: a manageable and well-understood improvement scope; sound project management practices and executive commitment to the effort's end-goals. Service Improvement Management should also work to ensure that current

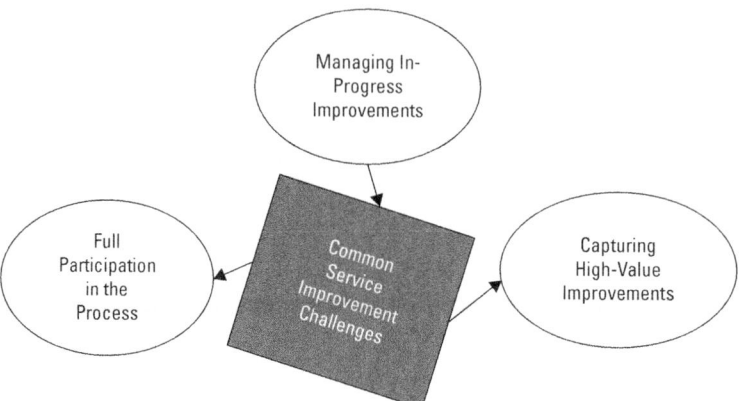

Figure 15.6 Service Improvement challenges and considerations

improvement proposals complement existing development activities across the enterprise so that conflicts or redundancies do not result.

15.10. Typical assets and artifacts of a Service Improvement program

A set of documented assets and artifacts will need to be created in support of your Service Improvement program. Assets are the program materials that bound the way the program is governed and run. Artifacts are those work products that emerge when improvement teams engage in program activities. Following is a list of some common assets and artifacts that you would find in a typical Service Improvement program. While your program may require some of these, you will probably wish to create some things not described here; but this list, while not exhaustive, is typical.

Service Improvement policy

This is an executive policy that stipulates the goals and objectives of the Service Improvement program. The policy, which ideally should be no longer than a few pages, documents at a high level the purpose of the program, the resources available to the program, the chief responsibilities of the program, quality targets, reporting hierarchies, and program measures. Endorsed by executive management, the policy is a demonstration of organizational commitment to the value and importance of service improvement activities.

Service Improvement Plan template

This template provides a structural guide for creating the organization's Service Improvement Plan (SIP). The template outlines the contents and sections that a properly documented plan should contain. Such plans usually identify the following kinds of information: purpose and scope of Service Improvement, resources assigned to the initiative, management and other key stakeholders, improvement objectives, identified improvement opportunities, expected improvement outcomes (ROI), schedule of improvement activities, improvement milestones, and status, reporting, and communication channels.

Service Improvement Plan
This is the organizational plan, based on the template above, that – once approved and adopted – specifies how Service Improvement activities will be conducted over a set period of time.

Service Improvement process
This is a process that details the workflows inherent in the Service Improvement program. Establishing this process in an effective way is important; it will serve as the heart of the program. The process defines how all improvement activities work. Such a process would usually define separate flows for improvement planning, assessment planning, assessment results reporting, managing performance issues, and communicating with both Service Management and senior IT management. The process would also describe entry criteria, exit criteria, inputs, and outputs; it would also identify the people needed to execute each defined activity. The process might also be supported by lower level procedures or work instructions.

Service Improvement Measurement Plan
Periodic product and process measures are needed if a Service Improvement program is to be effective. The Service Improvement Measurement Plan is a tool for doing this. It identifies and defines the metrics to capture in order to assess the performance of IT services, management processes, and the work products they produce. A typical plan will describe the set of measures, define how to collect them, specify where the pulled data is to be stored, and provide formulae for analyzing the data. The measures you select for this plan will depend naturally on the needs of your IT organization, but the CSFs and the KPIs described in this chapter may be helpful examples of the kinds of measures you may wish to set up for your Service Improvement program.

NOTE: Organizations often include the Service Improvement Measurement Plan as part of its overall Service improvement Pan.

Service Improvement reporting and distribution procedure
This is a documented procedure that describes how Service Improvement reports are created, how often they are generated, and to whom they are to be distributed. This procedure can be seen as an extension of the Service Improvement Plan and Service Improvement Measurement Plan described above. Together these artifacts provide the kind of information needed by IT management and customer groups to understand the effectiveness of Service Improvement and Service Management activities and identify opportunities for improvement.

Organizational chart

This is a chart that shows the structural make-up of the Service Improvement operation. As with other organizational charts, its purpose is to identify teams, team relationships, and hierarchical flows. The shape of this chart will naturally depend on the general shape of your organization, and your Service Improvement program. Most organizational charts of this sort tend to be fairly simple. Senior IT management is indicated at the top with a line down to the Service Improvement Manager. A dotted line extends from the Service Improvement Manager to the Service Improvement Process Owner (if the role is separate from the Service Improvement Manager). Below the Service Improvement Manager are PQA analysts, who are responsible for planning and conducting assessments. Sometimes it is also helpful to have a dotted line extending from the Service Improvement Manager over to Service Managers off in another parallel spot.

Roles and responsibilities matrix

This matrix is an extension of the organizational chart. It describes the various roles and responsibilities the organization has assigned to support the Service Improvement program. The roles typically include such positions as Service Improvement Process Owner, Service Improvement Manager, and PQA analyst. Along with the job role definitions you should have descriptions of the responsibilities each role should account for, and references to how the roles interrelate and communicate. The matrix might take one of several forms: a spreadsheet, a series of database records, or a version-controlled text document. Ownership of this artifact is usually shared between IT management and Human Resource management.

16. Implementing a basic Process Quality Assurance function

The focus of Continual Service Improvement is to regularly look for ways to make service design, delivery, operation, and management more effective. The best way to do this, of course, is to measure the service mix over time. Through this you can develop a quantitative picture of performance, and from this picture assess ways toward improvement. As we have seen with the eleven processes featured in this book, measurement is an important aspect of ITIL. Key performance indicators (KPIs) and critical success factors (CSFs) constitute a planned approach to Service Management. But there is an additional facet that could benefit from being measured, a facet apart from the services themselves; that is the Service Management program, the program that includes any set of these eleven processes. This is where the function of process quality assurance (PQA) enters the picture.

PQA is not a defined process of ITIL, but it is an implied activity under the Service Improvement and Service Reporting processes. It is also the industry-recognized manner in which IT governance is introduced into an organization. The task of PQA is probably familiar to most people. It is to periodically assess IT teams to measure how well they are using the IT Service Management program. PQA looks for two main things:
- The level of performance across the organization relevant to policies and processes
- The degree to which the program is furthering IT missions and goals.

From the PQA activities will come assessment results. Because an IT Service Management program is ultimately owned by senior management, these reports provide insight into patterns of organizational activity necessary for decision-making. Importantly, the data provides objective feedback and directly supports the mission of Continual Service Improvement.

Some form of PQA presence is essential for the introduction and growth of any process program. (CMMI-Dev, CMMI-Svc, PMBOK, Six Sigma, ISO/IEC 20000 all set out PQA practices.) In this chapter we will look at how a basic function might be set into place in a way that will integrate easily with the Service Improvement process described in Chapter 15.

16.1. Objectivity and independence

Before we look at the activities associated with PQA we should take a moment to focus on two concepts: objectivity and independence. The goal of PQA is to provide senior management with *objective* insight into organizational behavior. That is, insight that is not skewed or prejudiced by conflicting agendas. For example, you would probably not ask your IT service managers to assess their own adherence to design and operation methodologies. Objectivity can be achieved in two ways. The first is through *independence*. Here a party separate and distinct from the party being assessed conducts the inspections. This should remove conflicts of interest. This is a proven way to promote objectivity but is does have one drawback: it requires an additional resource. With small organizations, especially, those extra resources may be hard to find.

But there is a way around this. And particularly for new or expanding ITIL programs this may even be a better way to go. That is to make the PQA assignment a part-time or shared one and to add to that an additional layer of objectivity. This is achieved by making the assessment results strictly factual and binary (yes/no answers with no qualification such as 'partially', 'largely' and so on), so that there is no scope for subjective interpretation of the data. This approach provides clean assessment data. As your plan your PQA program you will need to look at the structure and shape of your IT organization, evaluate available resources and determine the blend of objectivity and independence that makes the best sense.

A typical reporting chain might look like this:

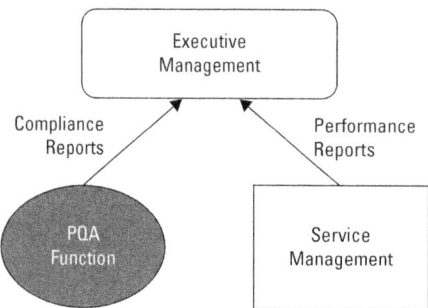

Figure 16.1 PQA reporting chain

16.2. PQA activities

The PQA function is a logical component of an organization's Service Improvement process. But the main audience for this function's work is senior IT management. Four responsibilities are typically assigned to this task, and they are intended for the production of specialized (i.e., process-oriented) management reports. The four responsibilities are:
- Planning process quality assurance assessments
- Conducting quality assessments
- Reporting on program performance
- Identifying opportunities for improvement

PQA planning

With planning, an appointed PQA Analyst works with service managers to collaboratively develop a PQA plan. The plan is a contract of agreement about when quality assessments will occur and what they will cover.

A simple PQA plan will contain the following kinds of detail:
- Purpose of PQA within the organization
- Resources assigned to conduct PQA activities
- IT service teams that will be assessed
- Assets and artifacts that will be included in assessment inspections
- Expected inspection results
- Schedule of assessments and assessment results reports
- Performance issue management procedures
- Corrective action procedures
- Commitment (signature)

The plan is important for three reasons. First, it sets a level of expectation between Service Management, quality management, and senior management about the policies and processes that should be followed. Next, it provides a performance baseline that service managers can use in order to plan for performance targets within their own teams and prepare for the assessments. Lastly, it is a guide for senior management to use for validating that the essential elements of IT operations are being tracked and measured.

Once a plan has been formulated and drafted it should be reviewed by all relevant stakeholders, revised as necessary based on the review, formally approved, and then placed under change control.

PQA assessment

According to schedule the assessments should take place as planned. A traditional assessment stream will cover the following sub-practices:
- The assessor sends notification of an upcoming assessment to relevant participants.
- The assessment occurs.
- Use of process assets is verified.
- Creation of work products is verified.
- Interviews with team members validate performance levels.
- The assessor records results and manages performance issues as they may be encountered.
- The assessor reviews preliminary results with team members before finalizing the results. Discussions and adjustments may contribute to the shape of final results.

PQA reporting

Reporting presents the results of assessment activity in official, finalized form. Once the assessor and assessed team agree on the findings, the results should be published and distributed to Service Management, quality management, and senior IT management. The results may also be stored in a repository of other performance metrics.

Identifying opportunities for improvement

This final activity links PQA solidly with Service Improvement. The assessment results will naturally point the way to opportunities for improvement, which can be grouped in three categories. First are opportunities to improve policies and processes (Service Management). Next are opportunities to improve how people interact with the policies and processes. And then there are opportunities for how the IT services themselves might be improved. These opportunities should be identified and then sifted for further analysis and action into the Service Improvement process.

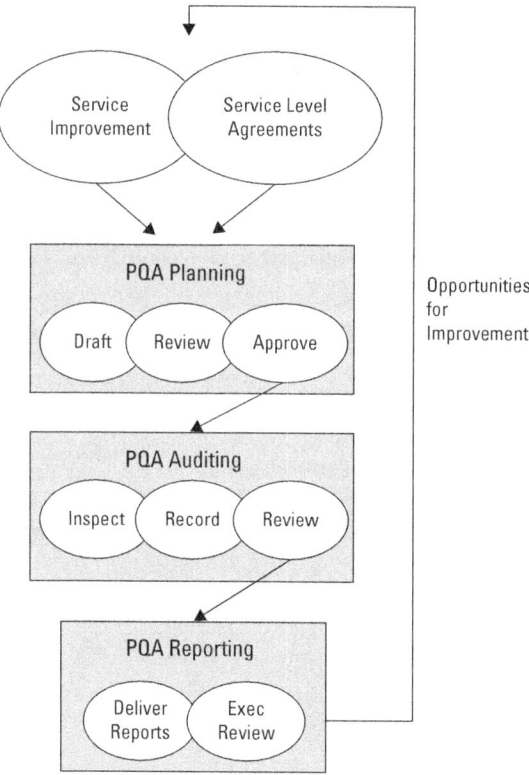

Figure 16.2 Typical PQA responsibility flow

16.3. The value of PQA

Though it may sometimes slip 'under the radar', the organization should not underestimate the value the PQA function brings to Service Management. Here we describe the value that the PQA function can bring to the organization when it is implemented in a considered and well-designed manner.

Promotes adoption and institutionalization

Visible PQA activities on the IT organization's shop floor demonstrate management's commitment to the ITIL-based program. They provide the opening for service teams to receive help (coaching and mentoring) using the various components of the program. PQA's visibility can provide a reminder of the program's importance to senior management. When consistently applied over time, this function can go a long way toward promoting enterprise-wide process adoption and ensuring that organizational practices become institutionalized within design, development, and operation teams.

Provides insight into program effectiveness

It can be difficult to judge how well a process is working if the process is not measured. The PQA function is a way to measure process. When a certain process proves to be working contrary to expectations it can be for one of these reasons: people are not using it, people are using it incorrectly, and the process itself is faulty. A PQA program that is targeted to the purpose and shape of your processes can reveal, through the assessment metrics, where a program's strengths and weaknesses lie. These metrics can also provide pointers to the sources of strong performance and the causes of weak performance. From analyses of this information you can identify and formulate opportunities for improvement.

True objective insight

The primary value of the PQA function is that it provides second-party insight into organizational performance. This insight is not only structured to be objective but it represents what can be called an expert opinion. The PQA analysts who conduct the assessments should be trained in the process areas under inspection and familiar with the IT services relevant to those domains. When assessment results are completed they should paint a representative picture of performance. This other-side-of-the-coin view benefits management's work to drive the enterprise toward its goals.

16.4. Summary: ensuring success

Adopting ITIL as an improvement framework and then creating a quality system based on it requires a sustained organizational commitment. The task of the PQA function is to help see that commitment realized in institutionalization. This is where the Service Management program becomes after a time invisibly embedded in the corporate culture. It becomes simply the way things are done. The watchful eye of

PQA can guide your program down that path. To make that journey as smooth as possible here are some tips for how you might shape your program's PQA function.

Communicate the importance of performance
This tip takes us back to Chapter 2, where we discussed success tips for implementing an ITIL-based program in general. The topic here, once again, is executive commitment. For your program to be successful people are going to have to use it, and in order for that to happen they will need to be encouraged to use it. This is why this executive communication is so important. Senior management should disseminate the message that process performance is important, that PQA is more about insight than oversight, and that the organization needs the help of its team members to reach the program's goals.

Promote cooperative PQA planning
Process quality plans are not something that quality analysts should develop in isolation, apart from service teams. PQA plans should instead be cooperatively developed by service managers and quality analysts working together toward common agreement. When this is the path taken, both parties emerge with an approach to quality that is not only likely to be realistic but one whose expectations are shared across stakeholders.

Begin with gradient performance goals
Though it may be a natural temptation to do so, it is not necessary to expect performance levels of 100% right from the start. This may be necessary for some IT organizations, but others may consider – at least early on – lower goals. This may help shape adoption so that it seems less daunting to teams, provide for some early wins, and thus win confidence for the program. You can then gradually increase performance expectations as the organization matures.

Focus on the essentials
When beginning a PQA effort, do not feel compelled to have to assess everything in the environment, down to the last detail. Focus primarily on the important things, on those tasks and work products that deliver the strongest benefits. This will help keep the initial assessments to a manageable scope and allow teams to meet performance targets more quickly. Later on as the essentials have been taken care of, you can expand the assessments to cover more territory.

Provide coaches, not cops
A common mistake made when implementing a PQA function is to treat assessors as policeman or judges- that the job at hand is to weed bad practice. That is the wrong attitude of course. Better is to shape it as a coaching function. PQA's job is to help teams adopt and stay on process. The assessments simply reveal a measure of how well this is going. The assessment results inform management as to how they make the adoption go smoothly, how they might apply resources toward that end. Programs that take the 'cop' approach can easily instill anxiety in the workplace, and that is not good for adoption or productivity.

Reward performance

The goal of PQA is not solely to single out instances of performance issues and weak performance. It should also be used to identify areas of strength within the organizations. These can include teams with high levels of adoption and program components proving very effective. In order to promote the idea across the enterprise that the service program is essential to long-term success, management should – when it discovers such pockets of excellences – reward those involved. The rewards should be both valuable and visible, so that others will recognize them and be encouraged to follow.

Continue over time

Continual improvement is not so much a goal as it is an operational philosophy. Well-managed PQA practices can provide you with the methods and techniques, and thus the insight, needed to appreciate how well the IT Service Management program is performing - that is, how well it is meeting the needs of both IT and the customer base. Though it will not happen immediately, every quality assurance step can be used to move the IT organization toward better and better efficiencies, and greater and greater effectiveness. The key is to stay with the journey, to follow the course it takes down a natural path to productivity.

ITIL Books

Foundations of ITIL®

Now updated to encompass all of the implications of the 2011 refresh of ITIL, this ITIL Foundations book looks at Best Practices, focusing on the Lifecycle approach, and covering the ITIL Service Lifecycle, processes and functions for Service Strategy, Service Design, Service Operation, Service Transition and Continual Service Improvement.

ISBN 978 90 8753 674 9 (english edition)

Passing the ITIL® Foundation Exam

A complete and thorough explanation of all key concepts for ITIL Foundation Exam, this title contains sample questions and practical examples. Endorsed by APMG, it has been designed to follow the official ITIL Foundation Exam syllabus.

ISBN 978 90 8753 069 3 (english edition)

ITIL® - A Pocket Guide

A concise summary to ITIL®, providing a quick and portable reference tool to this leading set of best practices for IT Service Management.

ISBN 978 90 8753 676 3 (english edition)

Van Haren Publishing is a leading international publisher, specializing in best practice titles for IT management and business management. Van Haren Publishing publishes in 14 languages, and has sales and distribution agents in over 40 countries worldwide: www.vanharen.net

ISO/IEC 20000

ISO/IEC 20000 - An Introduction
Promoting awareness of the certification for organizations within the IT Service Management environment.

ISBN 978 90 8753 081 5 (english edition)

English €49.95 excl tax

Implementing ISO/IEC 20000 Certification - The Roadmap
Practical advice, to assist readers through the requirements of the standard, the scoping, the project approach, the certification procedure and management of the certification.

ISBN 978 90 8753 082 2 (english edition)

English €39.95 excl tax

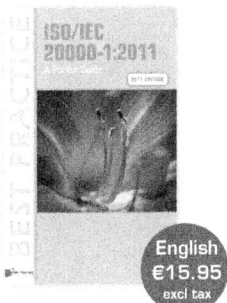

ISO/IEC 20000-1:2011 - A Pocket Guide
A quick and accessible guide to the fundamental requirements for corporate certification.

ISBN 978 90 8753 682 4 (english edition)

English €15.95 excl tax

www.vanharen.net

Other leading ITSM Books

Metrics for IT Service Management
A general guide to the use of metrics as a mechanism to control and steer IT service organizations, with consideration of the design and implementation of metrics in service organizations using industry standard frameworks.

ISBN 978 90 77212 69 1

Metrics for Service Management: Designing for ITIL
This title is the sister book to the global best-seller Metrics for Service Management. Taking the basics steps described there, this new title describes the context within the ITIL 2011 Lifecycle approach.

ISBN 978 90 8753 648 0 (english edition)

The ITIL® Process Manual
Covers the basic approaches to the fundamental processes – companies will find the concise, practical guidance easy to follow and implement.

ISBN 978 90 8753 650 3 (english edition)

The Service Catalog
Practical guidance on building a service catalog, this title focuses on IT community relationship with the business and users. Including useful templates on key documents such as OLAs and SLAs, this is definitive guide for all those delivering this tool.

ISBN 978 90 8753 571 1 (english edition)

www.vanharen.net

Printed in Great Britain
by Amazon

47480112R00215